Basic Books in the Mass Media

Basic Books in the Mass Media

An Annotated, Selected Booklist Covering
General Communications, Book Publishing,
Broadcasting, Editorial Journalism, Film,
Magazines, and Advertising

SECOND EDITION

Eleanor Blum

University of Illinois Press

Urbana Chicago London

LIBRARY OF CONGRESS CATALOGING IN PUBLICATION DATA

Blum, Eleanor.
  Basic books in the mass media.

  Includes indexes.
  1. Mass media — Bibliography. I. Title.
Z5630.B55   1980   [P90]   016.3022'3
ISBN 0-252-00814-6   80-11289

To Fred Siebert, one of the first
and finest scholars in communication law,
to whom all of us owe so much.

Contents

I. General Communications 1

II. Books and Book Publishing 67

III. Broadcasting 96

IV. Editorial Journalism 187

V. Film 233

VI. Magazines 301

VII. Advertising and Public Relations 317

VIII. Indexes to Mass Communications Literature 344

Subject Index 353

Author-Title Index 373

Preface

This new edition of <u>Basic Books in the Mass Media</u> has
been updated, greatly revised, and expanded from 665
entries to 1,179, to reflect the growth of the field. A
number of the old entries have been deleted, and of those
retained the annotations have often been rewritten,
especially for new editions and annuals. Although the
majority of the new entries were published after the cut-
off date of the first edition, April, 1971, I have also
picked up some older titles which the wisdom of hindsight
tells me should have been included previously. For the
most part, the older entries are books which, in my
opinion, have not dated, or which possess historical
significance, or which are classics in the field.

This edition, like the previous, has three primary
purposes: to serve as a reference tool; to suggest materials for research; and to provide a checking or buying
list for libraries. This time around I have kept a
secondary purpose in mind: to put together a bibliography which will allow the user, through judicious
browsing, to piece together an informal history of the
literature of mass communications and the authors/
scholars who have shaped its direction.

Many of the titles are primarily reference materials
such as handbooks, directories, guides, manuals, reports,
bibliographies, yearbooks. Others are surveys, anthologies, texts, studies, histories. All, however, give
information about some aspect or aspects of communi-
cations--theory, background, economics, structure,
function, research, contents, effects. None deals with
techniques or is mainly methodological. Most entries
contain footnotes and bibliographies. When they do, the
annotation says so.

All entries have one common factor: they treat the
subject in broad, general terms. For example, I have
included books about news agencies, but not about a
specific agency; I have included histories of newspapers,
but not of individual papers. For this reason there are

no biographies, either personal or institutional, and
no books which treat too narrow an aspect of a subject.
Also, the entire contents must concern communications:
those with only partially relevant content are not
included.

The first section is general and deals with theory,
popular culture, law, public opinion, and propaganda,
and with books that treat three or more media. The
other six sections deal with book publishing, broadcasting, film, editorial journalism (covering news, whether
print or broadcast, or even, in the case of newsreels,
film), magazines, and advertising (which, although not
a medium in itself, affects the others in varying
degrees). The list of periodicals in the 1972 edition
has been omitted because a comprehensive one is now
readily available in the Aspen Handbook on the Media:
A Selective Guide to Research Organizations and Publications in Communications, published every two years.
However, the annotated list of indexes to periodicals,
newspapers, and dissertations has been retained. For
this edition, it was compiled by Frances Goins Wilhoit,
Journalism Librarian at Indiana University, Bloomington.

A partial list of specific topics covered, in addition to the more general, includes telecommunications, the
underground and alternative presses, the black press,
minorities (including women), concentration of media
ownership, children and advertising, educational training, access, developing countries, ethics, satellites,
public broadcasting, various film genre including experimental and underground film, and too many others to
mention all. The detailed subject index will provide a
background and will guide the user to whatever topic is
wanted.

Certain subjects, however, are not covered individually. Among them are censorship, copyright, printing,
typography, comics, information science and computers,
the post office, instructional broadcasting, and telephone and telegraph (although these last two sometimes
enter in connection with telecommunications, just as
printing does with history, or censorship with law and
regulations, or, indeed, most of the others in connection with related subjects).

A number of the books contained here are out of
print--a fact no longer so important as formerly because
of the prevalence of paperback and hardcover reprints
and the possibility of obtaining photoreproductions or
borrowing through interlibrary loan.

Because price varies with edition and value on the
secondhand market, I have not attempted to include it,
nor the various editions of a title, which come and go.

Nor have I given publishers addresses unless they may
prove difficult to find. Most of them can be easily
obtained through such sources as the <u>Literary Market
Place</u> and the <u>American Book Trade Directory</u> and their
foreign equivalents. In this edition, however, I have
specified the number of pages, except in cases of
multivolume works.

In any work of this kind many titles could have been
included, and, conversely, many could have been omitted.
Selection inevitably becomes somewhat eclectic and
arbitrary, reflecting the compiler's knowledge and
leanings. My criteria for inclusion varied. Sometimes,
although not always, a criterion was that elusive attri-
bute, quality. The determination of quality, however,
is subjective as well as elusive, and some books which
I feel lack it in greater or lesser degree have their
place because little else exists on the subject or
because they cover aspects not covered previously.
Also, to limit a bibliography to works of indubitable
merit (and opinions differ as to what constitutes merit)
would narrow its scope and usefulness. Even hackneyed
anthologies may contain some essays of value, and
mediocre surveys may contain factual material not easily
found elsewhere.

I have also followed the practice of grouping works
by the same author together in cases where they are in
the same section and concern the same subject matter.

In conclusion, I would like to thank Professor George
Gerbner of the Annenberg School of Communications, University of Pennsylvania, for his suggestion years ago
that this bibliography was needed; Professor Theodore
Peterson of the University of Illinois, who--again years
ago--convinced the University of Illinois Press that it
should be published; Professor Nancy Allen of the University of Illinois for invaluable help on the film section;
Hal Fuson of the legal department of the <u>Los Angeles
Times</u> for his equally invaluable help with the books on
communication law; and the members of the University of
Illinois Library faculty who frequently assisted me in
tracking down innumerable details as well as, in many
cases, the books themselves. I also owe a great deal to
my skillful and patient editor, Cynthia Mitchell. Most
of all I want to thank Hugh Atkinson, the University of
Illinois Librarian, who provided me with the most favor-
able of working conditions.

I
General Communications

---

1. American Indian Media Directory. Washington 20036: American Indian Press Association, Room 206, 1346 Connecti-
   cut Ave., N.W., 1974. 49p.

   Lists the following: newspapers; magazines; school and
   college publications; special interest publications which
   include information about such things as art, history,
   prisons, religion, medicine, legislation and law, land,
   etc.; news services; printing; companies and outlets where
   music can be found; radio broadcasts; television training
   centers; cable television; monitors, telecasters, technicians; video systems administered by the Bureau of Indian
   affairs; film production and an actors association; and
   Indian theater. Information varies and is never extensive,
   but is enough for identification and contact. Indexed.

2. AMIC List of Theses: Studies on Mass Communication in
   Asia. Singapore 11: Asian Mass Communication Research
   and Information Centre, 39 Newton Road, annual. (1971--.)

   In three compilations: 1971, 1972, and 1973-74 in one
   volume. Entries, which are abstracted, attempt to list
   all M.A. and Ph.D. theses submitted to colleges and universities in Asia and abroad on various aspects of mass communication in Asia. Countries in the 1972 edition include
   Afghanistan, Bangladesh, Hong Kong, India, Indonesia, Japan,
   Korea, Pakistan, the Philippines, Sri Lanka, Taiwan, Thailand, the U.S., Vietnam. The 1973-74 edition has broadened
   its base to include Australia, Canada, England, Finland,
   France, Malaysia, and Yugoslavia. Subjects covered are:
   general; advertising, management, and public relations;
   broadcast media; communication--social aspects; education,
   film and other audio-visual media; print media; and rural
   communication. A fourth compilation includes theses for
   1975 and 1976, and any titles since 1971 not caught in the
   earlier volumes.

3. Asian Mass Communication Bibliography Series. Singapore 11:
   Asian Mass Communication Research and Information Centre,
   39 Newton Road, 1975--.

   In these annotated bibliographies communication is
   defined broadly to include relevant material from such areas
   as agriculture, anthropology, community development, economics, education, law, political science, population, public
   administration, sociology, social psychology, and urban
   studies. Types of material covered are books, pamphlets,
   conference reports, seminar papers, theses and dissertations, research studies, surveys, government annual reports,
   commission reports, and periodical materials. Some of these
   are unpublished. Ten of the series have appeared thus far:

   Mass Communication in Malaysia. Lim Huck Tee, comp.,
       assisted by V. V. Sarashandran. 1975. 91p. (No. 1.)
   Mass Communication in India. The Indian Institute of Mass
       Communication, comp., coordinator, R. K. Mehrotra. 1976.
       216p. (No. 2.)
   Mass Communication in Hong Kong and Macao. Timothy L. M.
       Yu, comp. 1976. 30p. (No. 3.)
   Mass Communication in the Philippines. Emilinda V. de
       Jesus, comp., assisted by Ameria J. Gloria and Aida B.
       Pecans. 1976. 335p. (No. 4.)
   Mass Communication in Taiwan. Shou-Jung Yang, comp. 1977.
       65p. (No. 5.)
   Mass Communication in Korea. Taeyoul Hahn, comp. 1977.
       67p. (No. 6.)
   Mass Communication in Singapore. AMIC, comp. 1977. 60p.
       (No. 7.)
   Mass Communication in Nepal. Narendra R. Panday, comp.
       1977. 34p. (No. 8.)
   Mass Communication in Sri Lanka. H. A. I. Goonetileke,
       comp. 1978. 77p. (No. 9.)
   Mass Communication in Indonesia. Mastini Hardjo Prakoso,
       comp. 1978. 61p. (No. 10.)
   Mass Communication in Pakistan and Mass Communication in
       Thailand are in process.

4. Asian Mass Communication Institutions, Teaching, Training
       and Research: A Directory. Singapore 10: Asian Mass
       Communication Research and Information Centre, 39 New-
       ton Road, 1973--. Looseleaf.

   An ongoing series which identifies as many Asian institutions as possible which are engaged in teaching, training,
   and research, with details like address, telephone number,
   date founded, objectives, activities, names of staff, type
   of research, examples, and facilities. Countries included
   are Hong Kong, India, Indonesia, Iran, Israel, Japan, Korea,

Lebanon, Malaysia, Pakistan, Philippines, Singapore, Sri
Lanka, Taiwan, Thailand, Vietnam (Saigon only). Contains
indexes to institutions and persons.

5. _Asian Press and Media Directory: Press, Radio, Television,
Advertising, Public Relations, Government Information,
Suppliers to Media_. Manila: Press Foundation of Asia
P.O. Box 1843, annual. (1974--.)

For twenty-six countries gives pertinent details about
daily newspapers and selected periodicals, news agencies,
associations, correspondents, public relations, training
institutions, broadcasting, satellite link-ups, advertising, government information sources, and equipment and
sources. There is a special section for regional media.
The section on the press goes into greater detail than
the others. Countries included are Afghanistan, Australia,
Bangladesh, Brunei, Burma, China, Hong Kong, India, Indonesia, Japan, Khmer (now Democratic Kampuchea), North and
South Korea, Laos, Malaysia, Nepal, New Zealand, Pacific
Islands, Pakistan, Philippines, Singapore, Sri Lanka,
Taiwan, Thailand, North and South Vietnam.

6. Aspen Handbook on the Media: A Selective Guide to Research,
Organizations and Publications in Communications. New
York: Praeger and the Aspen Institute, biennial.
(1973--.)

With each edition the coverage in this valuable reference book gets bigger and better. The 1977-79 volume
brings together extensive factual information about the
media not available in any other single source. Contents
include: universities with research programs in communications; nonacademic institutions conducting communications
research; organizations supporting communications research;
communications organizations (advertising and public relations, broadcasting, educational/instructional media, film
and photography, journalism, new communications technologies, print media, and related and general); media action
groups; a guide to government policymaking bodies in communications in the U.S. and Canada; communications law
courses; international and overseas communications organizations; a guide to special libraries and resources on
communications; communications periodicals--an annotated
list covering annuals, directories, and indexes; a selected
bibliography on communications and a selection of communications bibliographies; a selection of films on communications.
All entries give appropriate information to enable the users
to get in touch with a given source or order specific materials. Indexed. The 1977-79 edition is edited by William
L. Rivers, Wallace Thompson, and Michael J. Nyhan.

3

7. Atwan, Robert, Barry Orton, and William Vesterman, eds.
   American Mass Media: Industries and Issues. New York:
   Random House, 1978. 475p.

   An introductory reader in which a variety of scholars
   and professionals discuss the environment of media industries in terms of audiences, advertising, and government
   regulation, and then in terms of the various kinds of
   media--books, newspapers, magazines, radio, recordings,
   film, television, and "personal" media. This latter covers citizen feedback, telephone, CB radio and CB television, public access cable TV, and finally graffiti (about
   which Norman Mailer writes). Contains a brief bibliography
   of books and an index.

8. Australia National Commission for UNESCO. Entertainment
   and Society. Canberra: Australia National Commission
   for UNESCO, 1977. 242p.

   Report of a UNESCO seminar held to allow key personnel
   and organizations from the entertainment field to discuss
   the interplay between entertainment and society, especially
   in shaping societal and individual behavior. Discussions
   center around the high/popular culture relationship; funding and subsidy of performance; administration; and the
   purposes and meaning of the various forms of entertainment.
   Specific areas include popular entertainment in general;
   the media; sports; and the performing arts, with special
   emphasis on music.

9. Baer, Walter S., and others. Concentration of Mass Media
   Ownership: Assessing the State of Current Knowledge.
   Santa Monica, Cal.: RAND, 1974. 202p.

   A RAND Corporation study which has as its aim "to sift
   the literature systematically, and as dispassionately as
   possible, with two goals in mind: first, to determine what
   factual evidence there is on the effects of media ownership
   and its relevance to present government policies; and
   second, to suggest what additional data and analysis are
   needed to strengthen the basis for future policymaking."
   Discussion is concentrated around the issues of the public's
   stake in the mass media; federal concern with ownership;
   concentration--status and trends; its influence upon performance; and the problem of measuring performance. It is
   prefaced by a five-page summary. The books, monographs,
   reports, journal articles, dissertations, government documents, and other materials used cover a nineteen-year period
   from 1945 to the mid-seventies and form a comprehensive
   twenty-five-page bibliography--one of the best on the subject.

10. Bagdikian, Ben H. The Information Machines: Their Impact
    on Men and the Media. New York: Harper & Row, 1970.
    359p.

    A critical estimate of the past, present, and future of
    the communication media, sponsored by the RAND Corporation.
    Bagdikian discusses communication satellites, computers,
    conglomerates, the future of print, and the long-range
    impacts of high-density communication intervention on Amer-
    ican society.
    His analysis is backed with statistics and summaries of
    important studies, including those in broadcast as well as
    newspaper journalism. The list of references serves as a
    bibliography, and there is an index.

11. Basic Issues in Canadian Mass Communication. Developed
    under the supervision of Gertrude Joch Robinson. Mon-
    treal H3A 2T5: McGill University Book Store, Box 6070,
    1974. 13 booklets.

    A series of thirteen teaching modules about various
    aspects of Canadian communications, suitable for upper
    high school or introductory college courses. The quality
    varies somewhat, but most of these are well organized,
    well and simply written, and interestingly illustrated.
    Each contains, in addition to a factual survey, a biblio-
    graphy and suggested research projects. Titles are: Who
    Does What to Whom? How to Study Mass Media Effects; Where
    the Moose Run Loose: Carry On Canadian Film; Wired for What?
    Communications Technology in Canada; Freedom to Do What?
    The Press in Canada; Knock, Knock, Who's There? How to
    Study the Audience; For Love or Money: Broadcasting in
    Canada; Locking the Barn Door: Regulation and Control in
    Canadian Mass Media; Recording Stars with Stripes: The
    Record Industry in Canada; The Pit and the Pedestal: A
    Horror Story--Women in the Canadian Media; Hundreds of Doc-
    tors Recommend: Advertising in Canada; Perils, Problems
    and Potential: The Cable TV Industry in Canada; Snow Job:
    Communication in the Canadian North; and Under the Alter-
    native Counter: Styles and Motives of Alternative Media.

12. Bate, Michèle. The Media in France. London: Harrap, 1977.
    16p. (Life French Style.)

    This booklet, intended for secondary school students
    studying French, gives a simplified, thumbnail account of
    French newspapers, magazines, television, and radio.

13. Beasley, Maurine, and Sheila Silver. Women in Media: A
    Documentary Source Book. Washington 20008: Women's
    Institute for Freedom of the Press, 3306 Ross Place,
    N.W., 1977. 198p.

The authors, out of their experience in teaching a "Women and Mass Communications" course, have assembled the kinds of documents they feel best tell the historical development of women's role in communications in the United States from colonial times forward. The authors plan another volume which will include documents on women's role in the development of the arts, minority women journalists (other than black, who are covered in one of the documents in this volume), and women involved in the media in Canada and other countries. Bibliographical footnotes.

14. Berelson, Bernard, and Morris Janowitz, eds. Reader in Public Opinion and Communication. 2d ed. New York: Free Press, 1966. 788p.

Collection of over fifty articles by well-known social scientists on various phases of communication, grouped under the following headings: (1) theory of public opinion; (2) formation of public opinion; (3) impact of public opinion on public policy; (4) theory of communication; (5) communication media: structure and control; (6) communication content; (7) communication audiences; (8) communication effects; (9) public opinion, communication, and democratic objectives; (10) toward comparative analysis; (11) research methods.

15. Bibliography of Works on Mass Communication Published by Scandinavian Scholars in English and List of Scandinavian Communication Researchers. SF-33101 Tampere 10, Finland: Nordicom, P.O. Box 607, University of Tampere, 1975. 64p.

First bibliography of works on mass communication published in English by Scandinavian scholars. Includes, for Finland, works published both in Finland and abroad; for Denmark, Norway, and Sweden, mainly works published in those countries themselves. A list of communication researchers in Denmark, Finland, Norway, and Sweden is also included. For the first three countries it covers most of the active researchers; for Sweden the list in this edition is incomplete, but will be larger in a later edition. The bibliographical entries are unannotated; the entry for researchers contains the institute with which he or she is connected and its address, the researcher's field of interest, and a very brief theme of the project or projects on which work is currently being done.

16. Bigsby, C. W. E., ed. Approaches to Popular Culture. Bowling Green, Ohio: Bowling Green University Popular Press, 1976. 280p.

In the first part of this reader a number of writers outline possible academic approaches to popular culture (through sociology, structuralism, linguistics, Marxism, cultural

science, historical evidence); in the second part are
diverse examples of criticism. The former is especially
useful to laymen wishing a partial overview of theories
of popular culture in various disciplines.

17. Black List: The Concise and Comprehensive Reference Guide
    to Black Journalism, Radio, and Television Educational
    and Cultural Organizations in the USA, Africa, and the
    Caribbean. 2d ed. 2 vols. New York 10017: Black List,
    Box 3552, 1974-75.

   Black media is broadly defined to include broadcasting
stations--radio, television, and CATV--aimed at black listeners although not necessarily owned by blacks; newspapers,
periodicals, and publishing houses of various types; literary agents; theaters; and a large miscellaneous section of
media. Each entry has only the name and address and head;
in the case of periodicals frequency is given. There is a
lengthy introductory section consisting of articles, lists,
and statistics. Among them: an article by the chairman of
the FCC, "The FCC and Broadcasting; Matters of Concern to
Blacks"; one on television station employment practices;
"The Status of Minorities and Women 1974," which excerpts
reports; and figures on employment of blacks in broadcasting. Vol. I deals with the U.S.; Vol. II with Africa, the
Caribbean, and parts of Latin America.

18. Blake, Reed H., and Edwin O. Haroldsen. A Taxonomy of Con-
    cepts in Communication. New York: Hastings House, 1975.
    158p.

   The authors describe and classify some of the major concepts in communication--for example, cybernetics, information theory, rumor, content analysis, gatekeeper--along
with a number of such mass communication terms as news,
public relations, propaganda. Their aim is to provide new
students, or any laymen, with a vocabulary that will enable
them to discuss the subject more precisely. The terms
explained are the well-known ones; Blake and Haroldsen
state that they have not attempted to be definitive. But
this is a much-needed beginning. Emphasis is on the
behavioral approach. Arrangement is by broad subject categories, with an alphabetical listing of terms, a subject
index, and an author index of persons mentioned throughout
the book. Bibliography.

19. Bol, Jean-Marie van. Social Communication Media in Belgium.
    Brussels: Ministry of Foreign Affairs, External Trade
    and Cooperation in Development, 1975. 120p. (Memo from
    Belgium: "Views and Surveys" No. 169.)

   A concise survey of the Belgian media, including the
periodical press, weekly newspapers, and radio and

broadcasting. The author has given a great deal of background material such as history, regulation, unionization, associations, various forms of concentration, and other aspects. The various media are listed, and there are maps of daily newspaper and radio and television station locations. Each of the five chapters contains a bibliography.

20. Bol, Jean-Marie van, and Abdelfattah Fahkfakh. The Use of Mass Media in the Developing Countries. 1000 Brussels: International Center for African Social and Economic Documentation, 7 Place Royale, 1971. 750p.

   Contains 2,500 annotated citations in many different languages. The Aspen Handbook on the Media calls it "the best bibliography on the subject to date."

21. Boyle, Deidre, and Stephen Calvert. Children's Media Market Place. Syracuse, N.Y. 13201: Gaylord Professional Publications, P.O. Box 61/ Neal Schuman Publishers, 1978. 411p.

   This can be likened to a combination of Literary Marketplace and Audio-visual Marketplace, aimed at children, with other pertinent information about the market place added-- for example, libraries and television. It is divided into two parts: (1) Directory of Children's Media Sources and (2) Names and Numbers index to Children's Media Sources. Arrangement is by twenty areas of interest: The first two, Publishers, and Audiovisual Producers and Distributors, identify some 800 sources of children's materials, with each section followed by classified indexes locating materials by subject, type of format, and special interests. Magazines (Sections 3-6) give periodicals for children, professionals, and parents; review journals and services; and reviewers of children's media. Other sections are (7) wholesalers; (8) juvenile bookstores; (9) juvenile book clubs; (10) agents for children's properties; (11) sources for children's TV programs, including TV stations; (12) TV programs, with a title index; (13) organizations; (14) public library coordinators of children's and young adult services; (15) state school media officers; (16) examination centers; (17) calendar of events for 1978; (18) federal grants for children's media; (19) children's media awards; and (20) an annotated bibliography of selection tools and reference guides. The editors plan to produce future editions, and it is to be hoped that they will do so.

22. Branscomb, Anne W. The First Amendment as a Shield or a Sword: An Integrated Look at Regulation of Multi-Media Ownership. Santa Monica, Cal.: RAND, 1975. 114p.

   Examines the different ways in which the First Amendment has been applied with respect to concentration of control over the mass media; reviews the existing and proposed regulations; discusses the viability of alternative policies which would assure a diversity of information reaching the public regardless of ownership or control of the transmission facilities; and projects, from recent judicial decisions, what directions government policy might take to promote a diverse marketplace of ideas.

23. Bretz, Rudolf. A Taxonomy of Communication Media. Englewood Cliffs, N.J.: Educational Technology Publications, 1971. 168p. (A RAND Corporation Research Study.)

Defines twenty-eight specific communication media; discusses the difference between information and instruction, instructional media, and instructional aids; and proposes a set of criteria by which media may be distinguished from non-media.

24. Briggs, Asa. Mass Entertainment: The Origins of a Modern Industry. Adelaide, South Australia, Australia: The Griffin Press, 1960. 30p. (John Fisher Lecture in Commerce, University of Adelaide.)

This brief pamphlet gives a deeper insight into popular culture than many much longer works. Briggs approaches the development of mass entertainment from an economic and technological viewpoint, analyzing underlying conditions that make it an industry, and specifically tracing its growth in the nineteenth and twentieth centuries, with emphasis on film and broadcasting in the latter.

25. Brown, Charlene J., Trevor R. Brown, and William L. Rivers. The Media and the People. New York: Holt, Rinehart & Winston, 1978. 472p.

This useful book has a distinguished genesis. It is descended from Mass Media and Modern Society by Theodore Peterson and Jay Jensen (1965), which also came out in a second edition (1970), co-authored by William Rivers. The authors of this present book have based it on the earlier one, using basically the same structure, retaining the interpretative and essayist style, and drawing on "the insights of Professors Jensen and Peterson's literate and persuasive description and analysis of mass communication while reorganizing the contents to reflect the changes in the mass media in the late 1970s." A blend of description and theory, with emphasis on history, it remains one of the best of the introductions to mass communications. Contains notes and a bibliography. Frances Goins Wilhoit has compiled and annotated a list of periodicals about mass media. There is a name and a subject index. Those who have the older version in either edition should keep it; there is enough difference to merit it.

26. Burnet, Mary. <u>The Mass Media in a Violent World</u>. Paris:
    UNESCO Publications Center, 1974. 44p. (Reports and
    Papers on Mass Communication No. 63.)

    Report of a symposium conducted by twenty-three special-
    ists in various disciplines of the social sciences who
    represent eighteen countries. Emphasis is worldwide as mem-
    bers attempt to answer three questions: (1) What is meant
    by violence? (2) What is commonly assumed and what is
    actually known about the relation between violence in the
    mass media and violence in real life? (3) How can the media
    carry out their traditional mission of informing, educating,
    and entertaining in such a way that their influence will
    tend to reduce rather than increase violence? The develop-
    ing countries come in for special attention. Discussion
    centers around structure and theory rather than empirical
    studies.

27. Butler-Paisley, Matilda, Sheridan Crawford, and M. Violet
    Lofgren, comps. <u>Directory of Women and Minority Men in
    Academic Journalism/Communication</u>. Stanford, Cal. 94305:
    Women in Communication, Stanford University, 1976. Un-
    paged.

    For each entry gives address, degrees, teaching special-
    ties, media and research experience. Indexed according to
    teaching and research interests.

28. Canada. <u>Report of the Royal Commission on Violence in the
    Communications Industry</u>. Toronto: The Commission, 1977.
    7 vols. (Obtain from Renouf Publishing Co., Ltd., 2182
    St. Catherine St., W., Montreal, Quebec H3H 1M7.)

    The purpose of this study, sponsored by the government
    of Ontario, is fourfold: (1) to study the effects on soci-
    ety of the increasing exhibition of violence in the commu-
    nications industry; (2) to determine if there is any con-
    nection or a cause-and-effect relationship between this
    phenomenon and the incidence of violent crime in society;
    (3) to hold public hearings to enable groups and organiza-
    tions, individual citizens, and representatives of the
    industry to make known their views on the subject; and
    (4) to make appropriate recommendations, if warranted, on
    measures that should be taken by the government of Ontario
    or other levels of the Canadian government, the general
    public, or the industry. To accomplish this the past fifty
    years of research on the subject have been covered and
    applied to Canada. Because U.S. and Canadian media are
    interconnected, many of their findings are pertinent to
    this country as well. Vol. I contains <u>Approaches, Conclu-
    sions and Recommendations</u>; Vol. II, <u>Violence and the Media:
    A Bibliography</u>; Vol. III, <u>Violence in Television Films and</u>

News; Vol. IV, Violence in Print and Music; Vol. V, Learning from Media; Vol. VI, Vulnerability to Media Effects;
Vol. VII, The Media Industries: From Here to Where? In
addition to the master bibliography in Vol. II, other volumes contain individual bibliographies.

29. Canada. Senate. Report on the Mass Media. 3 vols.
    Ottawa: Information Canada, 171 Slater St., 1970.

   Vol. I, The Uncertain Mirror, summarizes and evaluates
the economics of the media in Canada and makes proposals,
one of which involves the teaching of journalism. Vol. II,
Good, Bad, or Simply Inevitable, gives raw data on the
economics of newspapers and advertising. Vol. III, Words,
Music and Dollars, is a questionnaire distributed in an
effort to learn how Canadian people feel about the mass
media. Results are broken down by province. Although
much of the contents concerns broadcasting, more of the
emphasis is on newspapers because broadcasting was covered
in 1965 by the Report of the Committee on Broadcasting (No.
365). The three volumes constitute a comprehensive picture
of the structure and function of the media and how the
people feel about them. Contains appendices and an index.

30. Canadian Radio-Television Commission. Bibliographie,
    Études Canadiennes sur les Mass Media: Bibliography,
    Some Canadian Writings on the Mass Media. Ottowa K1A
    ON2: The Commission, 100 Metcalf St., 1975. 99p.

   An unannotated listing of 1,075 items, prepared by the
journalism department, Université Laval, Quebec, and the
research branch of the Commission. Works include books,
dissertations, journal articles, and government documents
concerning the Canadian mass media by Canadians or by
authors living in Canada, and works published by U.S. firms
with Canadian branches if published in Canada as well as
the U.S. Items are in straight alphabetical order, with a
subject index.

31. Casty, Alan, comp. Mass Media and Mass Man. 2d ed. New
    York: Holt, Rinehart & Winston, 1973. 304p.

   This anthology, intended as an undergraduate text or
for collateral reading, is divided into three parts: "Mass
Media and Society"; "Mass Media and Culture"; and "Mass
Media and Information," with social issues that blend, overlap, or relate to the other two categories. A final section
contains topics and questions for further study, analysis
and research, and a bibliography. There is an author and a
title index. This second edition does not so much supersede
the first as supplement it, with some of the old articles
retained but many new ones added.

11

32. Chaffee, Steven H., and Michael J. Petrick. Using the Mass
    Media: Communication Problems in American Society. New
    York: McGraw-Hill, 1975. 264p.

    The authors discuss "major problem areas, which represent
    four distinct types of social goals that people try to
    achieve by means of the mass media"--public information,
    influencing behavior, social control, and social change.
    Intended "to some extent" as a textbook. Indexed.

33. Chatterjee, Rama Krishna. Mass Communication. New Delhi:
    National Book Trust (India), 1973. 222p. (Distributed
    by Thomson Press, India.)

    The author deals with mass communication in general,
    with emphasis on developments in India since its indepen-
    dence. Media include newspapers and periodicals, broadcast-
    ing, and film. There are discussions of press freedom, the
    role of mass communication, press laws, advertising, mass
    communication in the border areas, and mass communication
    and technology. Indexed.

34. Cherry, Colin. World Communication: Threat or Promise? A
    Socio-Technical Approach. New York: Wiley-Interscience,
    1971. 229p.

    Using a global and social approach, Cherry bridges the
    gap between writings on the subject by technical experts and
    by social scientists. He discusses the nature of human com-
    munication; ancient and modern communication; the communica-
    tion explosion; communication as pleasure and as politics;
    communication and wealth; and some social aspects. As he
    touches on these various sides of the media, we see the
    underlying structure of the systems that gave rise to them.
    Numerous charts, tables, and maps, a bibliography, and an
    index.

35. Chu, Godwin C., ed. Popular Media in China: Shaping New
    Cultural Patterns. Honolulu: University of Hawaii Press,
    1978. 263p. (An East-West Center Book from the East-
    West Communication Institute.)

    The authors have focused on five media--revolutionary
    children's folk songs, revolutionary serial pictures, revo-
    lutionary opera, short stories, and tatzepao, a form of
    poster art--to show how traditional popular-culture forms
    are being transformed to reflect the values of a new
    society. Bibliography and index.

36. Chu, Godwin C., and Brent Cassan, comps. Modern Communica-
    tion Technology in a Changing Society: A Bibliography.
    Honolulu: East-West Center, Communication Institute,
    1977. 162p.

One thousand articles, books, dissertations, and papers
from 1930 onward, covering a wide spectrum of the social
sciences including sociology, anthropology, economics, and
communication, are arranged under twelve categories: communication satellites, social effects of communication,
social structure and communication processes; communication
and national development; communication for community
development; communication for rural development; communication for information dissemination and innovation;
educational media; mass media systems; family planning
communication; CATV and communication technology; and
bibliographies. Entries are not annotated. A second section consists of abstracts of certain titles, with the
abstracts taken or sometimes modified from Sociological
Abstracts, Communication Research, and Dissertation
Abstracts International. Author index.

37. Commission on Freedom of the Press. Reports. 6 vols.
    Chicago: University of Chicago Press, 1946-47.

The following group of studies resulted from an inquiry
financed by Time, Inc., and Encyclopedia Britannica, Inc.,
with funds disbursed through the University of Chicago.
The aim of the Commission, composed mostly of some of the
leading university educators of the day and chaired by
Robert M. Hutchins, chancellor of the University of
Chicago, was to investigate the flow of public information
through the press as comprised of radio, newspapers, motion
pictures, magazines, and books. Equal emphasis was placed
on the flow of ideas. Recommendations, though not dramatic,
went further than freedom of the press, and urged owners
and managers to be aware of their responsibility to American culture and the American people--in short, they
advocated the social responsibility theory. The studies
listed below go deeply into history, structure, problems,
and principles of the individual media or of press freedom.
They are:

A Free and Responsible Press: A General Report on Mass
    Communication: Newspapers, Radio, Motion Pictures,
    Magazines and Books. (No. 68.)
Peoples Speaking to Peoples: A Report on International
    Mass Communication. By Llewellyn White and Robert D.
    Leigh. (No. 212.)
American Radio: A Report on the Broadcasting Industry in
    the United States. By Llewellyn White. (No. 620.)
Freedom of the Press: A Framework of Principle. By
    William Ernest Hocking.
Government and Mass Communications. By Zechariah Chafee, Jr.
Freedom of the Movies: A Report on Self-Regulation. By
    Ruth A. Inglis. (No. 888.)

13

(Because Chaffee and Hocking deal exclusively with censorship they are not entered separately.)

38. Communication/Journalism Education in Asia: Background and
    Status in Seven Asian Areas. Jack Lyle, ed. Honolulu
    96822: East-West Road, 1971. 84p.

    Background papers compiled for a teachers' seminar in
    which Taiwan, Hong Kong, India, Indonesia, Korea, the
    Philippines, and Thailand participated. The information
    about each country varies considerably, since the contri-
    butors were allowed to comment upon salient points in their
    particular situations rather than requested to follow a
    standard format. Topics common to most articles were pro-
    grams, facilities, research, service, government support.
    Lyle summarizes the seminar in a concluding section. There
    is a list of participants.

39. Communication Policies in . . . . Paris: UNESCO, 1974--.
    An untitled series of studies whose aim is an analysis
    of communication policies in various countries as they
    exist at public, institutional, and professional levels,
    with information presented in a way that enables compari-
    son. Countries covered thus far are the following:

    Furhoff, Lars, Lennart Jonsson, and Lennart Nilsson. Com-
        munication Policies in Sweden: A Study Carried out by
        the Swedish Journalism School. 1974. 76p.
    Mahle, Walter A., and Rolf Richter. Communication Policies
        in the Federal Republic of Germany: A Study Carried
        out by the Arbeitagemeinschaft fur Kommunikationforschung.
        1974. 86p.
    Szecsko, Tamas, and Gabor Fodor. Communication Policies in
        Hungary. 1974. 58p.
    Stapleton, John. Communication Policies in Ireland: A
        Study Carried out by the Institute of Public Administra-
        tion, An Foras Rairachain. 1974. 58p.
    Comargo, Nelly de, and Virgilio B. Noya Pinto. Communica-
        tion Policies in Brazil. 1975. 80p.
    Lekovic, Zdravko, and Mihailo Bjelica. Communication
        Policies in Yugoslavia: A Study Carried out by the
        Yugoslav Institute of Journalism. 1976. 66p.
    Desai, M. V. Communication Policies in India. 1977. 88p.
    De Silva, M. A., and Reggie Siriwardene. Communication
        Policies in Sri Lanka: A Study Carried out by a Com-
        mittee Appointed by the Ministry of Education. 1977.
        59p.
    Fonseca, Jaime M. Communication Policies in Costa Rica.
        1977. 89p.
    Kato, Hidetoshi. Communication Policies in Japan. 1977.
        57p.

Ortega, Carlos, and Carlo Romero. Communication Policies
in Peru. 1977. 68p.
Alajmo, Alberto Carrizosa. Communication Policies in
Colombia. 1977. 50p.
Bae-Ho, Hahn. Communication Policies in the Republic of
Korea. 1978. 50p.

40. Communication Yearbook. New Brunswick, N.J.: Transaction
Books, annual. (1977--.)

A series, sponsored by the International Communication
Association, whose purpose is to give an overview and
synthesis of the field by means of reviews and commentaries
from the various disciplines that constitute it; overviews
of subdivisions within each; and current research selected
to represent the interest areas. Divisions selected for
inclusion are information systems, interpersonal communication, mass communication, intercultural communication,
political communication, and instructional communication.
Each article lists references. In Vol. I an appendix gives
a history of the International Communication Association.
Brent D. Ruben edited the first two volumes. Topic and
author index.

41. Connor, Walter D., and Zvi Y. Gitelman, with Adaline
Huszezo and Robert Blumstock. Public Opinion in European Socialist Systems. New York: Praeger, 1977. 196p.

Concentrates on the U.S.S.R., Poland, Czechoslovakia,
and Hungary, describing the emergence of opinion polls, the
ups and downs and the reasons behind them, and the ways in
which they are conducted. Although data obtained from the
polls occupies a large space, primary emphasis is on a
social analysis of the process and its effects, with the
regimes of the four countries examined both as subject act-
ing to maintain itself and as object being evaluated by the
public. Contains chapter notes and an index.

42. Contemporary Authors: A Bio-Biographical Guide to Current
Writers in Fiction, General Nonfiction, Poetry, Journal-
ism, Drama, Motion Pictures, Television, and Other Fields.
Detroit: Gale Research Co., 1975. (Vol. I.)

Formerly Contemporary Authors, this has now been expanded
to include "significant personalities from all media." Complete coverage is obviously impossible, and although the
editor claims to have covered "major TV Capitol and foreign
correspondents, wire service reporters and bureau chiefs,
important by-line contributors to newspapers and magazines,"
as well as "newspaper and TV reporters, columnists, prominent newspaper and periodical editors, syndicated cartoon-
ists, screenwriters, TV script-writers," an examination of

15

the 1977 volume shows that many who come obviously to mind--
Norman Podhoretz, Bernstein and Woodward, Katherine Graham,
for example--are not included. Mark Vonnegut is in, but not
his father, Kurt. For whatever reasons, the reach of this
publication is high, its grasp incomplete. Even so, it
covers several thousand personages. Information about each
individual is grouped under headings which vary somewhat,
probably depending on what material he/she turned in; "personal" and "career" are constant. Other subjects include
"writings," "work in progress," "member," and "sidelights."
Personal facts come under the latter heading.

43. Curran, James, Michael Gurevitch, and Janet Woollacott, eds.
    Mass Communication and Society. London: Edward Arnold
    in association with The Open University Press, 1977.
    479p.

    "The central concern of this Reader is with whole soci-
    eties, their class structure and forms of class dominance
    and an exploration of the role of the media as ideological
    and signifying agencies within that whole. The concept of
    ideology is therefore of central concern," say the editors
    in their anthology. This is a very different approach from
    the empirical Lasswellian research formula: "Who says what
    in which channel to whom with what effect?" Divided into
    three sections: Section I presents the relationships
    between the media and society from different ideological
    perspectives; Section II focuses on the organizational
    structure of the media; Section III reflects a variety of
    approaches to "ideology" and the communication of "culture."
    Most of the articles were especially commissioned. Each is
    followed by extensive references. Indexed.

44. Current British Research on Mass Media and Mass Communica-
    tion: Register of Ongoing and Recently Completed
    Research. Connie Ellis, comp. Leicester, England LE1
    7RH: University of Leicester, 1976. 74p. (Leicester
    Documentation Centre for Mass Communication Research.)

    Summaries and other pertinent information (name of
    researcher, project title, sponsor where applicable,
    research institution, etc.) for 162 projects. Divided
    into two parts: Part I deals with entries on specific
    media--television, radio, the press, cinema and film,
    books, music, and entries covering more than two media;
    Part II is broken down by subject area--advertising,
    international studies, education, politics, psychology,
    and statistics.

45. Danielson, Wayne A., and G. C. Wilhoit, Jr., comps. A Com-
    puterized Bibliography of Mass Communication Research,

<u>1944-1964</u>. New York 10022: Magazine Publishers Asso-
ciation, Inc., Magazine Center, 575 Lexington Ave., 1967.
399p.

A monumental undertaking subsidized by the MPA, this computerized print-off bibliography leads the user to thousands
of articles relating to the mass media from 1944 through 1964
which appeared in forty-eight social science periodicals.

46. Davison, Walter Phillips, and Frederick T. C. Yu, eds. <u>Mass
    Communication Research: Major Issues and Future Direc-
    tions</u>. New York: Praeger, 1974. 246p.

    This anthology concerns itself with two questions: What
    is the current state of knowledge about research in this
    area? What might be the most fruitful direction for future
    research? Among aspects discussed are the structure of the
    field; the uses of mass communication by the individual;
    mass communication and socialization; the function of the
    media for organizations, mass communication, and the nation
    state; mass communication and the political system; profes-
    sional personnel and organizational structure in the media;
    management; implications of new information technology; and
    priority areas for future research. Other authors in addi-
    tion to the editors are Elihu Katz, Jay Blumler, Michael
    Gurevitch, Herbert Hyman, Daniel Lerner, Davis B. Bobrow,
    Ben Bagdikian, Leo Bogart, Edward B. Parker, and Forrest
    Chrisman. Bibliography and index.

47. Davison, Walter Phillips, James R. Boylan, and Frederick
    T. C. Yu. <u>Mass Media: Systems and Effects</u>. New York:
    Praeger, 1976. 245p.

    The aim of the authors is to evaluate the merits and
    demerits of mass media in the U.S. vis à vis the public
    interest. With this in mind they present "an introduction
    to the history of the mass media in the United States, an
    overview of information about their functioning and effects,
    and a brief comparison of the American media system and
    other media systems." Following an introductory historical
    chapter they synthesize major studies about the problem of
    private versus government control, the factors that shape
    content, the availability of channels, the ways in which we
    receive content, the effects, and certain facts about the
    media which the average viewer, listener, or reader should
    know. An appendix gives statistics on journalism and
    journalists--numbers, characteristics, incomes, working
    conditions. Lengthy list of references and an excellent
    index.

48. DeFleur, Melvin L., and Sandra Ball-Rokeach. <u>Theories of
    Mass Communication</u>. 3d ed. New York: McKay, 1975.
    288p.

"The intention of this book is to see the mass media within the context of society--with a special focus on American media and American society" and "to provide students with a guide and overview . . . with broad theoretical perspectives." Within this framework the authors discuss the various media and the media in general. There is a chapter on television and violence. The final chapter is "Toward an Integrated Theory of Mass Media Effects." Contains footnotes and an index.

49. Dennis, Everette E. The Media Society: Evidence about Mass Communication in America. Dubuque, Iowa: William C. Brown, 1978. 166p.

   Analytical commentary on the mass media in the U.S. which synthesizes much systematic research and perceptive observation on the subject. In three parts: "The Impact, Influence and Effect of the Media," "Looking Inside, the Media as Social Institutions," and "Media Criticism and Analysis." There are prolific notes after each chapter and a bibliography.

50. Dennis, Everette E., and William L. Rivers. Other Voices: The New Journalism in America. San Francisco: Canfield Press, 1974. 218p.

   Comprehensively surveys trends away from traditional journalism as it has existed for most of this century, and describes new and alternate forms, as well as the revival of an old form. Covers muckraking, journalistic nonfiction, advocacy journalism, the counterculture, alternative broadcasting, and precision journalism. There is also a chapter on journalism reviews. The authors have compiled an extensive annotated bibliography of articles and books. Indexed.

51. Dennis, Everette E., Arnold H. Ismach, and Donald M. Gillmor, eds. Enduring Issues in Mass Communication. St. Paul, Minn.: West Publishing Co., 1978. 380p.

   An anthology which places the media in an interesting framework. Part I, "The Impact of Society," gives perspectives on the role of the media as it has changed over the years. Part II, "Media Roles and Performances," examines the forces that shape content, including styles, values, and economics. Part III, "Media Reforms and Innovations," deals with technological, legal, and philosophical forces and issues today. Articles are well chosen, but have been extensively abridged. Notes and bibliographies follow each.

52. Developing Information Media in Africa: Press, Radio, Film, Television. Paris: UNESCO, 1962. 57p. (Reports and Papers on Mass Communication No. 37.)

Report of a meeting of 200 experts (and part of a continuing survey by UNESCO encompassing underdeveloped areas
on a worldwide scale) in which participants discuss methods
by which mass communications may be strengthened and, where
necessary, developed in Africa. Includes news agencies and
newspapers, film, radio and television broadcasting, training, and research on mass communications.

53. Emery, Michael C., and Ted Curtis Smythe, comps. Readings
    in Mass Communication: Concepts and Issues in the Mass
    Media. 3d ed. Dubuque, Iowa: William C. Brown, 1977.
    483p.

    A college textbook in which the compilers have organized
    their material around three aspects of the mass media:
    (1) changing concepts of function and role, including
    access, criticism, reporting practices, and legal restraints
    on news; (2) new ideas, technologies, and attitudes within
    and about the media; and (3) new issues. A second table of
    contents arranged around the media is included. A brief
    essay introducing students to leading bibliographies,
    indexes, periodicals, and a useful handbook precedes the
    text, and short bibliographic essays follow each chapter.
    Indexed.

Encyclomedia. (See No. 1103.)

54. Ernst, Morris L. The First Freedom. New York: Macmillan,
    1946. 316p.

    One of the earliest examinations of monopoly in the com-
    munications industry, which was then chiefly press, radio,
    and motion pictures. Updated in 1968 by Rucker's book by
    the same name, which concentrates on newspapers and broad-
    casting monopoly up to 1968 (No. 174).

55. Explorations in Communication: An Anthology. Edmund Car-
    penter and Marshall McLuhan, eds. Boston: Beacon, 1960.
    210p.

    Before Marshall McLuhan became well known, he and Car-
    penter were using a journal, Explorations, published at the
    University of Toronto between 1953 and 1959, as a sounding
    board for new and different approaches to communication.
    (Issues are now rare collectors' items.) All the essays in
    this anthology appeared in Explorations. They probed the
    grammars of such languages as print, the newspaper format,
    and television, arguing that revolutions in the packaging
    and distribution of ideas and feelings modified not only
    human relations but also sensibilities. They further
    argued that we are largely ignorant of literacy's role in
    shaping Western man, and equally unaware of the role of

electronic media in shaping modern values. These ideas are current today, but were for the most part pioneered by the contributors who included, in addition to Carpenter and McLuhan, David Reisman, Robert Graves, S. Gideon, Stanley Edgar Hyman, and Gilbert Seldes, among others.

56. External Information and Cultural Relations Programs of France. Harold J. Kaplan, comp. Washington: United States Information Agency, Office of Research & Assessment, 1972. 85p.

57. External Information and Cultural Relations Programs of the Federal Republic of Germany. F. Gunther Eyck, comp. Washington: United States Information Agency, Office of Research & Assessment, 1973. 94p.

58. External Information and Cultural Relations Programs of Japan. Kenneth Bunce, comp. Washington: United States Information Agency, Office of Research & Assessment, 1973. 125p.

59. External Information and Cultural Relations Programs of the People's Republic of China. Washington: United States Information Agency, Office of Research & Assessment, 1973(?) 339p.

60. External Information and Cultural Relations Programs of the Union of Soviet Socialist Republics. Washington: United States Information Agency, Office of Research & Assessments, 1973. 153p.

61. External Information and Cultural Relations Programs of the United Kingdom. Washington: United States Information Agency, Office of Research & Assessments, 1973. 192p.

Although the primary aim of this series is to describe strategies and structures of programs aimed at foreigners, it nonetheless gives facts and insights about the organization, administration, and programming of the national media in the countries described in addition to their propaganda techniques. Contents of each vary. Most of the publications contain charts and tables; some have bibliographic footnotes.

62. Felsenthal, Norman. Orientations to Mass Communication. Palo Alto, Cal.: Science Research Associates, 1976. 54p.

Intended as a textbook for late high school or early college years, this fifty-four-page booklet contains an amazing amount of capsuled information about mass communication: its nature, its content, the various theories, the societal effects, the control and regulation. It should also serve well to give the adult layman a concise overview. There is an excellent bibliography.

63. Fischer, Heinz-Dietrich, and John C. Merrill, eds. <u>Inter-national and Intercultural Communication</u>. 2d ed. New York: Hastings House, 1976. 524p.

A survey whose purpose is to show through a collection of readings the broad and varied aspects of international communication. The authors have presented articles and portions of books and theses which stress overall inter-national concerns rather than specific national ones. Material is grouped under the following headings: "Com-munication Systems and Concepts"; "The World's Media"; "Problems of Freedom and Responsibility"; "National Develop-ment and Mass Media"; "International News Flow and Propa-ganda"; "Advertising and Public Relations"; "Supranational Communication Efforts"; "Intercultural Communication"; "Theory and Research in International Communication." Among the authors are Fischer and Merrill, Leo Bogart, W. Phillips Davison, Willard P. Dizard, Wilbur Schramm, Raymond Nixon, Ralph Lowenstein, Mary Gardner, Jacques Ellul, Paul Lazarsfeld, L. John Martin, Hamid Mowlana, Kaarle Nordenstreng. Contains a bibliography of biblio-graphies from various countries and a name-subject index.

64. <u>Foremost Women in Communications: A Biographical Reference Work on Accomplished Women in Broadcasting, Publishing, Advertising, Public Relations, and Allied Professions</u>. Ed. by Barbara J. Love. New York: Foremost Americans Publishing Corp., 1970. 788p.

Gives biographical profiles of more than 7,000 women prominent in communications fields. Contains geographical and subject cross-indexes.

65. Francois, William E. <u>Mass Media Law and Regulation</u>. 2d ed. Columbus, Ohio: Grid, 1978. 616p.

A text in which the aim of the author is to present the broad scope of mass media law to the journalism student: press freedom, pornography, reporter's privilege, the Fair-ness Doctrine, libel, licensing, privacy, access, antitrust law and media competition, copyright. He discusses impor-tant court cases and analyzes majority and dissenting opin-ions. Summaries are given at the end of each chapter. Appendices describe the court system and the appellate decision-making process, and define legal terms. Contains a name and a subject index.

66. Franklin, Marc A. <u>Cases and Materials on Mass Media Law</u>. Mineola, N.Y.: Foundation Press, 1977. 878p.

In this casebook the author states as his purpose "to acquaint students with major aspects of media law and to

provide an extended look at the tensions between legal regulation and the First Amendment." Contents include: "The
Development of the Concept of Freedom of Expression"; "Business Aspects of Mass Media Enterprises"; "Legal Problems of
Gathering Information"; "Restrictions on Content of Communication"; "Distribution Problems of Non-Broadcasting Media";
"Introduction to Broadcasting"; "Broadcast Licensing"; "Legal
Control of Programming—Sources and Content." There is a
statutory appendix, "The Communications Act of 1934." Contains a table of cases and an index. The author's The First
Amendment and the Fourth Estate deals with the same material
in a simplified manner.

67. Franklin, Marc A., in collaboration with Ruth Korzenik Frank-
     lin. The First Amendment and the Fourth Estate: Communi-
     cations Law for Undergraduates. Mineola, N.Y.: Founda-
     tion Press, 1977. 727p.

    In this excellent work the object of the authors—one a
lawyer, the other a journalist—is to clarify major legal
doctrines that affect the mass media, to explain their
origins and asserted justifications, and to evaluate their
soundness. They approach the problems as journalists might
view them rather than as lawyers might. Appendices give the
Constitution, excerpts from the Communications Act of 1934,
the Sigma Delta Chi Code of Ethics (1973), and an organizational chart of the FCC.

68. A Free and Responsible Press: A General Report on Mass Com-
     munication: Newspapers, Radio, Motion Pictures, Magazines,
     and Books. Chicago: University of Chicago Press, 1947.
     138p.

    A summary and critique of the findings of the six-volume
report of the Commission of Freedom of the Press, with "press"
interpreted broadly. It emphasizes the responsibilities of
owners and managers to use their media for the common good—
the "social responsibility" theory.

69. Friedman, Leslie J. Sex Role Stereotyping in the Mass Media:
     An Annotated Bibliography. New York: Garland, 1977.
     324p.

    "This bibliography brings together the many studies, con-
tent analyses and published opinions concerning sex stereotypes in the media in order to put past research into
historical perspective and to offer direction for future
research," says Friedman. Entries run the gamut from pure
academic scholarship to speeches, statistical evidence
gathered by women's and church groups, consciousness-raising
slide programs and films, and works tracing the imagery of
women throughout the history of film, rock music, and women's

magazines. There are even twelve articles defending sexism—
all the author could find. Sections cover the mass media in
general, advertising, broadcast media, film print media,
popular culture, media image of minority group women and of
men, children's media, and the impact of media stereotypes
on occupational choices. Includes books, articles from
books, pamphlets, and other types of materials as well as
journal articles. An author and a subject index.

70. Gadney, Alan. Gadney's Guide to 1800 Contests, Festivals &
    Grants in Film & Video, Photography, TV-Radio Broadcast-
    ing, Writing, Poetry & Playwriting, Journalism. Glendale,
    Cal. 91219: Festival Publications, P.O. Box 10180, 1978.
    578p.

    Described as the premier edition of a reference source
for all those wanting to "enter their work in national &
international contests, festivals, competitions, salons,
exhibitions, markets, tradefairs, and other awards & sales
events; apply for grants, loans, scholarships, fellowships,
residences, apprenticeships, internships, training & personal-
benefit programs." Information for each entry varies according to media and the contest itself, but always includes such
essentials as full address, date, entry fee, and deadline.
Eligibility, nature of awards, and manner of judging are
included in the majority of cases, and there is always more-
than-adequate descriptive material where necessary. Contains
an alphabetical event/sponsor/award index and a subject/cate-
gory index.

71. Gallup, George H. The Gallup Poll: Public Opinion, 1935-
    1971. 3 vols. New York: Random House, 1972.
    _____. The Gallup Poll: Public Opinion, 1972-1977.
    2 vols. Wilmington, Del.: Scholarly Resources, Inc.
    1978.

    These two publications contain the findings of Gallup Poll
reports from the founding of the organization in 1935
through 1977. The five volumes give the results of each
survey by percentages, but lack of space in the first three
volumes forced the elimination of the editorial and interpretive material which usually accompanies the report. The
last two volumes, however, have included it. Arrangement
is chronological by date of release to newspapers, and the
final volume of each set has a comprehensive name-subject
index. Preferatory material in each set has a record of
Gallup's accuracy, and a chronology of events. Although
the primary purpose of this comprehensive work is to give
the American viewpoint on social and political issues, it
has a secondary use equally important—it shows what the
issues were.

23

Another compilation of opinion polling, of historical
interest, is Public Opinion, 1935-46, edited by Hadley
Cantril (Princeton University Press, 1951), which groups
under various subject headings the findings of twenty-
three polling organizations in sixteen countries. The
names of the participating organizations also form a useful list of international polling organizations of that
decade.

72. Gandy, Oscar H., Jr., Susan Miller, William L. Rivers, and
    Gail Ann Rivers. Media and Government: An Annotated
    Bibliography. Stanford, Cal.: Stanford University
    Institute for Communication Research, 1975. 93p.

"Although most research focuses on the impact of the
media on the public or on the election process, we try here
to encourage more research on the relationships between
journalists and officials," say the authors. In four parts,
with Part I organized around the nature of the news media;
Part II, government information sources; Part III, the
impact of government on the media; and Part IV, the impact
of the media on government. Both monographs and articles
are included, as well as a brief description of the methodology of each entry and an abstract of the content.

73. Gans, Herbert J. Popular Culture and High Culture: An
    Analysis and Evaluation of Taste. New York: Basic
    Books, 1974. 179p.

Gans, advocate of cultural pluralism and devil's advocate to those who maintain that popular culture threatens
the existence of high culture, here states his case.
Within a sociological framework he defends popular culture
against some of its attackers, arguing for cultural democracy and against the idea that only the cultural expert
knows what is good for people and for society. Finally,
he makes policy proposals for more cultural pluralism.
Footnotes and index.

74. Georgi, Charlotte. The Arts and the World of Business: A
    Selected Bibliography. Metuchen, N.J.: Scarecrow Press,
    1973. 123p.

Although the relationship of business and the arts is
peripheral to the mass media, it nevertheless verges on them
so closely and so little material exists on the subject that
this bibliography fills a niche in the literature. One section, "The Mass Media: Radio, Television and Film," cites
forty-five titles, most of which will be already familiar to
the expert. But other sections such as "Culture, Leisure
and the Arts," "Government and the Arts," "Labor and the
Arts," "Foundations, Grants and Fund-Raising," provide less

well-known material. There are also lists of indexes to
journal and periodical literature, recommended journals and
newsletters, reference sources, bibliographies, and associations, councils, and other organizations. Entries are
limited to books and are unannotated. Publishers' addresses
are given, and there is an author index.

75. Gerbner, George, ed. Mass Media Policies in Changing Cul-
    tures. New York: Wiley-Interscience, 1977. 291p.

    An anthology which examines international trends, new
directions, and theoretical developments in mass media
policies around the world in order to give a multinational
comparative perspective. Part I surveys international
trends, with various articles describing early Western
leadership and recent shifts in the balance of power. Part
II explores new directions in communications policy in
traditional, transitional, and revolutionary societies,
highlighting some of the issues involved in conflicts and
controversies. Part III presents developments in theory
and research to show the different ways cross-cultural media
studies have been approached. Each article is footnoted,
and there is an index.

76. Gillmor, Donald, and Jerome A. Barron. Mass Communication
    Law: Cases and Comments. 3d ed. St. Paul, Minn.: West
    Publishing Co., 1979. 997p.

    A casebook text. Contents include: the impact of the
First Amendment in terms of theory, practice, and problems;
libel and the journalist; privacy and the press; the journalist's privilege; the law of news gathering; free press and
fair trial; pornography; and regulation of radio and TV
broadcasting, focusing on some problems of law, technology,
and policy. There are also less specific problems of law
and journalism which are discussed in terms of examples.

77. Glattbach, Jack, and Mike Anderson. The Print and Broadcast-
    ing Media in Malaysia. Kuala Lumpur, Malaysia: South
    East Asia Press Centre, 230, Jalan Ampang, 1971. 33p.
78. _____. The Print and Broadcasting Media in Singapore.
    Kuala Lumpur, Malaysia: South East Asia Press Centre,
    230, Jalan Ampang, 1971. 18p.

    A general description of the newspaper press and broad-
casting systems of both countries, with concise data about
the general background, including literacy, manpower, equipment, news agencies, advertising, and other pertinent data.
The two pamphlets differ slightly as to information. An
introductory section of the one on Malaysia contains the
structure of the two media and some of their problems; an

appendix to the one on Singapore gives literacy levels and readership and listenership figures.

79. Golding, Peter. The Mass Media. London: Longman, 1974. 134p.

Golding, a sociologist at the Leicester University Center for Mass Communication Research, analyzes evidence produced by the social sciences about the mass communication process in contemporary Britain and the development and structure, the media's relationship to one another and to other agencies of society, and wider sociological implications of organizational and technological changes taking place within them. Contains a bibliography and an index.

80. Gordon, George N. Communications and Media: Constructing a Cross-Discipline. New York: Hastings House, 1975. 209p.

What is communication? What areas does it include? Is it a discipline? These are the questions Gordon sets out to answer. First of all, he takes an intellectual inventory—the technological involvement; the viewpoints of some of the thinkers on the subject; the categories into which it falls in terms of subject, processes, theories, and so on. Then he examines what he terms the conduits of communication—the press, cinema, broadcasting; and the controls exercised by industry, the government, and the audience. Last, he evaluates the disciplinary claim. Throughout he comments on the artistic, scientific, and technological aspects. Each section has a list of recommended readings, and there are notes and an index.

81. Gordon, George N. The Communications Revolution: A History of Mass Media in the United States. New York: Hastings House, 1977. 338p.

In this one-volume historical review of mass media in the U.S. in breadth rather than depth, the author's aim is to give equal emphasis to print, film, and broadcasting, taking into account print's considerable head start. Organization, although chronological, treats the media simultaneously with short sketches of technological developments and biographical material on important figures. Gordon places emphasis on "the growth and social assimilation of each medium, the cultural climate in which each evolved, and the empathetic understanding of why people expect what they expect from their books, movies, newspapers, television receivers, radios, recordings, and other gadgetry." Contains a bibliography and an index.

82. Gordon, Thomas F., and Mary Ellen Berna. Mass Communica-
    tion Effects and Processes: A Comprehensive Biblio-
    graphy, 1950-1975. Beverly Hills, Cal.: Sage, 1978.
    229p.

    A bibliography of research with emphasis on the social-
    ization effects of the media. Entries are in alphabetical
    order, with a detailed subject index, and include journal
    articles and books and some other types of monographs. As
    a rule there are no annotations, except for the sake of
    clarity, to indicate scope of importance, or for other rea-
    sons. Subjects excluded are law and regulation, historical
    development, economics and business, technical operations,
    and management and professional training. An overview of
    the literature precedes the entries.

83. Gowans, Alan. The Unchanging Arts: New Forms for the
    Traditional Functions of Art in Society. Philadelphia:
    Lippincott, 1970. 433p.

    Stretching the term art broader than many traditional-
    ists would, Gowans treats seriously the aesthetics of some
    of its more popular manifestations today in photography,
    commercial design, illustration (including narrative paint-
    ing and prints), comics, movies, television, cartoons,
    advertising. The section about each discusses the "high"
    and "low" forms. Emphasis is on the graphic.

84. Hachten, William A. Muffled Drums: The News Media in
    Africa. Ames: Iowa State University Press, 1971.

    Examination of the news media--newspapers, radio, tele-
    vision, magazines--in contemporary Africa, focusing on them
    as institutions, and describing their establishment, their
    effectiveness, and their relations with the government.
    Emphasis is on news and public information rather than cul-
    tural and educational roles.
        Hachten has also compiled Mass Communication in Africa:
    An Annotated Bibliography (University of Wisconsin, Center
    for International Communication, 1971, 121p.), which is a
    comprehensive guide to his source material.

85. Hall, Stuart, and Paddy Whannel. The Popular Arts. Chica-
    go: Hutchinson Educational, 1964. 480p.

    This book is intended to educate younger readers, or for
    that matter any interested layman, about today's mass cul-
    ture, and even though it was written some years ago it is
    so firmly grounded in verities that it has not dated. Part
    I defines the media's relation to society, minority art,
    folk art, and popular art and relates popular art to mass
    culture. Part II suggests topics for study--"Violence on

27

the Stage," "Falling in Love," "Fantasy and Romance,"
"Popular Forms and Popular Artists," among others. Part
III discusses social themes—the institutions, the critics
and defenders of mass society, society and the hero, and
the world of pop, and so on. Some of these are suggested
as teaching projects. Appendices contain bibliographies
of books and journals, records, films and television
materials, and organizations. Indexed.

86. Halloran, James D. <u>Mass Media in Society: The Need of
    Research</u>. Paris: UNESCO, 1970. 33p. (Reports and
    Papers in Mass Communication No. 59.)
87. Halloran, James D., ed. <u>Mass Media and Socialization:
    International Bibliography and Different Perspectives</u>.
    International Association for Mass Communication
    Research, 1976. 130p. (Obtain from headquarters,
    IAMCR.)

One of Halloran's several trademarks is his interest
in the international aspects of mass communications
research. In the first of these two monographs he discusses the state and organization of communication research
in the context of the hardware likely to be available and
commonplace within the next century, and its social impact.
He stresses throughout the need for cooperation at national
and international levels.
    The second title is an unannotated fifty-six-page bib-
liography of books, articles, reports, studies, etc.,
consisting of titles submitted by scholars from many
countries, which explores different approaches in perspective, both methodological and cultural, in mass communications research. Three essays accompany the bibliography:
"Changing Perspectives in the Study of Mass Media and
Socialization" by Robin McCron of the University of
Leicester; "Mass Information Processes and Problems of Per-
sonality Socialization" by Yury Sherkovin of Moscow State
University; and "Toward a Global System of Documentation
and Information Centres" by Kaarle Nordenstreng of the
University of Finland. Halloran has written the introduction: "The Mass Media and Socialization: An Introduction
to the Theme of the Monograph."

88. Halmos, Paul, ed. <u>The Sociology of Mass-Media Communica-
    tors</u>. Keele, Staffordshire, England: University of
    Keele, 1969. 248p. (<u>The Sociological Review</u>: Mono-
    graph No. 13.)

Emphasis here is divided between the theoretical and the
practical. Some of the essays broadly examine the factors
which underlie a number of aspects of the communications
system as it functions today; others concentrate upon

television. All articles probe beneath the surface. There
are footnotes at the end of each article but no bibliography.

89. Hammel, William, ed. The Popular Arts In America: A
Reader. 2d ed. New York: Harcourt Brace Jovanovich,
1977. 501p.

An examination in which a variety of writers from the
present and past discuss "Music," "Television and Radio,"
"Popular Music," and "Popular Print" (newspapers, magazines,
popular reading). The first section is a general examination of "sense and sensibility" in the popular arts.
Intended as a text to be used in English, speech, or communication courses, this is aimed at developing critical
judgment.

90. Harasymiw, Bohdan, ed. Education and the Mass Media in the
Soviet Union and Eastern Europe. New York: Praeger,
1976. 130p.

Studies selected from among those presented at the First
International Slavic Conference held in Banff, Canada, in
1974 which are concerned with public policy in Communist
countries as it involves education in relation to the mass
media (particularly the news agencies) and public opinion
(especially in the Soviet Union).

91. Hellack, Georg. Mass Media in the Federal Republic of Germany. Bonn-Bad Godesberg: Inter Nationes, 1974. 36p.

A thirty-five-page pamphlet which gives a brief but
informative rundown on newspapers, magazines, books, broadcasting, and film in West Germany. Includes such aspects
as freedom of the press, legal position, tendencies toward
concentration, publishers' and journalists' organizations,
Press and Information Office, advertising, and prospects
and future development. Useful as a brief survey or a
starting point, although there is no bibliographic information to use as leads.

92. Hindley, M. Patricia, Gail M. Martin, and Jean McNulty.
The Tangled Web: Basic Issues in Canadian Communications. Vancouver: J. J. Douglas, 1977. 183p.

The primary issues besetting Canadian communications,
as the authors see them, are U.S. domination of production,
promotion, and distribution capabilities; the tension
between public and private ownership; and the search for
Canadian identity. Against this background they discuss
book and magazine publishing; film; broadcasting, including
cable TV; telephony; computers; and satellites. Contains
chapter notes and a bibliography.

93. Hoggart, Richard. The Uses of Literacy: Aspects of Working-Class Life with Special Reference to Publications and Entertainment. New York: Oxford University Press, c1957, 1970. 319p.

In the earlier (1957) publication, this socio-literary study was subtitled Changing Patterns in English Mass Culture. It concerns changes in working-class culture during the last thirty or forty years preceding the 1960s, telling in particular how these changes were being encouraged by mass publications. Emphasis is on periodicals and popular music, although the author believes he would have obtained similar results if film and commercial broadcasting had been used. Contains "Notes and References," "A Select Bibliography," and an index.

94. Hohenberg, John. The Pulitzer Prizes: A History of the Awards in Books, Drama, Music and Journalism, Based on the Private Files over Six Decades. New York: Columbia University Press, 1974. 434p.

An analysis as well as a history, set forth in depth, describing mistakes as well as achievements. Appendices give members of the Advisory Board, awards by category, and a summary of the dates prizes were withheld and in which categories. Notes and comments, bibliography, and detailed index.

95. Hollander, Gayle Durham. Soviet Political Indoctrination: Developments in Mass Media and Propaganda Since Stalin. New York: Praeger, 1972. 244p.

Against the background of the Soviet political system the author analyzes the structure, content, and audience of book publishing, newspapers and magazines, broadcasting, film, and agitation and propaganda. Notes follow each chapter, and there are maps, tables, notes on Soviet sources, and an extensive bibliography.

96. Holloway, Harry, and John George. Public Opinion: Coalitions, Elites, and Masses. New York: St. Martin's Press, 1979. 286p.

A text in which the authors hinge their analysis of public opinion upon three basic concepts—coalitions, elites, and masses, with coalitions being major political groupings like the old New Deal alliance, elites being "those who are set apart from the bulk of ordinary mortals in positions of leadership and authority," and masses, "the ordinary mortals who make up most of a society's population." Within this framework they discuss the political process and mass opinion. An appendix tells "What Pollsters Do and How They Do

It." One chapter is entitled "The Media: From Quality
Press to Campaign Spots." Each chapter contains suggestions for further reading. Indexed.

97. Holmgren, Rod, and William Norton, eds. The Mass Media
Book. Englewood Cliffs, N.J.: Prentice-Hall, 1972.
421p.

The editors intend this anthology "to offer the student a critical overview of mass media in America today."
It is divided into two parts, "The News Media" and "The
Entertainment Media." Some of the contributors are
reporters and commentators from the mass media themselves;
some are critics; some, like Spiro Agnew, are merely
critical; some are university professors. As a whole the
articles are well chosen and well written, and the collection is rounded. Bibliography.

98. Hulteng, John L. The Messenger's Motives: Ethical Theory
in the Mass Media. Englewood Cliffs, N.J.: Prentice-
Hall, 1976. 262p.

After placing journalistic behavior within a larger context and then reviewing the literature on journalistic
ethics, Hulteng discusses in a broad sense the particular
problems confronting the profession. Intended for the consumer of journalism as well as the producer, although
widely used in journalism classes as a text. Annotated
bibliography and index.

99. Hulteng, John L., and Roy Paul Nelson. The Fourth Estate:
An Informal Appraisal of the News and Opinion Media.
New York: Harper & Row, 1971. 356p.

Covers the print media--newspapers, magazines, news
photography, cartoons, and books--and advertising and public relations. Some of the dominant issues connected with
them are presented--the Fairness Doctrine, ethics, objectivity, for example. Indexed.

100. Inkeles, Alex. Public Opinion in Soviet Russia: A Study
in Mass Persuasion. 2d ed. Cambridge, Mass.: Harvard
University Press, 1958. 393p.

The last two-thirds of this book is an analysis of the
structure, function, and contents of the Soviet press,
broadcasting, and films. The fact that there have been
more recent studies--Hopkins's Mass Media in the Soviet
Union (No. 696) and Markham's Voices of the Red Giants
(No. 135)--in no way invalidates its usefulness. Contains
bibliographic notes, a bibliography, and an index.

101. Innis, Harold A. <u>Empire and Communication</u>. Oxford:
     Clarendon Press, 1950. 230p.
102. _____. <u>The Bias of Communication</u>. Toronto: University
     of Toronto Press, 1951. 226p.
103. _____. <u>Changing Concepts of Time</u>. Toronto: University
     of Toronto Press, 1952. 142p.

One of Marshall McLuhan's outstanding contributions has
been to bring into prominence the works of the late Canadian
economist, Harold Innis. Innis's writings are best treated
as a group. His thesis is that the communications systems
of empires have influenced their rise and fall. In <u>Empire
and Communication</u> he discusses the possibility, with emphasis on economics, that communication may occupy a crucial
position in the organization and administration of government and in turn of empires and of Western civilization.
<u>The Bias of Communication</u> is a collection of papers support-
ing this theory in more detail. <u>Changing Concepts of Time</u>
attempts to show that the communication system of a given
culture can affect the way in which its people regard space-
time concepts.

104. International Commission for the Study of Communication
     Problems. <u>Documents for the Study of Communication Prob-
     lems</u>. 90 parts (approx.) Paris: UNESCO, 1979.

Series of pamphlets of varying lengths from eight to
fifty pages, resulting from a mandate by the Commission to
make a critical analysis on a global level of the state of
communication in the world today. Among topics treated are:
summary of statistics and of recent research; various
aspects of news agencies, with analysis of nineteen specific
ones; dissemination of information in a pluralistic world;
treatment of information and imbalances among nations; planning; strengthening the Third World press; technology; communication in traditional societies as illustrated by some
of the African and Asian nations and the Arab states.
Emphasis is on the needs of the developing nations. Pamphlet No. 7 is a bibliography.

105. Jacobs, Norman, ed. <u>Culture for the Millions? Mass Media
     in Modern Society</u>. Princeton, N.J.: Van Nostrand, 1961.
     200p.

Can pure culture survive the mass media and mass society?
This question is considered by a notable list of contribu-
tors whose comments do not date: Paul Lazarsfeld, Edward
Shils, Leo Lowenthal, Hannah Arendt, Ernest van den Haag,
Oscar Handlin, Leo Rosten, Randall Jarrell, James Baldwin,
Stanley Edgar Hyman, Arthur Schlesinger, among others.

106. Joan, Polly, and Andres Chesman. <u>Guide to Women's Publish-</u>
     <u>ing</u>. Paradise, Cal. 95969: Dustbooks, P.O. Box 100,
     1978. 296p.

     Comprehensive coverage of feminist journals; women's
     newspapers; feminist "small press" publishing, including
     all-women print shops and women printers; the non-sexist
     children's press (which concerns itself with sons as well
     as daughters); and distribution outlets for feminist writ-
     ing, with a listing of women involved in distribution.
     Ends with a section on additional resources of directories,
     review publications, libraries and archives, organizations,
     bookstores, and mail order. Index.

107. Jones, Greta, Ian Connell, and Jack Meadows. <u>The Presenta-</u>
     <u>tion of Science by the Media</u>. Leicester, England LE1
     7RH: University of Leicester, Primary Communications
     Research Centre, 1978. 76p.

     A study whose aim is to show how interpretations of
     science in the media are constructed. The authors have
     concentrated on an examination of the activities of those
     people involved in the presentation of science to the pub-
     lic by means of newspapers, radio, or broadcasting. Con-
     tains a bibliography.

108. Kato, Hidetoshi. <u>Japanese Research on Mass Communication:</u>
     <u>Selected Abstracts</u>. Honolulu: University of Hawaii
     Press, 1974. 128p.

     Contains ninety-eight abstracts of statistical studies
     giving data on a variety of subjects, among which are audi-
     ence, children's media, "the politically concerned public,"
     the use of radio by the blind, and changes in media taste
     throughout the years of television's growth. Contains a
     list of Japanese periodicals on mass communication and a
     subject index.

109. Katz, Elihu, and Paul F. Lazarsfeld. <u>Personal Influence:</u>
     <u>The Part Played by People in the Flow of Communications</u>.
     New York: Free Press, 1955. 400p.

     A theoretical analysis, backed by an empirical study,
     of the effect of face-to-face personal communication as
     distinguished from the effects of mass communication and
     their important interrelationships. Although a quarter
     of a century old, the findings remain valid. Contains
     bibliographic notes, a bibliography, and an index.

110. Katzen, May. <u>Mass Communication: Teaching and Studies at</u>
     <u>Universities: A World-Wide Survey on the Role of Univer-</u>
     <u>sities in the Study of the Mass Media and Mass Communica-</u>
     <u>tion</u>. Paris: UNESCO, 1975. 278p.

A thoroughgoing appraisal of the state of formal education in the field, with thirteen pages of conclusions.
Individual countries are dealt with by continent. An
appendix gives a note on the survey methods used. There
is an extensive list of references.

111. Katzen, May. Trends in Scholarly Communication in the
     United States and Western Europe. Leicester, England
     LE1 7RH: University of Leicester, Primary Communica-
     tion Research Centre (PCRC), 1978. 31p.

     Deals with the production and dissemination of informa-
     tion--the status, cost, cooperation, and other aspects--on
     an international level.

112. King, Josephine, and Mary Scott, eds. Is This Your Life?
     Images of Women in the Media. London: Virago, Ltd.,
     in association with Quartet Books, 1977. 199p.

     A group of women writers investigate the attitudes and
     images various media (radio, advertising, newspapers,
     comics, bestselling fiction, films, television, pop music,
     and erotic and women's magazines) offer readers, viewers,
     and listeners. Comparing their version of women's roles
     with the realities of changing times, they attempt to
     identify stereotypes and to search for ways in which atti-
     tudes are conditioned and perhaps manipulated. Illustrated
     by cartoons. Index.

113. Klapper, Joseph T. The Effects of Mass Communication. New
     York: Free Press, 1960. 302p.

     Many effects studies have been made in the years since
     this book was published and television has become a force,
     but Klapper's book is still important as the initial effort
     to synthesize existing knowledge on the subject. The first
     part is a report of the way the mass media change or rein-
     force opinions and the differences among the various media
     in bringing this about; the second part deals with probable
     effects of specific types of material--for example, crime
     and violence and escapist categories, and adult TV fare when
     viewed by children. Contains a bibliography and an index.

114. Kline, F. Gerald, and Phillip J. Tichensor, eds. Current
     Perspectives in Mass Communication Research. Beverley
     Hills, Cal.: Sage, 1972. 320p. (Sage Annual Reviews
     of Communication Research, Vol. I.) (1972--.)

     Articles in this anthology are selected to illustrate
     research perspectives in major departments and schools of
     journalism dealing with mass communication--the subjects
     they are treating and the methodologies they are using.

Among the subjects are gatekeeping, information diffusion, socialization, political campaigns, the urban poor, sex, and violence. There are also chapters on the interpersonal context of mass communication and on communication theory. Bibliographies at the end of each chapter, a general biblio graphy, and a subject index. Further volumes of the series deal with other aspects of communication research, both interpersonal and intrapersonal. Beginning with the 1981 edition, editors are James W. Carey and Peter Miller.

115. Kraus, Sidney, and Dennis Davis. The Effects of Mass Com-
    munication on Political Behavior. University Park:
    Pennsylvania State University Press, 1976. 308p.

    "Our purpose is to provide students, scholars and even politicians who study political communication with a review and commentary on what is known about the field, what is not yet known, what ought to be known, and how we assess and evaluate the effects of mass communication on political behavior." Chapters relate mass communication to social- ization, the electoral process, political information, the political process, and the construction of political real- ity in society. There is also an examination of methods of political communication research. The authors conclude with a discussion of the current state of knowledge. Each chapter contains abstracts and a bibliography. Author index and subject index.

116. Lasswell, Harold D., Daniel Lerner, and Hans Speier, eds.
    Propaganda and Communication in World History. Vol. I.
    The Symbolic Instrument in Early Times. Honolulu: Uni-
    versity of Hawaii, East-West Center, 1979. 631p.

    First of three volumes. Here scholars from many disci- plines and countries examine the impact of communication on history from its beginnings in primitive and tribal com- munities through the formation of centralized empires to the feudal system of medieval Europe, reconstructing the ways in which social communication was practiced, codified, and transmitted. This first volume emphasizes world reli- gions—Judaism, Christianity, Buddhism, and Islam—as major forces in transmission. Contains chapter notes and index. Future volumes will be The Emergence of Public Opinion in the West and A Pluralizing World in Formation.

117. Lasswell, Harold D., Ralph D. Casey, and Bruce Lannes Smith,
    comps. Propaganda and Promotional Activities: An Anno-
    tated Bibliography. Chicago: University of Chicago
    Press, c1935, 1969. 460p.
118. Smith, Bruce Lannes, Harold D. Lasswell, and Ralph D. Casey,
    comps. Propaganda, Communication, and Public Opinion:

A Comprehensive Reference Guide. Princeton, N.J.:
Princeton University Press, 1946. 435p.
119. Smith, Bruce Lannes, and Chita M. Smith, comps. Inter-
national Communications and Political Opinion: A
Guide to Literature. Princeton, N.J.: Princeton
University Press, 1956. 225p.

These three bibliographies covering the early days of
communications bring together thousands of references
from books and periodicals in both English and foreign
languages, especially French and German. Although they
concentrate largely on propaganda and public opinion, in
doing so they deal with symbols, channels, contents, and
effects of communication in general. While not up-to-
date they are certainly not out-of-date.
In the first volume Lasswell, one of the most distinguished scholars to pioneer the field, has written a long
essay, "The Study and Practice of Propaganda." In the
second volume, Smith, Lasswell, and Casey have contributed
four essays on the nature, contents, and effects of communications, with special emphasis on propaganda.

120. Laudon, Kenneth C. Communications Technology and Democratic Participation. New York: Praeger, 1977. 116p.

An examination of social and technological forces which
the author contends hold the promise of a renewal of political democracy in the form of more accountable elites and
a less alienated and more active citizenry, and at the same
time a threat of new "telefacism" which makes demagogy
easier. In examining the new communication technologies
(some of which are little known as yet), he draws a picture
of what may be tomorrow's brave new world. Chapter notes.

121. Lent, John A. Asian Mass Communications: A Comprehensive
Bibliography. Philadelphia: Temple University, School
of Communications and Theater, 1975. Supplement, 1978.
619p.

Lent calls this "the first attempt to make available in
one place as much as possible of what has been written on
all aspects of mass communications, both in Asian institutions and those abroad." Divided by region into four sec-
tions--Asia (general), East Asia, Southeast Asia, and
South Asia--and subdivided by country. Under each nation,
special divisions deal with the mass communications
research institutes available and types of research accomplished at these centers, and the bibliographies and periodicals published about or in that nation. Includes
articles from most mass communications journals around the
world, books, academic theses and dissertations, monographs,

36

bibliographies, conference and symposia proceedings, lectures, speeches, and fugitive materials such as academic term papers and other unpublished manuscripts. Entries, of which there are thousands, are not annotated. The supplement of 10,000 new entries includes previously unavailable material on Mongolia, Nepal, Brunei, and Laos. There is also a section entitled "China Watching," and one on satellite communications.

122. Lent, John A. <u>Philippine Mass Communications Before 1811,</u> <u>After 1966.</u> Manila: Philippine Press Institute, 1972(?) 179p.

A historical survey, covering broad territory in its 179 pages: the newspaper press as a whole, the provincial press, press freedom, magazines, radio, television, motion pictures, book publishing, advertising, and journalism education. Contains footnotes, a nine-page bibliography, and an appendix giving the libel law.

123. Lent, John A. <u>Third World Mass Media and Their Search for</u> <u>Modernity: The Case of Commonwealth Caribbean, 1717-</u> <u>1976.</u> Lewisburg, Pa.: Bucknell University Press, 1977. 405p.

". . . an attempt to examine historical, cultural, economic, and political aspects of all Commonwealth Caribbean mass media, from the time of the first newspaper in 1717 until 1972," says Lent, who explains their characteristics and practices in terms of the history of the region and relates them when applicable to theories of communication and national development. Appendices include a list of known newspapers in Commonwealth Caribbean; a one-page description of the advent of television on Bermuda; a chronology of significant dates; "The Allfrey Story," a description of a typical day the author spent with the two editors of a rather untypical newspaper; facilities and operations of cable and wireless in Commonwealth Caribbean relative to regional communications, 1968; UNESCO conclusions concerning Commonwealth Caribbean mass media; recommendations for further research. There is a comprehensive bibliography and an index.

Levin, Harvey J. <u>Broadcast Regulation and Joint Ownership of</u> <u>Media.</u> (<u>See</u> No. 480.)

124. Lippmann, Walter. <u>Public Opinion.</u> New York: Macmillan, 1922. 272p.

Years have not dated Lippman's basic concepts. His discussions of stereotypes, of the role of newspapers, and of various other aspects remain classic. Indexed.

125. <u>Literary Taste, Culture and Mass Communication</u>. Peter
      Davison, Rolf Meyersohn, and Edward Shils, eds. 14
      vols. Teaneck, N.J.: Somerset House, 1978.

   In this imaginative and wide-ranging collection of
over 200 articles, books, lectures, and reviews reprinted
in fourteen volumes, the editors had several purposes in
mind. They wanted to highlight the different approaches
taken by American, British, and to some extent Continental
scholars to the study of the mass media and popular culture, and to do so in such a way that readers of this generation would better understand the development of what
they were studying and what it has meant to those writing
in earlier decades. They also wanted to present material
from a number of viewpoints. In the words of the editors:
"In selecting what should be reprinted it was thought
there would be considerable advantage if work from many
different standpoints could be juxtaposed: literary,
sociological, cultural, and political; American, British,
and Continental; initial groupings and final analysis;
scholarly studies, journalistic articles, and the comments
of creative writers," and "that the very juxtaposition of
materials might provide new insights." Because their
approach is historical (although not chronological), the
materials begin as far back as the 1920s and carry through
the 1960s, but seldom into the 1970s, mainly because
recent works tend to be readily available and also because
in some cases there were copyright difficulties. Vol. XIV
contains a bibliography and an index, and each volume has
a "Further Reading" section, as well as individual bibliographies accompanying some of the articles.
   A partial list of authors gives an idea of the quality
of the series: Theodor Adorno, Dwight Macdonald, Susan
Sontag, F. W. Bateson, Robert Escarpit, Richard Hoggart,
F. R. Leavis, E. M. Forster, Stuart Hall, Leslie Fiedler,
Max Horkheimer, Maurice Janowitz, Bernard Berelson,
Richard D. Altick, Raymond Williams, H. G. Wells, Marshall
McLuhan, George Orwell, Andre Malraux, Stephen Spender,
George Steiner.
   Volumes shown in numerical order include:
<u>Culture and Mass Culture</u>
<u>Mass Media and Mass Communication</u>
<u>Art and Social Life</u>
<u>Art and Changing Civilization</u>
<u>Literature and Society</u>
<u>The Sociology of Literature</u>
<u>Content and Taste: Religion and Myth</u>
<u>Theater and Song</u>
<u>Uses of Literacy: Media</u>
<u>Authorship</u>
<u>The Writer and Politics</u>

Bookselling, Reviewing and Reading
The Cultural Debate Part I
The Cultural Debate Part II and Indexes.

126. Liu, Alan P. L. Communications and National Integration in Communist China. Berkeley: University of California Press, 1971. 225p.

Although the primary purpose of this study is to define the roles that the mass media play in achieving integration in China, it also serves as an excellent survey of radio, the press, book publishing, and film. In addition it details propaganda methods. Appendices give statistics. Contains notes, a bibliography, and an index.

127. McCombs, Maxwell E., and Lee B. Becker. Using Mass Communication Theory. Englewood Cliffs, N.J.: Prentice-Hall, 1979. 148p. (Perspectives in Mass Communication.)

The authors contend that students in journalism learn much about writing and something about reporting, or "message production," as they term it, but little about the influences that shape this phase of their work or the social context of the process. In the belief that this knowledge is important to the student, they provide, in the form of a survey of empirical research studies, an overview of factual knowledge about the interaction of mass communication and society, organized from the point of view of the practicing journalist.

128. McGarry, K. J., ed. Mass Communications: Selected Readings for Librarians. Hamden, Conn.: Linnet Books, 1972. 255p.

Although intended for librarians, this anthology is by no means limited to them. The author, who teaches at the College of Librarianship in Wales, has included some good articles which are not too familiar in the U.S., and some which are familiar and will bear repeating. Most of them are concerned with the structure, problems, and audience of the media, with emphasis on books, which too many anthologies ignore or treat in a once-over-lightly fashion. Among authors are Raymond Williams, Wilbur Schramm, Asa Briggs, James Curran, Lord Annan, Jurgen Ruesch, and Gregory Bateson. Indexed.

129. McLuhan, Marshall. The Gutenberg Galaxy: The Making of Typographic Man. Toronto: University of Toronto Press, 1962. 263p.

130. _____. Understanding Media: The Extensions of Man. New York: McGraw-Hill, 1964. 359p.

These are McLuhan's two best-known books. The Gutenberg Galaxy is a lively and unconventionally organized history of print, beginning with Gutenberg's press and skipping about eclectically through time and literature. For example, here are a few headings for brief chapters: "King Lear Is a Working Model of the Process of Denudation by Which Men Translated Themselves from a World of Roles to a World of Jobs," "Schizophrenia May Be a Necessary Consequence of Literacy," "The Greek Point of View in Both Art and Chronology Has Little in Common with Ours but Was Much Like That of the Middle Ages."

Understanding Media is the best single source of his theory.

131. McQuail, Denis. Toward a Sociology of Mass Communications. London: Collier-Macmillan, 1969. 122p.
132. _____. Sociology of Mass Communications. Harmondsworth, Middlesex, England: Penguin, 1972. 477p.
133. _____. Communication. New York: Longman, 1975. 299p.

Whether concerned with the mass media or individual communication, McQuail deals with communication from the aspect of the sociologist. In Toward a Sociology of Mass Communications his aim is to acquaint the layman with the field and to suggest guidelines for more detailed study. Covering in breadth rather than depth, he points out major issues and assesses the current state of discussion and research about the media and discusses the empirical tradition and new directions for studies.

Sociology of Mass Communications is an anthology of conceptual articles which have important theoretical implications for the mass media or are reflective in character. Emphasis is on issues of social policy and concern. Contributors include, among others, Dallas Smythe, George Gerbner, Franklin Fearing, Philip Elliott, Jeremy Turnstall, Elihu Katz, Herbert Gans, Kaarle Nordenstreng.

The third book, Communication, is a part of the Aspects of Modern Sociology series and deals with communication as a social process--its relation to society, its various theories, its operation, structure, and influence. There is also a chapter on mass communication. The conclusion treats communication problems and social research.

All three books contain bibliographies and indexes.

134. McWhinney, Edward, ed. The International Law of Communications. Leyden, Holland: Sijthof/Dobbs Ferry, N.Y.: Oceana, 1971. 170p.

What international laws will govern communications, and what forces will shape these laws? These are the questions

which this anthology examines. Special emphasis is placed
upon telecommunications and direct satellite broadcasting.
The essays grew out of a special colloquium on the new
international law of communications, held in the Institute
of Air and Space Law, McGill University, Montreal, in 1970.
Footnotes.

135. Markham, James W. <u>Voices of the Red Giants: Communications in Russia and China</u>. Ames: Iowa State University Press, 1967. 513p.

Investigation of Communist mass communication systems
as exemplified by the Russian Soviet and Communist Chinese
models. The author covers magazines, newspapers, radio
and television, the news agencies, and advertising. A
drawback is the use of secondary rather than primary
sources. Contains bibliographic notes and an index.

136. <u>Marxism and the Mass Media: Towards a Basic Bibliography</u>.
5 vols. in 2. New York 10013: International General,
P.O. Box 350, 1976.

An ongoing series whose aim is to compile a global,
multilingual, annotated bibliography of Marxist studies
on all aspects of communications. Entries date from the
nineteenth century and cover capitalist countries, socialist countries, and the third world, in the English, French,
and Italian languages. Contains a subject index, an author
index, and a country index. Vol. III (1974) includes Vols.
I-II; Vol. IV-V are bound together.

137. <u>Mass Media and Violence: A Report to the National Commis-
sion on the Causes and Prevention of Violence</u>. Robert
K. Baker and Sandra J. Hall, comps. Washington:
Superintendent of Documents, U.S. Government Printing
Office, 1969. 613p. (Staff Report 9 to the National
Commission on the Causes and Prevention of Violence.)

Vol. IX in a series dealing with the various aspects of
the problem of violence in American society. This one is
concerned with the media. First it approaches the problem
from a historical perspective. Then it analyzes factually
and often critically certain accepted values and practices
such as function and credibility, intergroup communication,
the marketplace myth (access to the mass media), coverage
of civil disorders, journalism education. And finally it
deals with television entertainment vis-à-vis violence,
with emphasis on our limited knowledge of effects. Programming is analyzed and contrasted with the reality of
violence in daily life.
Each section has discussions, conclusions, and recommendations, as well as factual appendices. Among these are:

codes, guidelines and policies for news coverage; a review
of recent literature on psychological effects of media portrayals of violence; the content and context of violence
in the mass media, with opposing views as to possible
effects; content analysis procedures and results; the
views, standards, and practices of the television industry.
Includes bibliographical references.

138. Mass Media Booknotes. Christopher H. Sterling, comp.
      Philadelphia 19122: Temple University School of Commu-
      nications and Theater, Department of Radio-Television-
      Film, monthly. (1969--.)

      This bibliography is an indispensible guide to the cur-
rent literature in various areas of communication. Sterling defines "mass media" broadly to cover a number of
aspects of the field in addition to the standard ones of
editorial journalism, broadcasting, and film. Among other
areas covered are communication theory and research, media
regulation and law, photography, popular culture (including popular music), book publishing, etc. Many of his comments are evaluative. His annual issue on government
publications deserves special attention because government
publications are not well publicized, nor is the literature
about them which the government puts out easy to follow.
In particular, librarians buying in the field with little
previous knowledge will find it especially valuable and can
use back issues to build up a collection.

139. Mass Media in C.M.E.A. Countries. H-1525 Budapest:
      Nemzetkozi Ujsagiro Szervezet (International Organiza-
      tion of Journalists), Interpress Kiado es Nyomda V.,
      Pf.-100, 1976. 255p.

      Hard facts about press, radio, and television in Coun-
cil of Mutual Economic Assistance (C.M.E.A.) countries--
Bulgaria, Cuba, Czechoslovakia, East Germany, Hungary,
Mongolia, Poland, Romania, and the U.S.S.R. Data include
concentrated information about central and regional papers,
weeklies and magazines (title, publisher, circulation,
thumbnail profile), press agencies, and radio and television, with a brief description of programming. Material
on each country differs somewhat.

140. The Media and Business. Howard Simmons and Joseph A.
      Califano, Jr., eds. New York: Vintage, 1979. 227p.

      Report of a seminar held in 1977 in which influential
American business executives met with leaders of press and
television for a weekend seminar to discuss in detail
their fundamental conflicts and to exchange beliefs and
biases.

141. The Media and Terrorism: A Seminar Sponsored by the Chi-
     cago Sun-Times and Chicago Daily News. Chicago 60811:
     Chicago Sun-Times/Chicago Daily News, 401 N. Wabash
     Ave., 1977. 38p..

     Law-enforcement officers, newsmen, journalism educators,
     and lawyers discuss coverage of acts of terrorism by the
     media, and come up with guidelines pro and con, and with
     standards.

142. Media Law Reporter. Washington 20037: Bureau of National
     Affairs, Inc., 1231 25th St., N.W., weekly with periodic
     cumulations. (1977--.)

     A looseleaf service which provides current texts of
     decisions of the courts and selected rulings of federal
     agencies in the field of communication law. Each weekly
     issue also contains brief notes and an index on the cover.
     The cumulated bound volume appears at intervals which
     average about nine months.

143. Media Studies in Education. Paris: UNESCO, 1977. 92p.
     (Reports and Papers on Mass Communication No. 80.)

     The teaching of the mass media in the secondary schools
     in France, Italy, the Federal Republic of Germany, the
     Netherlands, the United Kingdom, Denmark, Finland, Sweden,
     the U.S.S.R. and the U.S. Contains a list of international
     organizations and a bibliography.

144. Meeting of Experts on Development of Information Media in
     Latin America. Paris: UNESCO, 1961. 37p.

     Report of a meeting held in Santiago, Chile, at which
     participants discussed the status of news agencies, news-
     papers, periodicals, radio broadcasting, television, film,
     training of journalists, and scientific research.

145. Melody, William F. The Economics of Media Systems. Paris:
     UNESCO, 1973. 12p.

     An address given at the UNESCO Meeting on Management and
     Planning of New Communications Systems, in which Melody
     comments briefly on some relations between communications
     technology, institutions, and communications opportunities,
     contrasting technology in developing countries with that in
     developed countries and discussing satellite communication.
     Bibliography.

146. Mendelsohn, Harold. Mass Entertainment. New Haven, Conn.:
     College and University Press, 1966. 203p.

A theoretical analysis of the role of entertainment in
our lives, with emphasis on the kind of entertainment
derived from the mass media. The author discusses its
origins; its sociological and psychological functions; the
pleasure paradigm; aesthetics, culture, and entertainment;
the search for standards of excellence. Bibliography and
index.

147. Merrill, John C., and Ralph D. Barney, eds. Ethics and
the Press: Readings in Mass Media Morality. New York:
Hastings House, 1975. 338p.

Part I is concerned with ethical foundations--the problem of quality and objectivity and "truth," among others;
Part II concerns specifics. Contributors are practicing
journalists, teachers, politicians, authors. Among them:
Jacques Ellul, Lee Hills, Nat Hentoff, Barry Goldwater,
Wilbur Schramm, Michael Novak, Edward Jay Epstein, the two
editors. Contains a lengthy bibliography.

148. Merrill, John C., and Ralph L. Lowenstein. Media, Messages and Men: New Perspectives in Communication. 2d
ed. New York: Longman, 1979. 264p.

The authors' aim is to "involve the reader in thought-
ful consideration of the basic issues in journalism (and
in communication generally) as they relate to individual
men and women and their society." They do not attempt to
survey the field, but rather to probe certain problem
areas and issues, grouped within broad categories: the
changing roles of the media, the communicator and his
audience, and media concepts and ethics. An annotated bibliography and an index.

149. Murray, John. The Media Law Dictionary. Washington 20023:
University Press of America, 1978(?). 139p.

A vocabulary book whose purpose is to bring together
words and phrases commonly used in media law and intended
as an adjunct book to mass media courses dealing with law
questions or for journalists interested in First Amendment
issues. Contains a bibliography and a list of cases from
which terms are taken.

150. Nelson, Harold L., and Dwight L. Teeter, Jr. Law of Mass
Communications: Freedom and Control of Print and Broadcast Media. 3d ed. Mineola, N.Y.: Foundation Press,
1978. 675p.

For those unfamiliar with this legal text, its genealogy
needs tracing. The first edition (1969) was heralded as a
fifth edition of an old classic, Frank Thayer's Legal

Control of the Press (1962), but was actually a new and
different book with an almost complete reorganization and
presentation of largely new material. Now in its third
edition, it maintains the same organization as the first
but has been expanded and revised to include recent cases
and the most recent thinking on such issues as privacy,
free press-fair trial, contempt, obscenity, access to
information, regulation of advertising, and the Copyright
Act of 1976. Appendices include abbreviations, selected
court and pleading terms, a bibliography, advertising
standards from the Television Code, and Zurcher v. Stanford
Daily: A Right to Rummage. There is a table of cases and
an index, and a separate eighty-five-page publication by
David Gordon for teachers, "Programmed Instructions," for
use with the text.

151. Nordenstreng, Kaarle, and Herbert I. Schiller, eds.
     National Sovereignty and International Communication.
     Norwood, N.J.: Ablex, 1979. 304p.

     Sixteen experts representing Latin America, the third
world, Europe, Israel, Canada, and the U.S. examine from
their various viewpoints the new problems that have arisen
in international communications. Their articles challenge
conventional thinking on concepts such as free flow of
information, cultural integrity, the role of communications
in national development, the right of nations to control
their own cultural/communication space, the current makeup
of the international system of information transfer. In
four parts: "Communication and National Development:
Changing Perspectives"; "Direct Satellite Broadcasting:
Examplar of the Challenge of National Sovereignty"; "International Law: Conditions of Fundamental Principles";
"International Communication in Transition: The New Global
Balance."

152. Nye, Russel. The Unembarrassed Muse: The Popular Arts in
     America. New York: Dial, 1970. 497p.

     The author terms this "a historical study of certain
American popular arts, the arts of commercial entertainment." It relates many aspects of mass culture today and
yesterday: popular fiction (the Tarzan series and Zane
Grey, among other books), the pulps, radio and television,
comic books and comic strips, the Wild West show, vaude-
ville, film, musical comedy, poetry, even the "dream
palace" architecture of movie theaters in the 1930s. He
explores some of the myths about our culture not widely
discussed elsewhere. In addition to its reference value,
the book makes interesting reading. Contains a "Bibliography and Sources" and an index.

153. Owen, Bruce M., and David Waterman, comps., with the
     assistance of Andrew Wechsler. Mass Communication and
     Economics: A Bibliography. Stanford, Cal.: Stanford
     University, Center for Research in Economic Growth,
     470 Encina Hall, 1973. 68p. (Studies in Industry
     Economics No. 31; Research Memorandum No. 156.)

     Updates but does not replace A Selected Bibliography in
the Economics of the Mass Media (1970). The scope of this
present bibliography is broader, being expanded to cover
libraries, motion pictures, book publishing, and the postal
service, and it has excluded much of the material of interest primarily to students of journalism. The compilers
state that they have been highly selective of works published before 1960, much less selective with items dated
1960-70, and often undiscriminating with very recent items.
Included are books, articles, and government publications
dealing with television and radio, cable television, newspapers, magazines, book publishing and libraries, motion
pictures and TV program production, advertising, and freedom of expression. In order to permit greater breadth of
coverage, items are not annotated.

154. Pelletier, Gerad. Proposals for a Communications Policy
     for Canada: A Position Paper of the Government of
     Canada. Ottawa KIA 059: Information Canada, 17 Slater
     St., 1973. 35p.

     The Minister of Communications has presented a concise
outline of objectives and activities in the field of telecommunications which the Canadian government feels may
best benefit citizens. Proposals are purposely sketchy
and are intended to form a basis for public discussion.
Text is in both English and French.

155. Pember, Don R. Mass Media in America. 2d ed. Chicago:
     Science Research Associates, 1977. 389p.

     An update of the 1974 edition in which Pember has
brought the book in line with happenings of the three
intervening years and added a new chapter, "Masscomm
Research and Theory." But he has kept his theses intact:
Mass media in the U.S. remain first and foremost businesses, and media censorship is bad, no matter who is
censoring or for what reason. He also emphasizes the
argument that audiences are becoming more selective,
resulting in greater fragmentation. There are references at the end of each chapter, and an index.

156. Pember, Don R. Mass Media Law. Dubuque, Iowa: William
     C. Brown, 1977. 484p.

Mass Media Law, says Pember, is not really a law book
but rather a journalism or mass media book about law.
Under pertinent headings he has synthesized various aspects
of it as it pertains to journalism--freedom of the press;
libel; invasion of privacy; copyright; contempt; free press
and fair trial; journalists, broadcasters, and their news
sources; obscenity, pornography, and other dirty words;
regulation of advertising; broadcasting regulation; access
to information. Each synthesis is followed by a substantial bibliography.

157. Piepe, Anthony, Sunny Crouch, and Miles Emerson. Mass
     Media and Cultural Relationships. Westmead, Farnborough,
     Hants., England: Saxon House, Teakfield, 1978. 168p.

     Although this study is limited geographically to the
city of Portsmouth, England, its scope and conclusions go
much farther. The aim of the authors is to examine the
ways in which social differences connected with class and
housing influence community patterns and uses of mass media.
Emphasis is on television, but some of the studies about
other media are summarized as well, some going as far back
as the 1940s. In interpreting their findings the authors
lean heavily upon the theories of early sociologists. Bibliographic notes and index.

158. Pool, Ithiel de Sola. The Influence of International Com-
     munication on Development. Cambridge, Mass.: Massachu-
     setts Institute of Technology, 1976. 17p.

     A conference paper in which Pool makes a case for the
free flow of information to developing countries even
though the governments of these countries do not always
believe this to be to their advantage. He discusses this
thesis in terms of the merits and demerits of various kinds
of communications, especially radio, satellites, and computers.

159. Pool, Ithiel de Sola, Wilbur Schramm, and others, eds.
     Handbook of Communication. Chicago: Rand McNally,
     1973. 1,011p.

     Each of the thirty-one chapters of this 1,000-page hand-
book is a review of the studies and findings in a different
area of communication research. Part I describes the basic
process; the concept of a system; verbal, nonverbal, and
interpersonal communication; the mass media and their
audience; the impact of communication on children, and on
persuasion and propaganda. Part II examines the operation
of the process in various settings: the mass media; small
groups; bureaucracies; advertising; political parties;

scientific institutions. It also compares communication
in Western democracies, Communist countries, the developing
world. Part III reviews current methods of communication
research, particularly aggregate data analysis and experimental studies of communication effects. Contains a name
and a subject index.

160. Press, Film, Radio. 5 vols. and supps. 1-2. Paris:
      UNESCO, 1947-51. (Reports on the Facilities of Mass
      Communications.)

      A UNESCO survey originally designed to determine the
   extent of damage suffered by the equipment of news agencies,
   newspaper printing works, broadcasting stations, and cinemas during World War II in the war-devastated countries, as
   well as the nature and extent of those countries' technical
   needs in these fields of communication. This original purpose was later broadened to include all countries and territories, and information was extended to cover existing
   technical resources of mass communication. At the completion of the study 157 countries and territories had been
   surveyed. A few could not be surveyed—Albania, Bulgaria,
   Byelo-Russian SSR, USSR, and Yemen. In addition, certain
   British and Portuguese colonies failed to respond in time
   for inclusion of their data.
      Information, especially for the larger countries, is
   detailed and thorough, with historical background, tables,
   figures, and maps. For a follow-up, concerned with newspapers only, see The Daily Press: A Survey of the World
   Situation in 1952 (No. 656).

161. Rahim, Syed A., ed. Communication Policy and Planning for
      Development: A Selected Annotated Bibliography. Hono-
      lulu: East-West Communication Institute, East-West
      Center, 1976. 285p.

      Contains 395 entries from monographs, articles, theses,
   annual reports, and other sources which cover a variety of
   problems and issues relating to communication policy and
   planning in fifty-three countries. Indexed by subject, by
   country or region, and by author.

162. Rao, Y. V. Lakshmana. The Practice of Mass Communication:
      Some Lessons from Research. Paris: UNESCO, 1972. 52p.
      (Reports and Papers in Mass Communication No. 65.)

      The author calls this "an attempt at synthesizing and
   presenting in relatively uncomplicated form, communication
   research findings for the use of mass media practitioners
   and administrators of communication campaigns, especially
   in developing countries." He also shows possible uses for
   these findings.

163. Read, William H. *America's Mass Media Merchants*. Balti-
     more: Johns Hopkins University Press, 1976. 204p.

     The author, an experienced journalist and former
     regional director for the Voice of America, examines impli-
     cations as the mass media penetrate the globe, bringing
     American values into ethnic cultures. He begins with an
     overview of our transnational mass media and follows with
     more detailed exploration of the "visual media merchants"
     and the "print media merchants." Next he discusses the
     various influences of the media and the ill will often
     generated by it. He concludes with a critique. A well-
     documented scholarly work with many footnotes. Indexed.

164. Richstead, Jim, ed. *New Perspectives in International Com-
     munication*. Honolulu: East-West Communication Insti-
     tute, East-West Center, 1977. 241p.

     A report on the Conference of Fair Communication Policy
     for the International Exchange of Information, with par-
     ticipants discussing objections and alternatives to the
     concept of "free flow of information" as it affects devel-
     oping nations. A final section is devoted to more general
     knowledge about and analysis of international communica-
     tion flows. Contains "Notes and References" to the indi-
     vidual talks.

165. Rivers, William L., and Wilbur Schramm. *Responsibility in
     Mass Communication*. Rev. ed. New York: Harper &
     Row, 1969. 314p.

     A discussion of the role of the press in society in
     terms of ethical issues both direct and indirect. Appen-
     dices include radio, television, motion picture and public
     relations codes, and the American Society of Newspaper
     Editors' "Canons of Journalism." Chapter notes, biblio-
     graphy, and index. A considerably revised update is in
     preparation, with Clifford Christians an added co-author.

166. Robinson, Glen O., ed. *Communications for Tomorrow: Pol-
     icy Perspectives for the 1980s*. New York: Praeger,
     1978. 526p.

     "In communications, emphasis on technology always seems
     to be put ahead of concern about quality of substance and
     content. Technology has outpaced the formation of atti-
     tudes, understanding and public policy. We need policies
     that will promise to use the new communications technology
     most effectively. This book is concerned with the crea-
     tion of such policies." With these introductory remarks
     Robinson sets the tone for this book, which examines
     broadly the social, economic, and legal implications of

the new communications systems; the policy options they offer; and the capabilities of existing policymaking institutions to address them. The various articles carry notes and in some cases bibliographies. Indexed.

167. Rogers, Everett M., ed. <u>Communication and Development: Critical Perspectives</u>. Beverly Hills, Cal.: Sage, 1976. 148p. (Sage Contemporary Social Science Issues No. 32.)

A decade or so ago communication scholars believed that the spread of communications and its new technologies into developing countries would insure their development. But this has not proved the case. This anthology considers various alternative conceptions. References accompany each article.

168. <u>Role of the Mass Media in American Politics</u>. John L. Martin, ed. Philadelphia: American Academy of Political and Social Science, 1976. (Annals of the American Academy of Political and Social Science, Vol. 427.)

Topics discussed include mass media coverage, image building, adversary roles, perspectives, and effects. Discussants include journalists, broadcasters, and academicians from communications and political science.

169. Rosenberg, Bernard, and David Manning White, eds. <u>Mass Culture: The Popular Arts in America</u>. New York: Free Press, 1957. 561p.
170. _____. <u>Mass Culture Revisited</u>. New York: Van Nostrand-Reinhold, 1971. 473p.

This collection of fifty-one essays designed to show the interplay between the mass media and society was the first anthology to deal with popular culture, and remains, in spite of its age, one of the best. Contributors include literary critics, social scientists, journalists, and art critics whose work in this area has been scattered in relatively inaccessible scholarly journals and "little magazines." Not all are contemporary; for example, there are essays by de Tocqueville and Walt Whitman. Among more contemporary authors are Ortega y Gasset, Dwight Macdonald, Edmund Wilson, David Reisman, George Orwell. Among topics are books, magazines, detective fiction, comics, radio and television, motion pictures, and advertising. Contains a list of further readings at the end of each section and bibliographic notes following most of the articles.
<u>Mass Culture Revisited</u> updates its predecessor, with twenty-seven articles, some appearing for the first time. It takes into account the many changes between 1957 and 1970, including the increased impetus of television, comic

strips in the underground press, and new trends in established media like films, magazines, and newspapers. One
section, "The Overview," is general. Among the contributors are Hannah Arendt, Nicholas Johnson, Mordecai Richler,
Nathan Blumberg, Diana Trilling, and Fred Friendly.

171. Rothstein, Larry. New Directions in Mass Communications
     Policy: Implications for Citizen Education and Partici-
     pation. Washington: U.S. Department of Health, Educa-
     tion and Welfare, 1978. 34p. (HEW Publication No. (OE)
     78-07003.)

     Summarized results of a workshop held by the USOE Cit-
izen Education Staff which discussed the role of the media
in citizen education. While stressing the importance of
free speech and a free press, the conferees emphasized the
importance of access to the media for all sectors of
society; support for developing professional production
abilities for those seeking access; and expansion of the
number of outlets to present greater diversity of views.

172. Rubin, Bernard. Media, Politics, Democracy. New York:
     Oxford University Press, 1977. 192p.

     Deals with the way the media handle political events
and processes, with emphasis throughout on the need for
reform. Rubin analyzes five topics, showing how the media
environment itself creates political problems: communications objectivity and public understanding of political
reality; the connection between social values and programming alternatives confronting media managers; the concept
of media freedom; popular participation in media organizations and adequate media coverage of minority interests;
and media politics as they relate to elections. Contains
footnotes and an index.

173. Rubin, Bernard, and associates. Big Business and the Mass
     Media. Lexington, Mass.: Lexington Books, 1977. 185p.

     Five academics who have also had experience in the mass
media examine aspects of the relationship between business
and the press. Rubin writes on "Advocacy, Big Business
and Mass Media," Otto Lerbinger on "Corporate-Media Relations," Robert Rutherford Smith on "Corporate Access to
the Electronic Media," Robert Baram, "Newspapers: Their
Coverage and Big Business," and Roger Kahle, "Opinion
Leader Attitudes on Media-Business Relations." Each chapter contains notes.

174. Rucker, Bryce W. The First Freedom. Carbondale: Southern
     Illinois University Press, 1968. 322p.

In 1946 Morris Ernst, the author-lawyer, published a
study about monopoly in the newspaper, radio, and motion
picture industries, The First Freedom (No. 54). The present book by the same title is an updating, done at Ernst's
request, with emphasis on newspapers and broadcasting.
     Appendices contain a great deal of data. Sources of
information are cited. Numerous footnotes and a bibliography.

175. Salinas, Raquel. Communication Policies: The Case of
     Latin America. SO102 30 Stockholm 6: Institute of
     Latin American Studies, Odengatan 61, 1978. 39p.
     (Paper No. 9.)

     The author's aim is to relate Latin America to a search
for a new information order in the context of both the
developed and underdeveloped countries. She discusses the
nature of the forces opposing change and how they are also
manifest in industrialized countries. There is a bibliography of references.

176. Sandford, John. The Mass Media of the German-Speaking
     Countries. London: Oswald Wolff, 1976. 235p.

     An introduction to the mass media of West and East Ger-
many, Austria, and Switzerland which discusses for each
country the historical background and the present structure of the press and broadcasting systems. Comparisons
are drawn between the media systems within the four
countries dealt with and between their systems and those
of the English-speaking world. An appendix briefly
describes eleven of the major magazines and newspapers.
There is also a glossary of German words and abbreviations
used in the text, a bibliography, and an index.

177. Sandman, Peter M., David M. Rubin, and David B. Sachsmand.
     Media: An Introductory Analysis of American Mass Com-
     munications. 2d ed. Englewood Cliffs, N.J.: Prentice-
     Hall, 1976. 483p.

     A text designed primarily to acquaint consumers, whether
journalists or nonjournalists, with the world of mass communications. The approach is by function: development,
responsibility, role of each medium, and coverage; and the
aim is to produce better informed readers and viewers.
Each subsection contains a bibliography in the form of
footnotes and suggested readings. Indexed.
     The following year the authors published Media Casebook:
An Introductory Reader in Mass Communications (Prentice-
Hall, 277p.), an anthology of examples taken from books,
magazines, and newspapers where each presents a major problem or characteristic of the American mass media. Although
this can be used alone, it seems to supplement the text.

Sarkar, Chanchal. Challenge and Stagnation: The Indian Mass Media. (See No. 759.)

178. Schiller, Herbert I. Mass Communications and the American Empire. New York: Augustus M. Kelley, 1969. 170p.
179. _____. The Mind Managers. Boston: Beacon Press, 1973. 127p.
180. _____. Communication and Cultural Domination. White Plains, N.Y.: International Arts and Sciences Press, 1976. 127p.

All of Schiller's writings are radical, well documented, and skeptical of the status quo of the communications industries. In Mass Communications and the American Empire he critically examines the economic and political structure of the broadcasting industry in the U.S., from the period of radio to the period of the satellite, and finds it organized primarily to serve the military-industrial complex.

In The Mind Managers he makes a case that America's media managers "deliberately produce messages that do not correspond to the realities of social existence." In Communication and Cultural Domination he is concerned with the "sources, character, and contents of the communication stream that passes between nations and on the flow that is generated inside national states." Here again he feels the "haves" tend to influence and sometimes dominate the "have nots." All three volumes are copiously footnoted and are indexed.

181. Schramm, Wilbur, ed. Mass Communications: A Book of Readings. 2d ed. Urbana: University of Illinois Press, 1960. 695p.

Communications students of the 1950s and 1960s grew up on the articles in this anthology (the first edition came out in 1949). For this if nothing else it is important. But there are other reasons. The articles, which are as a whole well chosen, represent the thinking of some of the scholars who were then shaping the study of mass communication, and much of what they said holds today in the face of new technology, theory, and research. Among topics dealt with are development, structure, function, control and support, process, content, audience, effects, and responsibility of newspapers, broadcasting, magazines, and film. A number of articles in the 1949 edition are not duplicated in this one. Appendices in the first edition give statistical data, outdated but historically useful. The second contains a brief analysis of mass communication in other countries, accompanied by figures, and an excellent bibliography. Both are indexed.

53

182. Schramm, Wilbur L. Men, Messages, and Media: A Look at
     Human Communication. New York: Harper & Row, 1973.
     341p.

This synthesis of much important communication research
and theory is meant for the layman and beginning student
rather than the scholar, and emphasizes breadth rather than
depth. Among aspects covered are development, functions,
signs, codes, structure, social control, effects, and
models. It also deals with the mass media, particularly
audiences, control, some of the effects including political
impact, and possible future. This is a good starter to
acquire an overall knowledge of the field. Notes and references enable the user to go further.

183. Schramm, Wilbur, and Donald F. Roberts, eds. The Process
     and Effects of Mass Communication. Urbana: University
     of Illinois Press, 1971. 586p.

First published in 1954, this revised edition contains
only four articles from the original volume. It repre-
sents the enormous amount of communication research and
theory produced during the last fifteen years, as well as
the work done earlier in this century by prominent social
scientists. Subjects discussed include media, messages,
and audiences of mass communication; the effects of communication on attitudes, politics, public opinion, and
social change; and the technological future of mass communication. Contains a bibliography of 100 titles for
further reading and an index.

184. Seldes, Gilbert. The Seven Lively Arts. New York: Har-
     per, 1924. 306p.
185. _____. The Great Audience. New York: Viking, 1951.
     299p.

Gilbert Seldes was the first person in the twentieth
century to take popular art seriously. In a period when
film had just come into its own, it held great promise to
him as an innovative art form. He was also excited about
the quality of entertainment in general--the comic strip,
popular music, the Broadway comedians. Among the "lively
arts" he even includes Picasso.
   In the years that followed he lost much of his optimism.
But The Seven Lively Arts stands as one of the best descriptions of popular mass culture during and preceding the 1920s.
   When, a quarter of a century later, he reexamined the
state of mass entertainment--its character and the character
of the special type of audience it had created--he found it
wanting. Much emphasis is on radio and on television, which
was just appearing. Both books are perceptive studies which
have held up over the years.

186. Sellers, Leonard L., and William L. Rivers, eds. <u>Mass
     Media Issues</u>. Englewood Cliffs, N.J.: Prentice-Hall,
     1977. 370p.

   An anthology with brief commentaries on each article
by the editors and two tables of contents which categorize
the material differently--one by media and the other by
more general headings like news, economics, regulation,
structure and process, affect and effect. A number of the
articles are written in a popular or semipopular vein. A
good reader for undergraduates and laymen.

187. Seymour-Ure, Colin. <u>The Political Impact of Mass Media</u>.
     London: Constable/Beverley Hills, Cal.: Sage, 1974.
     296p.

   The author believes that <u>effects</u> has commonly been
defined too narrowly. Using a broader framework he has
examined and illustrated varieties of political effects
caused by the mass media. Illustrations are drawn mainly
from Britain and the U.S. Part I is an analysis of what
media effects comprise, the different ways they are produced, and the kinds of political relationship that may
result. Part II explores in some depth specific examples.
These complement Part I, but can be read on their own.
They include a study of the relationship between press
systems and party systems; a survey of the impact of the
media on British elections and electioneering since 1945;
studies of the mass media vis-à-vis Enoch Powell; the
political role of Private Eye; the role of the London
<u>Times</u> in the appeasement of Hitler; and the mutual influ-
ence of broadcasting and Parliament. Contains a list of
references, a bibliography, and an index.

188. Siebert, Fred S., Theodore Peterson, and Wilbur Schramm.
     <u>Four Theories of the Press</u>. Urbana: University of
     Illinois Press, 1956. 153p.

   "The thesis of this volume is that the press always
takes the form and coloration of the social and political
structures within which it operates. Especially, it
reflects the social and political structures whereby the
relations of individuals and institutions are adjusted."
In the light of this theory Siebert discusses both the
authoritarian and liberatarian theories, Peterson the
social responsibility theory, and Schramm the Soviet Communist theory.
   Press is interpreted broadly to include all media of
mass communication, although emphasis is primarily upon
print because it is the oldest. <u>Four Theories</u> has not
dated, and is still widely used.

189. Signitzer, Benno. Bibliography of Austrian Mass Communica-
     tion Literature, 1945-1975. A 5033 Salzburg, Austria:
     Wolfgang Neugebauer, Postfach 64, 1978. 349p.

     Contains approximately 4,600 annotated entries from
     monographs, journal articles, and newspapers, covering the
     newspaper, broadcasting, film, book, and recording industry
     as well as the more general areas of communication research,
     news agencies, public relations, journalism education,
     advertising, communication policy, and law. Contains sub-
     ject, author, and name indexes. In both German and English.

190. Singer, Benjamin, ed. Communications in Canadian Society.
     2d ed. Toronto: Copp Clark, 1975. 486p.

     A reader which considers "the broad sociological forces
     conditioning communications institutions; the problem of
     control and how it is asserted; the issue of Canadian
     identity; and some of the critical areas subsumed under the
     broad rubric of social problems." Various articles discuss
     Canadian newspapers; the telephone system; broadcasting;
     social planning; use of mass media in the classroom; the
     system of ownership and control; the Davey report on the
     media; public opinion and propaganda in Canada; censorship;
     violence and terrorism in relation to the media; and other
     topics. Also contains a descriptive listing of colleges
     and universities offering communication programs, and
     province-by-province structure and government. There is a
     useful bibliography of articles and books, and an index.
        A 1969 anthology, Mass Media in Canada, edited by John
     A. Irving (Toronto: Ryerson Press, 236p.), assesses the
     state of newspapers, books, film, broadcasting, and adver-
     tising, and discusses their development and problems.

191. Smith, Anthony. The Politics of Information: Problems of
     Policy in the Modern Media. London: Macmillan, 1978.
     252p.

     In this group of perceptive essays about various aspects
     of broadcasting and the print press, Smith's theme is that
     the media could serve the public better than they are doing.
     He proceeds to tell why he feels this to be the case.
     Orientation is British and Continental, but comments are
     applicable to Western countries in general. Indexed, with
     notes and references.

192. Sobel, Robert. The Manipulators: America in the Media Age.
     New York: Doubleday/Anchor, 1976. 458p.

     A former reporter, now professor of history, charts the
     growth of America's five media industries (newspapers, radio,
     movies, television, and college, which he considers a form of

show business), and tells the means by which they have come
to possess great power which is all too often used to manip-
ulate. He details how this is done. Among other things,
this is an unusual approach to the history of the media and
a challenging interpretation of their role in our society.
Footnotes, a lengthy bibliography, and an excellent index.

193. Stanley, Robert H., and Charles S. Steinberg. The Media
      Environment: Mass Communications in American Society.
      New York: Hastings House, 1976. 306p.

      The authors' aim is "to provide the reader with an
informational frame of reference that will permit the formation of sound critical judgments" about the institutions
of mass media in the U.S., particularly newspapers, motion
pictures, and radio and television. With this in mind,
they consider several basic questions: How did the current
media structure evolve? Who controls the vast information
and entertainment apparatus? In what way does economics
affect content? What are the legal foundations of the
media's current regulatory structure? How effective are
government and self-regulatory controls? Each medium is
treated chronologically. One chapter discusses public
broadcasting. There are also special chapters on mass
media and the Supreme Court; the U.S. and global communication; the media and minorities; public relations and advertising; and the impact of the new technology. At the end
is a lengthy bibliography. Indexed.

194. Sterling, Christopher H. The Media Sourcebook: Compara-
      tive Reviews and Listings of Textbooks in Mass Communica-
      tions. Washington: National Association of Educational
      Broadcasters, 1974. 53p.

      An evaluative overview of some 350 textbooks and books
suitable for texts which might be used in college and university courses in broadcasting and general mass media
topics. It is aimed potentially at two audiences: teachers
on the lookout for suitable textbooks, and potential authors
or publishers surveying the field to see what needs to be
written. There are six chapters in all, each covering a
time span of about a year; the first four are headed "Broadcasting Textbooks," with Chapter I covering "Industry and
Effects," II covering "Production and Performance," III
covering "Foreign and International," and IV covering "General Mass Media." Chapters V and VI are broadened to take
in textbooks in the media. Each heading is subdivided into
subject categories. All six chapters have appeared in Public Telecommunications Review, formerly Educational Broadcasting Review, which updated the texts in the February 1975
issue and has continued to do so in subsequent February
issues.

195. Sterling, Christopher H., and Timothy R. Haight. The Mass
     Media: Aspen Institute Guide to Communication Industry
     Trends. New York: Praeger, 1978. 457p.

   Here is a book that has been needed for a long time.
It brings together in a single reference source the most
significant statistics describing communication industry
trends in the U.S. since 1930, with more than 300 tables
of data supplemented by a brief interpretative text, an
analysis of source reliability and validity, and a listing
of sources of further information in each subject area.
Figures were gathered from all available sources--govern-
ment, business and trade, academic, and private correspondence. Material is divided into seven sections: growth;
ownership and control; economics; employment and training;
content trends; size and characteristics of audiences; and
U.S. media industries abroad. Media covered include books
(publishing, bookstores, book clubs, and libraries); newspapers; magazines; motion pictures; radio and television.
Those government publications which are the most frequently
used for communication statistics are discussed in a
special section, and there is an extensive bibliography.
Organizations which are a fruitful source of statistics are
also listed. Contains a subject index. All in all, this
is a comprehensive, thoroughly researched addition to the
literature of mass communications.

196. Stokke, Olav, ed. Reporting Africa. Uppsala: Scandinavian
     Institute of African Studies/New York 10003: Africana
     Publishing Corp., 101 Fifth Ave., 1971. 223p.

   Report of a seminar which explored the manner in which
African news is presented by the European press. In two
parts: "The Mass Media in Africa" and "Reporting Africa
by the International Mass Media." In the first part,
emphasis is on the English-speaking African nations--Ghana,
Kenya, and Nigeria--although there are chapters on the
African mass media as institutions of African political
systems, and on the freedoms and functions of mass communications in Africa. The second part deals with the way
selected European nations present African news, with a chapter each on the British, French, and North American mass
media, a single chapter on the Soviet and Czechoslovak
presses, and four chapters on Scandinavian broadcasting systems (including Finnish). Part II also contains sections
on the problem of cultural translation in the reporting of
African social realities, and the problems confronting correspondents specializing in Africa.

197. Strentz, Herbert J., and others. The Critical Factor:
     Criticism of the News Media in Journalism Education.
     Association for Education in Journalism, 1974. 40p.

(Journalism Monographs No. 32.) (Obtain from AEJ headquarters.)

Three articles assessing the role of journalism schools
as media critics: "The Journalism Educator as Critic:
His Contribution, Concern and Competence" by Strentz;
"Media Criticism in Classroom and Community" by Kenneth
Starck; and "Criticism of the Media, with the Media" by
David L. Anderson and Loren Ghiglione. A summary and conclusions and a selected bibliography follow. Three of the
contributors teach journalism; the fourth, Mr. Ghiglione,
is an editor and publisher.

198. Tebbel, John. The Media in America. New York: Crowell,
     1974. 422p.

     Tebbel pegs this survey of publishing, newspapers, maga-
     zines, and broadcasting to the concept of freedom of the
     press. Arrangement is chronological in four parts: "The
     Media and the Idea of Freedom," "Freedom Defined," "The
     Media and the Rise of Technological Society," and "The
     Media in the Twentieth Century." Intended for the lay
     reader, including university and college students. Bib-
     liography and index.

199. Trager, Robert, and Donna L. Dickerson. College Student
     Press Law. Urbana, Ill. 61801: ERIC Clearinghouse on
     Reading and Communication Skills, 1111 Kenyon Rd.,
     1976. 87p.

     Describes pertinent legal cases and decisions, with
     interpretive commentary.

200. Training for Mass Communication. Paris: UNESCO, 1975.
     44p. (Reports and Papers on Mass Communication No.
     73.)

     A highly practical report, intended for developing
     countries, which surveys in general terms the status of
     communication training, pinpointing deficiencies and
     identifying potentially influential trends. Discusses the
     nature of training, the institutions, the operational prob-
     lems, and course planning and curriculum. Appendices
     include "A Program for Action"; "Module Specification
     Sheet"; and "ETV Training Modules."

201. The Training of Journalists: A World-wide Survey on the
     Training of Personnel for the Mass Media. New York:
     UNESCO Publications Center, 1958. 222p. (Press, Film,
     and Radio in the World Today.)

     Gives training programs for journalists in twenty-one
     countries and contains discussions of UNESCO's role in

journalism education and a series of eight articles by
authorities on various aspects of journalism training,
including a comparative analysis of recent curricula
trends. Useful as a historical document.

202. Tunstall, Jeremy. The Media are American: Anglo-American
     Media in the World. New York: Columbia University
     Press, 1977. 352p.

     As its title indicates, Tunstall's theme is cultural
     imperialism. To quote him: "This book covers a lot of
     media, a big time span and most of the world's larger
     countries. . . . The main thesis is mainly at the begin-
     ning and the end, while particular countries come in the
     middle." Among countries he discusses are the British
     Commonwealth and ex-Commonwealth, which includes India and
     portions of Africa; Italy; Germany; France; Japan; the
     Communist countries; the Arab countries; the Middle East;
     Latin America; and of course the U.S. The big question he
     poses: Can countries, especially developing ones, find
     other forms and content for their media more suited to
     their culture than the form and content of ours? He also
     goes into detail about the structure of the present system
     from the standpoint of economics and distribution. There
     are a number of tables, an extensive bibliography, and an
     index.

203. Tunstall, Jeremy, ed. Media Sociology. Urbana: Univer-
     sity of Illinois Press, 1970. 674p.

     Anthology of twenty-five essays intended for students
     taking introductory courses dealing with the media, which
     in this anthology include newspapers, magazines, radio,
     records, television, and books. Although intended pri-
     marily for British students, articles by and about the
     American media are included as well. Contains a section
     citing "Notes and Sources" on which the articles are based,
     a bibliography, and name and subject indexes.

204. U.S. Bureau of the Census. Census of Manufactures.
     Industry Statistics 1972: Newspapers, Periodicals,
     Books and Miscellaneous Publishing. Washington: Super-
     intendent of Documents, U.S. Government Printing Office,
     1976. 43p.

     Detailed tables covering many aspects of production and
     consumption of printed media. Compares figures of current
     with previous editions--in this case 1967, although some
     tables go back to 1958. It is published every five years
     and runs several years late. Also included as part of
     Census of Manufactures. Vol. II. Industry Statistics
     Part 2. SIC Major Groups 27-34.

205. Viet, Jean. Thesaurus: Mass Communication. Paris:
     UNESCO, Mass Communications Documentation Centre, 1975.
     2 parts. 158p, 58p.

     This multilingual thesaurus in English, French, and
Spanish provides a "documentation language" developed at
the request of the Division of Communication Research and
Planning of UNESCO. Precise terms designed to be used in
post-storage retrieval of computerized documents are con-
sistent with international documentation systems in related
fields. The first part is a subject arrangement; the
second part, an alphabetical listing.

206. Wechsler, Andrew R. Economics and Freedom of Expression:
     A Bibliography. Palo Alto, Cal.: Stanford University,
     Department of Economics, 1974. 55p. (Studies In Indus-
     try Economics No. 38.)

     A listing of approximately 600 books, reports, articles,
court decisions, and laws dealing with issues of freedom
of speech, access, and antitrust regulation of the mass
media. Even though the entries are unannotated, and
arrangement is alphabetical in two listings by form--i.e.,
books, reports, and articles in one alphabet; court decisions and laws in another--this is valuable for the
thoroughness with which it covers the area. The author
says that in general only obviously significant pieces
published before 1960 have been included.

207. Weibel, Kathryn. Mirror, Mirror: Images of Women Reflected
     in Popular Culture. New York: Anchor/Doubleday, 1977.
     256p.

     A historical survey of the changing images of women in
our society and the motives behind the change, as revealed
on TV and in movies, magazines, advertising, and fiction.
Notes and an index.

208. Welch, Susan, and John Comer, eds. Public Opinion: Its
     Formation, Measurement, and Impact. Palo Alto, Cal.:
     Mayfield, 1975. 541p.

     The aim of the editors is to gather together in one
anthology the "constellation of incredibly diverse topics"
which constitute public opinion--the psychological factors
behind individual attitudes; the sociological antecedents
of mass opinion; the impact of opinion on policymaking; its
influence on political culture; the techniques of sampling
and measuring; the characteristics of voters. Each chapter
has copious bibliographical "End notes," and there is a
subject and a name index.

209. Wells, Alan, ed. <u>Mass Communication: A World View</u>. Palo
     Alto, Cal.: National Press Books, 1974. 276p.

     "What is attempted here," says the author, "is the pre-
     sentation of a sampling of geographic regions and issues."
     Articles are arranged in two parts: Part I provides mate-
     rial on overseas media systems, Part II, international
     facilities and influences. Among countries and regions
     included are China, Russia, Africa, Japan (NHK), Asia
     (newspapers), the United Arab Republic (government control).
     Among the topics: an international cable system, Intelsat,
     international news agencies, international film and pro-
     paganda, propaganda through printed media in developing
     countries, the international commercialization of broad-
     casting. Footnotes and bibliography.

210. Wells, Alan. <u>Mass Media and Society</u>. 2d ed. Palo Alto,
     Cal.: Mayfield, 1975. 412p.

     Designed to serve as a basic text for general liberal
     arts courses in mass communications on a college level,
     with emphasis on the factual and controversial rather than
     the technical or empirical. There are essays on the press,
     radio and recording, TV, film, advertising, content and
     effects of mass media, objectivity, bias and propaganda in
     the news, crime, violence and the media, public issues,
     politics and the media, racism, sexism and the media.

211. Whetmore, Edward Jay. <u>Mediamerica: Form, Content, and</u>
     <u>Consequences of Mass Communication</u>. Belmont, Cal.:
     Wadsworth, 1979. 332p.

     "<u>Mediamerica</u> concentrates on what <u>is</u> and not what <u>should</u>
     <u>be</u>," says Whetmore. In this text for journalism undergrad-
     uates he deals not only with the <u>New York Times</u> and other
     of the more traditional products, but also with the <u>National</u>
     <u>Enquirer</u>, and with such popular offshoots of the media as
     <u>Roots</u> and <u>Jaws</u> and <u>Star Trek</u> and rock music and disc jockeys.
     This is simply written without being "written down," and is
     pertinently illustrated with good references to further read-
     ing at the end of each chapter. It should give students
     food for thought, pleasantly presented.

212. White, Llewellyn, and Robert D. Leigh. <u>Peoples Speaking to</u>
     <u>Peoples: A Report on International Mass Communication</u>
     <u>from the Commission of Freedom of the Press</u>. Chicago:
     University of Chicago Press, 1946. 122p.

     A detailed analysis of the means by which information,
     especially news, is gathered, controlled, and distributed
     internationally. Source notes.

213. Wilcox, Dennis L. <u>Mass Media in Black Africa: Philosophy</u>
     <u>and Control</u>. New York: Praeger, 1975. 170p.

A descriptive, comparative survey of press-government
relationships in independent black Africa, defined as
those thirty-four nations south of the Sahara with black-
majority governments. Areas still under colonial or white-
minority governments in early 1974 are excluded. The
author systematically analyzes formalized press controls
exerted by government to try to find a pattern of evolving
press philosophies and to show the function and role of
the press in each country. An appendix compares in tabular form the media in Africa with other continents; another
gives names and ownership of daily newspapers in independent black Africa. Contains an extensive bibliography and
an index.

214. Wilhoit, Frances Goins, and D. Craig Mitchell. Mass Media
     Periodicals: An Annotated Bibliography. Bloomington:
     Indiana University, Center for New Communications of the
     School of Journalism, Ernie Pyle Hall, 1978. 33p.

     Includes approximately 125 journals, indexes, and statis-
     tical yearbooks intended as an introduction to the study of
     the media. Focus is on print and broadcast journalism,
     although it also includes the major journals which examine
     other aspects of the media. Tells where each of the jour-
     nals is indexed. Contains a list of indexes and abstracts
     annotated in the bibliography, and a subject index to the
     periodicals. (See also No. 25.)

215. Williams, Raymond. Communications. Rev. ed. London:
     Chatto & Windus, 1966. 196p.

     This book first appeared in 1962 as a part of Penguin's
     Britain in the Sixties series. Its contents, however,
     have a much broader application than a given country or
     decade, and summarize much of Williams's philosophy of com-
     munications, which he defines in broad terms of social and
     cultural policy. His approach is basically Marxist,
     although in no party sense. From this vantage point he
     examines the history and content of the various media, and
     differing ideas about mass and class culture. He concludes
     with a chapter on proposals which relates more directly to
     England than the rest of the book. There is a bibliography,
     "Further Reading," and two appendices: "Methods in TV
     Education" and "A Policy for the Arts."

216. Williams, Raymond. Culture and Society, 1780-1950. New
     York: Columbia University Press, 1958. 363p.
217. _____. The Long Revolution. Westport, Conn.: Green-
     wood, c1961, 1975. 396p.

     "The organizing principle of this book is the discovery
     that the idea of culture, and the word itself in its general

modern uses, came into English thinking in the period which we commonly describe as that of the Industrial Revolution. The book is an attempt to show how and why this happened, and to follow the idea through to our own day. It thus becomes an account and an interpretation of our responses in thought and feeling to the changes in English society since the late eighteenth century. Only in such a context can our use of the word culture, and the issues to which the word refers, be adequately understood," explains Williams of Culture and Society, in which he pursues this thesis in terms of the novelists, the economic and political philosophers, and the critics of the nineteenth and twentieth centuries.

He follows this with The Long Revolution, in which he further examines factors which have shaped culture, with particular emphasis on the Industrial Revolution in relation to print media. The first part of the book deals with the nature of the creative mind, and with culture and society in general. The second part is concerned with education, the reading public, the popular press, the novel, and writers. The third part surveys the 1960s.

Although Williams's orientation is British throughout both books, his analyses are universal. A Penguin edition of The Long Revolution appeared in 1965 with few revisions and amendments, and added notes. Both books have reading lists and indexes.

218. Winick, Charles, ed. Deviance and Mass Media. Beverly Hills, Cal.: Sage, 1978. 309p. (Sage Annual Reviews of Studies in Deviance, Vol. II.)

The fourteen reports in this volume tackle the relationships between deviance and the media. Contents are grouped into four categories: content-oriented media studies; a report on deviant media study; comparative studies; and analysis of the role of media in contributing to deviance. Among topics treated are drug abuse, obesity, illness, death, crime and law enforcement, rape, character assassination, transsexualism, and nonvoting—some of which are not commonly thought of as deviance in the usual sense. Each chapter lists references.

219. Winston, Brian. The Image of the Media. London: Davis-Poynter, 1973. 112p. (Dangling Conversations, Book I.)
220. _____. Hardware Software: A Background Guide to the Study of the Mass Media. London: Davis-Poynter, 1974. 160p. (Dangling Conversations, Book II.)

The first two of a projected series of four works designed to provide systematic underpinnings for a broad understanding of the media. Book I examines the dominant

approaches--through sociology, through culture, through
Marshall McLuhan's theories, through information theory.
Book II deals with the human sensory mechanisms and the
evolution of hard and software systems. Book III will
outline the history of the development of media forms,
Book IV will attempt to examine present media output on
a new basis.

The Working Press of the Nation. 5 vols. (See Nos. 626, 788,
    1074, 1075 1076.)

221. World Communications: A 200-Country Survey of Press,
    Radio, Television and Film. 5th ed. Epping, England:
    Gower Press, 1975. 533p.

    In the years that have passed since the fourth edition
of this comprehensive reference book appeared, great
changes have taken place that are reflected in the structure of the media and that have been incorporated into
the fifth edition. The first thirty-four pages are
arranged by media: the press, news agencies, broadcasting, and film, with broad overall continent-by-continent
surveys; the rest of the more than 500 pages are by continents, broken down by countries. Media statistics are
given for each country followed by discussion of trends
in the press, news agencies, radio, television, film,
space communication satellites, flows and exchanges, education for mass communication, professional associations,
and patterns of control. Data come from the information
regularly supplied to UNESCO by governments of member
states in reply to an annual statistical questionnaire
and can be found in the UNESCO Statistical Yearbook. Bibliography.

222. Wright, Charles R. Mass Communication: A Sociological
    Perspective. 2d ed. New York: Random House, 1975.
    179p.

    "If our sociological perspective has a scheme," Wright
says of his book, "it is the need to examine mass communications within the broader framework of social structure
and cultural context." From this orientation point he
deals with "The Nature and Functions of Mass Communications"; "Mass Communications as Social Institutions";
"Sociology of the Mass Communicator"; "Sociology of the
Audience"; "Informal Communication and the Mass Audience";
"Cultural Content of American Mass Communications"; "Social
Effects of Mass Communications." This is one of the finest
theoretical texts in the field for undergraduates and laymen. Extensive footnotes, a bibliography, and an index.

223. Zuckman, Harvey, and Martin J. Gaynes. <u>Mass Communication Law in a Nutshell</u>. St. Paul, Minn.: West Publishing Co., 1977. 431p. (West Nutshell Series.)

The authors, both lawyers and teachers, intend this to be a basic text for communications law students who need a general outline of the subject. Part I deals with the First Amendment and mass communications, Part II with regulation and the media. Apart from its possible use as a text it supplements fuller case studies such as Franklin's <u>Cases and Materials on Mass Media Law</u> (No. 66) and his <u>The First Amendment and the Fourth Estate</u> (No. 66), or Gillmor and Barron, <u>Mass Communication Law: Cases and Comment</u> (No. 76). It is also an excellent reference source to answer laymen's questions. Contains a subject index.

II
Books and Book Publishing

224. About Face: Toward a More Positive Image of Women in Text-
    books.   Toronto M5G 1Z6:   Ontario Status of Women Coun-
    cil, 1974.   10p.

    Survey of the contents of recommended textbooks,
    intended to assist teachers, publishers, and community
    groups in their efforts to improve the somewhat unreal-
    istic image of women presented in texts.   (See also
    About Face: Toward a Positive Image of Women in Adver-
    tising (No. 1078).)

225. The Accidental Profession: Education, Training, and the
    People of Publishing.   New York 10016:   Association of
    American Publishers, One Park Ave., 1977.   103p.

    The purpose of the AAP's Committee on Professional Edu-
    cation for Publishing is to survey the state of training
    for, in, and about book publishing.   In accomplishing this
    they have gone deeply into the condition and structure of
    the industry--the job market, including statistics and
    their reliability and the quality of applicants; the kinds
    of formal training courses available; in-house training;
    the literature of publishing and the lack of it; publish-
    ing education abroad; and the need for layman education
    about book publishing.   A by-product of the study is that
    it provides an understanding of the various facets of the
    profession.   Appendices give curricula for three new book-
    publishing institutes and models of in-house training pro-
    grams and outside programs.

226. African Book Publishing Record.   The African Book World
    and Press: A Directory.   Repertoire du Livre et de la
    Press en Afrique.   Hans M. Zell, ed.   Detroit: Gale
    Research Co., 1977.   296p.

    A listing of libraries, publishers and the retail book
    trade, research institutions with publishing programs,

book industry and literary associations, and the major
periodicals and newspapers published throughout the African continent. In all, it gives a total of 2,347 institutions and organizations, arranged alphabetically by
country, with varying data according to the nature of the
institution, but always including such essentials as
address, telephone number, and staff. In most cases considerable other information is given. Appendices include
a subject index to special libraries and to periodicals
and magazines; listings of book clubs, literary prizes,
and awards; a calendar of book trade events; a directory
of government printers and major commercial printers;
principal dealers in African books in Europe and the U.S.;
and a bibliography on publishing and book development in
Africa.

227. Altbach, Philip G. Publishing in India: An Analysis.
     New York: Oxford University Press, 1975; Delhi:
     Oxford University Press, 1975. 115p.

     In spite of the emphasis on India in the title, the
author treats all third world countries, but specifically
deals with India by using it as a case study to examine
historical development of the industry, its economics, and
distribution, copyright, "public" and "private" publishing,
foreign influences, regional language publishing, academic
publishing, and publishing and the intellectual community.
Footnotes and an extensive bibliography.

228. Altick, Richard D. The English Common Reader: A Social
     History of the Mass Reading Public 1800-1900. Chicago:
     University of Chicago Press, 1957. 430p.

     "This volume is an attempt to study, from the historian's
viewpoint, the place of reading in an industrial and increasingly democratic society," says the author in this systematically analyzed and documented work. In his approach he has
not fallen back upon anecdotes nor attempted to analyze the
appeal of the period's most popular authors. Rather, he has
discussed the social background of the century--its religion,
its prevailing philosophy, its education, its labor movements, and its book, periodical, and newspaper trade.
     Appendices include a chronology of the mass reading pub-
lic, 1774-1900; a chronology of best sellers with sales
figures and notes; and another chronology of periodical and
newspaper circulation. Contains a bibliography and an index.

229. American Book Trade Directory: Booksellers and Publishers
     in the United States, Great Britain, Ireland, and Canada;
     Wholesalers in the United States and Canada; Foreign Book
     Dealers. New York: Bowker, biennial. (1915--.)

Deals primarily with the various agencies involved in
bookselling and, to a lesser degree, with those involved
in book publishing. Lists currently about 12,000 retail
outlets in the U.S., giving address, telephone number,
owner, manager, buyer, branch stores, types of books carried, and, beginning with the 1975-76 edition, a separate
list of the shop's specialities and sidelines. Booksellers
in Canada, Great Britain, and the Republic of Ireland are
also listed, with address and telephone number only.

Some other features include a list of wholesalers in
the U.S. and Canada; a directory of book publishers in the
U.S., Canada, and Great Britain; and such further information as auctioneers of literary property, appraisers of
library collections, dealers in foreign language books,
exporters, importers, rental libraries, and chains. It
also brings together a list of former publishers, now
inactive, out of business, or merged, which is difficult
to obtain.

230. American Publisher's Directory: Guide to Publishers of
      Books, Journals, Magazines, Directories, Reprints, Maps,
      Microeditions, Braille Books and Book Clubs. New York:
      K. G. Saur, 1978. 390p.

      Contains more than 25,000 entries, listing for each
      address, telephone and telex number, ISBN prefix when
      available, and area of specialization when applicable.
      In addition to the categories in the subtitle, it also
      covers wholesalers and publishers whose yearly production
      involves fewer than five books or periodicals. The under-
      ground press is also included.

231. Anatomy of an International Year. Book Year--1972. Paris:
      UNESCO, 1974(?). 37p. (Reports and Papers on Mass Com-
      munication No. 71.)

      This is "a digest and appraisal of the initiatives taken
      and techniques employed during International Book Year with
      a view to making the most advantageous use of this informa-
      tion for the future." Includes need, origins, mechanics,
      the ways in which the program was carried out, a program
      for the future, an appraisal, and a summing up. An appen-
      dix gives resolutions adopted by the UNESCO General Confer-
      ence.

232. Anderson, Charles B., ed. Bookselling in America and the
      World: Some Observations and Recollections in Celebra-
      tion of the 75th Anniversary of the American Booksellers
      Association. New York: Quadrangle, 1975. 214p.

      The publishers call this commemorative miscellany "a
      book of praise to booksellers." Its range is wide and

roving, from a brief history by John Tebbel to reminiscences
by famous booksellers to a musical tribute by Michael
Flanders and Donald Swan, and, of course, a history of the
American Booksellers Association--this by Chandler Grannis.
Contains a list of officers of the ABA from 1900 through
1975 and the Board of Directors from 1930 to date.

233. Astbury, Raymond, ed. <u>Libraries and the Book Trade</u>. Lon-
     don: Clive Bingley, 1968. 194p.

     Survey of the British book trade, centering around pub-
lishing, censorship, and bookselling. A final chapter
includes the book trade and the role of the library.

234. Bailey, Herbert S., Jr. <u>The Art and Science of Book Pub-
     lishing</u>. New York: Harper & Row, 1970. 216p.

     "The ideas presented here . . . are meant to focus
analytically on the problems of management: organization,
communication, external and internal relationships, types
of decisions, work flow, personnel, finances, planning,
new technologies, and so on." So says the author, drawing
upon his experience as director of the Princeton University Press. The result is one of the best possible inside
views of the structure and economics of book publishing.
One appendix suggests useful business forms for publishing
houses; another is a bibliography. Indexed.

235. Baker, John. <u>The Book Business</u>. London: John Baker,
     1971. 88p.

     An insider who has spent his life in the book trade com-
ments about some of the often mysterious and illogical ways
in which book publishing works. His love of his profession--
"half a trade and half a vocation"--shows through as he
explains such matters as publishing policies, booksellers,
libraries, authors, reviewers, and what he calls "the frus-
trated reading public." A slim, but not slight, book.

236. Barker, Ronald E. <u>Books for All: A Study of International
     Book Trade</u>. New York: UNESCO Publications Center, 1956.
     102p.

     On a worldwide basis, the author covers facts and figures
on the structure and economics of book publishing, import
and export, tariffs, copyright, translations, libraries, and
book exchanges. Contains a bibliography and an index.
     Although a sequel to Barker has been written (No. 269),
its orientation is sociological rather than statistical. In
1952 and from 1954 through 1961 UNESCO published <u>Basic Facts
and Figures</u>, which gave data on production of print media,
film, and broadcasting. This has now been incorporated in

UNESCO Statistical Yearbook: Annaire Statistique, the best source for current data. Statistics are found under the heading of "Culture" rather than "Communication" (which encompasses telephone, telegraph, and mail traffic), organized by country and by language.

237. Barker, Ronald E., and Robert Escarpit. The Book Hunger. Paris: UNESCO, 1973. 155p.

A brief survey of the role of the book in developing countries in terms of needs, demand, production, distribution, and copyright. An appendix gives the "charter of the book."

238. Benjamin, Curtis G. A Candid Critique of Book Publishing. New York: Bowker, 1977. 187p.

Lively and provocative essays that have grown out of the author's half-century in book publishing. They deal with the many facets of the trade--the problem of definition; the attractions; the relationship between author and publisher; the art of keeping--and stealing--authors; marketing and promotion; subject publishing; paperbacks; mergers; copyright; foreign markets; multinational publishing; helping indigenous publishers in needy countries; trade associations; the role of government; the number of and the future of books. Notes, references, an excellent bibliography, and an index.

239. Bennett, H. S. English Books and Readers [1475 to 1640]. 3 vols. 2d ed. Cambridge, England: Cambridge University Press, 1965, 1969, 1970.

History of the book trade in England for the period covered. Vol. I deals with the years from Caxton to the incorporation of the Stationers' Company; Vol. II, the reign of Elizabeth I; Vol. III, the reigns of James I and Charles I.
The author discusses the kinds of books being published, why they were written, and for whom they were intended; the growth of printers and booksellers; and the relationships of printers, authors, patrons, and readers. Each volume contains a bibliography and an index.

240. Bonham-Carter, Victor. Authors by Profession. Vol. I. From the Introduction of Printing until the Copyright Act 1911. Los Altos, Cal.: William Kaufmann, 1978. 252p.

Bonham-Carter has summarized the contents of his book in the subtitle: "How authors and dramatists have practiced their profession; their contractual and personal relations with patrons, publishers and promoters; their situation under the law of copyright; their standing with the public; their part in the trade of books and periodicals and presentation of stage plays; their professional organizations." Orientation is British, and there is discussion of the Society of Authors, the Net Book Agreement, various authors who have in one way or another influenced the economics of authorship, and other interesting highlights and sidelights. Notes, bibliography, and index. Vol. II, which will take the work to the present, is in preparation.

241. Book Development in Africa: Problems and Perspectives. Paris: UNESCO, 1969. 37p.

Report on a meeting of experts who discussed problems and implications in terms of what was and should be the economic and social role of books and book publishing in Africa.

242. Book Development in Asia: A Report on the Production and Distribution of Books in the Region. Paris: UNESCO, 1967. 72p. (Reports and Papers on Mass Communication No. 52.)

Part I assesses Asia's book needs and the problems involved in meeting them and discusses production, promotion, and distribution; the international flow of books; and the need for training, research, and cooperation of professional organizations. Part II gives facts and figures and a general summary.

The report includes the UNESCO member states only: Afghanistan, Burma, Cambodia, Ceylon, Taiwan, India, Indonesia, Iran, Nepal, Pakistan, Philippines, Singapore, Thailand, and the Republic of Vietnam.

243. The Book Industry in Yugoslavia: Report of the Delegation of U.S. Book Publishers Visiting Yugoslavia October 18-November 1, 1963. New York: American Book Publishers Council and the American Textbook Publishing Institute, 1964. 41p.

244. Book Publishing and Distribution in Rumania: Report of the Delegation of U.S. Publishers Visiting Rumania October 1-10, 1965. New York: American Book Publishers Council and American Textbook Publishers Institute, 1966. 60p.

245. Book Publishing in the U.S.S.R.: Report of the Delegation of U.S. Book Publishers Visiting the U.S.S.R. August 20-September 17, 1962. New York: American Book Publishers Council and American Textbook Publishers Institute, 1963. 112p.

Three studies of the booktrade in countries which have a common Communist orientation. Facts differ somewhat for each, but all deal comprehensively with the many aspects of production and distribution of trade books as well as belles lettres, scientific, technical, professional books, etc. There are also sections on translations, exports and imports, copyright, and similar important subjects. Statistics accompany texts.

246. Book Publishers Directory: An Information Service Covering New and Established, Private and Special Interest, Avant-Garde and Alternative, Organization and Institution Presses. Detroit: Gale Research Co., quarterly. (1977--.)

Keeping up with the many publishers of diverse kinds spreading throughout the country is increasingly difficult. This welcome directory lists hundreds of publishers not usually included in conventional sources. Entries provide the following information where appropriate: name, address, and phone number, date founded, ISBN prefix, affiliation, principal personnel, number of titles a year, brief descriptions, subjects covered, discount and return policies, imprints, divisions, subsidiaries, articles about the firm, examples of titles, magazines, journals, or serials published. Indexes, which are cumulative, include publishers and personnel, a geographic breakdown beginning with the second issue, and subject specialization.

247. The Book Trade of the World. Vol. I. Europe and International Section. Sigfried Taubert, ed. New York: Bowker, 1972. 543p.
    The Book Trade of the World. Vol. II. The Americas, Australia, and New Zealand. Sigfried Taubert, ed. New York: Bowker, 1976. 377p.

A country-by-country systematic description of some of the basic facts about book publishing which are necessary to know in order to conduct business on an international level and useful for other purposes as well. Each country was asked to give information about itself under the following categories: general, history, retail prices, organization, the trade press, book trade literature and address services, sources of information, international membership, market research, books and young people, taxes, clearing houses, training, copyright, national bibliographies and national libraries, book production, translation, book clubs, paperbacks, design, publishing houses (not a listing), literary agents, wholesale trade, retail trade, mail order, antiquarian book trade and auctions, imports, exports, book fairs, public relations, bibliophilism,

literary prizes, book reviews, and miscellaneous. Obviously
not all of these facts were filled out by every country, but
the total adds up to a great deal of data. In addition the
first volume has an international section in which much of
the information in that volume is summarized under these
same catagories. Vol. II has a long section on book production and number of translations, both for 1968; the UNESCO
Florence Agreement; the book trade answer code; and a listing of members of the Berne and the Universal Copyright conventions.

248. The Bookman's Glossary. Jean Peters, ed. 5th ed. New
York: Bowker, 1975. 169p.

The Bookman's Glossary first appeared in serial form in
the July 12, 1924, Publishers Weekly. Since that time it
has been revised and enlarged to reflect the expanding and
changing terminology of the book trade, but its object has
not changed. Like its predecessors this edition is
designed to provide a practical guide to the terminology
used in the production and distribution of books in words
in common usage in the bookstore, in the publisher's office,
in a library, or among book collectors. This time the
terminology has been broadened to take in the area of computer typesetting. People prominent in the technology of
printing have been included. There is a selected reading
list and a list of proofreader's marks.

249. Books for the Developing Countries. Asia. Africa. Paris:
UNESCO, 1965. 31p. (Reports and Papers on Mass Communication No. 47.)

Consists of two articles: "The Production and Flow of
Books in South East Asia" by Om Prakash and "The Production
and Flow of Books in Africa" by Clifford M. Fyle. Both
authors emphasize such social aspects as literacy level and
language difficulties and such economic aspects as copyright, trade barriers, and raw materials.

250. Books in East Africa. Alden H. Clark. New York: Franklin
Books Programs, 1964. 16, 9p.
251. Books in West Africa: Report and Recommendations. William
E. Spaulding, Simon Michael Bessie, and Datus C. Smith,
Jr., comps. New York: Franklin Books Programs, 1964.
44p.

Both reports assess socioeconomic, geographic, and other
conditions in East and West Africa as they relate to the
possibility of setting up an indigenous book-publishing and
-distribution system.

252. Bowker Annual of Library and Book Trade Information. New
     York: Bowker, annual. (1955--.)

     Although devoted mainly to libraries this contains
     lengthy sections on the book trade which vary slightly
     from year to year. The 1977 volume includes "Book Trade
     Statistics," "International News/Book Trade," and
     "Directory of Book Trade Organizations." Among data are
     estimated sales by category; book outlets; statistics on
     the number of books reviewed in prominent reviewing media;
     the year's mergers; prices of U.S. and foreign materials;
     the report of the Association of American Publishers' Com-
     mittee on Education for Publishing; news of the inter-
     national book trade which includes statistics and pro-
     grams; literary awards; trade associations. The 1976
     edition has a cumulative index for 1972-76.

253. Bowker Lectures on Book Publishing. New York: Bowker,
     1957. 389p.

     A collection of the first seventeen Bowker Memorial
     Lectures on book publishing covering 1935-56. Even
     though a few are personal reminiscences and most of them
     are somewhat out of date, a number give a broad overview
     and all give a historical perspective of their various
     subjects. The lectures delivered since 1956 are available
     as monographs from the New York Public Library.

254. The Business of Publishing: A PW Anthology. New York:
     Bowker, 1976. 303p.

     Articles from Publishers Weekly about the economics of
     book publishing, publisher-author relations, manufacturing,
     advertising and promotion, paperbacks, distribution, mail
     order, remainders, and other aspects. Indexed.

255. Cain, Michael Scott, ed. Co-op Publishing Handbook.
     Paradise, Cal.: Dustbooks, P.O. Box 1056, annual.
     208p. (1978--.)

     As major-league book publishing becomes more and more
     a conglomerate industry with emphasis on mass-market best
     sellers and the book as a packaged product, a substantial
     number of writers have found an alternative in cooperative
     publishing. Here a number of such groups tell why and how
     they got started. The book is both philosophical and
     practical, exploring the impetus and needs behind the
     growth of co-ops and describing the nuts and bolts. Var-
     ious kinds of cooperative publishing are represented--
     large well-established ones like Fiction Collective, the
     regional groups, the social-political groups, the oddities,
     the independents, the unclassifiable. The editor has

written a substantial introduction about the movement and
a summing-up.

256. Cassell's Directory of Publishing in Great Britain, the
Commonwealth, Ireland, South Africa and Pakistan,
1976-1977. 8th ed. London: Cassell, 1976. 581p.

The British counterpart of Literary Marketplace (No.
287). In two parts: "The Publishing and Promotion of
Books" and "Representatives and Services." Over half of
the book is given to a listing of publishers with full
information: telephone, telex, cable numbers, directors,
personnel, subject area, parent company, allied and subsidiary companies, overseas representatives. The rest
gives publishers' overseas representatives in Great
Britain; British publishers classified by fields of activity; British paperback publishers and imprints; government
agencies concerned with the industry; trade associations
and agencies connected with the industry and others of
interest to publishers; book societies and book clubs;
literary foundations; a calendar of events; a list of periodicals and reference books; and even literary luncheons.
Under "Representatives and Services" come authors' agents;
British representatives overseas; commercial artists and
their agents in London; picture, photo, and lecture agents;
television and radio organizations; remainder merchants;
translators; book packagers; consultancies; research;
indexing; and a variety of other similar services. There
are indexes of subjects and of names of publishers and
literary agents. An interesting feature is an endpaper
map showing location of publishers and agents in central
London, and another of postal districts.

257. Cave, Roderick. The Private Press. London: Faber &
Faber, 1971. 376p.

Since the invention of printing, private presses have
played an important part in literary and political history
as well as in the graphic arts. In this handsome and comprehensive book Cave describes some of the most important
presses and amateur printers, and the social or aesthetic
roles they have played from the beginning of printing to
the present. Among these are the quasi-official or
patron's press; the scholarly press; the aristocratic
plaything; the author as publisher; bibliomania; clandes-
tine presses used for religious and political reasons
and such illegal work as counterfeiting; printing as a
hobby; William Morris and his Kelmscott Press, and later
fine presses in Britain; fine printing in America and on
the European continent, etc. Concluding chapters discuss

the contemporary scene. There are handsome illustrations
of presswork, a lengthy bibliography, and an index of names
and titles.

258. Cazden, Robert E. German Exile Literature in America 1935-
     1950: A History of the Free German Press and Book Trade.
     Chicago: American Library Association, 1970. 250p.

Describes the growth of a large and dynamic anti-Nazi
press and book trade on an international scale; tells how
thousands of German-language books and journals published
outside the Third Reich were imported to the U.S.; and discusses the fate of the German emigré author in America.
There are three bibliographic appendices: "Retail Distributors of Free German Publications in the United States
1933-1950"; "Free German and Free Austrian Newspapers and
Periodicals in the United States 1933-1950--A Checklist";
"Free German Books and Pamphlets Published in the United
States 1933-1954--A Checklist." There is also an extensive bibliography, footnotes following each chapter, and
an index.

259. Cheney, O. H. Economic Survey of the Book Industry 1930-
     31. New York: Bowker, c1931, 1960. 356p.

Since Cheney wrote his economic analysis of book publishing five decades ago, many changes have taken place:
the paperback revolution, the decline of the independent
publisher, the concept of the book as a product to be tied
in with motion pictures and television shows and often
written both for and from them, and other trends too numerous to enumerate. But some of the problems remain the
same--for example: too many titles? what to do about
remainders; who buys books? are popular books bad? the
good book without a market. Cheney touches tellingly upon
these and many others, ending each chapter with recommendations and making final overall recommendations. Newer
books, notably Dessauer's (No. 263), do not displace this;
it is essential for anyone wanting a knowledge of the past
as a frame for the present or for its own sake. The 1960
reprint contains a new bibliography and an introduction by
Robert Frase comparing the book industry in 1930 with the
industry in 1960.

260. Clair, Colin. A Chronology of Printing. New York:
     Praeger, 1969. 225p.

". . . being an attempt to set in chronological order
those matters judged most important in the history of the
printed book, its manufacture, design and dissemination,"
says the author as he follows printing year by year from
its introduction into Europe and its spread throughout

the world to the present. His aim is to give a wide spread
of information rather than to study any portion in depth.
Entries are grouped nationally. A comprehensive index of
more than 10,000 items pulls the facts together.

261. Compaine, Benjamin M. The Book Industry in Transition: An
     Economic Study of Book Distribution and Marketing. White
     Plains, N.Y.: Knowledge Industry Publications, 1978.
     235p.

     Those who fear that the book will soon be antiquated
should take heart at this cool appraisal of the book-
publishing industry in which the author is guardedly optimistic that there is room for the production of books of
all kinds. Drawing from market research that Knowledge
Industry Publications has done for its clients, he has
updated some of the topics Cheney (No. 259) tackled four
decades ago. In his own words, the study is meant to be
"a detailed description of how general books get to various
markets, how the economics of this distribution work, what
the strengths and weaknesses of the current practices are,
what changes are affecting the book industry, and what may
be the future of the industry." In nontechnical language
he discusses the market in terms of structure and readers,
with much emphasis on the ways the various kinds of books
are distributed. In conclusion he presents some brief profiles of publishing companies, wholesalers, and retailers.
There are a number of tables and charts; a brief bibliography; an appendix, "Knowledge Industry Publications Book
Buyers Survey"; and an index.

262. Dahl, Svend. History of the Book. 2d English ed.
     Metuchen, N.J.: Scarecrow Press, 1968. 270p.

     The author describes his aim in the preface: "Most of
the existing works on the history of the book present its
various phases--manuscripts, printing, binding, illustra-
tion, the book trade and libraries--separately. In this
work I have attempted to present them all in a unified
account so that their interrelationship will become apparent and the history of the book will appear in perspective
as an essential factor in the history of culture." Contains a bibliography and an index.

263. Dessauer, John P. Book Publishing: What It Is, What It
     Does. New York: Bowker, 1974. 231p.

     An ideal introduction to the structure of a complicated
subject by one of the foremost authorities on the economics
of the industry. He treats book publishing under the following categories: "The Past Is Prologue," a short history;

"A Broad Perspective," a discussion of the issues, activities, and associations; and more specifically, "How Books Are Created," "How Books Are Manufactured," "How Books Are Marketed," "How Books Are Stored and Delivered," "How Publishers Finance, Plan and Manage," and in conclusion, "What Does the Future Hold?" Glossary of terms, index, and bibliographic notes.

264. Dessauer, John P., Paul D. Doebler, and E. Wayne Nordberg. Book Industry Trends 1977. Darien, Conn. 06820: Book Industry Study Book, P.O. Box 1174, 1977. 333p. (Research Report No. 4.)

"Can the uncertainty resulting from an accelerating rate of change somehow be reduced to the point that management can plan and take adequate anticipatory actions?" asks John Dessauer, official statistician for the Association of American Publishers and the Association of American University Presses, in this analysis and projection of trends in the book industry, in three parts. Paul D. Doebler, publishing management consultant, deals with "Recent and Anticipated Events, Developments and Perceptions in the Book Industry"; E. Wayne Nordberg, economic consultant to the Book Manufacturers' Institute, discusses "Economic Trends and the Book Industry: 1976 and Beyond"; and Dessauer examines "Book Industry Markets 1972-1981." This is tough going and not for the uninitiated, consisting as it does almost entirely of sales figures broken down by sources of distribution—libraries, general retailers, direct to consumer, export, etc.—and within this framework, by type of book—trade, religious, professional, book clubs, etc. However, it is invaluable for depth knowledge of an industry which has lacked this kind of systematic analysis. Barbara O. Slanker has written a final section, "The Need for Future Research."

265. Directory of British Publishers and Their Terms Including Agents for Overseas Publishers. London SW1W 9TZ: The Booksellers Association of Great Britain and Ireland, 154 Buckingham Palace Rd., annual. (1954--.)

Basic trade terms and publishing personnel relevant to the bookselling business, including over 1,000 publishers. In addition to agents it includes top personnel; names of publishers for whom they serve as distributors; ISBN prefix; types of books published; policy on returns; basic trade terms.

266. The Directory of Private Presses and Letterpress Printers and Publishers. Sacramento, Cal. 95825: Press of Arden Park, 861 Los Molinos Way, 1979. 56p.

79

Contains 305 listings of U.S., Canadian, British, German, and Latin American private presses. Each entry tells proprietor, address, phone number, type of equipment used, typefaces, kinds of work produced, willingness to exchange with other presses, date of establishment, and goals and philosophy.

Directory of Small Magazine/Press Editors and Publishers. (See No. 1046.)

267. Duke, Judith S. The Children's Literature Market, 1977–1982. White Plains, N.Y.: Knowledge Industry Publications, 1976. 241p.

An analysis of the structure of the juvenile publishing industry as it is today: the demographic, economic, and social trends affecting it and the economics of the industry itself: market trends; books clubs; magazines; the audiovisual market; current trends; predictions for future sales. There are also profiles of twenty-five of the leading publishers in the field.

Enser, A. G. S. Filmed Books and Plays: A List of Books and Plays from Which Films Have Been Made. (See No. 848.)

268. Ernst & Ernst. The Book Publishing and Manufacturing Industry in Canada: A Statistical and Economic Analysis. Ottawa: Government of Canada, 1970. 172p. (Prepared for the Department of Industry, Trade, and Commerce.)

Highlights the main characteristics of the book-publishing and -manufacturing industry from a statistical and economic rather than a cultural or sociological viewpoint. It discusses the methodology used, gives a profile of the industry, tells about both English- and French-language publishing, and examines book manufacturing. Findings are summarized at the beginning. Ernst and Ernst had access to a number of private documents to supplement their research.

269. Escarpit, Robert. The Book Revolution. London: Harrap; Paris: UNESCO, 1966. 160p.

Although intended as a sequel to Barker's Books for All (No. 236), The Book Revolution, by a well-known French sociologist, makes no effort to update statistics but rather focuses on broad trends in general and the fate of the literary book in the mass market in particular. The result is a series of provocative essays about the way in which belles lettres fare in various countries.
There is no bibliography as such, although notes at the

end of each chapter contain references to other works, many of them European; there is no index.

270. Febvre, Lucien, and Henri-Jean Martin. David Gerard, tr. The Coming of the Book: The Impact of Printing 1450–1800. London: NLB; Atlantic Highlands, N.J.: Humanities Press, 1976. 378p.

This volume, first published in French in 1958, goes far beyond the history of printing; it is a cultural history of the book by a distinguished French historian whose approach is interdisciplinary. In his preface he states that his object is to study the changes the printed book brought into the world, their causes and effects, and to show how the printed book became something the manuscript could never become, for reasons which he analyzes in detail. He takes up the introduction of paper into Europe; technical problems of printing and their solution; the visual appearance of the book; the book as a commodity; journeymen, masters, printers, booksellers, and authors; the geography of the book as it spread from western and middle Europe into the Slavic countries, the New World, and the Far East; the book trade; and the book as a force for change. Febvre died before completing his work; the completion was done by his collaborator and disciple, Martin. There is an introductory chapter on manuscripts by Marcel Thomas. Contains extensive notes and an index.

271. Feehan, John M. An Irish Publisher and His World. Cork: Mercier, 1969. 137p.

Books about contemporary Irish publishing are rare. The author emphasizes the problems that differentiate book publishing there from publishing in other countries and concludes with a chapter about his own press, Mercier.

272. Fulton, Len. The Psychologique of Small Press Publishing. New Brunswick, N.J.: Rutgers University, Graduate School of Library Science, 1976. 16p. (Occasional Papers No. 76–3.)

An authority whose life has been devoted to the small press movement and whose small publishing house, Dustbooks, has been called "the R. R. Bowker-H. W. Wilson" of the small presses briefly traces the growth of the movement. In discussing his own house he describes the directories it publishes (Nos. 1046 and 1052) and other valuable reference books Dustbooks alone has made available.

273. Glaister, Geoffrey Ashall. Encyclopedia of the Book. New York: World Publishing Co., 1960. 484p.

"Terms used in paper-making, printing, bookbinding and publishing, with notes on illuminated manuscripts, biblio-philes, private presses, and printing societies"--Subtitle. In its coverage of book publishing, it not only defines terms but also identifies trade journals, prizes and awards, private (but not commercial) presses, and organ-izations from the Stationers' Company to the American Book Publishers Council (now the Association of American Publishers). Although the emphasis is British, coverage for the U.S. is thorough. Much of the contemporary infor-mation has of course dated as private presses, publica-tions and awards, trade journals, printing societies, and organizations have gone, and new ones have come, but terminology has changed little, and enough of the informa-tion is historic to make the book still useful.

274. Gorokhoff, Boris I. Publishing in the U.S.S.R. Blooming-ton: Indiana University Research Center in Anthro-pology, Folklore and Linguistics, 1959. 306p.

"This study seeks to present a survey of book, period-ical, and newspaper publishing in the Soviet Union, includ-ing some related topics such as censorship, copyright, and the book trade"--Preface. Emphasis is on science and technology. Contains bibliography and index.

275. Grannis, Chandler, ed. What Happens in Book Publishing. 2d ed. New York: Columbia University Press, 1967. 491p.

"This edition, like the first, is an outline of proce-dures in book publishing, not a how-to book," says the editor of this anthology. Many changes have taken place since 1967, but enough holds true to make it valuable still. Aspects included are the creation of the trade book: securing and selecting the manuscript, copyediting, design, production and manufacturing; distribution of the trade book: selling, advertising, publicity, business management and accounting, order fulfillment, subsidiary rights and permissions; and special areas of publishing: children's books, religious books, textbooks, technical, scientific, and medical publishing, university presses, mass-market paperbacks, trade paperbacks, mail order, reference books, "vanity" publishing. There are also articles on the legal aspects and distribution of American books abroad. Indexed.

276. Greenfeld, Howard. Books from Writer to Reader. New York: Crown, 1978. 211p.

Not "how to" but rather "how it is done" by an author and publisher who obviously does not feel that the book is about to be supplanted by the computer. He takes the

book through its various stages at a fast gallop--the
writer, the literary agent, the publishing house, the
decision to publish, the editor, the illustrator, the
copyeditor, the designer, the jacket designer, the production supervisor, the compositor, the proofreader and the
indexer, the printer, the color printer, the binder, the
route from the warehouse to the bookstore and from the
bookstore to the reader. There is a glossary, a bibliography, and an index.

277. Gross, Gerald, ed. Publishers on Publishing. New York:
      Bowker, 1961. 491p.

     "The basic editorial concept of Publishers on Publish-
ing was to present a series of professional self-portraits
of the great publishers, past and present, active and
inactive," says Gross. Taking his selections from memoirs,
autobiographies, and articles, sometimes by the publisher
under discussion, Gross shows attitudes of (in most cases)
yesterday's publishers toward such aspects of the business
(and art) as agents, writers, editors, and advertisers.
Some of the excerpts deal with the history of publishing.
Gross has added commentaries and biographical notes about
author-publishers.

278. Hackett, Alice Payne, and James Henry Burke. 80 Years of
      Best Sellers 1895-1975. New York: Bowker, 1977. 265p.

     Since 1950 this compilation has appeared each decade.
Its purpose is to present facts and figures, based on Publishers Weekly's count, and to interpret and comment
briefly upon the statistics and trends, but not to evaluate from a literary point of view. The main portion of
the book is a year-by-year listing, followed by brief comments; shorter sections organize best sellers by sales
figures in three groups--hardbound, paperbound, and combined, and also by subject. Other features include a
history of best sellers, a discussion of them before 1895,
and books and articles about best sellers. This is not
the book for those wanting a depth study of the phenomenon,
but nothing else is so useful for breadth. Figures before
1912 come from The Bookman; after that, from Publishers
Weekly. Users should be aware that PW includes only books
distributed to bookstores and libraries, not those sold
through mail order or book clubs.

279. Hart, James D. The Popular Book: A History of America's
      Literary Taste. New York: Oxford University Press,
      1950. 351p.

     Relates America's popular reading to the social back-
ground of the times, from the mid-sixteenth century (Institutes of Christian Religion by John Calvin) to the late

1940s (This I Remember by Eleanor Roosevelt). The author
pegs his discussions around specific books. Contains a
bibliographical checklist, a chronological index of books
discussed (but no sales figures), and an index.

280. Hasan, Abul. The Book in Multilingual Countries. Paris:
UNESCO, 1978. 40p. (Reports and Papers on Mass Communication No. 82.)

Views each link in the publishing chain--its creation
by the writer; its production, distribution, and promotion processes, etc.--from the standpoint of a multilingual
context, especially in developing countries. Based on the
proceedings of a symposium on the subject held in Moscow.
Contains a bibliography and guidelines.

281. Hepburn, James. The Author's Empty Purse and the Rise of
the Literary Agent. London: Oxford University Press,
1968. 135p.

Beginning with the historical background in Elizabethan
times, Hepburn shows early informal origins of the literary agency, then centers on the appearance of the modern
agency at the turn of this century and its development
into a literary institution. Emphasis is British, with a
chapter on the U.S. There is a bibliography of 500 items,
often briefly annotated. Indexed.

International Directory of Little Magazines and Small Presses.
(See No. 1052.)

282. International Literary Marketplace. London and New York:
Bowker, annual. (1965--.)

A listing of 160 book-publishing houses by country.
Typical information for each firm includes address, telex
number, leading personnel, subject matter, number of titles,
date of founding, and ISBN prefix. In addition it gives
pertinent general and business information about the country itself--language(s), religion, population, public
holidays, banking hours, currency, mailing information,
and exports/imports. There is also a list of trade book
organizations and of reference books and journals about
the trade. The international section contains information
on copyright conventions, international publishing organizations, trade bibliographies, literary prizes, and an
explanation of the ISBN system.

283. Kerr, Chester. A Report on American University Presses.
Washington, D.C.: The Association of American University Presses, 1949. 291p. (Obtain through University
of North Carolina Press, Chapel Hill.)

A report giving the results of a survey conducted in
1948-49 by the Association of American University Presses.
Gives the history of university presses in this country,
their status at the time of the report, their selection
of manuscripts, their economics, their production and
distribution, and their nonbook activities. A fifty-one-
page supplement appeared in 1956. The October, 1969,
issue of Scholarly Publishing carries a twenty-five-page
article by Mr. Kerr, "The Kerr Report Revisited."

284. Kingsford, R. J. L. The Publishers' Association 1896-
     1946, with an Epilogue. London: Cambridge University
     Press, 1970. 228p.

This story of England's book trade association from
its founding to the mid-1940s, with an epilogue of six
pages bringing it up to 1962, is also the story of the
major events of the British book trade during the period.
Appendices give the first rules of the Association,
the founding members and first Council, and the officers
and secretaries from 1896 to 1962. There is a bibliography and an index.

285. Kurien, George Thomas. The Directory of American Book
     Publishing from Founding Fathers to Today's Conglom-
     erates. New York: Simon and Schuster, 1975. 386p.

A reference book modeled on J. Kirchner's Lexikon des
Buchwesena. "Publishing," says the author, "is basically
a mosaic and does not lend itself easily to an integrated
narrative," but rather to a dictionary-type reference
book. He has grouped his entries under the following
headings: "Founding Fathers and Their Enterprises";
"Today's Publishing Houses"; "Conglomerates"; "Multiple
Publishing Houses"; "Book Trade Associations"; "Major
Prizes, Awards, Events." Each entry contains a succinct
account of salient facts. Although an attempt has been
made to include publishing houses founded before 1968 and
all university presses irrespective of size, the list is
by no means all-inclusive nor intended to be. Appendices
give commonly used publishing abbreviations; a glossary
of publishing terms; and two bibliographies--one of general references, biographies, and memoirs; the other of
company histories and company addresses. Indexed.

Lazarsfeld, Paul F. Radio and the Printed Page. (See No. 473.)

286. Lehmann-Haupt, Hellmut, in collaboration with Lawrence C.
     Wroth and Rollo G. Silver. The Book in America: A
     History of the Making and Selling of Books in the
     United States. 2d ed. New York: Bowker, 1951. 431p.

A history in which the author chronicles book production
and distribution from the colonial period, beginning in
1638, to about 1950. Excellent for its identification and
discussion of printers, publishers, and publishing houses
in the U.S. during the time covered. For the crowded events
of the next fifteen years, see Madison (No. 289); and for a
much fuller account of the years between 1630 and 1940, see
Tebbel's multi-volume history (No. 315).

287. Literary Marketplace; with Names and Numbers: The Direc-
     tory of American Book Publishing. New York: Bowker,
     annual. (1941--.)

An appropriate subtitle for this compendium might also
have been The Bible of American Book Publishing. Perhaps
its most used feature is an alphabetical list of the most
active book publishers in the U.S. (vanity publishers
excluded), with addresses, telephone numbers, and personnel;
a concise summary of the kinds of publications each firm
produces; the number of yearly titles; foreign representatives; and trade associations to which each firm belongs.
Further lists classify the publishers both by location and
by type. Another important feature is "Names and Numbers,"
an alphabetical listing of firms and leading figures in
book publishing, with addresses and telephone numbers.
(This was formerly a separate volume.)
A partial list of other information: agents; artists
and art services; book reviewers; exporters and importers;
prizes and awards; courses in book publishing; magazines,
newspapers, and news services useful to publishers or free
lancers; sales representatives; translators; wholesalers;
writers' conferences; direct mail and promotion services;
editorial services; employment agencies; photographers;
public relation services.

288. McMurtrie, Douglas. The Book: The Story of Printing and
     Bookmaking. 3d ed. New York: Oxford University Press,
     1943. 676p.

Because of the close relationship between printing and
publishing, this account of book design from the time of
primitive human records to the present is a good source
for information about the historical development of the
book, early printers, publishers, and presses, and so on.
Contains extensive bibliographies and an index.

289. Madison, Charles A. Book Publishing in America. New York:
     McGraw-Hill, 1966. 628p.

A chronological and descriptive account from book publishing's colonial beginnings to 1965, with major emphasis
on the period after 1900, and detailed information about

major firms, past and present. Appendices contain "Chronology of Publishing Events," "All-Time Best Sellers," and a bibliography. Indexed.

290. A Manual on Bookselling: How to Open and Run Your Own Bookstore. Charles B. Anderson and G. Royce Smith, eds. 2d ed. New York: Harmony Books, 1974. 336p.

Although this manual sponsored by the American Association of Booksellers is basically a host of "how to" techniques, it covers bookselling so succintly and efficiently that it is not only useful for reference, but also gives an insight into the book industry. Successful booksellers describe the various categories of bookstores and tell about opening new ones, operating and financing, stocking and ordering, carrying sidelines, promotion and advertising, and continuing education, trade tools for the bookshop, ABA conventions, the booksellers' school, publisher relations, obscenity and the law. Bibliography, glossary, and index.

291. Meeting of Experts on Book Development Planning in Asia, Singapore, 1968. Final Report. Paris: UNESCO, 1968. 15p.

Skeletal resumé which pinpoints what had been done to develop a book-publishing industry in those Asian countries where little existed, with recommendations for the future.

292. Mott, Frank Luther. Golden Multitudes: The Story of Best Sellers in the United States. New York: Bowker, c1947, 1960. 357p.

The author establishes a simple arithmetical formula for determining best sellers and discusses them chronologically in their social and literary context, from Michael Wigglesworth's Day of Doom in 1662 to Kathleen Winsor's Forever Amber in 1945.

293. Mumby, Frank A., and Ian Norrie. Publishing and Bookselling. 5th ed. London: Jonathan Cape; New York: Bowker, 1974. 685p.

Frank Mumby's first edition, which deals with publishing and bookselling in England, first appeared in 1930 and has been updated to about 1956. This latest is a hefty volume, in which Norrie uses Mumby's first thirteen chapters, up to 1870, and carries into contemporary times from there. Mumby has dealt with publishing and bookselling in the ancient world and the Middle Ages, and from that point oriented himself around England. Norrie discusses, among other topics, the recent acceleration of takeovers and

mergers, the obscenity laws, international copyright, and
restrictive practices. Both authors have written in detail
about individual British publishing firms. Appendices contain tables of sales broken down by subject category for
1937, 1943, 1955, 1960, 1970; officers of England's Publishing Association from 1896 through 1975, and the same
for the Booksellers Association of Great Britain and Ireland from 1895 to 1973; U.K. book sales broken down by
home and export for 1939, 1949, 1959, 1965, and 1966-70.
There is a detailed sixty-page bibliography and an author-
title index with occasional subject entries.

294. Myers, Robin. The British Book Trade from Caxton to the
     Present Day. London: Deutsch in Association with the
     National Book League, 1973. 405p.

     "This book consists of a classified and annotated selec-
     tion of works indicating the way in which the book trade
     evolved, with a historical bias which reflects that of the
     libraries [the National Book League and St. Bride's Insti-
     tute] on which it has been based. I took the invention of
     printing from movable type in Europe as a starting point,
     although trading in books goes back at least to the fifth
     century B.C. The contents are limited to organized com-
     merce in books, excluding the non-commercial book world
     such as libraries and librarianship . . . , and other
     forms of printed communication. . . ." Emphasis is Brit-
     ish, but the book trade being what it is, other countries
     are inevitably drawn in. Contents include authorship,
     bookselling, binding, design and production, illustration,
     history of the book trade, children's books, laws relating
     to the book trade, the Net Book Agreement, printing paper
     and ink, private presses, publishing. Each section and
     some subsections have introductions which summarize and
     explain where necessary. Annotations are detailed and
     often evaluative. Author-title-subject index.

295. Nemeyer, Carol A. Scholarly Reprint Publishing in the
     United States. New York: Bowker, 1972. 262p.

     The author has described her work concisely: ". . .
     the main focus is on hardcover, small edition, facsimile
     reprinting. The primary goal of this normative survey
     has been to discover and report the overall dimensions
     and the particular characteristics of the reprint indus-
     try in this country. A general overview and details of
     the industry's procedures, programs, problems, and rela-
     tionships with libraries are represented." Chapter III
     is a historical survey from early times into the present
     century. Appendices include a directory of reprint

publishers and an index to subject specialties. Contains
a lengthy bibliography and an index.

296. Nunn, Godfrey Raymond. Publishing in Mainland China. Cam-
     bridge, Mass.: M.I.T. Press, 1966. 83p. (M.I.T.
     Report No. 4.)

     "This study attempts to analyze the organization of book
     and periodical publishing in China from 1949 to the end of
     1964, with particular reference to publications in the
     natural, applied, and social sciences."--Introduction.
     Gives as much information as could be obtained from
     sources at Hong Kong about the structure of the industry,
     the size of publishing houses, the relative amounts of
     literature published in minority and foreign languages,
     and the relative amounts published by subjects. It also
     deals with distribution systems--retail, direct, and
     through libraries. Contains four appendices, a biblio-
     graphy, and an index.

297. Page, Roger. Australian Bookselling. London: Deutsch,
     1970. 175p.

     A survey, including a historical retrospect, of the
     Australian book trade as it affects booksellers. Contains
     chapters on educational and library business and the trade
     in English, American, and locally published books. The
     author is manager of the Royal Melbourne Institute of
     Technology bookshop and a former president of the Austra-
     lian Booksellers Association. Contains appendices, a
     bibliography, and an index.

298. Perspectives on Publishing. Philip G. Altbach and Sheila
     McVey, eds. Philadelphia: American Academy of Polit-
     ical and Social Science, 1975. (Annals of the American
     Academy of Political and Social Science, Vol. 421.)

     A different look at book publishing--particularly
     scholarly publishing--in which a number of authors from
     both academe and book publishing contribute articles
     placing it within a social, cultural, and international
     perspective. The table of contents gives an idea of its
     nature and scope: "Publishing and the Intellectual Sys-
     tem," "Publishers as Gatekeepers of Ideas," "Role of the
     Publisher in the Dissemination of Knowledge," "Shapers of
     Culture: The Editor in Book Publishing," "Demythologiz-
     ing Scholarly Publishing," "College Textbook Publishing
     in the 1970s," "Nineteenth Century America: Publishing
     in a Developing Country," "Pity Poor Pascal: Some Sober-
     ing Reflections on the American Book Scene," "Independent
     Publishing: Today and Yesterday," "Scholarly Publishing

89

in Western Europe and Great Britain: A Survey and Analysis," "Publishing in the USSR and Yugoslavia," "The Bright Promise of Publishing in Developing Countries," "Who Controls Book Publishing in Anglophone Middle Africa?" Footnotes and an author-title-subject index.

299. Plant, Marjorie. The English Book Trade: An Economic History of the Making and Sale of Books. 3d ed. London: Allen & Unwin, 1974. 520p.

The author's comprehensive historical analysis is mainly economic and, as the title states, British. It is divided into two parts--the age of hand printing and the age of the mechanical printer. This latter section extends to 1970. Among topics discussed in a depth often lacking in publishing histories are labor, labor organizations, paper and binding materials, and an extensive treatment of copyright. Statistical and other data have been revised, and new sections have been included on public lending right, paperbacks, photocopying, and the rise of international publishing. Extensive footnotes and a subject index.

300. Publishers' International Directory; with a Supplement: International ISBN Publishers' Index. 7th ed. New York: Bowker; Munich: Verlag Dokumentation, 1977. 620, 270p.

Lists more than 38,000 publishers, giving as much of the following information as available: address, telephone and telex numbers, ISBN number, and subjects published. In this edition the editors have included "even those publishers whose yearly production is very limited, the so-called mini-publishers, and the institutes which issue publications in book form."

301. Publishing in Africa in the Seventies. Edwina Oluwasanmi, Eva McLean, and Hans Zell, eds. Ife-Ife, Nigeria: University of Ife Press, 1975. 377p. (Proceedings of an International Conference on Publishing and Book Development held at the University of Ife, Ife-Ife, Nigeria, 16-20 December, 1973.)

The recommendations, summaries of the various sessions, and a selection of the papers read at this conference attended by more than 100 African writers, publishers, booksellers, librarians, printers, and teachers give a succinct account of the history and hopes of African publishing. Among topics discussed are the cultural and social factors of book reading and publishing in Africa; a frank explanation as to why indigenous publishing has trouble getting started; the mechanics of acquiring library materials--African and otherwise; the role of

government; the role of Christian publishing houses; and
the problems faced by writers, distributors, and booksellers.

302. Publishing in Nigeria. Benin City, Nigeria: Ethiope Pub-
     lishing Corp., 1972. 71p.

     An anthology in which each individual article represents
     an aspect of book publishing in a country where, for eco-
     nomic rather than political reasons, it is under government
     control. Among the topics: the African publisher, the
     non-indigenous publisher, the university press, publishing
     for children, African books in print, and book development.

303. Sankaranarayanan, N., comp. and ed. Book Distribution and
     Promotion Problems in South Asia. Paris: UNESCO, 1964.
     278p.

     Survey of distribution and promotion in Ceylon, Burma,
     Iran, East and West Pakistan, North and South India, as
     well as in three highly developed countries by way of con-
     trast--Holland, the United Kingdom, and the U.S.

304. Scholarly Publishing in Asia: Proceedings of the Confer-
     ence of University Presses in Asia and the Pacific Area.
     Shigeo Minowa and Amadio Antonio Arboleda, eds. Tokyo:
     University of Tokyo Press, 1973. 172p.

     ". . . the (two) types of (existing) university presses,
     the medieval (i.e., Cambridge and Oxford models) and the
     modern (i.e., the American university press model) are
     being supplemented in certain countries by a third type, a
     new concept of university press," says Minowa. These
     proceedings--in two parts, "The Asian Experience" and "The
     International Experience"--discuss problems particular to
     sixteen countries in the Asia-Pacific region and the pos-
     sibilities of international cooperation. Not all countries
     are "developing"--for example, India, Australia, and Japan--
     although the rest qualify. Of particular interest is an
     appendix, "Report on the Formation of the Asian University
     Presses and Scholarly Publishers Group."

305. Shaffer, Susan E. Guide to Book Publishing Courses:
     Academic and Professional Programs. Princeton, N.J.:
     Peterson's Guides, 1979. 150p.

     Published in cooperation with the Education for Publish-
     ing Committee of the Association of American Publishers,
     this guide lists and gives information about all academic
     and professional courses and programs in the U.S. Informa-
     tion varies, but is sufficient to provide a comprehensive
     idea about each. Samuel S. Vaughan has written a dis-
     cussion of publishing as a career. Appendices list

institutions offering comprehensive programs; institutions offering courses on particular aspects; a geographical breakdown; a bibliography; and a directory of administrators.

306. Sheehan, Donald. This Was Publishing: A Chronicle of the Book Trade in the Gilded Age. Bloomington: Indiana University Press, 1952. 288p.

A history of the crucial years between the Civil War and World War I when foundations were laid for modern publishing. This is not a chronicle of firms but rather an analysis of conditions. Contents show the author's broad overview: "The Philosophy of Publishing," "The Business of Publishing," "The Antagonisms and Friendships of Publishing," "Contracts between Author and Publisher," "Private Publishing and Public Speech," "The Machinery of Wholesale Distribution," "The Assault on the Consumer," "The Problems of Competition and the Self-Regulation of the Book Trade." Conclusions, notes, bibliography, and index.

307. Smith, Datus C., Jr. A Guide to Book Publishing. New York: Bowker, 1966. 244p.

308. _____. The Economics of Book Publishing in Developing Countries. Paris: UNESCO, 1977. (Reports and Papers on Mass Communication No. 79.)

Two books which treat from different angles book publishing in developing countries. The 1966 volume deals explicitly with techniques which will help developing countries to establish book-publishing programs. It traces the various steps from beginning to end, including economics and specialized publishing, encouragement of literacy and reading development, the role of libraries, rights and contracts, and distribution, this latter encompassing retail bookstores and training. It contains a bibliography and an index.

The 1977 publication is based on the findings of a detailed survey of publishers in Africa, Asia, Latin America, and the Middle East, which pinpoints problems and gives a general picture of publishing in each of these areas. Contents include, first, an overview containing facts from the survey--manufacturing, editorial and overhead cost, list price, discount, sales income, profit, loss, and break-even point; and second, an analysis and commentary, consisting of such subjects as pricing policy and long-term planning, book development, the issues of national languages and self sufficiency, possibilities of co-publishing, cooperation with government, and determination of greatest needs. In his preface Smith lists six books he considers basic to the subject.

309. Smith, Roger H. Paperback Parnassus: The Birth, the Development, the Pending Crisis . . . of the Modern American Paperbound Book. Boulder, Colo.: Westview, 1976. 111p.

An expanded version of a series of articles on mass-market paperback distribution which appeared in Publishers Weekly.

310. Steinberg, S. H. Five Hundred Years of Printing. New York: Criterion Books, 1959. 286p.

This excellent one-volume history of printing is as well a history of the book trade and its concomitant areas, such as the growth of a reading public, best sellers and steady sellers, censorship, libraries, popular series, technical progress, etc. Dates cover 1450 to roughly 1950. Notes, bibliography, and index.

311. Stiehl, Ulrich. Dictionary of Book Publishing, with 12,000 Sample Sentences and Phrases. German-English. Munich: Verlag Dokumentation, 1977. 538p.

A German-English dictionary covering books and other media (periodicals, newspapers, and audiovisual materials), authors and readers, the book industry in general, book publishing in specialized fields, book art, editing and copyright, production, marketing, and library science. Includes as examples 8,000 complete sample sentences in English and several thousand illustrative phrases drawn from various sources.

312. Strauss, Victor. The Printing Industry: An Introduction to Its Many Branches, Processes and Products. New York: Bowker, 1967. 814p.

Encyclopedic treatment of printing, involving not only printing itself but also publishing, advertising, and manu-facturing of printed materials. Contains notes and refer-ences, a selective bibliography, and a subject index.

313. Sutherland, J. A. Fiction and the Fiction Industry. Atlantic Highlands, N.J.: Humanities Press, 1978. 231p.

An examination of the material conditions under which the contemporary English novel is produced and consumed. The first section, "Crisis and Change," considers the economic and institutional conditions under which novels are produced and applies to both England and the U.S. The second, "State Remedies," dealing with public lending right, the Arts Council, and writers in universities, dis-cusses England in the first two chapters and both countries in the third. The final section, "Trends, Mainly American," selects several major trends affecting both--paperbacks, packaged literature, book clubs, genre fiction, independent publishing, the telenovel. Throughout, Sutherland is always concerned with the economics of authorship, with libraries as a market, and with whether or not, in Kingsley Amis's phrase, "more makes worse." A literate and provocative book by an author who knows contemporary literature and its economic background.

314. Taubert, Sigfred. <u>Bibliopola: Pictures and Texts about the Book Trade</u>. 2 vols. New York: Bowker, 1966.

Vol. I includes 306 illustrations with texts arranged by themes such as symbols of the book trade, the antiquarian bookman, the author, bookshop interiors, and even headings like "Drink" (the bibulous bookseller, with woodcut: "An early specimen, this woodcut suggests that drinking is another tradition among booksellers, though less violent than the 16th-century artist would have us believe"). Vol. II contains 258 plates arranged chronologically, along with an anthology of writings covering the book trade over the past 2,000 years. Text is in French and German as well as English; illustrations are charming.

315. Tebbel, John. <u>A History of Book Publishing in the United States</u>. Volume I. <u>The Creation of an Industry, 1630-1865</u>. New York: Bowker, 1972. 646p.
_____. <u>A History of Book Publishing in the United States</u>. Volume II. <u>The Expansion of an Industry, 1865-1919</u>. New York: Bowker, 1975. 813p.
_____. <u>A History of Book Publishing in the United States</u>. Volume III. <u>The Golden Age Between Two Wars, 1920-1940</u>. New York: Bowker, 1978. 744p.

Tebbel's encyclopedic history of American book publishing traces its development from small and eclectic colonial beginnings to its growth as a major American industry in 1940 (though still small in comparison with such other American industries as automotive or food, for instance.) His method is chronological and narrative; his approach, which varies somewhat from volume to volume, centers around firms, figures, and categories of subject specialization, with sections devoted to such trends and aspects as censorship, copyright, technology, advertising, graphics, etc. Vols. II and III each have three appendices. Vol. II: "American Book Title Output, 1880-1918," "A Graphic Survey of Book Publication," and "Directories of Publishers, 1888, 1900, 1919." Vol. III: "An Economic Review of Book Publishing, 1915-1945," "PW Profiles of Children's Editors,"

by Muriel Fuller, and "Best Sellers, 1920-1940." A fourth
volume is in process, tentatively titled Book Publishing
Since 1940, which will carry on to the present.

This is a formidable addition to the literature of book
publishing in the U.S. and a valuable reference tool. In
addition it contains vignettes about various colorful
personalities which make good reading indeed. All volumes
are well indexed.

316. Vanier, Dinoo J. Market Structure and the Business of
Book Publishing. New York: Pitnam, 1973. 213p.

Applying technical theory and statistical analysis to
the structure of the book-publishing industry, Vanier
treats demand, distribution, production, pricing, costs,
profits, and promotion. The text is liberally sprinkled
with charts and tables, and there is an appendix of tables,
"Regression Analysis of Book Demand." Bibliography and
index.

317. Vaughan, Samuel S. Medium Rare: A Look at the Book and
Its People. New York: Bowker, 1977. 39p. (Fourth of
the R. R. Bowker Memorial Lectures, New Series, November 4, 1976.)

Are too many books published? What are the book's
unique characteristics? Will it survive in competition
with other media? What is its role in journalism, history,
politics? The author brings his long experience in book
publishing and his knowledge of communication history and
theory to bear in his answers to these questions. Bibliography.

318. Walker, Gregory. Soviet Book Publishing Policy. Cambridge,
England: Cambridge University Press, 1978. 164p.

An examination of the operations and management of the
vast Soviet publishing industry in the light of governmental
policy and its effects on creation, content, production,
manufacture, and distribution. Appendices give authors'
fee scales and all-union book retail prices. There are
notes, a bibliography, and an index.

319. Watt, Ian. The Rise of the Novel: Studies in Defoe, Rich-
ardson and Fielding. London: Chatto & Windus, 1957.
319p.

The bounds of this study far exceed the literary. In
tracing the development of the novel, the author tells
about social developments which made a new form of communication necessary. Extensive footnotes and an index.

III

Broadcasting

---

320. Action for Children's Television: The First National Sym-
     posium on the Effect of Television Programming and
     Advertising on Children. New York: Discus/Avon, 1971.

     An anthology of short articles in which a number of
     writers report what they feel television is doing to child-
     ren and what can be done about it.

Adams, William, and Fay Schreigman, eds. Television Network
     News. (See No. 629.)

321. Adler, Richard, and Walter S. Baer, eds. The Electronic
     Box Office: Humanities and Arts on the Cable. New
     York: Praeger and the Aspen Institute, 1974. 139p.
     (Sponsored by the Aspen Program in Communication and
     Society.)

     Authorities discuss the potential of cable for increas-
     ing the diversity and quality of television programming
     available to the public. Adler, Baer, Douglass Cater, and
     other authorities give pros and cons such as the financial
     boost cable could give the performing arts as opposed to
     the opposition it will probably meet from commercial broad-
     casters and theater owners, and specific FCC rules designed
     to keep off pay cable programs that might threaten them.
     Also discussed are unions, the economics of pay TV, experi-
     mental video groups, and the danger that no "bold vision
     of what can be accomplished" will present itself or be
     accepted if it does. There is much emphasis on economics
     throughout. Indexed.

Alfred I. Dupont-Columbia University Survey of Broadcast Jour-
     nalism. (See No. 630.)

322. Allard, T. J. The C.A.B. Story 1926-1976: Private
     Broadcasting in Canada. Ottawa K1P 552: Canadian Asso-
     ciation of Broadcasters, Box 627, Station B, 1976. 68p.

A commemorative booklet, published by the Canadian Association of Broadcasters on its fiftieth anniversary, telling
the history of the organization of stations existing outside
of the framework of nationalization. Appendices give
officers and officials of the C.A.B. for the years covered,
and a summary of structural changes in the Board of Directors.
There is also brief biographical material on C.A.B. presidents
and chairmen.

323. Allerton Park Institute No. 19, 1973. CATV and Its Impli-
cations for Libraries: Proceedings of a Conference.
Cora Thomassen, ed. Urbana: University of Illinois
Graduate School of Library Science, 1974. 91p. (Spon-
sored by the Illinois State Library, the University of
Illinois Graduate School of Library Science, and the
University of Illinois Office of Continuing Education
and Public Service.)

Articles examining ways in which cable TV can be used
by libraries and some of the problems and procedures.
Includes discussions of the role of industry; franchising
problems and procedures; information access; potentials of
interactive cable TV; cable TV as an information tool; a
video policy statement; and a public-access workshop. A
few of the chapters give references and there is a index.

The American Film Institute. Guide to College Courses in Film
and Television. (See No. 792.)

324. The Annan Report: An ITV View. London W1P CAU: Independent Television Books, 247 Tottenham Court Rd., 1977. 58p.

A submission to the Home Secretary in response to the
Annan Report (No. 426), which makes some general observations; comments on the recommendations; discusses ITV 2,
the fourth channel; and briefly remarks on other pertinent
topics such as the pros and cons of competition, ITV company profits, advertising to children, public hearings by
broadcasting authorities, a broadcasting complaints commission, independent production, TV and the press. It
also corrects what it considers certain errors of fact in
the Annan Report.

325. An Annotated Bibliography of UNESCO Publications and Documents Dealing with Space Communication 1953-1977. Paris:
UNESCO, 1977. 102p.

Provides a consolidated list of papers, reports,
articles, and publications produced by UNESCO in the field
of space communication, incorporating two previous bibliographies compiled in 1970 and 1973. Most of the documents
are not available for free distribution or for sale,

although a few recent issues can be purchased. In this
case price is indicated. Others can be consulted in
UNESCO's Mass Communication Documentation Centre and are
also in most UNESCO depository libraries.

326. Annual Directory of Religious Broadcasting. Ben Armstrong,
     ed. Morristown, N.J. 07960: National Religious Broad-
     casters, Box 224R, annual. (1971--.)

   A geographic list of both radio and television stations
in the U.S., giving for each entry address, ownership, network, frequency, format, class, representative, and chief
personnel. Other features include listings of foreign
radio stations, cable TV, foreign program producers, affil-
iated services, agencies, book publishers, equipment,
record companies, and facts about National Religious Broadcasters. Radio station index, radio program index, and TV
and film index.

327. Australia. Parliament. Joint Committee on the Broadcast-
     ing of Parliamentary Proceedings. Television Inquiry.
     Canberra: The Government Printer of Australia, 1976.
     374p. (1974--Parliamentary Paper No. 62.)

   A debate in Parliament as to whether proceedings should
be televised which discusses not only that issue but much
else about Australian broadcasting.

328. Awasthy, G. C. Broadcasting in India. Bombay 1: Allied
     Publishers Ltd., 15 Graham Rd., Ballard Estate, 1965.
     268p.

   The author, a former employee of All India Radio, calls
this book "a critical narrative of AIR, its programmes,
its policies, its ambitions and its failures since 1946."
A five-page appendix deals with television.

329. Babe, Robert E. Cable Television and Telecommunications
     in Canada: An Economic Analysis. Michigan State Uni-
     versity, East Lansing: Division of Research, Graduate
     School of Business Administration, 1975. 287p.

   "Cable TV," says Babe, "is one wing of a seismic structural change in the organizational makeup of the general
telecommunications network and broadcasting," which offers
a potentially alternative mode that threatens the present
status of commercial television and telephone/telegraph.
He gives a cost analysis of cable TV, and discusses how an
alternative mode can be accomplished in relation to broad-
band communications and broadcasting. Included is an
analysis of the economics of broadcast advertising. It is
a thick, well-documented book filled with data not only

about broadcasting but also about the telephone and telegraph industry. There are many footnotes and a list of
works cited.

330. Baggaley, Jon, and Steve Duck. Dynamics of Television.
Farnborough, Hants., England; Lexington, Mass.: Saxon
House, 1976. 180p.

Believing that our concern with research centered upon
"mass" communication with emphasis upon content is the
wrong approach, the authors advocate an "analysis of the
effects upon the individual that stem from the conventions
and forms of a medium as opposed to its declared content--
in particular the ways in which these conventions and
forces affect the individual's processes of cognition and
social judgment." From this perspective they analyze
television as a medium--its imagery, its persuasiveness,
its power to teach, its control. Since their analyses
are based on a number of studies, the book is an excellent
source of review for the empirical literature in the field.
There are long lists of references at the end of every
chapter. Indexed.

331. The B and T Yearbook. Sydney 2001, Australia: Greater
Publications Pty Ltd., 340 Pitt St., GPO Box 2608,
annual. (1957--.)

Lists radio and television stations, advertising agencies, newspapers, and public relations consultants in
Australia, with pertinent information about each. It also
contains statistics, maps locating broadcasting stations,
recording studios, services, associations and clubs,
legislation, the composition of the Australian Broadcasting Commission, rules and standards, and a who's who. One
section describes New Zealand media and another section
contains thumbnail accounts of the structure and facilities
of radio and television in Fiji; Guam; the Marianas Islands;
Hong Kong; Malaysia; Japan; Singapore; Papua, New Guinea;
and the Solomon Islands.

332. Barcus, F. Earle, with Rachel Wolkin. Children's Television: An Analysis of Programming and Advertising. New
York: Praeger, 1977. 218p.

A content analysis, made for Action for Children's Television, which includes descriptions of racial, cultural,
and sexual representations; a measure of the incidence of
aggressive behavior; and a breakdown of advertising themes
and formats. Data is accompanied by an introduction and
references to other studies, and interpretation of findings.
An initial chapter explains methodology.

333. Barnouw, Erik. <u>A History of Broadcasting in the United</u>
    <u>States</u>. Vol. I. <u>To 1933: A Tower in Babel</u>. New
    York: Oxford University Press, 1966. 344p.
    _____. <u>A History of Broadcasting in the United States</u>.
    Vol. II. <u>1933-53: The Golden Web</u>. New York: Oxford
    University Press, 1968. 391p.
    _____. <u>A History of Broadcasting in the United States</u>.
    Vol. III. <u>From 1953: The Image Empire</u>. New York:
    Oxford University Press, 1970. 396p.

    A chronological overview of American broadcasting which
touches upon practically every major event, trend, and per-
sonality in its history. The author's style makes for
good reading. Appendices in each volume include a chronology in outline form, text of the major laws relating to
broadcasting, an extensive bibliography, and an index by
performer, program, and topic.
    In 1978 Barnouw condensed the three volumes into one,
which he updated, <u>The Tube of Plenty</u> (Oxford, 518p.). Like
its predecessor, it "stresses the emergence of television
as a dominant factor in American life and a component of
American influence in many nations." Here, too, a chronology, bibliographical notes, and an index follow the text.

Barnouw, Erik. <u>The Sponsor: Notes on a Modern Potentate</u>. (<u>See</u>
    No. 1089.)

334. Baron, Mike. <u>Independent Radio: The Story of Commercial</u>
    <u>Radio in the United Kingdom</u>. Lavenham, Suffolk, Eng-
    land: Terence Dalton Ltd., 1975. 194p. (Sound Radio
    Series.)

    A strictly factual history of Britain's independent
radio from the early days of "wireless broadcasting" to the
mid-seventies, with much attention to broadcasting politics.
Also contains a map, history, and description of the eighteen or so local stations. Appendices list addresses,
telephone numbers, and top personnel of the stations;
addresses of associations; technical information about the
various stations; and a discussion of the job market with
emphasis on disc jockeys. Indexed.

335. <u>BBC Handbook: Incorporating the Annual Report and Accounts</u>
    <u>1974-75</u>. London WIM 4AA: British Broadcasting Corpora-
    tion, 35 Marylebone High St., annual. (1928--.)

    Contents in the past have varied somewhat. Later edi-
tions are in three sections: Annual Report and Accounts
(beginning with 1974); Programme Review; and Reference.
As a whole the Handbook provides an overall yearly coverage of BBC activities and services in England, Scotland,

Wales, and Northern Ireland, with considerable general
information in addition. There is a bibliography and an
index of contents.

336. Belson, William A. Television Violence and the Adolescent
Boy. Westmead, Farnborough, Hampshire, England: Saxon
House, Teakfield Ltd., 1978. 529p.

Description and results of a study sponsored by Columbia Broadcasting System and carried out in England, in
which Belson measured the effects on adolescent boys of
exposure to TV violence. Findings lend support to the
case for making major changes in policy concerning the
broadcasting of violence. Belson's methodology is interesting; he uses a naturalistic, or real-life, approach
instead of a laboratory one. This is fully described.

337. Berger, Arthur Asa. The TV-Guided American. New York:
Walker, 1976. 194p.

What effect does television programming have upon the
thinking of the American people? What does it reveal to
us about our national self-image? Berger investigates
these questions through an examination of the characters,
plots, and themes of several of our more popular and long-
lasting shows. He also discusses news programs and commercials. There is neither a bibliography nor an index,
which this type of book needs if it is to be used for
reference purposes.

338. Berrigan, Frances J., ed. Access: Some Western Modern
Models of Community Media. Paris: UNESCO, 1977. 229p.

Discussion, with case studies, of different ways in
which communities in the U.S., Canada, and some of the
European countries have provided access for audience participation in broadcasting programming for both television
and radio. European countries are England, the Netherlands,
Denmark, France, Germany, Italy, Belgium, and as an appendix
"Yugoslavia--A Different Model." Contains a bibliography.

339. Birinyi, Anne E. Chronology of State Cable Television
Regulation, 1947-1978. Cambridge, Mass. 02138: Harvard
University, Program on Information Resources Policy,
1978. 20p.

An evaluation of cable TV regulation in the U.S. presented by means of a chronological and contextual matrix,
giving decisions made by state legislatures, state courts,
and state regulatory agencies, alongside decisions of the
federal courts and the FCC. In addition there are important position statements of stockholders and study groups

interested in cable, such as the National Association of
Regulatory Utility Commissioners (MARUC). The House Subcommittee on Communications and the Sloan Commission on
Cable Communications are included to illustrate the pro-
gression of cable TV regulatory philosophies over a thirty-
year period.

340. Black, Peter. The Biggest Aspidistra in the World: A Personal Celebration of Fifty Years of the BBC. London:
British Broadcasting Corp., 1972. 243p.

An informal history written around accounts of programs
and people associated with the BBC rather than around
policies. It is especially useful for the insight into
BBC radio and television content. Contains a bibliography
and an index.

341. Bogart, Lee. The Age of Television: A Study of Viewing
Habits and the Impact of Television on American Life.
3d ed. New York: Ungar, 1972. 515p.

The text of this book, first issued in 1956, discusses
the development of television as a cultural factor in
American life and details patterns of viewing habits; programming; interrelation with radio listening, reading,
movies, spectator sports, and advertising; political
effects; and the juvenile audience. The author has
updated it with a new introduction, a set of notes to be
read with the text, the latest statistics, and a new supplemental bibliography. Indexed by name and subject.

Boretsky, R. A., and A. Yurovsky. Television Journalism. (See
No. 644.)

342. Bower, Robert T. Television and the Public. New York:
Holt, Rinehart and Winston. 1973. 205p.

A continuation of the systematic study of popular attitudes toward the mass media that began with such works as
Paul Lazarsfeld's Radio and the Printed Page (1940) (No.
473), Lazarsfeld and Field's The People Look at Radio (1946)
(No. 474), and Gary Steiner's The People Look at Television
(1960) (No. 584). Like them, this one is based on interviews. There are sections on ten-year attitude changes;
television's audience and reactions to programs; television
news; and family viewing. Appendices give details about
the sampling and field-work procedure and some statistical
notes.

343. Boyd, Douglas A. Egyptian Radio: Tool of Political and
National Development. Association for Education in

102

Journalism, 1977. 33p. (Journalism Monographs 48.)
(Obtain from AEJ headquarters.)

Studies about Egyptian broadcasting are rare. This one
examines radio's role and Egypt's attempt, primarily under
Nassar, to disseminate the government's view of what is
best for the Arabs. Footnotes.

344. Brack, Hans. The Evolution of the EBU through Its Statutes
from 1950 to 1976. Geneva 20, Switzerland: European
Broadcasting Union, 1, Rue de Verembe, 1976. 179p.
(EBU Monograph 11, Legal and Administrative Series.)

An analysis of the European Broadcasting Union--its
founding, its structure, its financing, its achievements--
traced through its statutes. Appendices give the statutes,
1950 version (Torquay) and 1976 version (Helsinki), and a
table of the organizations that have held seats on the
Administrative Council between 1950 and 1976, together with
the names of the administrators and their alternates. Subject and name index.

345. Briggs, Asa. History of Broadcasting in the United Kingdom.
Vol. I. The Birth of Broadcasting. New York: Oxford
University Press, 1961. 525p.
_____. History of Broadcasting in the United Kingdom.
Vol. II. The Golden Age of Broadcasting. New York:
Oxford University Press, 1965. 663p.
_____. History of Broadcasting in the United Kingdom.
Vol. III. The War of Words. New York: Oxford Univer-
sity Press, 1970. 766p.
_____. History of Broadcasting in the United Kingdom.
Vol. IV. Sound and Vision. New York: Oxford Univer-
sity Press, 1979. 1096p.

A detailed history by one of England's foremost historians in the field of communications, this multivolumed
work puts broadcasting in its larger economic, political,
and social context. The first volume goes through 1926;
the second, from 1927 to World War II; the third, from 1939
to 1945; the fourth covers the ten years following World
War II. Each volume is complete within itself; together or
individually they make reading for the layman as well as
for those with an institutional or scholarly interest in
broadcasting. Footnotes, bibliographical notes, and
indexes in all volumes.

346. Brily, Sharon, and Shirley Kwan. Cable Television State
Regulation. Washington: Policy Review and Development
Division, Cable Television Bureau, Federal Communications
Commission, annual or twice a year. (1975--.)

A survey of franchising and other state laws and regulations on cable TV which gives a general overview followed
by a brief abstract of legislation by state, with date of
introduction and status at present.

347. British Broadcasting: A Bibliography. London WH1 4AA:
British Broadcasting Corp., 35 Marylebone High St., 1958.
35p.
348. British Broadcasting: A Selected Bibliography, 1922-1972.
London WH1 4AA: British Broadcasting Corp., 35 Marylebone High St., 1972. 49p.

The 1958 volume replaces Books about Broadcasting, which
was first issued in 1948. It covers books published in
Britain on sound and TV broadcasting, excluding those on
engineering. Included are periodical articles on BBC policy, the more important debates about the BBC in both
houses of Parliament, and all government and official publications relating to the BBC.
The 1972 volume contains more than 700 annotated references, divided into thirteen major categories, including
much material on the BBC's colonial broadcasting in Africa
and Asia and external broadcasting elsewhere. There is
also material on commercial broadcasting in Britain.

British Film and TV Yearbook. (See No. 822.)

349. Broadcasting: The Critical Challenges. Charles S. Steinberg, ed. New York: Hastings House, 1974. 315p.

A report of the significant discussions and findings of
the International Radio and Television Society at the Third
Annual Faculty Industry Seminar at which participants
appraise the condition of broadcasting in the first half of
the 1970s. Various problems are considered by well-known
figures in education, industry, government, and the press.
Among these problems: the future of television news,
counter-advertising, television and politics, broadcasting
criticism and aesthetics, and children's programming. Supplementary material includes an opinion survey of the faculty participants, a brief biography of all participants,
and a bibliography. Indexed.

350. Broadcasting and Cable Television: Policies for Diversity
and Change. New York 10022: Committee for Economic
Development, 477 Madison Ave., 1975. 120p. (Statement
by the Research and Policy Committee of the Committee
for Economic Development.)

A group of business executives and educators study what
they consider to be vital issues of communication policy.

Much of the discussion centers around ways of bringing about greater understanding of the interrelated policy problems facing commercial broadcasting, public broadcasting, and cable TV, and of actions necessary for achieving diversity in a period of transition from scarcity to abundance in electronic television.

351. Broadcasting Cable Sourcebook. Washington 20036: Broadcasting-Telecasting Bldg., 1735 DeSales St., N.W., annual. (1971--.)

A geographical listing of cable TV systems in the U.S. and Canada, giving for each the address, area served, subscribers, channel usage with summary of each system and TV stations carried by the system, common carrier microwave company (where pertinent), pay cable, automated origination, access channels, other origination, whether or not system accepts advertising and, if so, yearly revenue, other services offered, and ownership. More general features include "Anatomy of Cable Regulation," an outline of federal cable and television rules; multiple systems operators in the U.S. and Canada; broadcasters in CATV; CATV financial data; manufacturers and distributors of equipment; program supplies; consultants; associations; state regulatory agencies; personnel of NCTA (National Cable TV Association); and federal agencies and congressional committees.

352. Broadcasting from Space. New York: UNESCO Publications Center, 1970. 65p. (Reports and Papers on Mass Communication No. 60.)

Report of a UNESCO-sponsored conference which touched upon a number of aspects of space communications, among which are: free flow of information; action toward satellite television transmission (legal protection against uses not authorized by the originating body); assessment of the requirements of education, science, and culture in the future allocation of frequencies for space communication; and the respective roles of the UN and the International Communication Union. Concluding is an address by Arthur C. Clarke, "Beyond Babel: The Century of the Communication Satellite."

353. Broadcasting Yearbook. Washington 20036: Broadcasting Publications, Broadcasting-Telecasting Bldg., 1735 DeSales St., N.W., annual. (1935--.)

This yearly supplement to Broadcasting magazine is an indispensable source of data on radio and TV. Its main feature consists of separate directories of TV and radio stations in the U.S. and Canada, giving for each the date

of founding, address, ownership, personnel, and other
assorted information. Both public broadcasting and commercial stations are included.

It also provides a wealth of other information about
such facts as group ownership, including print as well as
broadcasting media; revenues; advertising; program specialization; Spanish programs; pending applications and
ownership transfers; Voice of America; NAB codes; networks
and affiliates; news service; major awards; distribution
and production services; professional services; FCC staff,
rules and regulations; a directory of education; satellites, etc. There is a section on public broadcasting,
and, as an introduction, a description of broadcasting--
how it evolved; how it works; how it is regulated, as
reported by the FCC; and a statistical overview of the
industry. The final section contains a bibliography of
the year's outstanding books and a brief summary of facts
about broadcasting in many countries--Russia and China
being notable exceptions, although in the latter case the
omission will probably be remedied.

354. Brooks, Jim, and Earl Marsh. Complete Directory to Prime
Time Network TV Shows 1946-Present. New York: Ballantine, 1979. 848p.

An alphabetical listing of nighttime talk shows, situation comedy, general drama, documentaries, news programs,
variety, sports, adventure, music, audience participation
shows, medical, children's shows, etc. between 1946 and
1978. Entries are in alphabetical order by title; information varies but is as full as possible, usually including all or most of the following: genre, first and last
telecast and date, broadcast history (date or dates,
network, time slot), cast and production, a summary of
content. Appendices include primetime schedules from
1946 on, award winners, and top-rated programs by season,
according to Nielsen.

355. Brown, Les. The New York Times Encyclopedia of Television.
New York: Times Books, 1977. 492p.

"As one who frequently combs the indexes of books and
rummages through clips from the Times' morgue in search of
an elusive fact, I have endeavored to fulfill my own wish
for a book that would bring together all the flickering
parts of television in stable print: the history, technology, programs, stars, creative talents, executives,
special language, FCC regulations, landmark legal cases,
networks and station groups, industry organizations, unions,
citizens' groups, syndications, cable TV, pay TV, public
television, the economics, the meaning and mechanics of

ratings, and the structure and content of foreign broadcast systems," writes the author, who for more than twenty
years has covered TV, first for Variety and now for the
New York Times. He has arranged all this information in
neat chronological form and tightly packed prose, with
illustrations here and there. Coverage is thorough.
There is a brief bibliography giving some of the key general books. Contains "see also" references but no index,
so that some of the minor references within articles can
be lost.

356. Brown, Ronald. Telecommunications: The Booming Tech-
     nology. New York: Doubleday, 1970. 191p.

     Intended for the layman, this is a simplified account--
     as untechnical as is possible--which extends from the
     growth of early telegraph systems to the communication
     satellite. Contains many illustrations, a bibliography,
     and an index.

357. Bunce, Richard. Television in the Corporate Interest.
     New York: Praeger, 1976. 150p.

     The author, a research sociologist, questions the
     structure of commercial television in relation to the pub-
     lic interest. Does it properly represent the diverse and
     often antagonistic segments of our society? How respon-
     sible are business corporations to these diverse segments?
     Is regulation by government the answer? These issues are
     examined and evidence presented, much of it economic.
     Part I, "The Logic of FCC Policy," discusses business
     pluralism and crossownership; Part II, "The Logic of Cor-
     porate Practice," discusses the meaning of business con-
     trol, multinational empire building, conglomerates, and
     television in the public interest. There are tables,
     footnotes, and a bibliography.

358. Buxton, Frank, and Bill Owen. The Big Broadcast, 1920-
     1950. New York: Viking, 1972. 301p.

     A new, revised, and expanded edition of Radio's Golden
     Age (1966) which lists alphabetically network radio pro-
     grams of the period. Information about each necessarily
     varies, being very scanty for some, but always including
     the type of program and, in almost every case, the date
     it began and the leading characters. In some cases there
     are complete casts, director, writer, network, a synopsis
     of the plot, and considerable other information. Now and
     then the history of the program is included, as, for
     instance, "Grand Ole Opry." All entries are series. In
     spite of its unavoidable unevenness, it is useful because
     so little information of this sort exists for radio.

There are also pictures of some of the performers, a bibliography, and a name index.

359. The Cable/Broadband Communications Book. Mary Louise
     Hallowell, comp. Washington 20036: Communications
     Press, 1346 Connecticut Ave., N.W., biennial. (1977--.)

     Designed for the layman as well as the professional who
     needs to keep abreast of the fast pace of happenings in
     cable, this handbook provides general background on the
     most significant current and emerging issues in cable tele-
     vision and the new technologies. Each volume varies some-
     what, but the general format consists of in-depth articles
     by experts from government, industry, and research who
     discuss governmental regulation and use of cable in rela-
     tion to minorities, schools, church, health, libraries,
     museums, and the arts, etc. Its predecessor was Cable
     Handbook 1975-1976: A Guide to Cable and New Communica-
     tion Technologies (1975).

360. Cable Communications and the States: A Sourcebook for
     Legislative Decision-Makers. Albany: New York State
     Senate, 1975. 487p.

     A compendium of information about cable television in
     the fifty states. Included are the following: background;
     intergovernmental relations; state involvement in regula-
     tion; legislation; pros and cons; guiding development (a
     broader view); and a bibliography.

361. Cable Television: Franchise Provisions for Schools.
     Washington 20036: National Education Association,
     1201 Sixteenth St., N.W., 1973. 33p.

     In addition to recommended franchise provisions, this
     book gives ownership options, a glossary, and appendices,
     "Rules and Regulations," and "Franchise Provisions at Vari-
     ance with FCC Cable Television Rules."

362. Cable Television in the Cities: Community Control, Public
     Access, and Minority Ownership. Charles Tate, ed.
     Washington 20037: Urban Institute, 2100 M St., N.W.,
     1972. 184p.

     Information concerning the technology, franchising,
     local program origination, strategies for community con-
     trol, community ownership arrangements, business develop-
     ment procedures and prospects, and other pertinent data.
     A final section is an eighty-page Reference and Resource
     Guide which gives a glossary of terms; facts and figures
     on the CATV industry; CATV regulation and policy develop-
     ment; special ordinance/franchise provisions; FCC

regulations and New York access rules; important federal agencies; organizations and associations; research and demonstration projects; information and technical assistance; trade journals and industry publications; and a bibliography of selected articles and books.

363. Cable Television Information Center. Publications Service. Washington 20037: 2100 M St. N. W., 1972-75.

This organization has published the following useful pamphlets designed to make information available to local officials and other decision makers involved in setting up and maintaining cable systems. Subject matter covers regulation, economics, local ordinances, and technology, among other topics. Available pamphlets include:

A Suggested Procedure: An Approach to Local Authorization of Cable Television. 1972. 14p.
Cable Economics. 1972. 14p.
The Use of Financial Analysis in Decision Making. 1975. 40p.
How to Plan an Ordinance: An Outline and Some Examples. 1972. 145p.
Technical Standards and Specifications. 1973. 71p.
Bibliocable. 1972, 1974. 59p.
A Glossary of Cable Terms. 1975. 28p.
Technology of Cable Television. 1973. 33p.
The Uses of Cable Communications. 1973. 47p.
Cable System Interconnection. 1974. 40p.

The center also publishes a quarterly newsletter, Notes from the Center, which reports on important developments on the federal and local level, and has a Special Reports Service which at present includes the following three publications: Regulating Cable Television Subscriber Rates: A Guide for Local Officials (1977. 57p.), Local Government Uses of Cable Television (1974. 66p.), and Educational Use of Cable Television (1974. 105p.). In addition it has issued three Miscellaneous Papers, one a report on an interconnection system in the Minneapolis-St. Paul area, and the other two entitled Fund Raising for Cable Television Projects (1974. 20p.) and Legal Bibliography: Synopsis of Cases on Cable Television (1974. 21p.).

364. Canada. Committee on Broadcasting. Report. Ottawa: Queen's Printer, 1965. 416p.

Popularly known as the Fowler Report after Robert M. Fowler, chairman of the committee, this is a full-scale investigation of practically all facets of Canadian broadcasting, including both the Canadian Broadcasting System and the private sector.

365. Canada. Royal Commission on Broadcasting. Report. 2 vols. Ottawa: Queen's Printer, 1957.

Inquiry, resulting from extensive hearings, into various facets of Canadian broadcasting in relation to Canada's geographic and socioeconomic situation. Numerous appendices give the data from which much of the text is taken. Vol. II, Basic Tables: Television and Radio Programme Analysis, compiled by Dallas W. Smythe, gives in tabular form a TV program log analysis.

366. Canadian Radio-Television Commission. Broadcast Programmes and Research Branches: A Resource for the Active Community. Ottawa K1A ON2: The Commission, 100 Metcalfe St., 1974. 125p.

A collection of articles gathered from people who have themselves been involved in community broadcasting in Canada. The Commission warns that their experiences and opinions do not express official CRTC policy or follow guidelines as to how expression might best be achieved. Articles range widely, from the practical and technical to the abstract and sometimes controversial philosophies of the communities represented. Contains a list of terms and a bibliography.

367. Canadian Radio-Television Commission. Canadian Ownership in Broadcasting: A Report on the Foreign Divestiture Process. Ottawa K1A ON2: Information Canada, 100 Metcalfe St., 1974. 44p.

Listing and discussion of the various companies whose holdings were involved in the extensive divestiture transactions across Canada which took place after passage of Direction of Foreign Ownership (P.C. 1969-2229). An introductory chapter traces historically the involvement of foreigners in Canadian broadcasting, followed by an account of each specific case. Appendices give specific figures.

368. Canadian Radio-Television Commission. Directory: Multilingual Broadcasting in Canada. Ottawa K1A ON2: Information Canada, 100 Metcalfe St., 1974. 117p.

A listing of Canadian stations which broadcast in languages other than English. Includes cable TV, off-air TV, AM radio and FM radio.

369. Canadian Radio-Television Commission. Lists Showing the Ownership of Radio and Television Stations Licensed by the Canadian Radio-Television Commission. Ottawa K1A ON2: Queen's Printer, 1970. Loose-leaf.

Gives names, addresses, directors and executive officers, stock shareholders, their citizenship, and the number of common and preferred shares each stockholder owns.

370. Canadian Radio-Television and Telecommunications Commission. Committee of Inquiry into the National Broadcasting Service. Report. Ottawa K1G 3J5: Canadian Broadcasting Corp., 1500 Bronson Avenue, 1977. 144p.

An evaluation of the CBC to investigate whether it is fulfilling its mandate to the Canadian public. Topics include an assessment of the immediate situation; treatment of news, information, and public affairs; the public view of the CBC; cultural apartheid; and the need for further inquiry. Appendices give CRTC announcements, CBC–Radio Canada documents sent to the committee, research reports prepared for the committee, and an extensive bibliography.

371. Canadian Radio-Television and Telecommunication Commission. Report on Pay Television. Ottawa K1A ON2: The Commission, 100 Metcalfe St., 1978. 56p.

Examines the issues posed by the possible introduction of pay television in Canada, outlining the historical context, describing and examining the most recent submissions for a system in Canada, and giving the Commission's conclusions and possible guidelines.

372. Canadian Radio-Television Commission. Research Branch. Symposium on Television Violence: Colloque sur la violence à la télévision. Ottawa K1A OS9: Printing and Publishing Supply Services, 1976. 252p.

Report of a forum hosted by the Canadian Radio-Television and Telecommunications Commission, in which representatives of the television industry, writers, social science scholars, and legal and lay experts voice diverse opinions, areas of agreement, and analyses of problems and possible solutions. Contents include "The Public Issue," "The Social Effects of Television Violence," "The Industry Perspective," and "Control and Improvement." Contains four bibliographies and footnotes which include the Canadian Code of Broadcast News Ethics of the Radio Television News Directors Association of Canada.

373. Case Studies on Broadcasting Systems. London: Routledge and Kegan Paul in association with the International Institution of Communications, 1977––.

A series of monographs, sponsored by the International Institute of Communications, which points out the main features of the communications patterns of a number of different countries. Emphasis is on the various structures and how they came into existence, landmarks in their histories, and alternative possibilities envisioned for the future. Studies thus far include:

Broadcasting in Sweden by Edward W. Ploman. 1977. 90p.
Broadcasting in Canada by E. S. Hallman and H. Hindley. 1977. 90p.
Broadcasting in Peninsular Malaysia by Ronny Adhikarya with Woon Ai Leng, Wong Hock Seng, and Khor Yoke Lim. 1977. 102p.
Broadcasting in the Netherlands by Kees van der Haak with Joanna Spicer. 1977. 93p.
Broadcasting in Ireland by Desmond Fisher. 1978. 120p.
Broadcasting in Guyana by Ron Sanders. 1978. 76p.
Broadcasting in Japan by Masami Ito. 1978. 125p.

374. Cater, Douglass, ed.; Richard Adler, project ed. Television as a Social Force: New Approaches to TV Criticism. New York: Praeger, 1975. 171p. (Sponsored by the Aspen Institute on Communications.)

375. _____; _____. Television as a Cultural Force. New York: Praeger, 1976. 191p. (Published with the Aspen Institute.)

The first of these titles contains essays which analyze from varying viewpoints TV's impact and its potential for influencing our concept of reality. Among the subjects considered are TV vis à vis "thinking people"; TV and public health; TV as a medium for communicating ideas; newspaper news and TV news; electronic journalism and politics; and the electronic community--a new environment.

In the second title, eight participants from the Aspen program's Workshop on Television examine the significance of its first twenty-five years in America, with special reference to American culture. Some of the areas discussed are TV as dream, as cultural document, as melodrama, as moral force, as news. There is a bibliography and a name and program index.

376. Cater, Douglass, ed.; Michael J. Nyhan, project ed. The Future of Public Broadcasting. New York: Praeger, 1976. 372p. (Published with the Aspen Institute Program on Communications and Society.)

Experts examine the many serious policy questions facing public broadcasting over the next decade, identifying problems, exploring possible solutions, and proposing future directions. Topics include the difficult business of building public broadcasting into an institution, the stations, public radio, instructional television, audience involvement, financing, audience and programming research, programming, program funding, the new technology. Christopher Sterling has compiled "A Selective Guide to Sources on Public Broadcasting." Glossary and index.

Catholic Press Directory. (See No. 649.)

377. CATV and Station Coverage Atlas and Zone Maps. Washington 20036: Television Digest, Inc., 1836 Jefferson Pl., N.W., annual. (1966-67--.)

Intended to provide a "quick portable guide to: (1) Communities and areas in relation to the predicted coverage of TV stations, as expressed by Grade B contours. (2) 35-Mile Zone Maps, depicting areas within 35 miles & 55 miles of TV markets, as employed by the Federal Communications Commission in its CATV rules." Both commercial and educational stations are included. There is also a variety of other information: industry statistics; cable systems with pay-cable operations; a copyright-office directory; state regulatory agencies; Bell System representatives; an NCTA (National Cable TV Association) directory; a directory of state and regional associations; the text of the FCC cable rules; TV stations being considered for purposes of cable carriage; equipment manufacturers; translator stations; multipoint distribution service stations; satellite earth stations serving cable systems and microwaves serving cable systems, and maps giving their location. The initial title was CATV Atlas.

378. Chin, Felix. Cable Television: A Comprehensive Bibliography. New York: IFI/Plenum, 1978. 285p.

The first section of this excellent bibliography lists general reference materials, periodicals, and indexes to periodicals and legal digests. The second, which is the main body of the book, contains citations (annotated unless the title is self-explanatory) under seven categories: general information and history, cable television regulation and policy, cable technology and channel capacity, cable television finances and economics, uses of cable television, cable television and education, and community control and franchises. The final section consists of more than 150 pages of appendices: a list of the fifty largest U.S. CATV systems and another of the top fifty CATV companies; a chronology of major decisions and actions affecting cable television; federal agencies and congressional committees dealing with CATV; national, regional, and state CATV associations and other organizations in CATV; state regulatory agencies for CATV; section headings of FCC rules; and a glossary of terms. An author and a subject index.

379. Citizens' Media Directory. Pamela Draves, ed. Washington
     20036: National Citizens Committee for Broadcasting,
     1977. 170p.

     A directory of groups which fall under the heading
     "media reform," defined broadly. Categories include both
     national and local groups, public access centers, alterna-
     tive news services, community radio stations, and film and
     video producers and distributors and services. Appendices
     include national trade associations, TV networks, and the
     FCC. Nicholas Johnson has written the introduction.
     The NCCB is also the publisher of Access, a professional
     media reformers' magazine started in 1974.

380. Codding, George A., Jr. Broadcasting without Barriers.
     New York: UNESCO Publications Center, 1959. 167p.

     A study to determine the extent to which radio broad-
     casting is available throughout the world as a means of
     communicating information and to examine ways of overcom-
     ing political, economic, and technological obstacles that
     impede its availability.
     Describes broadcasting systems in the various countries,
     broadcasting between countries, use of the radio spectrum,
     the sharing of frequencies, the quest for better techniques,
     and the impact of television on radio broadcasting. Con-
     tains a bibliography and an index.

381. Cole, Barry, and Mal Oettinger. Reluctant Regulators: The
     FCC and the Broadcast Audience. Reading, Mass.:
     Addison-Wesley Publishing Co., 1978. 288p.

     An in-depth study of the FCC showing conflicts and com-
     promises that influence it and various forces that operate
     behind these conflicts and compromises--the lobbyists, the
     Washington law firms handling FCC cases, the trade press,
     the concerned citizens' groups. In dealing with these
     latter, the authors pay particular attention to the efforts
     to improve children's television. They thoroughly examine
     the inner workings of the FCC and measure what it is sup-
     posed to do against the ways it actually operates. Appen-
     dices give an organizational chart, forms relating to
     license renewal, and the FCC Children's Policy Statement.
     There is no bibliography, probably because most of the
     material comes from close firsthand observation. This is
     one of the best possible sources for an overall picture of
     the agency.

382. Colino, Richard R. The INTELSAT Definitive Arrangements:
     Ushering in a New Era in Satellite Telecommunications.
     CH-1221 Geneva 20: European Broadcasting Union, 1, Rue

de Varembe, 1973. 196p. (Legal and Administrative
Series. Monography No. 9.)

The assistant vice-president in charge of international
affairs, Communications Satellite Corporation, discusses
in detail the arrangements, giving the background, the
process of negotiation, an analysis of key features, and a
commentary on the controversy between INTELSAT and other
satellite systems. Elaborate footnotes and supplementary
materials accompany the text of the agreement.

383. College Carrier Current: A Survey of 208 Campus-Limited
Radio Stations. New York 10028: Broadcast Institute
of North America, 147 E. 81 St., 1973. 12p.

An attempt by the Broadcast Institute of North America
(BINA) to identify and characterize current carrier radio
stations on college campuses. About half of the identified
stations questioned responded, a larger group than has
ever been listed in any one place before. The study summarizes the general findings under auspices and management, income and budget, programming and news. It concludes with findings and recommendations. The stations
queried are listed in an appendix. Very little other
work exists in this area.

Collins, Richard. Television News. (See No. 650.)

384. Commonwealth Broadcasting Association. Handbook. London
W1A 1AA: Broadcasting House, 1976. 122p.

Founded in 1945 as the Commonwealth Broadcasting Conference, this association of forty-five national broadcasting organizations in forty-two Commonwealth countries
is pledged to work for "the professional improvement of
broadcasting in member organizations through collective
study and mutual assistance, and of the technical facilities for transmission and reception of their services."
It holds frequent conferences to discuss problems and
developments. The Handbook records the origins of the
association, gives examples of practical cooperation, and
summarizes the proceedings of the General Conferences held
between 1945 and 1976. In addition it provides a short
history of each of the forty-five member organizations.
It will be revised and reissued from time to time.

385. Communications and the United States Congress: A Selectively Annotated Bibliography of Committee Hearings,
1870-1976. George D. Brightbill, comp. Washington
20036: Broadcast Education Association, 1771 N St.,
1978. 178p.

A much-needed key to a century of hearings on various
aspects of radio, TV, telecommunications, and films. For
reasons which Brightbill does not state, he has excluded
newspapers, magazines, and book publishing unless they
impinge on another subject such as "Obscenity." The
source of each entry is indicated. Page 2 of the Introduction, incidently, gives a list of these sources which
should be useful to any layman trying to chart a course
through the intricacies of government documents. The
Introduction also contains a brief but very useful paragraph, "Updating the bibliography."

386. Communications Technology for Urban Improvement. Washing-
     ton, D.C. 20418: National Academy of Engineering,
     2101 Constitution Avenue, Committee on Telecommunications,
     1971. 218p. (Report to the Department of Housing and
     Urban Development.)

     Defining communications as broadcasting only, this study
     discusses the problems and opportunities within the city;
     the role of telephone, videophone, telephone data networks,
     radio and TV broadcasting, public broadcasting, broadband
     cable networks, and interactive home terminals; project
     recommendations in the areas of education, health, pollu-
     tion, crime prevention, and so on; and a prediction about
     cities of the future. Appendices deal with broadband cable
     communications, mobile radio technical considerations, and
     the reaction of the cities to the proposals. Glossary of
     selected telecommunications terms.

387. Comstock, George, Steven Chaffee, Natan Katzman, Maxwell
     McCombs, and Donald Roberts. Television and Human
     Behavior. New York: Columbia University Press, 1978.
     581p.

     The co-authors have attempted "out of vanity and with
     a touch of arrogance" to cover the entire relevant scien-
     tific literature on television in English, examining more
     than 2,500 books, articles, reports, and documents, includ-
     ing some that fall beyond the usual boundaries of science,
     and recording their conclusions (some of which are tenta-
     tive) and their speculations. They have grouped their
     material under the following headings: "Overview," "What's
     On," "The Audience," "Living with Television," "One Highly
     Attracted Public" (children), "Four Highly Attracted Pub-
     lics" (women, blacks, the poor, and the elderly), "Politics
     and Purchases," "The Psychology of Behavioral Effects," and
     "The Future." There are forty-seven pages of references,
     a name index, and a subject index. This is the biggest
     single study of empirical evidence about television since
     the Surgeon General's Report in 1972 (No. 591).

This was preceded by three volumes of background and
bibliographic research, published by the RAND Corporation
in 1975: Television and Human Behavior: A Guide to the
Pertinent Scientific Literature (251p.) by Comstock and
Marilyn Fisher; Television and Human Behavior: The Key
Studies (120p.) by Comstock with the assistance of F. G.
Christen, M. L. Fisher, R. C. Quarles, and W. D. Richards;
and Television and Human Behavior: The Research Horizon
(344p.) by Comstock and George Lindsey.

388. Consumer Electronics: Annual Review. Washington 20006:
     Consumer Electronic Group, Electronic Industries Asso-
     ciation, 2001 Eye St., N.W., annual. (1968--.)

     Annual survey of the multi-billion-dollar consumer
electronics industry which began with radio over half a
century ago and now encompasses phonographs, television,
tape recorders, electronic household appliances, electronic clocks and watches, micro-wave ovens, and many
other similar electronic products. Tables and charts
give figures for production and sales, and short articles
elaborate. Emphasis is on radio and television. There
is a list of members of the Consumer Electronic Industry,
Allied Trade Associations.

389. Contreras, Eduardo, and others. Cross-Cultural Broadcast-
     ing. Paris: UNESCO, 1976. 49p. (Reports and Papers
     on Mass Communications No. 77.)

     A discussion of transnational broadcasting which explores
conditions, possibilities, and problems. Among them:
regional communications systems and cooperation in program
production; use of satellite broadcasting to achieve a wide
diffusion of television programming to multi-cultural audiences; international program sales which insure that programs are suitable for the cultures which they reach.
Political, cultural, linguistic, and psychological implications and possible effects are taken into consideration.
Footnotes and bibliography.

390. Control of the Direct Broadcast Satellite: Values in Con-
     flict. Palo Alto, Cal.: Aspen Institute Program on
     Communications and Society, 1974. 156p. (An Occasional
     Paper.)

     The prospect of technology (not yet in existence) which
could reach across national boundaries into the home without
the aid of expensive receiving apparatus has caused heated
debate in the U.N. and UNESCO as to form of control, with
U.S. opinions in the minority. This publication, consisting
of papers delivered at the Airlie House Conference on International Communication: The Free Exchange of Information

117

and Ideas and the Integrity of National Cultures, attempts
to explain some of the issues and viewpoints. Glossary,
bibliography, and index.

391. Costigan, Daniel M. Fax: The Principles and Practice of
    Facsimile Communication. Philadelphia: Chilton, 1971.
    270p.

    A survey of facsimile--its background, its technology,
    its economics, its standards, and speculations upon its
    future. Indexed.

392. Crane, Rhonda J. The Politics of International Standards:
    France and the Color TV War. Norwood, N.J.: Ablex,
    1979. 165p.

    Focusing on the adoption of color TV standards in France,
    the author examines the politics, technology, international
    trade relations, and bargaining involved in standard-setting,
    showing the degree to which technical standards are the
    result of political and economic factors. Some of the evi-
    dence is drawn from never-before-released declassified docu-
    ments. Appendices, a bibliography, and an author and a
    subject index.

393. Davis, Anthony. Television: The First Forty Years. London
    W1P OAU: Independent Television Publications, 247 Totten-
    ham Court Rd., 1976. 144p.
394. _____. Television: Here Is the News. London: Indepen-
    dent Television Publications, 1976. 159p.

    The word history has too scholarly a connotation to use
    in connection with these two informal chronological accounts
    of the development of television and of television news in
    Britain. Both are designed for laymen who want a quick
    overview or even entertainment. Emphasis throughout is on
    the contrast between ITV (the publisher) and BBC. The First
    Forty Years has a brief chapter on advertising and ITV's
    advertising code. Both contain a number of photographs and
    brief bibliographies, and are indexed.

395. Daytime TV's Star Directory. Paul Denis, ed. New York:
    Popular Library, 1976. 254p.

    An inexpensive paperback which gives leading members of
    casts, with biographies, and brief rundowns of plots for
    fifteen of the best-known daytime serials. Name index.

Desmond, Robert W. The Information Process: World News Reporting to the Twentieth Century. (See No. 658.)

118

396. The Development of Wireless to 1920. George Shiers, ed.
New York: Arno Press, 1977. Variously paged. (Historical Studies in Telecommunication.)

An anthology containing twenty articles published
between 1890 and 1967 on the "pre-history" of radio, showing the experimental and technological work.

397. De Vera, Jose Maria. Educational Television in Japan.
Tokyo: Sophia University; Rutland, Vt.: Tuttle, 1967.
140p.

De Vera's aim is to provide both information and interpretation, with the term educational covering both instructional TV to schools and more general instructional TV to
a wider audience. He first discusses the concept and philosophy of educational broadcasting in Japan, including
its history, then he proceeds to its content and audience,
its effects and its effectiveness in the learning process,
and finally gives an overall appraisal. Notes and bibliography.

398. Diamant, Lincoln, ed. The Broadcast Communications Dictionary. 2d ed. New York: Hastings House, 1978. 201p.

"This handy quick reference book is designed for every-
day assistance," says the author over-modestly about his
comprehensive dictionary of more than 4,000 terms intended
to assist both beginner and professional. Included are
technical, common, and slang words and acronyms in current
use in radio and TV programming and production, network and
station operations, broadcast equipment and engineering,
audio and video tape recording, performing talent, advertising procedures, media usage, research, and government
and allied groups. There are cross references to British
terminology.

399. Documents in American Telecommunications Policy. John M.
Kittross, ed. 2 vols. New York: Arno Press, 1977.
(Historical Studies in Telecommunications.)

A collection of important American articles, reports,
government documents, and other types of materials which
helped to shape telecommunications policy, and in some
cases have now become difficult to find. Arrangement is
chronological, covering the period from 1904 to 1957. In
his introduction Kittross gives the background of each
selection, which forms a brief history of telecommunications policy. Following this is "A Chronological List of
Selected Books on American Telecommunications Policy."

400. Drury, C. M. White Paper on a Domestic Satellite Communi-
        cations System of Canada. Ottawa: Queen's Printer,
        1968. 94p.

   Reviews the main factors involved in planning and
   establishing domestic satellite communications to meet
   Canada's needs, both in the immediate future and over the
   longer term. Appendices include a survey of satellite
   developments on an international level--INTELSAT, the
   Franco-German "SYMPHONIE," the U.S.S.R.'s satellite communication system, the European Launcher Development
   Organization (ELDO), and the European Space Conference.
   There is a glossary of terms. Text is in both English
   and French.

401. Dunn, Gwen. The Box in the Corner: Television and the
        Under-Fives. London: Macmillan, 1977. 160p.

   A British study in which the author observed children
   in their own homes to determine their reactions to television. Quoting extensively from their comments and
   reactions, she focuses on the intentional and unintentional
   effects of television on the mental and physical development of pre-school children and how it can best be used to
   the child's advantage. Bibliography.

402. Dunning, John. Tune in Yesterday: The Ultimate Encyclo-
        pedia of Old-Time Radio, 1925-1976. Englewood Cliffs,
        N.J.: Prentice-Hall, 1976. 703p.

   Intended as historical reference, a nostalgia reader,
   and an entertainment review, this book covers drama, comedy,
   and variety shows, listing them alphabetically, discussing
   each, and often going into considerable detail for well-
   known series. (One Man's Family runs to nine pages, complete with family tree.) Dunning explores interrelation-
   ships of characters and includes full biographical data on
   many of the stars. Among other items of information are
   dates, networks, sponsors, time changes, and personnel.
   Newscasters are covered only when they were billed regularly
   as semi-entertainment (for example, Walter Winchell and
   Hedda Hopper), and band leaders only when they had a regularly sustained variety show. Although the author says that
   a number of shows are discussed here for the first time, not
   all series from radio history are included. There is a
   name-show index.

Durham, F. Gayle. News Broadcasting on Soviet Radio and Tele-
     vision. (See No. 661.)

403. Durham, F. Gayle. Radio and Television in the Soviet Union.
        Cambridge, Mass.: Massachusetts Institute of Technology,

Center for International Studies, Research Program on
Problems of Communication and International Security,
1965. 122p. (Distributed by Clearinghouse for Federal Scientific and Technical Information, U.S. Dept.
of Commerce.)

Gives information on many aspects of Soviet broadcasting: structure, equipment, production and repair, subscription fees, programs and hours, educational television,
relations with Intervision, and audience. Detailed notes
refer to the original sources; and numerous charts, graphs,
and tables illustrate the text.
Amateur Radio Operation in the Soviet Union (71p.), also
by Durham and with the same publisher and date as Radio and
Television in the Soviet Union, tells the importance, structure, and extent of amateur radio, and contains bibliographic footnotes.

404. Dyer, Richard. Light Entertainment. London: British Film
Institute, 1973. 43p. (BFI Television Monograph No. 2.)

Relates the practice of TV light entertainment to the
ideals of abundance, energy, and community, and poses the
question of how far it is able to live up to these ideals.
Starting from an examination of the notion of light television, Dyer considers the nature of the television entertainment situation, the kind of aesthetics needed for its
analysis, and the ways in which we may attempt to understand its place in contemporary society.

405. Edmondson, Madeleine, and David Rounds. From Mary Noble to
Mary Hartman: The Complete Soap Opera Book. New York:
Stein and Day, 1976. 256p.

More a chronological analysis than a history, this
revised, updated, and expanded edition of The Soaps begins
with radio soaps and concludes with Beacon Hill and Mary
Hartman. The authors discuss the psychological appeals,
the writers and players, the economics and regulations that
have played a part in the development of the genre. There
are a few illustrations and a name index for persons and
shows.

406. Eguchi, H., and H. Ichinohe, eds. International Studies
of Broadcasting, with Special Reference to the Japanese
Studies. Tokyo: Japan Broadcasting Corp. (Nippon Hoso
Kyokai), Radio & TV Culture Research Institute, 1-10.
Shiba Atago-cho, Minato-ku, 1971. 301p.

One section is devoted entirely to Japanese research in
such areas as background, programs, public opinion, and
studies about children. The second section takes up trends

and developments in the U.S., Germany, France, Finland, England, and Canada—all written by nationals of these countries.

407. Ellmore, R. Terry. <u>The Illustrated Dictionary of Broadcast-CATV-Telecommunications</u>. Blue Ridge Summit, Pa.: G/L TAB Books, 1977. 396p.

This is much more than a dictionary of terminology; it contains identifying descriptions of law cases, commissions, associations—to name a few of the areas. It even defines <u>catharsis</u> as the term is used in relation to broadcasting. And there are countless acronyms. A few hundred engineering terms are included, but it is not intended to be primarily technical. It interprets telecommunications broadly and even deals with advertising, sales, scenery, research, history, and other wide-ranging aspects. Contains some illustrations.

408. Emery, Walter B. <u>Broadcasting and Government: Responsibilities and Regulations</u>. 2d ed. East Lansing: Michigan State University Press, 1971. 569p.

Discusses the various governmental agencies concerned with broadcasting and sets forth briefly their basic rules, policies, and any services they may provide to the American people. There are bibliographic notes at the end of each chapter; appendices which give important documents, requirements, definitions, codes, and so on; a selective bibliography; and an index.

409. Emery, Walter B. <u>National and International Systems of Broadcasting: Their History, Operation and Control</u>. East Lansing: Michigan State University Press, 1969. 752p.

Country-by-country examination of the broadcasting systems of twenty-nine countries and one continent, giving origin, development, regulation, programming patterns, quantitative dimensions. While some of the material has dated, much still holds. Countries include the U.S., Mexico, Canada, the United Kingdom, Ireland, Belgium, the Netherlands, Luxembourg, Denmark, Iceland, Norway, Sweden, Finland, France, Italy, Greece, Germany, Austria, Switzerland, Spain, the U.S.S.R., Hungary, Yugoslavia, Turkey, India, China, Japan, Australia, and the continent of Africa (an overview).
An appendix gives various broadcasting laws and acts, codes for several nations, membership of the European Broadcasting Union, and information on satellite communications. Detailed bibliography and subject index.

Encyclomedia. _Radio_. (See No. 1103.)

Encyclomedia. _Television_. (See No. 1103.)

410 English, Harry Edward, ed. Telecommunications for Canada:
     An Interface of Business and Government. Toronto:
     Methuen, 1973. 428p.

   A survey of the present state and plans for future development of the Canadian telecommunications industry. The
first part presents studies of general policy--the principal
issues, major policy options, the characteristics of the
industry and of regulatory principles and practice in Canada.
The second part deals with specifics--technology, demand and
cost (an empirical study of Bell Telephone of Canada),
accounting aspects of telecommunications regulation, telecommunications and the federal constitution of Canada, and
federal regulations. Footnotes.

Epstein, Edward Jay. _News from Nowhere: Television and the
   News_. (See No. 667.)

411. Fackelman, Mary P., and Kimberly A. Krekel. _International
     Telecommunications Bibliography_. Washington: U.S. Dept.
     of Commerce, Office of Telecommunications, 1976. Var-
     iously paged. (OT Special Publication 76-7.)

   The authors state that they have attempted to provide a
framework useful in defining the U.S. role or potential
roles within the international telecommunications community,
and have selected articles, books, and professional papers
on the technology, economics, industrial structures, and
legal aspects of telecommunications systems worldwide. All
entries are annotated. Few references pre-date 1970, and
the authors regret that they were not able to include U.N.
documents. Contains a glossary, a list of research facilities, and author and subject indexes.

412. Faenza, Roberto. _The Radio Phenomenon in Italy_. Stras-
     bourg: Committee for Out-of-School Education and
     Cultural Development, Council for Cultural Cooperation,
     Council of Europe/Conseil de l'Europe, 1977. 29p.
     (CCC/DC (76) 93-E.)

   A brief survey of the present state of broadcasting in
Italy, with an analysis of the use of radio as a social
force, its power, and its consequences in the Italian context.
   Another study on Italian broadcasting, made in the same
year by the same committee, is _Independent Television Networks in Italy at the Turning Point from Cable_, by

Francesco Cavalli-Sforza, Agnes Donati, and Hew Evans.
(36p. CCC/DC (76) 92-E.) It gives the story of the
emergence of local television, with six case studies and
some evaluation of the development and of its present
momentum. A map shows the distribution of independent
TV networks as of October, 1976, with brief information
about each.

413. Fifty Years of Japanese Broadcasting. History Compila-
tion Room, Radio & TV Culture Research Institute,
Japan Broadcasting Corporation, with cooperation of
the Mainichi Newspapers. Tokyo: Japan Broadcasting
Corp. (Nippon Hoso Kyokai) Radio & TV Culture Research
Institute, 1-10 Shiba Atagocho, Minato-Ku, 1977. 429p.

Although compiled and edited by Japan's public broadcasting organization, NHK, this relates the history and
development of commercial broadcasting as well. The
editors say that an additional aim is to bring into relief
the relationship between broadcasting and Japanese society.
Appendices include the provisions of the broadcast law,
standards of NHK's domestic and overseas broadcast programs, and thirty-two pages giving the annals of Japanese
broadcasting, 1885-1975. A map shows the NHK GTV network.

414. Forbes, Dorothy, and Sanderson Layng. The New Communications: A Guide to Community Programming. Washington:
Communications Press, 1978. 117p.

". . . gathers a range of services into a distinctive
philosophy of community television which identifies cable
television as an important community resource. It places
heavy emphasis on feedback, on the accomplishment of the
individuals who make community programming happen, and it
attempts to de-mystify the television medium in a way that
makes it an attractive vehicle of communication to the
layman."--Foreword. Bibliography.

Fowler Report. See Canada. Royal Commission on Broadcasting.
Report. (No. 365.)

415. The Future of Broadcasting: A Report Presented to the
Social Morality Council, October 1973. London: Eyre
Methuen, 1974. 100p.

The council states in the Introduction that "Our Report
has no official blessing or sponsorship, and has no pre-
tensions to be a substitute for the sort of wide-ranging
inquiry the British government has commissioned in the
past; it is merely an attempt by a few interested lay
people to make a socially and morally responsible examination of some of the important questions which issue from

broadcasting (particularly television)." In this light
they have examined goals, structure, accountability, and
relationship to education. Finally they make their
recommendations. Indexed.

Gans, Herbert J. Deciding What's News: A Study of CBS Evening News, NBC Nightly News, Newsweek and Time. (See
No. 675.)

416. Garnham, Nicholas. Structure of Television. London:
British Film Institute, 1973. 48p. (BFI Television Monographs No. 1.)

An analysis of the organizational structures of British
television, placed in relationship to the concepts of communication and democracy. Bibliography.

Gelfman, Judith S. Women in Television News. (See No. 677.)

417. Gerani, Gary, and Paul H. Schulman. Fantastic Television:
A Pictorial History of Sci-Fi, the Unusual and the
Fantastic from Captain Video to the Star Trek Phenomenon
and Beyond. New York: Harmony Books, 1977. 192p.

In two parts. "Fine Tuning" focuses on thirteen shows
which the authors feel to be the "very best" in the science
fiction/fantasy genre, and follows them from birth and
development to eventual demise. On the other hand, the
second section, "The Full Picture," is a brief treatment of
other representatives of the genre, giving in five or six
lines primary credits and a "nutshell" synopsis. Indexed.

418. Gerbner, George, Larry Gross, and others. Trends in Network Television Drama and Viewer Concept of Social
Reality, 1967-1976. Philadelphia: Annenberg School of
Communications, University of Pennsylvania, 1977. 29,
80p. (Violence Profile No. 8.)

Latest report in the well-known Violence Index series
which analyzes the content of television programs. Number
8 incorporates significant findings of previous reports
and supersedes them. The first part summarizes findings
and methodology; the second gives statistical tables.

419. Gibson, George H. Public Broadcasting: The Role of the
Federal Government, 1912-76. New York: Praeger, 1977.
236p.

Tells of the expansion of the role of the federal government in noncommercial educational broadcasting since about
1912 and describes in detail the work that presidents, con-
gressmen, the FCC, commissioners of education, the Department

of Health, Education and Welfare, foundations, and educational broadcasters have done at the federal level with regard to public broadcasting. Footnotes at the end of each chapter and an index.

420. Gillespie, Gilbert. _Public Access Cable Television in the United States and Canada, with an Annotated Bibliography._ New York: Praeger, 1975. 157p.

Intended as a reference for anyone involved or planning to be involved with public access. The author discusses apparent impact, its history as a concept, the factors which impede or corrupt its progress, and its future. Contains bibliographic notes, a chronology, and a long, annotated bibliography.

421. Ginsburg, Douglas H. _Regulation of Broadcasting: Law and Policy toward Radio, Television and Cable Communications._ St. Paul, Minn.: West Publishing Co., 1978. 741p. (American Casebook Series.)

Consists mainly of excerpts from major cases which have affected the electronic media--radio, television, and cable-- and is intended for use in law, public policy, and communications curricula. It is especially valuable in institutions without a law library. In three parts: introductory material; industrial organization; and content regulation. Appendices contain the selected provisions from the Communications Act of 1934; the Public Broadcasting Act; the Newspaper Preservation Act of 1970; the Copyrights Act; the Code of Federal Regulation, Title 47; and the case of Central Florida Enterprises, Inc., v. FCC. Indexed.

422. Glut, Donald F., and Jim Harmon. _The Great Television Heroes._ New York: Doubleday, 1975. 245p.

"We do not claim to have written a history of the medium, but rather a nostalgic look back upon the greatest and most exciting years of television--its infancy," the authors tell us in the Foreword. Even though strictly a nostalgia trip, the book nonetheless contains some useful information about the early heros--and heroines and character actors and actresses and programs as well.

423. Goodhardt, G. J., A. S. C. Ehrenberg, and N. A. Collins. _The Television Audience: Patterns of Viewing._ Lexington, Mass.: Lexington Books, 1975. 157p.

A study of the British audience, in which the authors use statistics to examine such aspects as programming, audience flow, channel loyalty, demography, repeat viewing, intensity of viewing, appreciation, the audience in the

U.S., and effects. An appendix describes audience-measurement procedures. There is a listing of Independent Broadcasting Authority (IBA) Reports from September, 1967, to January, 1975; two bibliographies giving suggested further readings and a list of references used, and an index.

424. Gordon, George N. Educational Television. New York
     10011: Center for Applied Research in Education,
     70 Fifth Ave., 1965. 113p.

History and appraisal which takes into account growth, financial structure, public service function, open- and closed-circuit television, television in schools, and effect studies. Contains a brief bibliography and an index.

Gormley, William T., Jr. The Effects of Newspaper-Television
Cross Ownership on News Homogeneity. (See No. 679.)

425. Great Britain. Committee on Broadcasting (1960). Report.
     London: Her Majesty's Stationery Office, 1962. 324p.
     Appendices 1-2. 1268p.

The Report, commonly known as the Pilkington Report, consists of an introduction which surveys the situation and states the purposes of broadcasting, followed by a lengthy discussion of services of all sorts provided, a constitution, finance, and technical considerations. The two appendices, which are books in their own right, consist of selected memoranda sent to the BBC by various organizations, including some from within the BBC itself. Others are government departments, BBC advisory bodies, Independent Television Authority, Independent Television Programme companies, staff and performers' associations, school and adult education associations, religious bodies, minority groups, national interests, advertising, technical and engineering, local and sound broadcasting, subscription television, relay services, cinematographic interests, miscellaneous organizations, and individuals.

426. Great Britain. Home Department. Committee on the Future
     of Broadcasting. Report of the Committee on the Future
     of Broadcasting. Lord Annan, chairman. London: Her
     Majesty's Stationers Office, 1977. 522p. (Cmmd 6753,
     6753-I.)

"The Annan Report" on British broadcasting discusses at length future strategy; various aspects of BBC and ITV; programming of all kinds; technical questions and development; services in Scotland, Wales, and Northern Ireland;

industrial relations; staff and performers; audience
research; copyright; program archives; and journals. Few
aspects are omitted. The final chapter gives conclusions
and a summary of recommendations. There are four appendices: "List of Organizations and Individuals Who Submitted Formal Written or Oral Evidence"; "Broadcasting
Use of Frequency Spectrum"; "Recommendations of the Crawford Committee on Broadcasting Coverage . . ."; and "Press
Interests in Commercial Television and Radio Companies."

A volume of separate appendices consists of five essays:
"The Intervention of Television in British Politics" by
Jay Blumler; "Research Findings on Broadcasting" by J. D.
Halloran; "The Profits of Advertising--Finances, Broadcasting" by B. V. Hindley; "The Population of Great Britain,
1961-1991" by Mrs. G. B. G. Tomas; and "The Relationship
of Management with Creative Staff" by A. Smith. Other
appendices will probably follow.

427. Green, Timothy. The Universal Eye: The World of Television. New York: Stein and Day, 1972. 276p.

Comprehensive work which surveys in detail the state
of TV in every nation that has TV available to any extent.
Covering Europe, Asia, Africa, North and South America,
and Australia, it examines programming, financing, the
availability of talent, the role of government, and the
possible future course of TV. Written by the former head
of Time's London Bureau, it is also extremely readable.
Contains a bibliography and an index.

428. Greenfield, Jeff. Television: The First Fifty Years.
New York: Abrams, 1977. 275p.

An outsized, coffee-table-type book of 500 pictures
accompanied by text which, in spite of its appearance, is
a serious and critical analysis of television. It examines
news, sports, commercials, soap operas, situation comedies,
and practically all kinds of programming in terms of what
the medium may be doing to us, for better or worse. The
pictures are chosen to illustrate points in the text rather
than vice versa. Greenfield laments his inability to document as fully as he would have liked the earliest programs
and commercials because broadcasts were live at that time
with no kinescopic recording or else the recordings have
been lost. Bibliography and index.

429. Grundfest, Joseph A. Citizen Participation in Broadcast
Licensing before the FCC. Santa Monica, Cal.: RAND,
1976. 195p.

"Describes some of the avenues open to citizens seeking
to influence FCC policies; describes the history of citizen

participation, through partition and settlement, in broadcast licensing; trances the evolution of an FCC policy
statement regarding citizen agreements and analyzes it,
especially in the light of four recent cases before the
FCC; makes recommendations for future commission policy
which suggest that considerable leeway remains for commission approval of citizen settlements, without infring-
ing on the rights and obligations of broadcasters."--
Preface. Footnotes.

430. Guimary, Donald L. Citizens' Groups and Broadcasting.
New York: Praeger, 1976. 170p.

An examination of the broadcaster's relationship with
his audience. The several issues discussed center around
three aspects. First, how should broadcasters ascertain
community interests and needs, how can majority and minority audiences convey these needs to the broadcaster, and
how can they express their satisfactions and dissatisfac-
tions with programs? Second, how should the FCC determine
if and when a licensee has served its community adequately,
and how can listeners get their views across to the commission? And third, by what means should the listening
public participate in and attempt to influence programming
decisions? Bibliography and index.

431. Hale, Julian. Radio Power: Propaganda and International
Broadcasting. Philadelphia: Temple University Press,
1975. 196p.

An introduction to the practice of overseas broadcasting as propaganda and the various ideological philosophies
back of it, in terms both of sender and receiver. Analysis
centers around Nazi Germany, the communist countries, the
U.S.'s Voice of America, Britain's BBC, and the undeveloped
parts of the world. A large section is devoted to factors
affecting success or failure. Appendices give a table of
radio sets and ownership around the world in 1973; external
broadcasting statistics in 1950, 1960, 1970, and 1973;
extracts from Internal Policy Guidelines of Radio Free
Europe and Radio Liberty; and extracts from a BBC unpublished monitoring report. Contains chapter notes, a bibliography, and an index.

432. Halloran, James D. The Effects of Mass Communication with
Special Reference to Television. Leicester, England
LEI 7RH: University of Leicester Press, 1964. 83p.
(Television Research Committee Working Paper No. 1.)
433. _____, ed. The Effects of Television. London:
Panther, 1970. 224p.

434. Halloran, James D., and P. R. C. Elliott. Television for Children and Young People: A Survey Carried Out for the European Broadcasting Union. 1211 Geneva 20, Switzerland: European Broadcasting Union, 1, Rue de Varembe, 1970. 134p.

435. _____, Roger L. Brown, and D. C. Chaney. Television and Delinquency. Leicester, England LEI 7RH: University of Leicester Press, 1970. 221p. (Television Research Committee Working Paper No. 3.)

The first title is an overview of the major social-scientific studies, experiments, and surveys that deal with the effects of television, especially upon children. Halloran deliberately omits certain aspects: the use of television in education (closed-circuit and school broadcasts) and its uses in propaganda and psychological warfare. He also limits himself to works with an empirical approach, and he stresses the gaps in verifiable evidence. Contains a bibliography and a rather sketchy index.

In the second title five British social scientists look at different areas of television from their own particular standpoint. Halloran gives a general introduction and a chapter on social effects; Jay G. Blumer handles political effects; Roger Brown, the arts; Peter Masson, effects on other media; Dennis McQuail, education. The authors point out that the subject is too elusive for definitive answers. But the essays cover much existing evidence and make speculations, some of which raise provocative questions. Each study has a bibliography. Indexed.

The third monograph is "a study and comparison of the hours of television devoted to out-of-school programs for children and young people, and policy regarding facilities and staff relative to other programme output." Questionnaires were distributed by all member institutions in the EBU countries (which include Japan and the U.S. as well as sixteen in Europe). Consists of description analysis and statistics.

Television and Delinquency sets the problem of delinquency in a wider context. The first part examines the nature and cause of delinquency. The second part consists of a report on an exploratory study of the television-viewing habits of adolescents placed on probation by the court. Footnotes and name and subject indexes.

436. Harmon, Jim. The Great Radio Heroes. New York: Doubleday, 1967. 263p.

A lighthearted book which gives an excellent though informal account of the popular radio serials of yesteryear. The title, incidentally, is a misnomer; heroines are included as well.

437. Harmonay, Maureen, ed. Promise and Performance: Children
     with Special Needs. ACT's Guide to TV Programming for
     Children. Vol. I. Cambridge, Mass.: Ballinger, 1977.
     255p. (Action for Children's Television Programming
     Series.)

An anthology which deals with television programming--its
pros and cons--as a medium for children with handicaps.
Articles by specialists discuss the way in which television
at present portrays the handicapped; the image that comes
across to those without handicaps and those with; the use
of television by and for specific types of disabilities.
Bibliography and index.

438. Harris, Paul. Broadcasting from the High Seas: The History
     of Offshore Radio in Europe, 1958-1976. Edinburgh: Paul
     Harris Publishing, 25 London St., 1977. 361p.

The mid-twentieth century has witnessed a new type of
piracy--unlicensed shipboard radio broadcasting. The author
(and publisher) of this history describes minutely the growth
and development of these stations--their squabbles with each
other and with the authorities, the legislation against them,
the pros and cons of their existence in social terms. Much
of Harris's material is based on his earlier work, When
Pirates Ruled the Waves.

439. Head, Sydney W., ed. Broadcasting in Africa: A Continental
     Survey of Radio and Television. Philadelphia: Temple
     University Press, 1974. 453p.

Thirty-five authorities, including the editor, have contributed essays which together give a comprehensive picture
of the structure of African broadcasting country by country,
and the role which non-Africans play in shaping it. Information given for each African nation includes population,
receivers per thousand, radio transmitter sites, area per
site. Otherwise information varies a bit, with longer discussions for larger countries. The authors discuss the
system against the background of such factors as geography,
politics, and language, and include broadcasting history
and, when available, audience data. The second half of the
book is concerned with the ways in which other nations are
influencing African broadcasting. Here are discussions of
international broadcasting agencies and programs, religious
broadcasting, foreign aid, training, research, educational
uses to which broadcasting is put, and the commerce of
broadcasting. Head concludes with an agenda for further
study. Appendices give technical problems of spectrum
utilization, the uses of broadcasting in African political
crises, historical and demographic data, a summary of

131

system facilities, and languages used in broadcasting. There is a lengthy bibliography and a comprehensive index.

In 1974 Head, with Lois Beck, also published The Bibliography of African Broadcasting: An Annotated Guide (Philadelphia: Temple University, School of Communication and Theatre. 60p.), which lists major books and articles from newspapers and magazines—458 items in all, with a list of periodicals in the field and a topical index.

440. Head, Sydney W. Broadcasting in America: A Survey of Television and Radio. 3d ed. Boston: Houghton-Mifflin, 1976. 629p.

Head's landmark one-volume history of broadcasting first appeared in 1956; the second in 1972; the third only four years later in 1976—a change of pace, he says, which reflects the accelerated growth of broadcasting studies. Each chapter has been reassessed and in large part rewritten, so that, in Head's words, "The third edition, therefore, is truly two removes from the first." Contents include a prologue chapter: "Broadcasting in America—and the World," dealing with comparative systems and U.S. influences abroad. Following this are sections on "Use and Management of Radio Energy," "Origin and Growth of Broadcasting," "Economics of Broadcasting," "Social Control of Broadcasting," and in conclusion, "Assessment: Influence of Broadcasting." Christopher Sterling has provided a comprehensive bibliographical section in which he cites background reading for each chapter, and Head has done a "Citations" section in which he lists alphabetically the sources he used and the sources cited by Sterling—some of which overlap. There is an index of names and subjects.

441. Heller, Melvin S., and Samuel Polsky. Studies in Violence and Television. New York: American Broadcasting Co., 1976. 503p.

A 500-page volume which gives the results of five years of empirical testing by the American Broadcasting Company to try to determine the effect of television violence upon the normal child and the emotionally disturbed child.

442. Higgins, Patricia Beaulieu, and Marla Wilson Ray. Television's Action Arsenal: Weapon Use in Prime Time. Washington 20006: U.S. Conference of Mayors, 1620 Eye St., N.W., 1978. 57p.

A study conducted "to fill a basic information gap in the television violence research literature, namely a

lack of information on the instruments of violence."
Appendices deal with the methodology.

443. Hill, Harold E. The National Association of Educational
     Broadcasters. Washington, D.C. 20036: National Asso-
     ciation of Educational Broadcasters, 1346 Connecticut
     Ave., 1954. 61p.

     Because of the close relationship of the NAEB to
     educational broadcasting in general, this history of the
     organization from its inception as the Association of
     College and University Broadcasting Stations in 1925 to
     the early 1950s serves also to trace the development of
     the movement in the U.S. Contains a bibliography.

444. Himmelweit, Hilde T., A. N. Oppenheim, and Pamela Vince.
     Television and the Child: An Empirical Study of the
     Effect of Television on the Young. London: Oxford
     University Press, 1958. 522p.

     Study based on a large sample of children in five
     cities who were questioned about their attitudes, inter-
     ests, and behavior and reexamined a year later to test
     changes that might have occurred. The authors looked
     for reactions to conflict, crime, and violence, and for
     effects on values, outlook, knowledge, school perform-
     ance, leisure, interests, and so on. Appendices describe
     methods and there is a bibliography, glossary, and index.
     For a study made in the U.S. shortly afterward, see Tele-
     vision in the Lives of Our Children by Schramm, Lyle, and
     Parker (No. 560).

445. Howe, Michael J. A. Television and Children. Camden,
     Conn.: Linnett Books, 1977. 157p.

     A study by a British psychologist in which he deals
     with what we know about television's various influences
     on children: their viewing habits; the kind of world
     they view; the informal learning that occurs; the effects
     of television violence; specific children's programs,
     including those like Sesame Street which are intended to
     help them learn; and finally, suggestions for dealing
     with problems the survey has brought to light. A biblio-
     graphy follows each chapter.

Hudson's Washington News Media Contacts Directory. (See
     No. 697.)

446. Hummel, Lani S. Cable Television: Issues of Congres-
     sional Concern. Washington: Library of Congress,
     Congressional Research Service, 1972. 55p.

133

Written "to provide the Congress with an overview of some of the major issues surrounding the growth of the new technology called 'cable television.'" Among these are the historical evolution of CATV; the conflict with TV; regulatory issues and issues of ownership and control; issues of legislative concern. An appendix lists specific Exploratory Research & Problem Assessment (ERPA) telecommunication projects, 1971-72, with the amount of research money designated. Footnotes and a brief annotated bibliography.

447. Instant World: A Report on Telecommunications in Canada. Ottawa K1A 059: Information Canada, 171 Slater St., 1971. 256p.

Summary of more than forty studies, covering the present state of Canadian telecommunications through the 1960s and the future propects. Divided into five parts: (1) The problem and the means; (2) Telecommunications and people; (3) Telecommunications today; (4) Telecommunications tomorrow; (5) The public interest. The complete list of studies from which this summary was made is given in an appendix. Indexed.

448. International Telecommunications Union. Catalogue of Films on Telecommunications, 1978-79. 6th ed. Geneva 20: ITU Film Library, Place des Nations, 1211, 1978. 65p. and supp.

An annotated listing of films available for loan from the ITU. Information for each film includes producer, language/languages, millimeters, length, black and white/color, and audience from whom intended--technical, semi-technical, entertainment. Indexed by subject, title, country, and language. Frequently updated.

449. International Television Almanac. New York 10019: Quigley Publishing Co., annual. (1929--.)

As in its companion volume, the International Motion Picture Almanac (No. 891), the term international is misleading. Except for a relatively few pages at the end of the book--"The World Market," "The Industry in Great Britain and Ireland," and "International Film Festivals"--emphasis is on the U.S. and Canada. Also, there is much duplication of material in both yearbooks, notably in the lengthy and valuable "Who's Who in Motion Pictures and Television," "Credit for Feature Films" of the year, "Film Distribution in Key Cities," "Services for Producers," "Feature Films from 1955 . . ." to the current year, and the international section. This is not to put down the usefulness of each volume, but to forewarn the user.

The "Who's Who" section is broad and includes producers, directors, writers, set designers, and other kinds of workers in film and broadcasting in addition to actors and actresses. Among other features are industry statistics; Emmy Award winners; talent and literary agencies; publicity representatives; companies (networks, set manufacturers, major producers, minor producers, major group station owners, cable TV); producer-distributors of programs, commercials, feature films, and shorts; commercial TV stations; advertising agencies; station representatives; organizations; primetime shows; new syndicated shows; trade publications and newspaper listings; and broadcasting codes.

450. Irwin, Manley R. The Telecommunications Industry: Integration vs. Competition. New York: Praeger, 1971. 223p.

Comprehensive study of vertical integration in the communications industry, providing an up-to-date analysis of the problem and demonstrating the interdependence of corporate conduct, regulatory and antitrust policies, and market structure. Contains tables and a bibliography of FCC dockets and reports; U.S. government reports, hearings, and studies; dockets and reports of state regulatory agencies; selected periodicals, conference papers, and books; judicial cases and decisions.

451. Issues in International Broadcasting. Charles Sherman and Donald Browne, eds. Washington 20036: Broadcast Education Association, 1771 N St., N.W., 1976. 171p. (Broadcast Monographs No. 2.)

A revision of papers originally given in a seminar. In the first section two participants debate cultural imperialism. Other sections contain broad-ranging discussions on the international flow of programs, national and international broadcasting systems, and teaching and research in international broadcasting. The appendix consists of a bibliography, "Comparative Systems of Broadcasting: A Bibliography, 1970-1973," by Benno Signitzer.

452. Jacobson, Robert E. Municipal Control of Cable Communications. New York: Praeger, 1977. 139p.

Should the cities take the initiative in developing cable communications systems? With this question in mind, Jacobson examines possible planning options, discussing the historical development of cable in an urban context, the possible role of telecommunications as a public good, the failure of private entrepreneurs to fill this role, and the means by which cities can have cable until their role is investigated. Appendices give three operating

135

public cable television systems. There are notes and a bibliography.

The Japanese Press. (<u>See</u> No. 701.)

453. Jennings, Ralph M., and Pamela Richard. <u>How to Protect</u>
    <u>Your Rights in Television and Radio</u>. New York 10010:
    United Church of Christ, Office of Communication,
    289 Park Ave. S., 1974. 167p.

    In preparing this comprehensive guide the authors
    clearly had in mind members of minority groups, organiza-
    tions, and institutions (such as the church) who as lay-
    men want to use broadcast facilities. They describe in
    detail the American system of broadcasting and the role
    of the public in making it work, and explain how to
    gather information and make effective use of it. Among
    topics they deal with are: regulation; the responsibil-
    ities of broadcasting, including the Fairness Doctrine,
    political broadcasting, advertising, contests, and the
    quality of broadcasting in general; the broadcaster's
    relationship with the public; Equal Employment Opportun-
    ities; how to start programming; renewal of broadcast
    licenses; FCC program reports and forms. Appendices
    contain a bibliography of FCC policies and other infor-
    mation about regulation, organizations offering assist-
    ance, license renewal dates, sample forms of reports,
    and selected FCC rules.

454. Johnson, Nicholas. <u>Test Pattern for Living</u>. New York:
    Bantam, 1972. 154p.

    In 1970 Johnson's <u>How to Talk Back to Your Television</u>
    <u>Set</u> (Little Brown) was published. In it Johnson, a
    maverick former member of the FCC, reminds the public that
    it owns the airwaves, gives facts about broadcasting as it
    exists in the U.S., and states what he feels can be done
    to improve it. <u>Test Pattern for Living</u> is a sequel and an
    update. Both books are essential reading for anyone who
    is not contented with the present state of television and
    wants to do something about it. Bibliography.

455. Johnson, Richard B. <u>Federal Regulations Relevant to the</u>
    <u>Structural Development of Telecommunications Industries</u>.
    Washington: Department of Commerce, Office of Telecom-
    munications, 1977. 61p. (OT Report 77-135.)

    Discusses major federal regulations and policies which
    have affected the structural development of telecommunica-
    tion industries, and provides a brief analysis of the FCC
    and judicial decisions which have interpreted the intent

of these regulations and policies. In addition, some of
the more significant non-FCC federal actions whose impact
may eclipse even the actions of the commission are discussed. Contains a list of FCC rulings and of legal citations.

456. Johnstone, Ian Anthony. The Right Channel. Dunedin, New
     Zealand: John McIndoe Ltd., 1968. 48p.

     A forty-eight page pamphlet which surveys TV in New
Zealand, with emphasis in the first portion on programming
and in the latter portion on questions of present and
future control.

457. Jones, William K. Cases and Materials on Electronic Mass
     Media: Radio, Television, and Cable. Mineola, N.Y.:
     Foundation Press, 1976. 474p.

     Cases and other documents, with explanatory discussion
by the author, which take up use of the radio spectrum,
licensing, functions of the FCC, concentration of control,
network practices, and regulation. Contains a table of
cases and statutory appendices giving the Communications
Act of 1934 and the Public Broadcasting Act.

458. Kaftanov, S. V., and others, eds. Radio and Television in
     the U.S.S.R. Washington, D.C.: U.S. Joint Publications
     Research Service, 1961. 243p. (Purchase photocopies
     from Photoduplication Service, Library of Congress.)

     Gives concise information about: radio and television
programs in the U.S.S.R.; some of the more important broadcasts of the central and local services; radio and television newspapers and magazines; the extent of the service;
the growing international ties; the activities of the All-
Union Scientific Research Sound Recording Institute and the
State House of Radio Broadcasting and Sound Recording in
Moscow; the basic material-technical means for radio broadcasting and television broadcasting.

459. Kahn, Frank J., ed. Documents of American Broadcasting.
     3d ed. Englewood Cliffs, N.J.: Prentice-Hall, 1978.
     638p.

     A collection of primary source materials in the field
of broadcasting history, regulation, and public policy,
including laws, speeches, FCC materials, industry codes,
decisions, reports, and other documents in their original
form. Most documents appear in their entirety, although
some have been abridged "to minimize the redundant and
irrelevant." An introduction and suggestions for further

reading precede each. The author has included a section, "Legal Citation and Glossary," for the uninitiated, and an index to legal decisions as well as a general index. There is a lengthy bibliography of references within the text. Some new material has been added to the third edition, and some old material deleted.

460. Kalba, Kas. The Video Implosion: Models for Reinventing Television. Palo Alto, Cal.: Aspen Institute Program on Communications and Society, 1974. 46p. (Series on Communications: An Occasional Paper.)

Kalba deals with TV as "a basic way of perceiving and communicating." He shows the manner in which technology expands the scope of the medium through low-cost production equipment, the emergence of cable, video-cassette programming outlets, and similar means, while at the same time practical difficulties place constraints on expansion. The evolution of video activity, the emerging institutional approaches, and the barriers which remain are discussed, as are some of the roles that government, industry, foundations, and community institutions might take to overcome obstacles. This is an interesting paper for anyone wishing to explore the larger significance of TV and its various technological manifestations.

461. Kamen, Ira. Questions and Answers about Pay TV. Indianapolis: H. W. Sams, 1973. 158p.

In question-and-answer format the author introduces the subject and gives its rules and regulations, its economics, the various over-the-air systems, the hotel and motel systems, and auxiliary services.

462. Katz, Elihu, and George Wedell. Broadcasting in the Third World: Promise and Performance. Cambridge, Mass.: Harvard University Press, 1978. 305p.

"The emphasis of our study is on process, on the dynamics of accommodating the phenomenon of broadcasting and its institutional forms to the surroundings of a developing country for which it was not in the first instance designed," say the authors. They are also interested in side effects, some of which were not anticipated. Basing their work on an extensive review of statistical and documentary data concerning broadcasting in ninety-one developing countries and on case studies of eleven of these, they assess the status quo in terms of structure, control, and social and cultural patterns. The eleven countries include Algeria, Brazil, Cyprus, Indonesia, Iran, Nigeria, Peru, Senegal, Singapore, Tanzania, and Thailand. Contains a number of tables of data throughout and an appendix of supplementary

tables. Two other appendices give methodology and levels
of development of the ninety-one selected countries. There
are numerous footnotes and an index. This is the most comprehensive review to date of the status of the media in
developing countries and of the implications. Winner of
the 1977 National Association of Education Broadcasters
Award.

463. Katzman, Natan, and Kenneth Wirt. Public Television Pro-
        gramming by Category, 1976. Washington: Corporation
        for Public Broadcasting, 1978. 135p.

        Second report on the numbers and characteristics of one
year of public television content, based on data provided
by public television licenses to CPB. Statistical data is
given in terms of hours for various kinds of programming--
instructional, general, news/public affairs, special or
target audiences, etc. It does not deal with individual
programs. Appendices give "secondary" schedules, methodology, and ITV grade level by subject matter. The first
of the series, Public Television Program Content, 1974
(CPB, 1975), also by Katzman, does the same thing for an
earlier period. Previously, starting in 1961, a series
of volumes entitled One Week of Educational Television was
produced by a variety of different people and organizations.

464. Kaye, Evelyn. The Family Guide to Children's Television:
        What to Watch, What to Miss, What to Change, and How to
        Do It. New York: Pantheon, 1974. 194p.

        This useful guidebook, prepared jointly by Action for
Children's Television and the American Academy of Pediat-
rics, answers many questions parents, teachers, and concerned adults ask. It includes the ratings of adult and
children's programs made by the National Association of
Better Broadcasting, an explanation of the structure of
broadcasting and the role of the FCC, discussions of violence and of commercials, and specific details of how and
to whom to protest. There is, in addition, a directory of
useful addresses in and outside of the U.S., a bibliography,
a list of the programs the National Association for Better
Broadcasting considers suitable for family viewing, and a
list of programs which contain excessive violence.

465. Kinsley, Michael E. Outer Space and Inner Sanctums: Gov-
        ernment, Business, and Satellite Communication. New
        York: Wiley, 1976. 280p.

        Makes an argument that cooperation between the legisla-
ture, the regulatory agencies, and the White House vis à
vis satellite communication is not in the best interest

139

either of technological advance in the field or of the
American people. It traces and documents the history of
U.S. communications satellites, beginning with the Communications Satellite Act of 1962, and analyzes what the
author contends is the bankruptcy of the semi-government
corporation. Footnotes and index.

466. Kittross, John M., comp. A Bibliography of Theses and
Dissertations in Broadcasting, 1920-1973. Washington:
Broadcast Education Association, 1978. 238p.

Has more than 4,300 main entries, each containing
author and title, degree awarded, institution, and date.
A serial number precedes each entry. There is a key word
index, a title-by-year index, and a topical index. Preceding the main entries Kittross has analyzed the theses
and dissertations according to schools and years and has
drawn some observations.

467. Klever, Anita. Women in Television. Philadelphia: West-
minster Press, 1975. 142p.

A slim volume written by a woman who is herself a producer, writer, and performer. She has interviewed thirty-
seven women in about as many jobs--station managers,
program directors, engineers, commentators, anchorwomen,
art designers, etc.--who tell very briefly how they "made
it" in a tough field and, having done so, how it feels.
Useful because it gives specific information about some
of the key women in broadcasting, including a few who got
there long before women's lib, and also because it gives
an idea of the range of jobs.

468. Koenig, Allen E., ed. Broadcasting and Bargaining: Labor
Relations in Radio and Television. Madison: University of Wisconsin Press, 1970. 344p.

A study on broadcasting unions covering four major
areas: a historical overview, legal decisions rendered
by the National Labor Relations Board and the courts,
specific problem areas confronting the industry and
unions, and a look at the future. Contains appendices:
"Report and Order of the FCC on Nondiscrimination in
Broadcast Employment Practices," and "Further Notice of
Proposed Rulemaking on Nondiscrimination in Broadcast
Employment Practices." Indexed and with footnotes at
the ends of sections.

469. Krasnow, Erwin G., and Lawrence D. Longley. The Politics
of Broadcast Regulation. 2d ed. New York: St. Martin's
Press, 1978. 213p.

Traces the historic development of broadcast regulation
and shows how regulations and public policy are determined
not only by the FCC but also by the courts, the broadcast
industry, citizens' groups, and the executive branch.
Each of these determinants is discussed at length. The
second half gives case studies involving FM radio, UHF
television, comparative license renewal policies, commercial time, and CB radio. A final chapter analyzes the
case studies and takes an overall look at broadcast regulation. There are footnotes, an annotated bibliography,
and an index.

470. Lackmann, Ron. _Remember Radio_. New York: Norton, 1970.
128p.

Intended to provide entertainment and provoke nostalgia
through photographs, scripts, and radio listings of programs in pretelevision days, this covers a range of popular
radio programs. Among other things, it provides about 300
pictures of characters known by voice rather than by face.

471. Land, Herman W., Associates, Inc. _Television and the
"Wired City": A Study of the Implications of a Change
in the Mode of Transmission_. Washington, D.C. 20036:
National Association of Broadcasters, Public Relations
Service, 1771 N St., N.W., 1968. 256p.

Prepared for the President's Task Force on Communications Policy by the National Association of Broadcasters,
this study reexamines the utilization of the useful
electronic spectrum in the light of present and future
technological breakthroughs such as communications satellites and coaxial cable transmission.

472. Laskin, Paul. _Communicating by Satellite: Report of the
Twentieth Century Fund Task Force on International
Satellite Communications_. New York 10021: Twentieth
Century Fund, 41 East 70th St., 1969. 78p.

A report which focuses on the way the international
community can best be served by the communications satellite rather than on who should own it.

473. Lazarsfeld, Paul F. _Radio and the Printed Page_. New York:
Duell, Sloan & Pearce, 1940. 354p.

Lazarsfeld pioneered in examining the role and effect
of broadcasting, at that time limited to radio. In this,
the first of half a dozen or more studies, he discusses
its interplay with reading.

474. Lazarsfeld, Paul. The People Look at Radio. Chapel Hill: University of North Carolina Press, 1946. 158p.
475. _____ and Patricia Kendall. Radio Listening in America: The People Look at Radio--Again. New York: Prentice-Hall, 1948. 178p.

Two studies conducted by the National Opinion Research Center in cooperation with the Bureau of Social Research are analyzed and interpreted by Paul Lazarsfeld (and Patricia Kendall on the latter). Both concern radio content and the communication behavior of the American people, with discussion on the role of criticism. Appendices give statistics. Indexed. Updated to 1963 by Steiner's The People Look at Television (No. 584).

476. Lazarsfeld, Paul F., and Frank N. Stanton, eds. Radio Research, 1941. New York: Duell, Sloan & Pearce, 1941. 328p.
477. _____. Radio Research, 1942-43. New York: Duell, Sloan & Pearce, 1944. 599p.
478. _____. Communications Research, 1948-1949. New York: Harper, 1949. 332p.

These are among the earliest anthologies (especially the first two volumes) in the new subject field of mass communications. The 1942-43 volume contains such classics as the articles on soap operas by Herta Herzog and by Rudolf Arnheim and Leo Lowenthal's "Biographies in Popular Magazines." It also has a section about radio in World War II.
The 1948-49 volume as well has some classic studies, among them "The Children Talk about Comics" by Katherine M. Wolf and Marjorie Fiske and "What Missing the Newspaper Means" by Bernard Berelson. Alex Inkeles has analyzed domestic broadcasting in the U.S.S.R. and Robert Merton and Lazarsfeld discuss research methodology. Both volumes are indexed.

479. Lent, John A., ed. Broadcasting in Asia and the Pacific: A Continental Survey of Radio and Television. Philadelphia: Temple University Press, 1978. 429p.

Asian and Pacific national broadcasting personnel and international communication scholars, trainers, and practitioners contributed to this anthology, which covers the instructional and functional foundations of broadcasting in forty-four countries, territories, and dependencies, ranging from Afghanistan on the periphery of West Asia to the South Pacific islands. All chapters are original except the introductory one, which is reprinted from the 1974 Asian Press and Media Directory, and many are by nationals from the countries described. For the most part topics covered are oriented to historical development,

control, ownership and pressures, programming and performance, facilities, financing and advertising, external services, audiences, training, and research. There is a long
section on cross-system functions which includes specialized
program services and international, regional, and national
assistance and cooperation. The bibliography lists primarily sources cited in the text; for further references
Lent refers us to his Asian Mass Communications: A Comprehensive Bibliography (No. 121). Indexed.

LeRoy, David J., and Christopher Sterling, eds. Mass News:
Practices, Controversies, and Alternatives. (See No. 716.)

480. Levin, Harvey J. Broadcast Regulation and Joint Ownership
of Media. New York: New York University Press, 1960.

Discusses the character of intermedia competition, the
pattern and trend of joint media ownership, the case for
separate ownership, economics of joint ownership, impact
of old media on new, competition in price and quality,
broadcast regulatory policy. Although some of this material has dated and the statistics have become historical,
its verities hold. An appendix giving sources of statistical data forms a bibliography, and there are indexes to
cases cited and to subjects.

481. Levin, Harvey J. The Invisible Resource: Use and Regulation of the Radio Spectrum. Baltimore: Johns Hopkins
Press, 1971. 432p.

Detailed account with emphasis on the technical and
economic. In four parts: the spectrum system, which discusses the technical basis of the problem, the major users
of spectrum, and potential goals of spectrum management;
the alternatives in spectrum allocation and management,
which discusses a free-market rather than a regulated
approach; the level of spectrum development; and
allocations-regulation-prices-service, which examines the
potential of competition as a means of preserving resources.

482. Lewels, Francisco J., Jr. The Uses of the Media by the
Chicano Movement: A Study in Minority Access. New York:
Praeger, 1974. 185p.

Chicanos feel that they and other minority groups are
denied access to the media because they lack funds and for
other reasons. This book documents the steps they have
taken and are taking to gain access, especially (although
not exclusively) to broadcasting. Contains detailed footnotes and a bibliography.

483. Lichty, Lawrence W., comp. World and International Broadcasting: A Bibliography. Washington: Association for Professional Broadcasting Education (now Broadcast Education Association), 1771 N St., N.W., 1971. 800p. (approx.).

A massive work encompassing close to 100,000 entries from 1920 through the 1960s, geographically and chronologically organized, unannotated, and covering about 150 countries and territories, excluding Great Britain, Canada, and the U.S., but including thirteen pages on China. Preceding and following this geographic listing are sections on bibliographies and general references; on general works; and on international ones. In addition to books and periodicals, there are articles from the New York Times. Lichty says that he has not been selective nor has he verified items, but has depended upon other bibliographies, indexes, and listings.

This work is updated by Benno Signitzer's "Comparative Systems of Broadcasting: A Bibliography, 1970-1973," an appendix to Issues in International Broadcasting (Charles Sherman and Donald Browne, eds. Washington: Broadcast Education Association, 1976. Broadcast Monograph No. 2). Signitzer has updated it further in International Communications, 1975-1977: A Selected Bibliography (Salzburg, Austria: University of Salzburg, Department of Mass Communications).

484. Lichty, Lawrence W., and Malachi C. Topping, comps. American Broadcasting: A Source Book on the History of Radio and Television. New York: Hastings House, 1975. 723p.

An anthology of ninety-three selections (one third of which were never before published), chosen to give "as complete and accurate" a picture as possible of American broadcasting from its prehistory to 1975. Divided into eight parts: technical, stations, networks, economics, employment, programming, audiences, and regulation, each preceded by the compilers' commentaries. There is a second table of contents, which is chronological, and more than fifty original tables.

485. Liebert, Robert M., John M. Neale, and Emily S. Davidson. The Early Window: Effects of Television on Children and Youth. New York: Pergamon Press, 1973. 193p.

The authors, all psychologists, have amassed an impressive amount of facts and data, statistical and otherwise, on TV and children, and have synthesized it not only to tell us some of its possible effects but also to explain briefly about its political and economic structure and its regulation. Among topics discussed are violence,

advertising, social stereotypes, and educational programs
such as "Sesame Street." An appendix abstracts sixty
studies. Also, each chapter lists references used. There
is an author-title index. Provides excellent background
for local groups who want to pursue the subject.

486. Lisann, Maury. <u>Broadcasting to the Soviet Union: Inter-
    national Politics and Radio</u>. New York: Praeger, 1975.
    199p.

    Deals chronologically with Soviet radio as it is influ-
    enced by governmental policies, and in a final chapter
    probes opinion and trends. Each chapter is footnoted and
    there is a lengthy bibliography and an index.

487. McCavitt, William E., comp. <u>Radio and Television: A
    Selected, Annotated Bibliography</u>. Metuchen, N.J.:
    Scarecrow Press, 1978. 229p.

    Contains 1,100 listings of books and other printed
    materials, including an extensive list of periodicals,
    associated with the various aspects of broadcasting and
    covering the period from 1920 to 1976. The author says
    that it is intended both to serve as a buying list and
    to suggest what is needed by showing what now exists, but
    a third use can also be included--to provide a starting
    place for laymen who need to explore a given area.
    Entries are arranged under twenty-one subject or form
    headings, most of which are further subdivided: surveys,
    history, regulation, organization, programming, produc-
    tion (here's where the "how to" books are found), minor-
    ities, responsibility, society, criticism, public broad-
    casting, audience, cable TV, research, broadcasting
    careers, international, technical, bibliographies,
    annuals, periodicals, and reference materials. Annota-
    tions are descriptive rather than evaluative, which is
    inevitable in a bibliography of this scope. A few items
    are unannotated, perhaps because McCavitt feels the titles
    give sufficient indication of contents. There is no sub-
    ject index, which limits its usefulness as a reference
    tool, although this is somewhat compensated for by the
    specificity of the subject arrangement. But these are
    small matters. This bibliography is a valuable contri-
    bution to the literature of broadcasting.

488. McGraw, Walter. <u>Toward the Public Dividend: A Report on
    Satellite Telecommunications and the Public Interest
    Satellite Association</u>. New York 10036: The Public
    Interest Satellite Association, 55 West 44th St., 1977.
    31p.

This fact-filled pamphlet gives a point of view not
often found in U.S. literature on satellites. The Public
Interest Satellite Association (PISA) contends that the
communication possibilities of satellites are enormous
and that their use in the public interest conflicts
sharply with the profits of the private interests. It
explains to the layman in terms as simple as possible why
PISA believes this is so and why it should be otherwise,
and provides a clear and concise picture of the technology, economics, regulation, and potential of satellites.
There is an outline in tabular form of "The World Scene"
and "The Home Market." It also gives the Consumer Federation of America Satellite Policy Resolution.

489. MacKay, Ian K. Broadcasting in Australia. Melbourne:
     Melbourne University Press, 1957. 216p.
490. _____. Broadcasting in New Zealand. Wellington,
     Australia: Reed, 1953. 150p.
491. _____. Broadcasting in Nigeria. Ibadan, Nigeria:
     Ibadan University Press, 1964. 159p.
492. _____. Broadcasting in Papua, New Guinea. Carlton,
     Australia: Melbourne University Press, 1976. 190p.

"This book," says the author in his Acknowledgments in
his latest in the series, Broadcasting in Papua, New Guinea,
"completes a quartet. Each book was written to provide a
description and appraisal of broadcasting in four countries
where I have worked." The volume on New Zealand predates
television.

493. Maclauren, W. Rupert, with R. Joyce Harman. Invention and
     Innovation in the Radio Industry. New York: Arno Press,
     c1940, 1971. 304p.

A history of radio and early TV, first published by
Macmillan, from the time of the scientific pioneers of
radio to 1940, with emphasis on the technology involved.
Appendices include "The Elements of Modern Radio Communication" and "Radio Patent Litigation." Bibliography and
index.

494. McMahon, Morgan E., comp. Vintage Radio: Harold Green-
     wood's Historical Album Expanded with More Old Ads,
     Illustrations, and Many Photos of Wireless and Radio
     Equipment. 2d ed. Palos Verdes Peninsula, Cal.:
     Vintage Radio, Box 2045, 1973. 263p.

In the early days of wireless and radio, a man named
Harold Greenwood put together a collection of pictures
from many sources illustrating the early apparatus used
for broadcasting and receiving, with textual explanations

when necessary. This book is now out of print. Morgan McMahon has compiled a similar one, described in the subtitle, with illustrations and materials of all sorts, drawn mainly from old ads and catalogs, which should prove useful to those interested in equipment used between the late nineteenth century and the first two decades of this one. In addition to the main text, which shows the many types of receivers and transmitters, there is a survey at the beginning and a guide to collecting. Indexed. A second book, A Flick of the Switch, 1930-1950, also published by Vintage Radio (1975), takes up where the earlier book leaves off, covering early television as well as radio.

495. Macy, John W., Jr. To Irrigate a Wasteland: The Struggle to Shape a Public Television System in the United States. Berkeley: University of California, 1974. 186p.

A capsule history of public broadcasting in America, with an inside account of recent developments and consideration as to how it may be financed without commercials or partisan control. Appendices give, among other things, a glossary of organizational terms in public TV's national organizations; public TV licenses, call numbers, locations; text of Public Law 90-129, Public Broadcasting Act of 1967; growth pattern--1969-72; characteristics of PTV station types, 1971; U.S. noncommercial compared with U.S. commercial TV stations; source of funds by PTV station type, 1966-71; TV service cost by country; public TV programming sources, 1971. Indexed.

496. Maddison, John. Radio and Television in Literacy: A Survey of the Use of the Broadcasting Media in Combating Illiteracy among Adults. Paris: UNESCO, 1971. 82p. (Reports and Papers on Mass Communication No. 62.)

Gives information on the uses of radio and TV in connection with literacy work in forty countries in various parts of the world.

497. Maddox, Brenda. Beyond Babel: New Directions in Communications. London: Deutsch, 1972. 288p.

"This book is about change and resistance to change in communications," says Maddox. Among the many new techniques and devices, she has chosen the three she feels will be "the ingredients of the revolution in communications," which can make possible--or has already made possible--cheap, portable, instantaneous two-way communication from one part of the world to another: satellites, cable television, and telephones. She discusses the case

147

of Intelsat in detail. Emphasis is historical and technological. There is a glossary of technological terms,
a bibliography, and an index.

498. Magnant, Robert S. Domestic Satellite: An FCC Giant Step
     toward Competitive Telecommunications Policy. Boulder,
     Colo.: Westview Press, 1977. 296p.

     The main hypothesis of this review of the factors that
have influenced the FCC's domestic satellite policy is that
the decision involved was possibly the most important and
complex in the FCC's history and carries a lasting potential for benefit to the public. Specifically, it discusses:
"Historical Foundations and Boundary Conditions," including
the regulatory origins of the FCC and the common carrier
industry, and the constraints placed upon them by business
and technology; "The Precedents of DOMSAT," including the
Communications Satellite Act of 1962 and space-age regulation, some of which involves international communications;
"The Development of DOMSAT Policy," including the basic
issues in terms of technology and competition, and the
policy makers; "DOMSAT Policy Today," including technological trends and the entry of IBM into the field with its
Satellite Business System (SBS) and potential competition
from AT&T. Contains a lengthy bibliography and appendices
consisting of letters, documents, and interviews from which
the author collected his data, a chronology of individuals
connected with DOMSAT, and further analysis of the ALOHA
concept.

499. Mankiewicz, Frank, and Joel Swerdlow. Remote Control:
     Television and the Manipulation of American Life. New
     York: Times Books, 1977. 308p.

     A damning array of facts compiled and conclusions drawn
from a wide variety of sources, including literally thousands of studies and a number of intensive interviews with
men and women in the profession. The authors examine TV
in the light of violence, family-hour programming, news,
sex roles, reading, learning and behavior in children, con-
sumership, and our political and quasi-political institutions. Their conclusions about the part TV plays in our
lives are not reassuring. There is a sizable bibliography
and an index.

500. Manning, Willard G., Jr. The Supply of Primetime Enter-
     tainment Television Programs. Stanford, Cal. 94305:
     Center for Research in Economic Growth, 470 Encina Hall,
     1973. 78p. (Research Memoranda series, Memorandum
     No. 152.)

A survey of the industry supplying entertainment programs to the TV networks and the syndication market,
analyzing quantitative data from various public services
in order to characterize the economic structure of the
industry and describing by means of theoretical models
the size, distribution, and types of firms. Includes
sources of programming supply, domestic syndication, com-
petitiveness of supply, prospects for cable. Appendices
include tables. Bibliography.

Marzio, Peter C. The Men and Machines of American Journalism.
    (See No. 723.)

501. Meeting of Experts on the Use of Space Communication by
        the Mass Media. New York: UNESCO Publications Center,
        1966. 32, 8p.

    Report of a UNESCO meeting at which a number of related
    subjects were discussed: technical capabilities, economics,
    social implications, transmission of news, radio and tele-
    vision broadcasting, education, cultural exchange.

Mehr, Linda Harris. Motion Pictures, Television, and Radio: A
        Union Catalogue of Manuscripts and Special Collections
        in the Western United States. (See No. 941.)

502. Mission and Goals, Tasks and Responsibilities. Washington:
        Corporation for Public Broadcasting, Office of Public
        Affairs, 1976. 14p.

    Guidelines for CPB made by its board of directors in
    1976.

Moment of Truth. (See No. 630.)

503. Morris, Norman S. Television's Child. Boston: Little,
        Brown, 1971. 238p.

    Explores possible effects of television on children and
    gives guidelines for parents. Evidence and suggestions
    are based upon extensive interviews with clinical psychia-
    trists and psychologists, educators, television executives,
    producers, performers, advertisers, parents, and children
    themselves. The author has pulled the various viewpoints
    together and has tried to maintain impartiality toward the
    medium, even though he is a newscaster. Bibliography.

504. Mosco, Vincent. Broadcasting in the United States: Inno-
        vative Challenge and Organizational Control. Norwood,
        N.J.: Ablex, 1979. 168p.

Mosco makes a case that established interests--primarily
the owners of radio and TV stations--have induced the FCC
to respond conservatively to FM radio, UHF TV, cable TV,
and subscription TV. He contends that this has resulted
in the concentration of political and economic power in the
hands of the broadcasting industry and has restricted the
audiences' choice of programs. He then reviews proposals
that have been made to change the regulatory structure, and
suggests new alternatives. Contains appendices, a bibliography, and an author and subject index.

505. Mullick, K. S. <u>Tangled Tapes: The Inside Story of Indian</u>
      <u>Broadcasting</u>. New Delhi: Sterling Publishers, 1974.
      159p.

      A detailed study of the structure and performance,
imprint on national life, and contribution to social, cultural, and economic progress of the All India Radio. The
author, who has spent thirty years with the organization,
feels that much of its potential has been stifled by
bureaucratic red tape. He suggests a pattern which he
feels would give AIR greater significance.

Murphy, Sharon. <u>Other Voices: Black, Chicano, and American</u>
      <u>Indian Press</u>. (<u>See</u> No. 730.)

506. Musolf, Lloyd D., ed. <u>Communications Satellites in Polit-</u>
      <u>ical Orbit</u>. San Francisco: Chandler, 1968. 189p.

      Beginning with the organization of the Communication
Satellite Corporation in 1962 and progressing through the
next half-decade, the editor has traced its history through
the use of official documents--testimony of interested
parties, both public and private, before congressional committees; reports made by these committees; interchanges
between protagonists on the floor of the House or Senate;
presidential messages and statements; and policy pronounce-
ments by administrative agencies. Through use of these
excerpts, he has been successful in revealing some of the
decision-making processes that structured an important
technological innovation. A valuable sourcebook.

507. Namurois, Albert. <u>Structure and Organization of Broad-</u>
      <u>casting in the Framework of Radiocommunications</u>.
      Ch-1211 Geneva 20: European Broadcasting Union, 1, Rue
      de Varembe, 1972. 211p. (Legal and Administrative
      Series, Monograph No. 8.)

      The author states that his aim has been "to assemble,
classify and coordinate a series of notions on the international regulation of radiocommunications, and to make
available a body of knowledge concerning the organization

of a broadcasting service that is based on firsthand
experience." He discusses first the general system of
telecommunications--sources of communication law, the
ITU, the structure of telecommunications and principles
governing international communications, the main rules
of radio, the ownership of space. The second part deals
with radio and TV services--evolution in the organization
and structure of radio and TV, definition and mission of
broadcasting service, promotional methods, structural and
organizational problems. A final section contains a bibliography of periodical articles and documents, one section of which is geographical; a list of diagrams,
acronyms, and abbreviations; a list of members; and the
text of Act No. 72-553 of 3 July 1972 providing for the
constitution of French broadcasting. (An earlier edition,
The Organization of Broadcasting, now out of print in the
English edition, appeared in 1964.)

508. NCTA Cable Services Directory. Washington 20006:
      National Cable Television Association, 908 Sixteenth
      St., N.W., annual. (1974--.)

      Formerly titled Local Origination Directory, this is
an annual statistical summary of programming activities
of the cable systems throughout the U.S. The major portion is taken up with a state-by-state profile of systems
involved in some form of local origination. Information
for each station includes the number of communities
served, subscribers and potential subscribers, equipment
capabilities, advertising, and kinds of programs. An
introduction summarizes survey findings, and a brief section discusses library uses. Final sections index programming by category and list colleges and universities
involved in cable TV.

Network Rates and Data. (See No. 1143.)

509. Newcomb, Horace. TV: The Most Popular Art. New York:
      Anchor, 1974. 272p.

510. _____, ed. Television: The Critical View. New York:
      Oxford University Press, 1976. 314p.

      In both of these books Newcomb approaches TV from a
humanistic vantage point. In the first title he applies
humanistic analysis to TV as popular culture--soap opera,
westerns, mystery and detective, sports, news, and various
other genres in TV programming--in order to find aesthetic
dimensions which will help to establish some of its cultural functions. He believes that the aesthetic and
social scientific viewpoints are not necessarily at odds,
but might supplement one another in an attempt to discover

151

the total meaning of the mass media. Bibliography and index.

In the second title he again seeks to establish and define the role of TV in American culture through twenty articles by TV critics and social scientists. In the broadest sense the approach is humanistic, but is backed by social science research. It is in three parts: the first, "Seeing Television," contains essays on specific popular shows like "The Waltons," "All in the Family," and "The Mary Tyler Moore Show"; the second, "Thinking about Television," considers how TV affects our view of the world and of ourselves; the third, "Defining Television," presents articles on the aesthetics of TV compared to other art forms and other media.

511. New Zealand. Committee on Broadcasting. The Future of Broadcasting for New Zealand: Report, 31 July 1973. Presented to the House of Representatives by Leave. Wellington: A. R. Shearer, Government Printer, 1973. 205p.

In the early 1970s the Minister of Broadcasting for New Zealand set up a committee to create a new system of control and operation of broadcasting (including TV) under publicly owned but competitive channels. This report contains its conclusions and the legislation it envisages. Included are plans for various types of radio and TV broadcasting--educational, religious, news, sports; revenues and finances; advertising and programming standards; transmission and technical services; and other aspects. Appendices give trends of finances in graph form; staff payments and numbers comparison; maps which show regional advisory committees, TV microwave linking systems, existing public national and concert station coverage, public commercial station coverage.

512. Noble, Grant. Children in Front of the Small Screen. Beverly Hills, Cal.: Sage, 1975. 256p.

A synthesis of literature on the subject of children and TV, with an introductory article, "Why Is Television So Popular?" Noble has some interesting theories, influenced by his experiences as a westerner contrasted with time he spent in India observing peoples whose lives were complete without mass media and even without literacy. Bibliography and index.

513. Noll, Roger G., Merton J. Pec, and John J. McGowan. Economic Aspects of Television Regulation. Washington: Brookings Institution, 1973. 342p.

The authors analyze the economic, technical, and institutional factors which determine the TV industry's performance with two objectives in mind: to examine the industry's
potential for improved performance, especially in the number, variety, and quality of programs offered; and to
evaluate FCC regulation vis à vis its efforts to improve
local programming. One chapter discusses TV in connection
with consumer welfare; others discuss commercials, subscription, cable, services, and public. An appendix deals with
instructional TV. Indexed.

514. Nordenstreng, Kaarle, and Tapio Varis. Television Traffic--
A One-Way Street? A Survey and Analysis of International
Flow of Television Programme Material. Paris: UNESCO,
1974. (Reports and Papers on Mass Communication No. 70.)

The first part of this study is a sixty-two-page international inventory of the composition of TV programs,
particularly from the point of view of program material
imported to a country from outside, and a survey of the
international networks for sale and exchange of program
material for TV. Included are numerous tables, charts,
and graphs. The second part is the essence of a symposium
held at the University of Tampere and is designed to comment upon the hard facts contained in the study, which was
also made at the University of Tampere.

Norland, Rod. Names and Numbers: A Journalist's Guide to the
Most Needed Information Sources and Contacts. (See No. 737.)

Overseas Press Club of America and American Correspondents Overseas, 1975 Membership Directory. (See No. 741.)

515. Owen, Bruce M., Jack H. Beebe, and Willard G. Manning, Jr.
Television Economics. Lexington, Mass.: Lexington,
1974. 218p.

"Glamour and social influence notwithstanding, television is a business," say the authors of this book
intended to make the intricacies of TV economics understand-
able to the general reader. It is in two parts, the first
emphasizing theory and analysis, the second emphasizing
policy. Among topics included are programming supply,
theories of program choice, behavior of networks, improving
TV performance with both limited and unlimited channels,
public TV, and related policy issues. There are many
tables, a bibliography, and an index.

516. Parish, James Robert. Actors' Television Credits, 1950-
1972. Metuchen, N.J.: Scarecrow Press, 1973. 869p.

517. Parish, James Robert, with Mark Trost. Actors' Television
     Credits. Supplement 1, 1978. 423p.

   Detailed credits on a selected list of TV performers
("those who have contributed most uniquely to the industry.
Due to space limitations the author has had selectively to
eliminate some of the more hardworking but less essential
actors . . ."). The main source used to gather the information was TV Guide, which the author and his associates
have virtually indexed by player. Names are arranged
alphabetically, with information as to the type of program
(a series, a single episode, a pilot, and so on) and the
nature of the role (hostess, narrator, etc.). Areas not
covered: documentaries, game shows, live special events,
news shows, quiz shows, sports shows, talk shows, theatrical motion pictures, variety shows.
   The supplement adds new entries and amplifies, corrects,
and deletes information in the earlier volume where necessary. Cut-off date is 1976.

518. Park, Rolla Edward, Leland L. Johnson, and Barry Fishman.
     Projecting the Growth of Television Broadcasting:
     Implications for Spectrum Use. Santa Monica, Cal.:
     RAND, 1976. 308p.

   The purposes of this study, prepared for the FCC, are
(1) to estimate the number of commercial UHF TV stations
that are likely to come on the air between the present and
1990, and (2) to determine whether spectrum resources
already allocated will be adequate to meet this demand.
Appendices include: "A Model of the Determination of the
Number of Viable UHF Television Stations," "The Relationship between Television Service and Television Viewing,"
"Television Market Revenue," "Individual Station Shares
of Television Market Revenue," "Television Station Profits," and "A Simultaneous Equations Model of Televison
Station Revenue and Expenditure" by Stanley M. Besen.

519. Parker, Derek. Radio: The Great Years. Newton Abbot,
     Devon, England; Pomfret, Vt.: David & Charles, 1977.
     160p.

   Light-hearted account of British radio, beginning in
1901. Indexed.

520. Patterns of Discrimination against Women in the Film and
     Television Industries: Special Report by the Associa-
     tion of Cinematograph and Television Technicians.
     London W1V 6DD: The Association, 2 Soho Square, 1975.
     62p.

154

A thorough investigation of all aspects of the problem.
The first part deals with such generalities as attitudes,
educational and social training and facilities, job structure and security, right to work and rights of work, repre-
sentation in the ACTT, and economic and legal position.
The second part deals more specifically with types of
position--laboratory, TV (ITV and BBC), film production.
Appendices include "Women in the BBC," "Educational Television," "Women in the French Film Industry," "The Working Women's Charter," "Maternity Leave Schedules," "Sources
of Information" (few of them books), "Glossary," "Recommendations," and tables on which much of the data is based.

521. Patterson, Thomas E., and Robert D. McClure. The Unseeing
     Eye: The Myth of Television Power in National Politics.
     New York: Putnam, 1976. 218p.

The authors asked themselves two questions: How manipulative is political TV? How informative is political TV?
Conducting nearly 2,000 hour-long interviews before, during,
and after the 1972 presidential campaign to determine how
voters' opinions changed, they came out with findings that
contradict previous prevailing assumptions about TV's power.
One factor emphasized in their research is the effectiveness of political commercials. Appendices describe methodology and give detailed tables of figures.

522. Paulu, Burton. British Broadcasting: Radio and Tele-
     vision in the United Kingdom. Minneapolis: University
     of Minnesota Press, 1956. 457p.
523. _____. British Broadcasting in Transition. Minneapolis:
     University of Minnesota Press, 1961. 250p.

The first book analyzes British broadcasting from the
standpoint of organization, history, type of programming,
and audience, and discusses in detail BBC and ITA. Its
sequel updates it and discusses the effects of competition
on British broadcasting. Both contain bibliographies and
indexes.

524. Paulu, Burton. Radio and Television Broadcasting in Eas-
     tern Europe. Minneapolis: University of Minnesota
     Press, 1974. 592p.

Describes and appraises the theory and practice of
radio and TV broadcasting in the Soviet Union, East Germany, Poland, Czechoslovakia, Hungary, Romania, Yugoslavia,
and Albania. Covers the following: basic information
theory, legal structure, finance, technical facilities,
stations and networks, program objectives, principal
program areas, audience research, and broadcasting for

listeners. Among program types discussed are news, current affairs, drama, music, documentaries, educational and entertainment film, and sports. There are comprehensive footnotes; a bibliography; and an index of persons, places, and subjects.

525. Peers, Frank W. The Politics of Canadian Broadcasting, 1920-1951. Toronto: University of Toronto Press, 1969. 446p.

526. _____. The Public Eye: Television and the Politics of Canadian Broadcasting, 1952-1968. Toronto: University of Toronto Press, 1979. 459p.

The first volume traces the beginnings and development of Canada's mixed system of private and public ownership of broadcasting, which was then almost exclusively radio. Peers gives particular attention to the reasons that Canadian radio diverged from the primarily commercial U.S. model and shows how and why it reflects values different from those prevailing in the British or U.S. system. The second volume traces the beginnings and development of TV from 1952 to the passing of the Broadcast Act in 1968, focusing on decisions made by governments on broadcasting activities and the circumstances under which they were made. Indexes in both volumes.

527. Pelton, Joseph N., and Marcellus S. Snow, eds. Economic and Policy Problems in Satellite Communications. New York: Praeger, 1977. 242p.

In this anthology the authors of the various articles document their contentions that "in the area of communications satellites, as elsewhere, scientific and technological capability has outstripped the ability to adapt technology to human well-being through an appropriate set of institutions and arrangements," with consequences that can be devastating. In Part I, Snow, Richard W. Nelson, and Kenneth B. Stanley discuss economic issues; in Part II, Pelton, Hamid Mowlana, and Jack Oslund deal with policy issues. Appendices give the world's communications satellite systems, existing and planned, and the major cable systems of the world. Chapters have bibliographic notes, as has the appendix giving satellite systems, and there is an index.

528. Perry, Martin Kent. Recent Trends in the Structure of the Cable Television Industry. Stanford, Cal.: Department of Economics, Stanford University, 1974. 40p. (Studies in Industry Economics No. 44.)

An examination of the increase of concentration and vertical integration since 1965, and implications of this
increase as it affects the public. The author uses brief
corporate histories of leading firms and industry statistics to make his point. Footnotes.

529. Piepe, Anthony, Miles Emerson, and Judy Lannon. Television and the Working Class. Lexington, Mass.: Saxon
House/Lexington, 1975. 170p.

An attempt to measure the social consequences of TV in
the flow and distribution of values in society--specifi-
cally, British society--as it relates to class and strat-
ification. Findings are based on the results of two
surveys. Of special interest is a lengthy review of the
literature, much of which deals with TV effects.

Pilkington Report. See Great Britain. Committee on Broadcasting (1960), Report (No. 425).

530. Pitts, Michael R. Radio Soundtracks: A Reference Guide.
Metuchen, N.J.: Scarecrow Press, 1976. 161p.

The purpose of this book is to provide information on
the collecting of oldtime radio entertainment broadcasts
which are still in existence, the forms in which they may
be obtained (i.e., tape recordings, LP records, compilation albums), and the sources from which they may be
bought. Arrangement is by form, with an index to shows.

531. Ploman, Edward W. A Guide to Satellite Communication.
Paris: UNESCO, 1972. 35p. (Reports and Papers on
Mass Communication No. 66.)

Brief survey intended to provide decision makers with
basic information about the characteristics, uses, and
implications of communication satellites.

532. Poindexter, Ray. Golden Throats and Golden Tongues: The
Radio Announcers. Conway, Ark. 72032: River Road
Press, 1978. 233p.

During recent years there has been considerable radio
nostalgia, with emphasis on comedians, singers, actors,
and musicians, but little or none on announcers, complains
Poindexter, who sets about to remedy the situation. His
aim in this book is to capture, in a paragraph or two
about each, the essense of the style of hundreds of
announcers in the heyday of radio. Indexed by name.

The Politics of Broadcasting, 1971-1972. (See No. 630.)

533. Poteet, G. Howard. Published Radio, Television, and Film
     Scripts: A Bibliography. Troy, N.Y.: Whitston, 1975.
     245p.

     The author tells us that although a few incomplete list-
     ings of film scripts exist, there is no index to the
     scripts used in radio and TV. This is the first attempt
     to index all three media. Both excerpts and complete
     scripts have been included. Texts come from monographs
     and collections. Arrangement is alphabetical by media.
     For radio and TV, transcripts as well as scripts are
     listed, as are dates on which each program was broadcast
     and the name of the author when available. For films,
     both complete works and fragments have been included, but
     no novelized scripts, music sheets, or picture books.
     Contains an author index.

534. Powledge, Fred. Public Television: A Question of Survival;
     A Report of the American Civil Liberties Union. Wash-
     ington: Public Affairs Press, 1972. 46p.

     Surveys concisely the problems facing public television
     at the time of this writing--the threats of censorship and
     lack of funds, and the even more basic problem as to how,
     or whether, federal money should support a free medium of
     communication. Appendices give the 1967 Public Broadcast-
     ing Act and tell where PBC's money goes.

535. Pre-School Children and Television: Two Studies Carried
     Out in Three Countries. Erentraud Homberg, ed. New
     York: K. G. Saur; Munich: Verlag Dokumentation Saur,
     1978. 78p.

     Presents summaries of two major studies: "Pre-School
     Children and Television," carried out by the Centre for
     Mass Communication at the University of Leicester under
     James D. Halloran, and "The Role of Television and Other
     Media in the Lives of Pre-School Children," carried by
     Sveriges Radio, Weiden, and directed by Leni Filipson
     from its Audience and Research Department. Each study
     presents the following information: significance, influ-
     ence, position relative to other media, response to con-
     tents, and popularity of particular programs.

536. Program Material Available from Government and Civic
     Agencies for Use by Radio Stations: A Source for Pub-
     lic Service Programming. Washington: National Asso-
     ciation of Broadcasters, 1973. 22p.
537. Program Material Available from Government and Civic
     Agencies for Use by Television Stations: A Source for
     Public Service Programming. Washington: National
     Association of Broadcasters, 1973. 46p.

Directories containing lists of transcriptions, tapes,
announcements, and other program material available from
government and civic organizations for local broadcasting.
All items are free unless a charge is specifically cited.

538. Prowitt, Marsha O'Bannon. Guide to Citizen Action in
      Radio and Television. New York 10010: United Church
      of Christ, Office of Communication, 289 Park Ave. S.,
      1971. 44p.

      Describes FCC standards for programming and performance
      and details effective public action. Appendices list
      organizations which give assistance in this area and sources
      from which materials can be obtained.

539. Public Perceptions of Television and Other Mass Media: A
      Twenty-Year Review, 1959–1978. New York 10022: Tele-
      vision Information Office, 745 Fifth Ave., 1979. 23p.

      A summary of twenty years of surveys by the Roper Organ-
      ization in which trend questions were asked about the pub-
      lic's attitude toward TV vis à vis other media (excluding
      film). Results have shown "the growing ascendancy of tele-
      vision as a primary news source. . . . We have also sought
      dimensions of opinion that would throw more light on the
      viewer's relationship," especially about bias and credi-
      bility, "dire effects and imputed powers," the commercial
      system and possible shortcomings, and the role of govern-
      ment agencies in determining content. In all questions
      commercial television comes out a winner.

540. Public Television: A Program for Action. New York: Har-
      per & Row, 1967. 254p.
541. A Public Trust: The Report of the Carnegie Commission on
      the Future of Public Broadcasting. New York: Bantam,
      1979. 401p.

      Two reports made twelve years apart, both of which
      examine public TV in its various aspects. The earlier one
      concerns prospects for a broader base. It defines the
      term, summarizes the report, and discusses the opportunity,
      the present system, the commission's proposal, and the
      specific type of programming that could emerge. There is
      a list of various stations operating as of the end of 1966,
      and supplementary papers by various experts concerning
      technology, costs, legal aspects, relations of stations
      with FCC, financial and operating reports for the previous
      year, and estimates of audiences, 1965, 1966.
      The later report designs a new structure for public
      television around four areas: programming, public partic-
      ipation, financing, and technology dissemination. This is
      preceded by a summary of findings and recommendations.

Appendices include a chronology of public broadcasting; a
statistical overview; an analysis of costs; discussions of
facilities, new technologies and services, and legal
status; and a listing of public TV and radio services.

542. Public Television: Toward Higher Ground; Report and Papers
     from the Aspen Institute Conference on Public Broadcast-
     ing. Palo Alto, Cal. 94304: Aspen Institute Program on
     Communications and Society, 770 Welch Road, 1975. 70p.

     A policy paper in the form of an anthology which recom-
     mends two essentials if public broadcasting is to move
     ahead: long-range federal funding and good programming.
     Indexed.

543. A Qualitative Study: The Effect of Television on People's
     Lives. Washington 20036: Corporation for Public Broad-
     casting, Communications Research, 1978. 91p.

     A four-city (Philadelphia, Minneapolis, Denver, Houston)
     study, conducted by means of discussion groups, to discover
     how representative television viewers "interacted with
     their television sets, what their viewing habits were, how
     they planned for their viewing time, which members of the
     family had a strong say-so in program selection, what type
     and what specific programs were liked and disliked and what
     programs or televised events had made a strong impact on
     them." Also, how they felt about the time spent watching,
     and their attitudes toward public television.

544. Queeney, K. M. Direct Broadcast Satellites and the United
     Nations. Winchester, Mass.: Sijthoff & Noordhoff,
     1978. 327p.

     Follows the treatment of the direct broadcast satellites
     issue within the U.N., showing the struggle for control by
     various factions in terms of both technical and international
     diplomatic regulatory trends. Appendices give important
     draft conventions and proposals to past U.N. work sessions to
     which reference is made in the text. Bibliographic notes.

545. Quicke, Andrew. Tomorrow's Television: An Examination of
     British Broadcasting, Past, Present and Future. Berk-
     hamsted, Herts., England: Lion, 1976. 240p.

     ". . . intended to give the general reader an insight
     into the complexities and the politics of the television
     world, and to explain some of the problems affecting the
     future of television in Britain that will have to be
     solved by the Committee looking into the future of tele-
     vision under the chairmanship of Lord Annan," says the
     author, who makes no claim to original research. Among

aspects he treats are "The Populists versus the Elitists," "The New Priesthood," "Television and Politics," "Television and Belief," "Sociology and the Mass Media," "Cassettes, Cable and Satellites," "Control and Censorship." Quicke is a television producer. Indexed.

Quinn, James. The Film and Television as an Aspect of European Culture. (See No. 977.)

546. Radio and Television Bibliography: A Guide to Reference Material on Radio and Television Broadcasting. Washington: National Association of Broadcasters, Public Relations Department, 1974. 24p.

An unannotated list, broken down by subject, of about 150 basic books in broadcasting. Headings include: General Interest; Advertising; Audience Interest; CATV; Management; News Broadcasting; Politics and Broadcasting; Programming, Production, and Performance; Public, Educational, and Instructional Broadcasting; Regulations; Technical Aspects; Yearbooks and Directories. There is also a list of trade publications and of sources for other materials.

547. The Radio Code. 21st ed. Washington: National Association of Broadcasters, 1978. 31p.
548. The Television Code. 20th ed. Washington: National Association of Broadcasters, 1978. 38p.

For both gives program standards, advertising standards, regulations, and procedures. The Radio Code has a "Broadcasting Creed"; The Television Code, a "Preamble." Each has a subject index.

549. Radio Programming Profile. 2 vols. Glenn Head, N.Y. 11545: BF/Communication Services, Plaza Bldg., 40 Railroad Ave., quarterly. (1967--.)

A geographic listing of AM and FM stations, intended to provide advertisers and public relations specialists with detailed programming in capsule form--for example, contemporary music, country music, ethnic shows, talk shows, news, etc. The stations themselves have supplied comments along with the data. Covers 200 markets.

550. RAND Cable Television Series. 4 vols. New York: Crane Russek, 1974.

A series addressed to local government officials, community group members, and others concerned with the development of cable TV in their communities. It is also intended to serve as a college and university text and

161

reference book. Titles include:

Baer, Walter. Cable Television: A Handbook for Decision-
    making. 244p.
    _____ and others. Cable Television: Franchise Consid-
    erations. 294p.
Rivkin, Steven R. Cable Television: A Guide to Federal
    Regulations. 371p.
Carpenter-Huffman, Polly, Richard C. Kletter, and Robert K.
    Yin. Cable Television: Developing Community Services.
    371p.

The first volume, by Baer, presents basic information
about cable TV and outlines political, social, economic,
legal, and technical issues communities face in cable
decision-making. In the second volume Baer and other contributors discuss federal regulations, with emphasis on
technological and legal aspects. In the third volume
Rivkin, a Washington lawyer, has put together relevant
documents on FCC rules and regulations and other pertinent
policies. These he updated in 1978 with A New Guide to
Federal Cable Television Regulations (MIT Press. 314p.)
because "by 1977 cable regulations had acquired an entirely
new empirical dimension through the actual resolution by
the FCC of several thousand 'certification' and interpretive proceedings as well as through ongoing rulemaking
refinements." Like its predecessor, it reproduces pertinent documents and contains an introductory "Summary and
Overview." The final volume by Carpenter-Huffman, Kletter,
and Yin explores the uses of cable for education, local
government services, and public access.

551. Report of the Task Force on Women in Public Broadcasting.
        Caroline Isber and Muriel Cantor, comps. Washington:
        Corporation for Public Broadcasting, 1975. 141p.

    A report, authorized by the CPB board of directors,
in which a task force monitored programs, collected and
analyzed data, interviewed, discussed, and recommended.
Appendices describe methodologies and instruments, and
present program content analysis tables, employment tables,
and other related tables.

552. A Report on Cable Television and Cable Telecommunications
        in New York City. New York: The Mayor's Advisory Task
        Force on CATV and Communications, 1978. 75p.

    Report of a committee, chaired by Fred Friendly, which
reviews present and future uses of telecommunications in
New York City and recommends policies and programs to
ensure that modern telecommunications technology is fully
exploited to further the city's economic activities and

social well-being. Much in the report is applicable to
other cities.

Rich News, Poor News. (See No. 630).

Robinson, Gertrude Joch. Tito's Maverick Media: The Politics
    of Mass Communication in Yugoslavia. (See No. 753).

553. Rose, Ernest D. World Film and Television Study Resources:
    A Reference Guide to Major Training Centers and Archives.
    Bonn-Bad Godesbert: Friedrich Ebert-Stiftung, 1974.
    421p.

    Describes in some detail approximately 375 schools and
eighty-five archives in seventy-six countries around the
world. Information under each entry varies, including for
schools all or some of the following items: address, telephone, date of founding, source of support, language of
instruction, program emphasis, length of program, award
upon completion, number admitted annually, school year
calendar, application procedures and deadline, special
requirements for foreign students, estimated living
expenses. For resource centers, information includes size
and type of holdings, address, director or curator, source
of support, description of library, publications screenings,
and other activities. Contains a lengthy bibliography
divided by country.

Ross Report. See Television Index. (No. 594).

Rosse, James N., Bruce M. Owen, and David L. Grey. Economic
    Issues in the Joint Ownership of Newspaper and Television
    Media. (See No. 757).

554. Rothafel, Samuel L., and Raymond Francis Yates. Broad-
    casting: Its New Day. New York: Arno Press, c1925,
    1971. 316p.

    In this book, written when radio was almost brand new,
the authors have tried to present "the bigger and more
vital issues on broadcasting and commercial radio." They
discuss directions it is taking, some of which are "Radio
and National Sport," "The New Force in Politics," "What
Radio Can Do for Education," "The Broadcast Drama, A New
Art," "Can We Talk to Mars?," "Radio and the Future of
America's Commerce," "Radio: The Invisible Crusader"
(its use in religious broadcasting). They also go into
technological problems, such as interference, and technological possibilities, such as communication with Mars
and the wire telephone.

555. Rovin, Jeff. The Great Television Series. Cranbury, N.J.:
     A. S. Barnes, 1977. 175p.

     A nostalgic history of the various TV series and their
     leading characters, useful for pinpointing facts but giving
     no larger picture.

556. Rutstein, Nat. "Go Watch TV!": What and How Much Should
     Children Really Watch? New York: Sheed and Ward, 1974.
     213p.

     "A major purpose of this book is to make parents appre-
     ciate what kind of force their children are interacting
     with when they turn on the TV set and what the consequences
     can be if parents make no attempt to control TV watching at
     home," states the author, as he demonstrates the good and
     the bad effects it can have. As a whole he finds that the
     bad outweighs the good. His facts are documented by evi-
     dence from studies and articles and are sprinkled with
     advice. Rutstein has worked nationally and internationally
     in television journalism for fifteen years and served as
     communications consultant to the White House Conference on
     Children. Contains footnotes.

557. Schramm, Wilbur L., and Lyle Nelson. The Financing of Pub-
     lic Television. Palo Alto, Cal. 94304: Aspen Program
     on Communications and Society, 770 Welch Rd., 1972. 59p.

     Gives concise facts and figures on the economic status
     and structure of public TV--its program services and cover-
     age from its beginnings to the early 1970s, its cost esti-
     mates, and its funding.

558. Schramm, Wilbur, Jack Lyle, and Ithiel de Sola Pool. The
     People Look at Educational Television: A Report on Nine
     Representative ETV Stations. Stanford, Cal.: Stanford
     University Press, 1963. 209p.
559. Lyle, Jack. The People Look at Public Television, 1974.
     Washington: Corporation for Public Broadcasting, Office
     of Communication Research, 1975. 66p.

     Schramm, Lyle, and Pool conducted more than 30,000 inter-
     views measuring audience composition and size, programs
     viewed and why, and how audiences felt about ETV. They
     also discussed potential audience. Twelve years later Lyle
     handles the same subject, presenting an overview based on a
     number of studies, some of which were part of an ongoing
     series sponsored by CPB. The 1963 volume contains a bib-
     liography and index; the later one contains charts about
     audience preferences and composition, and a listing of
     public television stations.

560. Schramm, Wilbur, Jack Lyle, and Edwin B. Parker. <u>Televi-sion in the Lives of Our Children</u>. Stanford, Cal.:
Stanford University Press, 1961. 324p.

This standard work analyzes the effects of television
on children, based on a study of over 6,000 children and
on information obtained from some 2,300 parents, teachers,
and school officials. An appendix gives statistics and
tabulations and data on related topics (including children's use of other mass media). There is an annotated
bibliography, an index of names, and a general index.
For its British counterpart see Himmelweit's <u>Televi-sion and the Child: An Empirical Study of the Effect of
Television on the Young</u> (No. 444).
In 1964 Schramm compiled a fifty-four-page annotated
bibliography, <u>The Effects of Television on Children and
Adolescents</u> (UNESCO, Reports and Papers on Mass Communication No. 43), with an introductory overview of research
reports, which was international in scope and included
books and periodical articles.

561. Seiden, Martin H. <u>Cable Television U.S.A.: An Analysis
of Government Policy</u>. New York: Praeger, 1972. 252p.

This detailed and somewhat technical study traces the
federal, state, and local regulation of cable TV from its
beginnings in the early 1950s to the early 1970s; examines
the industry's economics; summarizes five landmark court
cases affecting policy; discusses common carrier possibilities; and speculates upon the potential impact of space
satellites. The author emphasizes what he considers to be
the FCC's preoccupation with CATV. About ninety pages of
appendices are crammed with facts and figures.

562. Shanks, Bob. <u>The Cool Fire: Television and How to Make
It</u>. New York: Norton, 1976. 318p.

An excellent book to find out basic facts about the
workings of television--networks, staffs, syndication,
talent agencies, advertising agencies, script writing,
ratings, technology and equipment, basic economics, and
finally public, pay, cable, and cassette TV. The author
writes from experience; he has produced, directed, and
written television programs for ABC, CBS, NBC, and PBS.
Indexed.

563. Shapiro, Andrew O. <u>Media Access: Your Rights to Express
Your Views on Radio and Television</u>. Boston: Little,
Brown, 1976. 297p.

The aim of the author is to present a complete, impar-
tial guide through the maze of laws, FCC regulations and

rulings, and landmark court cases that define the American citizen's right of access to the broadcasting spectrum. Includes a complete set of legal citations for attorneys and cross references within the text. An appendix lists citizen organizations and public-interest law firms. Indexed.

564. Sharp, Harold S., and Marjorie Z. Sharp, comps. Index to Characters in the Performing Arts. Vol. IV. Radio and Television. Metuchen, N.J.: Scarecrow, 1973. 697p.

The object of this book is to identify radio and TV characters with the productions in which they appear. In all, about 2,500 major national broadcast programs are covered, and about 20,000 characters, with coverage extending from the inception of these media to about 1955 in the case of radio and to the fall, 1972, season for TV. Local programs, "specials," and most minor, short-lived programs are not included. It gives a little information about each character; shows whether such characters were real people (Jack Benny, Bob Hope, Walter Winchell) or fictitious characters (Archie Bunker, Ben Cartwright, Paladin); and indicates whether the production(s) in which they appeared were broadcast by radio, TV, or both. It also designates the type of each program, as "detective drama," "variety," "quiz," "Western," "situation comedy." Cross references take the user from specific programs or minor characters to the name of the major character under which the program is discussed--for example: "Doc Adams. See Dillon, Marshall Matt." Or "Gunsmoke. See Dillon, Marshall Matt." (The other three volumes deal with non-musical plays, operas and musical productions, and ballet.)

565. Shayon, Robert Lewis. The Crowd-Catchers: Introducing Television. New York: Saturday Review Press, 1973. 175p.

Shayon examines the TV industry pro and con and attempts to show why it is the way it is, highlighting the role of the station operators, the advertisers, and the government. He also discusses alternatives--technological and otherwise--which offer promise of more flexible telecommunication. Intended for the layman who has a more than superficial interest but is unfamiliar with the structure of the industry. Contains a glossary of selected terms and an index.

566. Shayon, Robert Lewis. Parties in Interest: A Citizens' Guide to Improving Television and Radio. New York 10010: Office of Communication, United Church of Christ, 289 Park Ave. S., 1974. 28p.

Guidelines designed to increase citizens' understanding
of the legal aspects of the American broadcasting system.
Includes examples of ways in which communities have
effected desired changes in discriminatory practices and
in quality of programming. Appendices list names and
addresses of organizations which local groups may call
upon for assistance, and government, trade, and general
publications.

567. Shiers, George, assisted by May Shiers. Bibliography of
the History of Electronics. Metuchen, N.J.: Scarecrow
Press, 1972. 323p.

Contains 1,820 listings of articles, books, and other
printed materials associated with the historical aspects
of electronics and telecommunications. Entries are
grouped under the following sixteen headings: General
Reference, Serial Publications, General Histories, Biographies, Broadcasting, Electricity and Electronics,
Electro-acoustics, Electromagnetic Waves, Electron Tubes,
Industrial Electronics, Radar, Radio, Solid-State Electronics, Telegraphy and Telephony, and Television and
Facsimile. Entries are annotated except when titles are
self-explanatory. There is an author index and a detailed
subject index.

568. Shulman, Milton. The Least Worst Television in the World.
London: Barrie and Jenkins, 1973. 180p.
569. _____. The Ravenous Eye. London: Coronet, 1975. 349p.

Shulman, a caustic and perceptive critic of TV, describes
his 1973 book as ". . . a personal survey of how television
in Britain has developed and, in my opinion, has deteriorated.
In such a tale of rise and decline, the compromises, the
shortcomings, the scandals of the medium tend to overshadow
the achievements and successes. If they do, my book may act
as some counter-weight to the load of complacency and self-
congratulation that is pumped out by the press officers of
the BBC and the commercial companies."
In the latter volume he has not changed his mind. "Six
years of working in television and eight years of writing
about it have convinced me that in its present primitive
phase in countries like Britain and America it does, on
balance, more harm than good." He proceeds to document his
views with surveys, studies, and statistics. Notes and
index.

570. Siepman, Charles A. Radio, Television and Society. New
York: Oxford University Press, 1950. 410p.

Siepman best tells in his own words the scope of his
analytical study of broadcasting, calling it an attempt

"to describe the facts about radio and television and to
combine these facts with a consideration of the social
and psychological effects of broadcasting." His first
purpose is "to bring to the general reader the history
of a cultural revolution and to show what has been discovered by research concerning the effects of radio and
television upon our tastes, opinions and values." His
second is "to deal with broadcasting as a reflection of
our time and to throw light upon the problems of free
speech, propaganda, public education, our relations with
the rest of the world, and with democracy itself." He
has succeeded well; his book remains an excellent examination of the role of broadcasting in society and is
especially suitable for undergraduates. Bibliographies
for each chapter and an index.

571. Skornia, Harry J. Television and Society: An Inquest
and Agenda for Improvement. New York: McGraw-Hill,
1965. 268p.

Skornia contends that a TV system controlled wholly
by business cannot be expected to put public interest
before profit. Bolstering his thesis with documents,
he discusses the structure of commercial TV--its leadership, its hidden economics, its rating system, its possible effects, including those on international relations. Chapter notes and index.

Skornia, Harry J. Television and the News. (See No. 762).

572. Sloan Commission on Cable Communications. On the Cable:
The Television of Abundance. New York: McGraw-Hill,
1971. 256p.

A report dealing with the significance of cable TV for
the home viewer. Makes recommendations concerning the
nature of regulation which should be established to give
the public the most service and satisfaction, and speculates upon the nature of the new elements that might be
part of an expanded and broadened TV system--such as pay
TV, community TV, public-access channels, new forms of
news and political coverage, and services to special
groups. Includes appendices on the technology of cable
TV, the economics of cable TV, and the uses of public-
access channels, together with abstracts of other papers
prepared for the commission.

573. Smith, Anthony, comp. British Broadcasting. London:
Newton Abbot; Devon: David & Charles, 1974. 271p.

"The purpose of this book is to show, through documents from official and other sources, how the

institutions of broadcasting in Britain were created and
developed in a context of public discussion," says the
author. He has selected nearly 100 key documents, concentrating on certain areas often inaccessible to the ordinary reader or student, including Parliamentary Papers,
Acts, memoirs, and commission reports. The introduction
and commentary are useful for those who need a historical
explanation of today's issues. Arrangement is chronological, beginning with the 1863 Electric Telegraphy Act and
ending with documents and BBC statements of principles in
the 1960s. There is an essay bibliography, "Suggestions
for Further Reading," and an index.

Smith, Anthony. The Politics of Information: Problems of
Policy in the Modern Media. (See No. 191).

574. Smith, Anthony. The Shadow in the Cave: The Broadcaster,
the Audience and the State. Rev. and enl. ed. London:
Quartet, 1976. 355p.

In this carefully documented analysis of the role of
broadcasting in society, the author's aim is to show the
ways in which it does not fulfill its potential to serve
the people. Using as examples the systems in Britain,
the U.S., France, Japan, Holland, and, more briefly, several other countries, he makes a case that the arguments
besetting it--bias, taste and lack of it, trivialization,
control of access, balance and fairness--are part of a
larger problem threatening democratic freedom. An appendix, "The Management of Television in a Democratic Society,"
presents a paper he gave at the Committee on Culture and
Education of the Council of Europe at Munich in 1974. A
second appendix, "The National Television Foundation,"
contains a plan for the fourth channel--evidence presented
to the Annan Committee on the Future of Broadcasting, 1974.
There are copious notes, a long and detailed bibliography,
and an index.

575. Smith, Anthony, ed. Television and Political Life: Studies
in Six European Countries. New York: St. Martin's,
1979. 288p.

In this anthology, political journalists and media
experts examine ways in which television has affected
national society and political culture in six European
countries. They show how this is brought about formally
by means of the structure and execution of the programming
and, more informally, by the interaction between political
leaders and television journalists and by the influence on
public opinion exerted by "styles" of politicians and

broadcasters. Countries assessed are Britain, France, Germany, Italy, Holland, and Sweden. Indexed.

576. Smith, Delbert D. Communication via Satellite: A Vision
     in Retrospect. Leyden/Boston: A. W. Sijthoff, 1976.
     335p.

The author's intent is to trace the strategy of communication satellite development from its origins in the 1800s, when its possibilities were undefined, to its present advanced state. Studying satellite progress in an institutional, legal, and social context, he interprets it in the light of governmental concern about its role in technological society, or "technology integration" as he terms it, referring to a complex economic, legal, and social process he claims is unique in the context of government-industry relationships. There is a list of acronyms and abbreviations, forty-one pages of footnotes, a twelve-page bibliography, and an index.

This is a companion work to the author's International Telecommunication Control: International Law and the Ordering of Satellite and Other Forms of International Broadcasting (Sijthoff, 1969. 231p.), which investigates legal controls and provides a framework for alternative concepts through "an examination of the relevant general principles of international law, the activities of the International Telecommunication Union and other organizations, unauthorized international telecommunication and the applicable control theories and legislation, regional broadcasting groupings and national policy alternatives, and the problems created by satellite telecommunication."

577. Smith, Robert Rutherford. Beyond the Wasteland: The
     Criticism of Broadcasting. Urbana, Ill. 61801:
     National Council of Teachers of English, Clearinghouse
     of Reading and Communication Skills, 1111 Kenyon Rd.,
     1976. 105p.

The main contention in this excellent book, intended to help laymen, and especially students, to be their own television critics, is that thus far very little criticism of the medium exists--a situation which encourages programs to thrive without the restraints needed to encourage taste, style, and excellence. The first part is concerned with the process of broadcast criticism, the second part with the issues involved. At the end of each chapter is a list of suggested readings.

578. Smythe, Ted C., and George A. Mastroianni, eds. Issues in
     Broadcasting: Radio, Television, and Cable. Palo Alto,
     Cal.: Mayfield, 1975. 430p.

Articles from trade and scholarly journals and the popular press, in which the editors have sought to present views on a variety of issues of the 1970s that deal with social criticism, professional problems, cable TV, public broadcasting, government regulation, international broadcasting, minority interests, and technological effects. Appendices give performances of network affiliates in the top fifty markets, the Corporation for Public Broadcasting/Public Broadcasting Service agreement, and a fact sheet on the PBS station program cooperative. Indexed.

579. Snow, Marcellus S. <u>International Commercial Satellite Communications: Economic and Political Issues of the First Decade of INTELSAT</u>. New York: Praeger, 1976. 170p.

The first book-length study of Intelsat by an economist and also the first to make intensive use of Intelsat financial data and other official documents. Part I describes its organization and technology and basic issues of its first years; Part II derives cost functions on the basis of a decade of operating data and documents and analyzes the various criteria of charging power it has followed; Part III deals with natural monopoly, scarce resource constraints, and economic developments; Part IV sums up the situation from an economist's standpoint. There is a bibliography of books and articles and an index.

580. Soares, Manuela. <u>The Soap Opera Book</u>. New York: Harmony, 1978. 182p.

This is a far cry from an empirical study, but Soares has made a worthy stab at giving us something more than a nostalgia trip. Her aim is to explore various aspects of soap operas not generally discussed in the fan magazines—where shows originate; how they are made; who watches and why; treatment of recurrent themes like love, marriage, sex, the family, divorce, death, etc. She also discusses some of the series themselves, catagorizing their style. There is also a who's who of characters and the actors and actresses who portray them, and an annotated list of twenty-five of radio's favorite operas. Definitely not for scholars, but useful for reference questions or students needing a handle on the subject.

581. Solberg, Janet. <u>Children's Television Programming: Some Prior Considerations and Research Designs for Canadian Broadcasts</u>. Toronto: Children's Broadcast Institute, 1977. 98p.

Intended neither as a textbook nor as a definitive work, this is a "selective and descriptive collection of material which we hope will encourage improvements in the creation, production and evaluation of children's programming." Discusses "The Contribution of Research," "Child Development," and "The State of the Art." Footnotes, bibliography, and a list of resource centers in Canada and in the U.S.

582. A Sourcebook on Radio's Role in Development. Washington 20037: The Clearinghouse on Development Communication, 1414 Twenty-second St., N.W., 1976. 85p. (Information Bulletin No. 7.)

A bibliography, international in scope, which abstracts about 600 items in an attempt to bring together in a single source the various project reports, country surveys, research and evaluation studies, bibliographies, and discussions concerning the application of radio to problems of education and development.

Spot Radio Rates and Data. (See No. 1143.)

Spot Television Rates and Data. (See No. 1143.)

583. Stein, Aletha Huston, and Lynette Kohn Freidrich. Impact of Television on Children and Youth. Chicago: University of Chicago Press, 1975. 72p.

Review of a large body of literature on observational learning and TV which is not limited to the study of violence, but discusses prosocial TV, cognitive function, and social knowledge and sterotypes as well. Contains an extensive bibliography of articles, books, theses and dissertations, documents, and other types of material.

584. Steiner, Gary A. The People Look at Television: A Study of Audience Attitudes. New York: Knopf, 1963. 422p.

Report of a study at Columbia University's Bureau of Applied Social Research in which the author conducted personal interviews with a sample of about 2,500 adults to determine each respondent's attitude toward programs and commercials as well as toward himself as a viewer. (See also Nos. 474 and 475.)

585. Sterling, Christopher H. Broadcasting and Mass Communications: A Survey Bibliography. 7th ed. Philadelphia: Department of Radio-TV-Film, Temple University, 1978. 32p.

A highly selective bibliography intended to provide a core collection in mass communication, with stress on broadcasting and with film and print titles excluded. Some of the old titles are dropped with each edition, but

Sterling has tried to keep the classics on the list and
has starred and double-starred books he considers especially important. Paperback editions are indicated.
There are no annotations. Arrangement is by subject
under sixteen classifications.

586. Sterling, Christopher, and John M. Kittross. Stay Tuned:
A Concise History of American Broadcasting. Belmont,
Cal.: Wadsworth, 1978. 562p.

"Our goal is to tell how American broadcasting got
where it is today, and, by analyzing principles, events,
and trends, suggest what directions it may take in the
future," say the authors of this comprehensive one-volume
history which emphasizes broad trends, important individuals, and basic principles rather than isolated facts.
Events are interrelated with developments in technology,
organization and structure of the industry, economics,
programming, audience research, public policy, and regulation. Arrangement is topical within a chronological
context. There are two tables of contents, one chronological and one topical. Appendices give a short chronology of American broadcasting, a glossary, historical
statistics, and a selected bibliography. Indexed.

Stokke, Olav, ed. Reporting Africa. (See No. 196.)

587. Summers, Harrison B. A Thirty-Year History of Programs
Carried on National Radio Networks in the United States,
1926-1956. Columbus: Ohio State University, Department of Speech, 1958. 228p. (Reprinted by Arno Press,
1971.)

Programs are listed by year and, within this framework,
broken down by type--comedy, variety, general variety,
hillbilly, minstrel, concert music, musical variety,
drama, thrills, news, commentary, public affairs talks,
religious, talk programs of various sorts. Information
about each includes as much of the following data as
available: sponsorship, number of seasons on the air,
network, program length, day, hour, and ratings.

588. Summers, Harrison B., Robert E. Summers, and John H.
Pennybacker. Broadcasting and the Public. 2d ed.
Belmont, Cal.: Wadsworth, 1978. 468p.

The purpose of the authors of this broadcasting text
is to provide an understanding of American broadcasting
as a social force and as a form of business enterprise.
Major topics include the characteristics of the system;
the directions in which broadcasting has developed over
the years; regulation, organization, and operation of

stations and networks; and the effects of economic considerations on those operations and on the selection of programs to be put on the air. Short lists of suggested
readings follow each chapter. Indexed.

Surgeon General's Report by the Scientific Advisory Committee
    on Television and Social Behavior. (See No. 591.)

Survey of Broadcast Journalism. See Alfred I. DuPont-Columbia
    University Survey of Broadcast Journalism. (No. 630.)

589. Technical Development of Television. George Shiers, ed.
    New York: Arno Press, 1977. 500p. (Historical Stud-
    ies in Communications.)

    A collection of thirty items which, taken as a whole,
surveys technical progress from the early proposals of
the late 1870s to the inception of modern color TV.
Materials include original papers by pioneers, contemporary articles, reports on individual and corporate
activities, accounts by historians, and national committee records. The selections constitute a record of
developments in Britain, Germany, Russia, and the U.S.
Material is divided into four sections: General History,
Mechanical Systems, Electronic Television, Color Television. The introduction includes a comprehensive list
of references to contemporary materials and a chronological list of ninety-one books published from 1925 to
1975.

590. Television and Radio. London SW3 1E8: Independent Broad-
    casting Authority, 70 Brompton Rd., annual. (1979--.)

    A guide to independent TV and independent local radio
in Britain. Contents include: ITV programming, regional
TV, radio programs, advertising, technical developments,
senior staff, audience research, creative aspects, a
chronology of important dates from 1952 onward, financing,
a bibliography, and an index.

591. Television and Social Behavior: A Technical Report to the
    Surgeon-General's Scientific Advisory Committee on
    Television and Social Behavior. John P. Murray, Eli
    A. Rubenstein, and George A. Comstock, eds. 5 vols.
    Washington: Superintendent of Documents, U.S. Govern-
    ment Printing Office, 1972.
592. Television and Growing Up: The Impact of Television Vio-
    lence. Washington: Superintendent of Documents, U.S.
    Government Printing Office, 1972. 279p.

    The editors of this series, popularly known as the Sur-
geon General's Report on Violence, call these five landmark

volumes "a broad scientific inquiry about television and
its impact upon the viewer." To this end more than fifty
scientists participated in research which produced over
forty scientific reports, with major emphasis on the
relationship between televised violence and the attitudes
and behavior of children. Vol. I, Media Content and Control; Vol. II, Television and Social Learning; Vol. III,
Television and Adolescent Agressiveness; Vol. IV, Television in Day-to-Day Life: Patterns of Use; Vol. V, Television's Effects: Further Explorations. Each volume
contains an overview paper which summarizes and relates
the papers in that volume. There are references at the
end of most chapters.

A part of the series, although not included as a volume,
is Television and Social Behavior: An Annotated Bibliography of Research Focusing on Television's Impact on
Children, edited by Charles K. Atkin, John P. Murray, and
Oguz B. Nayman and containing approximately 300 annotated
and 250 unannotated citations.

Television and Growing Up: The Impact of Television
Violence is a summary of the five volumes of the report,
with a lengthy bibliography of books and articles upon
which the authors of the articles drew.

593. Television Factbook: The Authoritative Reference for
     Advertising, Television, and Electronic Industries.
     2 vols. Washington 20036: Television Digest, 1836
     Jefferson Pl., N.W., annual. (1949--.)

One of the most detailed factual sources for information about geographic, economic, and legal aspects of TV
in the U.S. The first volume, Services, deals with allocations, associations, a variety of information about
CATV and CATV systems, colleges and universities offering
degrees, transfers of sales, Comsat, congressional committees, consulting engineers, electronics industries
association, European Broadcasting Union, FCC directory,
group station ownership, instructional TV, labor unions
and guilds, market and audience research organizations,
manufacturers, networks, publications, statistics, and
other similar information. The second volume, Stations,
is a comprehensive rundown on all TV commercial and public broadcasting stations in the U.S. and Canada, containing maps and such data as technical and recording
facilities, news wire and news film and facsimile services, licenses, ownership, personnel, a digest of the
rate card, net weekly circulation, total households, and
total TV homes.

175

594. Television Index. New York 10011: Television Index, Inc.,
      150 Fifth Ave., weekly. (1963, under present title;
      1949-63, Ross Reports.)

A guide to network television programs. In several
parts: the Network Program Report covers all commercial
network series debuting or returning during the current
week, with production credits, sponsors, and history;
also all network specials in each week, including varieties and documentaries, with credits and sponsors. The
Public Affairs section provides a continuing record of
guests and subjects of news, public affairs, religious,
and sports programs. The Program Performance Record provides performer, script, and other production credits for
the week's network programs that involve changes from
schedule and guest dramatic and variety performers and
talk-show guests. Network Program Reports has a quarterly
cumulative index.
      Television Index provides four other services, some of
which derive from Television Index:
      Television Network Movies (quarterly since 1973/74,
cumulative with annual index) is a spinoff from the Program Performance Record. It pulls together movies of
ninety minutes or more, whether made for theaters or
especially for television, giving for each the network,
running time, date of first showing, producer/distributor,
stars, writer, and director.
      TV Pro-log (weekly since 1972) is four digest-sized
pages of news and comment, with periodic special reports
in expanded issues based on interviews and surveys of
various aspects of the program production scene.
      Network Futures (weekly since 1966) gives calendar-
guide listings for upcoming series, debuts, returns, program specials, and schedule changes.
      Ross Reports Television (monthly since 1949) is a
directory, production, and casting guide, designed for
actors and writers, with information on major script
markets. Each issue is an update of the previous month.

595. Television Station Ownership: A Case Study of Federal
      Agency Regulation. Paul W. Cherington, Leon V. Hirsch,
      and Robert Brandwein, eds. New York: Hastings House,
      1971. 304p.

Experts examine the problem of spectrum regulation
from a number of angles. After an introduction and brief
history, they discuss forms of ownership vis à vis economic power, public opinion, and service to the needs and
interests of the community. Statistics throughout and
appendices.

596. Television Traffic--a One Way Street? A Survey and Analy-
     sis of the International Flow of Television Programme
     Material. Kaarle Nordenstreng and Tapio Varis, eds.
     Paris: UNESCO, 1974. 63p.

   An ambitious project in which the authors present the
structure of TV programming in various countries around
the world in terms of type of program and national origin.
The first part of the study contains the hard facts,
illustrated by graphs and tables; the second part is an
analysis and discussion of the international flow of TV
material, in which representatives from Finland, Egypt,
Israel, the U.S., and Canada discuss aspects of the situation. This is followed by a summary and further discussion.

597. Television Yearbook of the Republic of China, 1961-1975.
     English ed. Taipei, Taiwan: Television Academy of
     Arts and Sciences of the Department of China, 6, Lane
     51, Section 3, Ren-Ai Rd., 1976. 253p.

   This reference book (the use of the word yearbook is a
misnomer) is the first publication of its kind in Taiwan
and has as its aim to provide "a systematic presentation
of all the pertinent data about the development and growth
of the television enterprise in the country." Contents
include a brief history; a 140-page analysis of programming broken down by categories such as news, dramas, etc.;
engineering and industry; training of personnel; administration and pertinent regulations; international cooperation activities; advertising; a chronology of events; and
appendices containing (1) Broadcasting and Television Law
of the Republic of China; (2) Moral Code for the Television Enterprise in the Republic of China; (3) List of
Television Organizations and Advertising Agencies in the
Republic of China; (4) TV Books and Publications in the
Republic of China (in the Chinese language). The book
contains numerous illustrations and a great deal of data
in the form of tables, graphs, and maps.

598. Terrace, Vincent. The Complete Encyclopedia of Televi-
     sion Programs, 1947-1979. 2d ed. 2 vols. New York:
     Barnes, 1979.

   An alphabetical listing of entertainment TV programs
(excluding news specials and documentaries), giving for
each a brief synopsis, network, cast, length, date or
dates (if series), and syndication when necessary. The
first edition (1947-76) had no index and was intended
for the nostalgia trade. The addition of an index to
the new edition makes it much more useful as a reference
tool.

177

599. Thomas, Ruth. Broadcasting and Democracy in France.
     London: Bradford University in association with
     Crosby Lockwood Staples, 1976. 211p.

     Explores the history, structure, and economics of
     French broadcasting from 1945 onward; examines relations
     between broadcasting and government on the one hand and
     between broadcasting as a state monopoly and various
     commercial interests on the other; and analyzes the two
     central features of a democratic broadcasting system:
     information and citizen participation. Contains foot-
     notes and a bibliography.

600. Townsend, George R., and J. Orrin Marlowe. Cable: A
     New Spectrum of Communications. Spectrum Communica-
     tions, 1974. 102p.

     The authors, both cable TV operators, "tell it like
     it is," not in terms of future wonders cable may bring
     but rather in terms of what it is today--the political
     and economic climate which it faces. They give the
     historical background, the status quo, government regu-
     lations, the broadcaster versus the public interest,
     theater owners and pay TV, the impending conflict with
     the telephone companies, the availability of capital,
     and other challenges.

601. TV Broadcast Financial Data. Washington: Federal Com-
     munications Commission, annual. (1951--.)

     Consists of twenty-two tables of detailed financial
     data broken down by network-affiliated and independent
     VHF and UHF stations, and market data broken down by
     location. Some specifics include revenues, expenses,
     and income; financial data of TV networks, their owned
     and operated TV stations and other TV stations; number
     of commercial TV stations operating and reporting (UHF
     vs. VHF); detailed financial data for all stations, UHF
     and VHF network affiliated and independent stations;
     detailed financial data for major TV networks; number
     of TV stations reporting profit and loss by amount and
     by revenue; major principal expense items by revenue
     class; investment in tangible property; employment;
     and a great deal of market data. A preliminary page
     summarizes data. Supersedes in part the FCC's Broad-
     cast Financial Data for Networks and AM, FM and Tele-
     vision Stations. Between 1951 and 1962 the title was
     Final TV Broadcast Financial Data.

602. TV Season. Nina David, comp. and ed. Phoenix, Ariz.:
     Oryx Press, annual. (1975--.)

The bulk of this book gives information on each national TV program presented by ABC, CBS, NBC, and PBS during the year covered, as well as currently produced, syndicated shows with national distribution. Information on each regularly scheduled show includes name, network, type of show, descriptive material, and credits, such as executive producer, producer, director, writer, host, announcer, and stars and the characters they portray. Guests in specials are noted. Feature films made originally for theater distribution do not list casts and credits, but made-for-television films do whenever possible. PBS series and special shows are not included unless captioned for the hard-of-hearing. Other features include "Shows by Program Type," "Shows Captioned or Translated for the Hearing Impaired," "Shows Cancelled," "New Shows," "Summer Shows," "EMMY Awards," "Peabody Awards," and a "Who's Who in TV," which is a misleading heading, since it is really an index of names with no data.

TV Violence Index. See Gerbner, George, Larry Gross, and others. Trends in Network Television Drama and Viewer Concept of Social Reality, 1967-1977. (No. 418.)

603. Twomey, John E. Canadian Broadcasting History Resources in English. Toronto: Ryerson Polytechnical Institute, Canadian Broadcasting History Research Project, 1978. 72p. and appendices.

Results of a broadcast educator's investigation into the size and scope of available material reflecting Canadian broadcasting. Includes monographs, journals, bibliographies, scripts, archival materials in official sources, and private collections.

604. U.S. Congress. Joint Committee on Congressional Operations. Congress and Mass Communications: An Institutional Perspective. Washington: Government Printing Office, 1974. 81p.

A calendar print which goes briefly but thoroughly into opinions on the subject held over a period of time by executive and legislative branches of government, and the uses they have made of the mass media, especially broadcasting. In particular it covers previous hearings and broadcast access, and ends with proposals for the future. Appendices give bills and resolutions providing for broadcasting and televising which have been introduced; outstanding public TV coverage of local and state governments and public issues, October 1971 to March 1973; and broadcast coverage of congressional committees by national public radio, July 1971 to June 1972.

605. U.S. Department of Commerce. Office of Telecommunications. Cable Television for Europe. Sharon K. Black. Washington: Government Printing Office, 1974. 101p. and appendix. (OT Report 74-28.)

The author, who wrote this first as a master's thesis, describes the rising demand for cable TV in Europe and contends that its direction will be governed by the organizational structure of the separate national communication systems and by political systems. Evidence shows that its direction will be considerably different from its development in the U.S. She substantiates with facts and figures for the various European countries. Much of the information was gathered in interviews in 1972. An appendix contains a discussion of international program exchange organizations in Europe. Bibliography.

606. U.S. Foreign Broadcast Information Service. Broadcasting Stations around the World. Pts. I-IV. 26th ed. Washington: Superintendent of Documents, 1974.

Lists all reported radio broadcasting and TV frequency assignments with the exception of those in the U.S. which broadcast on domestic channels. Part I, "Amplitude Modulation Broadcasting Stations According to Country and City"; Part II, "Amplitude Modulation Broadcasting Stations According to Frequency"; Part III, "Frequency Modulation Broadcasting Stations," in two sections--one alphabetical by country and city and the other by frequency; Part IV, "Television Stations," also in two sections and with the same information as in the preceding parts plus additional data to distinguish audio, video, polarization, and other technical factors that apply. Appendices in Parts I and II give call-sign allocations and world time chart; an appendix in Part IV gives characteristics of VHF and UHF TV systems.

607. U.S. House. Committee on Interstate and Foreign Commerce. Subcommittee on Communications. International Communications Services. Washington: Government Printing Office, 1977. 550p. (Serial 95-56.)

Hearings on the need for an improved and expanded system of international telecommunications. Practically all the big telecommunications organizations (including, of course, the FCC) are represented. The general public is represented by two university professors.

608. U.S. House. Committee on Interstate and Foreign Commerce. Subcommittee on Communications. Sex and Violence on TV. Washington: Government Printing Office, 1978. 481p. (Serial 95-130.)

Hearings on the issue of TV violence and obscenity in
which individuals from the industry, academia, and action
groups testified and wrote. Contains tables of statistics
and research studies.

609. U.S. President's Task Force on Communications Policy.
     Final Report. Washington: Government Printing Office,
     1968. Variously paged.

"The report is organized around certain topics: the
organization of our international telecommunications
industry; policies to support and strengthen Intelsat;
telecommunications needs of less developed countries;
uses of domestic satellites; structure and regulation
of the domestic carrier industry; future opportunities
for television; spectrum use and management; and federal
government role in telecommunications--Introduction.
Appendices contain the President's message on communications policy, statements of partial dissent of the
task force's findings, and various other comments and
discussions.

610. U.S. Senate. Committee on Commerce, Science, and Trans-
     portation. Subcommittee on Communications. Inter-
     national Telecommunications Policies. Washington:
     Government Printing Office, 1978. 227p. (Serial
     95-54.)

Hearings to examine the present regulatory framework
and industry structure.

611. U.S. Senate. Committee on Finance. Subcommittee on
     Foundations. Role of Private Foundations in Public
     Broadcasting. Washington: Government Printing Office,
     1974. 153p.

Hearings giving facts and figures about the exact
involvement of foundations in public broadcasting.

612. Varis, Tapio. International Inventory of Television
     Programme Structure and the Flow of TV Programmes
     between Nations. Tampere, Finland: University of
     Tampere, Institute of Journalism and Mass Communica-
     tion, Research Institute, 1973. 264p. (No. 20/1973.)

More than fifty countries participated in this study,
which makes an international comparison of TV program
structure, describes the flow of information within and
between nations via TV, and analyzes the network structure through which material is exchanged by nations.

613. Vedin, Bengt-Arne. Media Japan. 103 14 Stockholm 2: Nord
     Video, Box 2144, 1977. 119p.

     A report on the development of the Japanese information
society which encompasses TV, video, telefacsimile, and
major experiments such as the Tama New Town "cable community" and the new Higashi-Ikoma optical fibre venture.

Violence Index. See Gerbner, George, Larry Gross, and others.
Trends in Network Television Drama and Viewer Concept of
Social Reality, 1967-1976. (No. 418.)

614. Webster, B. R. Access: Technology and Access to Communi-
     cations Media. Paris: UNESCO, 1975. 54p. (Reports
     and Studies in Mass Communication No. 75.)

     Emphasis here is on the extent to which technology can
assist in using open access for educational purposes. The
author discusses types of access; prerequisites and limitations on it; an approach to systems; the means of access;
technological developments; the future; systems planning
and low-cost technologies. Appendices give a technical
glossary, a summary of domestic cable developments, and a
summary of present and proposed developments of telephone
networks.

615. Wedlake, G. E. C. SOS: The Story of Radio Communication.
     New York: Crane, Russak, 1973. 240p.

     Beginning with Michael Faraday's discoveries in the
field of electrical science, this simply written account
for laymen traces developments in radio communication,
with attention to technical as well as social developments.
It is illustrated by both figures and photographs throughout. Appendices give particulars of early instruments and
a chronological table. There is a brief selected bibliography of books and an index.

616. Weil, Gordon L. Communicating by Satellite: An Inter-
     national Discussion. New York 10021: Carnegie Endow-
     ment for International Peace, Twentieth Century Fund,
     41 East 70th St., 1969. 78p.

     Report of an international conference, discussing regu-
lation and coordination of satellite communication, operation, and management and satellite broadcasting.

617. Weir, Earnest Austin. The Struggle for National Broad-
     casting in Canada. Toronto: McClelland & Stewart,
     1965. 477p.

     Lengthy history of Canadian broadcasting from 1919 to
the present. The author, who was with the Canadian

Broadcasting Corporation from its beginnings to his retirement, has used all available materials (he laments that
many of them have not been preserved) and has interviewed
a number of people who played prominent parts in the development of Canadian broadcasting.

618. Wells, Alan. Picture-Tube Imperialism? The Impact of U.S.
Television on Latin America. Maryknoll, N.Y.: Orbis,
1972. 197p.

A sociologist examines the cultural penetration of Latin
America by U.S. telecorporations, TV programs, and foreign
branches of Madison Avenue ad agencies. The first half of
the book deals with various aspects of communication, with
emphasis on consumerism; the second half with conscious
and unconscious manipulative uses by various agencies and
the media themselves. The book has a twelve-page bibliography and tables and diagrams.

619. Wertheim, Arthur Frank. Radio Comedy. New York: Oxford
University Press, 1979. 384p.

Discussion, accompanied by excerpts and photographs, of
many of the comedies of the 1930s and 1940s. Wertheim
explores the relationship between social history and radio
comedy, believing that it was popular not because it was
escapist fare but because it dealt with social issues.

Whatmore, Geoffrey. The Modern News Library: Documentation of
Current Affairs in Newspaper and Broadcasting Libraries.
(See No. 779.)

620. White, Llewellyn. The American Radio: A Report on the
Broadcasting Industry in the United States from the
Commission on Freedom of the Press. Chicago: Univer-
sity of Chicago, 1947. 260p.

A study of radio from its inception until the late
1940s made by the commission to determine possible need
for regulation and control. The author discusses history
and structure, the attempts to establish educational
broadcasting, academic and industrial research, and the
efforts toward regulation both by government and by the
industry itself. Appendices give regional networks and
excerpts from the codes of 1929 and 1939. There are
notes on sources.

White, Llewellyn, and Robert D. Leigh. Peoples Speaking to
Peoples: A Report on International Mass Communication
from the Commission of Freedom of the Press. (See No.
212.)

183

621. Williams, Arthur. Broadcasting and Democracy in West Germany. London: Crosby Lockwood Staples, 1976. 198p.

Traces the development of the German broadcasting system from 1945 onward, as its democratic foundations evolved. Material is presented in the context of West German society. Contains notes, a bibliography, and an index.

Williams, Francis. The Right to Know: The Rise of the World Press. (See No. 783.)

Williams, Francis. Transmitting World News: A Study of Telecommunications and the Press. (See No. 784.)

622. Williams, Raymond. Television: Technology and Cultural Form. New York: Schocken, 1974. 160p.

An exploration and a description of some of the relationships between TV as a technology and TV as a cultural form, in which Williams uses the medium as an outstanding example to comment not only upon it but also upon the interaction it brings about between technology, social institutions, and culture in general. He also discusses alternative technology and alternative uses of the medium. Throughout he brings a depth few writers on the subject can match. Bibliography and index.

623. Window Dressing on the Set: Women and Minorities in Television; A Report of the United States Commission on Civil Rights. Washington: U.S. Commission on Civil Rights, 1977. 181p.

Findings and recommendations derived from two content analyses which show the portrayal of women in dramatic programs and news, along with facts and figures concerning employment. Appendices give methodology used in collecting data on network entertainment programming; nonwhite characters identified by program, race, ethnicity, sex, and occupation, 1973 and 1974; network entertainment program sample, 1973 and 1974; sources of labor force and population data; and comments by the FCC on the report. This has been followed by Window Dressing on the Set: An Update (1979, 96p.), which deals with the late 1970s.

624. Winn, Marie. The Plug-in Drug: Television, Children and the Family. New York: Grossman, 1977. 231p.

A well-documented study in which the author contends that the act of watching TV can be bad, regardless of the nature of the content. Interviewing families, teachers, and child specialists and examining scientific studies,

she addresses herself to such questions as the effect of
TV on children's use of free time and on family relationships, the role of TV as surrogate parents, the possible
mental and physical dangers of passivity. She also suggests possible solutions which parents and educators might
adopt. Contains footnotes and an index.

625. Wolf, Frank. Television Programming for News and Public
      Affairs: A Quantitative Analysis of Networks and Sta-
      tions. New York: Praeger, 1972. 203p.

    The author contends that TV affects the political
socialization of children and adults and that the medium
itself is part of the political system. He attempts to
prove his thesis by analyzing the structure of ownership,
the regulatory environment, editorializing, and the economic determinents of news and public affairs programming.
Much of the material is based on questionnaires to stations.
Appendices show methodology, tell problems in procuring the
program data, and indicate joint ownership of other media
by television stations in the top fifty markets. Contains
footnotes and a ten-page bibliography.

626. The Working Press of the Nation: Radio and Television
      Directory. Vol. III. Burlington, Iowa 52601: National
      Research Bureau, 424 N. Third St., annual. (1947--.)

    Lists principal radio and television stations in the U.S.
and Canada, giving for each station call letters, address,
manager, and program director. Stations in cities of
150,000 or more get more detailed entries, with call letters, address, phone, power, network affiliation, air time,
and executive personnel. Other features include local
programming under type, principal stations listed by power,
networks and their personnel, and public/educational TV
stations in the U.S. Radio and TV are each in separate
sections.

627. World Radio TV Handbook: A Complete Directory of Inter-
      national Radio and Television. New York 10036: Bill-
      board Publications, One Astor Pl., annual. (1946--.)

    Detailed information by country of radio and TV sta-
tions and broadcasting organizations in 228 countries,
which, according to the editor, comprise all the countries
of the world. Data for each is prolific but hard for the
layman to find, although it would probably offer no problems to the expert. Among the items of information are
network organizations and stations by country with a great
deal of technical and program information crammed into a
very small space in very fine print. Shortwave, long-,
and medium-wave stations are listed separately by frequency

within continents. U.N. broadcasting is also included, but under the U.S. instead of separately. There is a great deal of information about organizations such as Voice of America and much else in broadcasting. The problem with this reference book, however, is the lack of adequate indexing, which makes individual items like these difficult to locate.

IV

Editorial Journalism

628. Adam, G. Stuart, ed. <u>Journalism, Communication and the</u>
     <u>Law</u>. Scarborough, Ontario: Prentice-Hall of Canada,
     1976. 245p.

     A group of essays divided into four sections. The
     first defines journalism and locates it within the domain
     of culture; the second concerns the process of journal-
     istic communication in Canada; the third discusses Cana-
     dian press law with special emphasis on press freedom;
     the fourth is a bibliography. In addition the articles
     are footnoted.

629. Adams, William, and Fay Schreibman, eds. <u>Television Net-</u>
     <u>work News</u>. Washington: George Washington University,
     School of Public and International Affairs, 1978. 231p.

     Brings together from a variety of disciplines discus-
     sions of some of the more important issues in the study
     of network news content. The three areas emphasized are
     the status of existing research, methodological issues,
     and future directions of research.

630. <u>Alfred I. Dupont-Columbia University Survey of Broadcast</u>
     <u>Journalism</u>. Marvin Barrett, ed. 6 vols. New York:
     Grosset & Dunlap (Vols. 1-3); Crowell (Vols. 4-6),
     1968--.

     The aim of the series is to consider and critique
     broadcast news of the preceding twelve months--how TV
     and radio report the news; how they serve the public; and
     how they live with politicians, advertisers, and the FCC.
     Their appraisals of the coverage of those years--years
     that saw assassinations, student unrest, Vietnam, Water-
     gate, and lesser events (among them, "Pope Barbara and the
     Greening of the FCC")--are a running commentary on the
     strengths and weaknesses of American journalism.
     Individual volumes in chronological order include:

     <u>Survey of Broadcast Journalism, 1968-1969</u>. 132p.

Survey of Broadcast Journalism, 1969-1970: Year of Chal-
   lenge, Year of Crisis. 156p.
Survey of Broadcast Journalism, 1970-1971: A State of
   Seige. 183p.
The Politics of Broadcasting, 1971-1972. 274p.
Moment of Truth. 274p.
Rich News, Poor News. 344p.

   The first five volumes are edited by Barrett; the sixth
is written by him. All are indexed.

631. Alphabetized Directory of American Journalists: Associated
   Press, United Press International, America's Daily
   Newspapers. Jack Barkley, comp. Kokomo, Ind. 46901:
   The author, P.O. Box 231, annual. (1977--.)

   Lists alphabetically by name approximately 20,000
writers, editors, managers, and other news-related personnel working for daily newspapers and the two major wire
services. A second section contains a geographic listing
of U.S. daily newspapers with addresses and telephone numbers.

632. American Newspapers, 1821-1936: A Union List of Files
   Available in the United States and Canada. Winifred
   Gregory, ed. New York: Wilson, 1937. 791p.

   A list of newspapers, beginning where Brigham (No. 645)
leaves off, giving their location in libraries of the U.S.
and Canada, dates when they began and ceased publication
(if no longer extant), and changes in names or mergers
that have occurred. Information about their history is
not, however, as full as in Brigham.

633. ANPA Foundation in cooperation with the Association for
   Education in Journalism. Education for Newspaper
   Journalism in the Seventies and Beyond. Proceedings.
   Washington 20041: American Newspaper Publishers Asso-
   ciation, P.O. Box 17407, Dulles International Airport,
   1974. 349p.

   Educators and newspaper executives meet and cover the
following aspects of journalism education: journalism and
a liberal education; non-verbal communication; professionalism of the press; the journalist's body of knowledge;
attitude formation; economics of the press; new technology;
social science reporting; professional media experience;
professional activity beyond the classroom; mastery of a
non-journalism discipline; the study of urban life; broad
understanding of major issues; objectives of journalism
schools; criticism of the press, and an evaluation of

journalism schools. Each paper is given in full and ver-
batim reports of the discussions that followed are also
included.

634 APS Directory. New York 10003: Alternative Press Syndi-
     cate, Box 777, 1976. 21p.

The Alternative Press Syndicate, a non-profit association of alternative newspapers and magazines, began in
1966 as the Underground Press Syndicate. It lists approximately ninety newspapers and periodicals in the U.S. and six
in Canada, giving for each the address, telephone number,
date of founding, frequency of publication, subscriptions
rates, and advertising rates--these latter two in detail.
A listing of members in Asia Pacific, Indo America, and
Europe follows. Preceding these is an explanation of the
APS and its impact, and a discussion of the alternative
press as a market, along with an explanation of advertising
standards, which are high. A similar directory was issued
in 1973 under the former title of the organization, the
U.P.S. Directory. (See also No. 774.)

635. Arndt, Karl J. R., and May E. Olson. The German Language
     Press of the Americas. New English ed. 2 vols. Munich:
     Verlag Dokumentation, 1973, 1976.

The first volume lists by geographic location German-
American newspapers published in the U.S.; the second volume lists those published in Argentina, Brazil, Bolivia,
Chile, Costa Rica, Cuba, the Dominican Republic, Ecuador,
Guatemala, Guyana, Mexico, Paraguay, Peru, Uruguay, and
Venezuela, with an addenda to Vol. I on the U.S. Data for
each entry vary but usually include frequency, date of
founding and expiration date for those no longer extant,
top personnel, library holdings, and publisher. Sometimes
there is a description of the publication. Some descriptions are direct quotes in German. Vol. II has a lengthy
bibliography of works consulted.

636. Ayer Directory of Publications. Philadelphia 19106: Ayer
     Press, 210 Washington Square, annual. (1868--.)

This is the one single source that lists together in
geographic arrangement daily and weekly newspapers and
periodicals published in the U.S., Puerto Rico, Virgin
Islands, Canada, the Bahamas, Bermuda, the Republic of
Panama, and the Philippines. Information about each varies according to type, but common to all is circulation,
founding date, subscription rate, frequency, format, and
price. Further data, where pertinent, can include political leaning and subject specialization. Brief gazetteer
information is given for each community.

There are a number of other valuable features. Among
them are names, addresses, and phone numbers of editors of
"the most popular features" appearing in newspapers with
100,000 circulation or over; and classified lists of the
following kinds of publications: agricultural, college,
foreign language, Jewish, fraternal, black, religious, and
general circulation magazines; trade and technical publications; daily, weekly, semiweekly and triweekly periodicals. A classified index breaking down specialized
publications into subjects and a straight alphabetical
index accompany this section.

Although Ayer has many uses, it is intended primarily
for advertisers, and therefore publications which do not
stress advertising, such as scholarly journals and literary magazines, are not usually included.

637. Back Talk: Press Councils in America. William L. Rivers,
William Blankenberg, Kenneth Starck, and Earl Reeves,
eds. San Francisco: Canfield, 1972. 146p.

An overview of the way press councils work, illustrated
by actual case studies. Chapter notes and bibliography.

Baechlin, Peter, and Maurice Muller-Strauss. Newsreels across
the World. (See No. 801.)

638. Balk, Alfred. A Free and Responsive Press. New York:
Twentieth Century Fund, 1973. 88p.

Consumerism, contends Balk, is becoming a force among
newspaper readers; they want a better press. He discusses
steps that have been taken in this direction, with emphasis
on press councils, and laments that too little has been
done. He describes the British Press Council, tells of
American efforts as a whole, and gives the structure of two
of the most ambitious in this country--those of Minnesota
and Honolulu. Appendices contain the constitutions of the
Minnesota and the British councils and the organization of
that of Ontario. The bibliography contains a bibliography
of books and of periodical and newspaper articles.

639. Baran, Paul. The Future of Newsprint, 1970-2000. Menlo
Park, Cal. 94025: Institute for the Future, 2725 Sand
Hill Road, 1971. 49p. (Special Industry Report R-16.)

Portion of a study which sought to develop a better
understanding of the factors that might change the demand
for newsprint within the next few decades. As the newsprint business is so much a part of the newspaper business,
the report focuses most attention on that area. Among
topics surveyed are basic facts about newsprint: its manufacture, distribution, ownership, etc.; substitute media;

demographics and economics of the newspaper; and ecological
considerations. Information was obtained by polling the
opinions of a panel of experts and, except for a five-page
introduction, takes the form of graphs and charts.

640. Benn's Press Directory. 2 vols. Tonbridge, Kent TN9 1RW:
    Benn Publications Ltd., annual. (1852--.)

    This is one of the world's oldest press directories.
Vol. I, United Kingdom, contains lists of newspapers and
periodicals, house journals, and directories, giving for
each date founded, address, head officers, proprietors,
personnel, and circulation, with a thumbnail sketch of
contents for most of the periodicals, which are classified
by subject. Other features in the first volume are a list
of publishers' groups and of agencies and services for the
communications industries. There is also a master index
for the U.K. Press.
    Vol. II, Overseas, emphasizes marketing, with a list of
newspapers and periodicals for about 180 countries and
territories. National information sources, both print and
broadcast, are also included. Other features are overseas
press and media associations, and international organizations with their official publications.

641. Bertrand, Claude Jean, comp. The British Press, an His-
    torical Survey: An Anthology. Paris: Office Central
    de Librairie, 65, Rue Claude-Bernard, 1969. 208p.

    Traces through documents and articles from contemporary
sources the growth of the British press from the introduction of printing to the present. A chronology, "Landmarks
in the History of the British Press," precedes the text.
Appendices in tabular form give circulation figures during
the last thirty years; an overview of newspapers broken
down into two categories--quality and popular--with circulation, political tendency, and controlling interest; the
periodical press divided into journals of opinion and mass
magazines, with political tendencies and circulation over
the last ten years. Bibliography.

642. Bhattacharjee, Arun. The Indian Press: Profession to
    Industry. Delhi: Vikas, 1972. 216p.

    This publication of the Press Institute of India, which
was started as separate individual surveys in 1969, takes
into account different facets of the Indian press. The
first of its three sections deals with press law in India,
which it briefly contrasts with press law in other countries; government assistance, which is sometimes called
"nationalization by the back door"; and the problem of

newsprint. The second section discusses the Indian news
agencies. The third treats Indian dependence upon imports
for paper and pulp mill machinery, television receiver and
equipment production, and photography and film equipment.
The book has a list of references and appendices giving
opinions of the Indian press by several political leaders,
the views of the Press Council, a very brief survey of a
feasibility study of a regional telecommunication network,
and circulation and newsprint figures.

643. Black Press Handbook. Washington 20045: National News-
     paper Publishers Association, 770 National Press Build-
     ing, 1977. 116p.

     A commemorative booklet to celebrate the 150th anniver-
sary of the founding of the first black newspaper, Freedom's
Journal, in 1827. A number of brief features describe various aspects, happenings, and personalities within the black
press. The main feature is a list of black newspapers which
are NNPA members, with addresses, advertising rates, personnel, date of publication, year of founding, and number of
employees. This was preceded by a 1974-75 edition with much
of the same information.

644. Boretsky, R. A., and A. Yurovsky. Television Journalism.
     Prague: International Organization of Journalists, Gen-
     eral Secretariat, 1970. 204p.

     The authors, both members of the Department of Journalism
at Moscow University, seek to explain TV reporting as a
system of mass information; to specify its place in society
(in this case, in a Communist society); and to discuss its
particular idiom as a genre, or rather, as a compound of
genres, because the authors feel that journalism is closely
akin to literature. There are also some pointers on news
gathering and production. All in all, this book gives the
Communist viewpoint to English-speaking journalists in
countries with a different ideology.

645. Brigham, Clarence S. History and Bibliography of American
     Newspapers, 1690-1820. 2 vols. Worcester, Mass.: Amer-
     ican Antiquarian Society, 1947.

     A geographical list of newspapers for the period covered,
locating the libraries where they may be found and giving
the history of each paper in a concise descriptive annotation. Brought up to date by American Newspapers, 1821-1936.
(See No. 632.) A fifty-page book of additions and corrections appeared in 1961. Each volume contains a list of
libraries and of private owners and an index of titles and
of printers; Vol. II has a general index.

A companion volume is Edward C. Lathem's Chronological
Tables of American Newspapers, 1690-1820: Being a Tabular
Guide to Holdings of Newspapers Published in America
through the Year 1820. (Barre, Mass.: American Antiquarian Society, 1972, 131p.) It consists of a series of
tables arranged geographically by state and then chronologically. By consulting columns representing the pertinent year or years, users can determine what papers may
exist, either for particular localities or generally.
Dates within the tables indicate each newspaper's span of
publication and current availability. After consulting
the tables the reader can go to Brigham for more detailed
information.

646. Brown, Lee. The Reluctant Reformation: On Criticizing
     the Press in America. New York: McKay, 1974. 244p.

     An analysis of press criticism, which takes in theories,
origins, social responsibility, new and old forms, the
National Press Council, and a look into the future. Appendices include a variety of codes of ethics, reports for a
National Press Council, Press Council operating rules,
critical attitudes toward the media, two surveys on the
image of the newspaper, and newspapers' use of internal
criticism. Bibliography and index.

647. Bryan, Carter R. Journalism in America before Emancipa-
     tion. Association for Education in Journalism Publica-
     tions Business Manager, 1969. 33p. (Journalism Mono-
     graphs No. 12.) (Obtain from AEJ headquarters.)

     A survey of very early examples of the black press,
including books, and its writers and editors. Footnotes
serve as a bibliography, and there is a checklist of
newspapers published before emancipation.

Bush, Alfred L., and Robert S. Fraser. American Indian Periodicals in the Princeton University Library: A Preliminary
List. (See No. 1041.)

648. Cannon, Carl L., comp. Journalism: A Bibliography. New
     York 10018: New York Public Library, 1924. 360p.

     Annotated list of books and magazine articles "intended
to be useful to the American newspaper man actively
engaged in his profession, or to the student of journalism."
The author has emphasized the present rather than the historical in his selections, which means that his bibliography
is now an excellent source for references to the state of
journalism in the early 1920s.

649. Catholic Press Directory. Rockville Center, N.Y. 11570:
     Catholic Press Association, 119 North Park Ave.,
     annual. (1923--.)

   Official media reference guide to Catholic newspapers,
magazines, and diocesan directories in the U.S. and
Canada. Most entries provide address, key personnel,
rates, and circulation.

Circulation: The Annual Geographic Penetration Analysis of
     Major Print Media. (See No. 1094.)

650. Collins, Richard. Television News. London WIV 6AA:
     British Film Institute, Educational Advisory Service,
     81 Dean St., 1976. 56p. (BFI Television Monograph 5.)

   Investigates some dominant assumptions and practices
which govern the production of news on British TV. Among
topics discussed are formation, function, and financing;
news values, principles, and practices; gatekeepers;
analysis of style and structure; and audience. Appendix
1 is a one-page rundown on the Eurovision News Exchange;
Appendix 2, a geographic chart. Bibliography.

651. Commission of Inquiry into High School Journalism. Cap-
     tive Voices: The Report. Jack Nelson, comp. New
     York: Schocken, 1974. 264p.

   The commission investigated four areas of high school
journalism: censorship, minority participation, educational and journalistic quality, and interest of editors
and other workers in the established media. Appendices
give "A Legal Guide to High School Journalism" and show
the methodology, ranging from questionnaires, whose
results are shown, to lists of the sources consulted.
Indexed.

Community Publication Rates and Data. (See No. 1143.)

652. Compaine, Benjamin M. Future Directions of the Newspaper
     Industry. 2 vols. White Plains, N.Y.: Knowledge
     Industry Publications, 1977.

   One of the best sources for statistics and financial
figures. Intended as a planning document, it "explores
the future by looking at some of the past of the newspaper and its rival media, then making a reasoned evaluation of what lies ahead." A five-page executive summary
gives a quick survey of contents. This is followed by
an overview and analysis of circulation, advertising,
competition and group ownership, new technology, labor
and labor unions, newsprint, and other pertinent

information. A special feature is a section of financial
profiles of sixteen major newspaper publishers and groups.

653. Cranfield, G. A. The Press and Society: From Caxton to
      Northcliffe. London/New York: Longman, 1978. 342p.

     A survey of the history of the British press in relation
to the development of British society, from the time of its
introduction into England in 1476 to the twentieth century.
Considerable emphasis is placed on the growth of the reading public. Includes not only newspapers proper but also
broadsides, ballads, pamphlets, serial fiction, penny
dreadfuls, and so on. Notes and bibliography.

654. Curran, James, ed. The British Press: A Manifesto. Lon-
      don: Macmillan, 1978. 339p.

     Essays by Raymond Williams, Stuart Hall, Anthony Smith,
Peter Golding, Philip Elliot, and others of the Acton
Society Press Group, which offer a critique of the British
press and proposals for reform. They challenge four commonly held assumptions: "the contentional view of press
freedom as property right; the belief that 'free market'
gives people what they want; the myth of the newspaper
'professional' who can distinguish fact from opinion; and
the traditional dictum that, in the words of Macaulay,
'government can only interfere in discussion by making
discussion less free than it would otherwise be.'" Chapter references and index.

655. Current South African Newspapers/Huidige Suid-Afrikaanse
      Koerante. Pretoria: The State Library, P.O. Box 397,
      1970. 17p.

     An alphabetical listing by place. For each entry gives
title (with any name changes), date of establishment,
address and telephone number, size, frequency, price, and
language (whether English or Afrikaans). Preceding this
are sections summarizing press law in South Africa, the
press union, the South African Press Association, and a
history of South African newspapers in broad outline.
Indexed.

656. The Daily Press: A Survey of the World Situation in 1952.
      New York: UNESCO Publications Center, 1953. 45p.
      (Reports and Papers on Mass Communication No. 7.)

     A follow-up, concerned only with newspapers, to the
five-volume series, Press, Film and Radio (No. 160). Consists of thirteen graphs and tables, with detailed explanatory texts, and covers the majority of countries and

territories throughout the world. Also lists countries
where no daily paper was published at that time.

657. Dann, Martin, ed. The Black Press (1827-1890): A Quest
for National Identity. New York: Putnam, 1971. 381p.

Although the editor's primary aim in this anthology of
the nineteenth-century black press is to provide an
insight into black history, it also tells a great deal
about the Negro press. A sizable portion--sixty-seven
pages--is taken up with its role; the five remaining
sections--"The Black View of American History," "The
Black Man and Politics," "The Black Man and Labor," "The
Black Exodus," and "Creating a Black Community"--present
in chronological order the articles, editorials, advertisements, and political cartoons of the period. Selections are almost exclusively from newspapers available
on microfilm in the Schomburg Collection of the New York
Public Library. Indexed.

Davis, Anthony. Television: Here Is the News. (See No. 394.)

658. Desmond, Robert W. The Information Process: World News
Reporting to the Twentieth Century. Iowa City: University of Iowa Press, 1977. 495p.

A factual history which follows news reporting in its
various forms chronologically from ancient times to the
beginning of the present century, ranging from the invention of the alphabet, paper and ink, and the printing
press; to the telegraph, cable, telephone and wireless;
to the creation of news agencies and the appearance of
photography. Footnotes, bibliography, and index.

659. Directory of Newspaper Libraries in the U.S. and Canada.
Grace D. Parch, ed. New York: Special Libraries
Association, Newspaper Division, 1976. 319p.

A project of the Newspaper Division of Special
Libraries Association, which its members plan to update
from time to time, this directory brings together a
listing, with information about personnel, services,
resources, group affiliation, hours, and date of founding. Indexes of newspapers and of personnel.

660. Directory of the College Student Press in America,
1977-78. Dario Politella, ed. 4th ed. New York:
Oxbridge, 1977. 659p.

The first edition of this directory, which appeared
in 1970, listed publications on some 650 campuses. This
edition contains 2,581. Arrangement is by state, with

institutions and their publications alphabetical. Brief
information about each college or university is given,
followed by its yearbooks, newspapers, and/or magazines.
Data for each varies according to its type, but generally
includes advisor, date founded, frequency, advertising
rates, budget or method of financing, size, method of
production, and for larger publications, incorporation,
copyright, and method of distribution. There are separate
indexes for magazines, newspapers, and yearbooks, a brief
history of the student press, and a list of award-winning
campus newspapers since 1972 selected by the Associated
Collegiate Press and its sister organization, the National
School Press Association.

661. Dunham, F. Gayle. <u>News Broadcasting on Soviet Radio and
 Television</u>. Cambridge, Mass.: Massachusetts Institute
 of Technology, Center for International Studies,
 Research Program on Problems of Communication and International Security, 1965. 63p. (Distributed by Clearinghouse for Federal Scientific and Technical Information,
 U.S. Dept. of Commerce.)

An introduction gives the Soviet conception of the function of broadcasting media and news. This is followed by
an analysis of the structure and content of radio news
broadcasting and a shorter chapter on TV broadcasting.
Contains copious bibliographical notes.

662. Duscha, Julius, and Thomas Fischer. <u>The Campus Press:
 Freedom and Responsibility</u>. Washington 20036: Ameri-
 can Association of State Colleges and Universities,
 One Dupont Circle, N.W., Suite 700, 1973. 115p.

Part I, by Duscha, outlines the history and development of the campus press, with an analysis of similarities
and differences between it and the general press. Part II,
by Fischer, is a historical and legal perspective on freedom of speech and the press, with a discussion of the particular problems in this area which may affect campus
presses. Important cases involving campus publications
are abstracted. Contains a section listing footnotes.

663. <u>Editor and Publisher Annual Directory and Syndicated Ser-
 vices</u>. New York 10022: Editor & Publisher Co.,
 575 Lexington Ave., annual. (1925--.)

Every year <u>Editor and Publisher</u> magazine carries a
special issue on syndicated services, listing them in
the following ways: by syndicate, giving name, address,
telephone, executives, and editors; by title of byline
features, giving author or artist; by author or artist;
and by subject.

664. Editor and Publisher International Yearbook. New York
    10022: Editor & Publisher Co., 575 Lexington Ave.,
    annual. (1921--.)

Properly subtitled "The Encyclopedia of the Newspaper
Industry," this annual supplement to Editor & Publisher
magazine is devoted primarily to a listing of daily
newspapers in the U.S. and Canada, with detailed information about editorial personnel and advertising. In
addition it tells addresses, telephone, circulation,
date of founding, special editions, mechanical facilities
available, broadcast affiliates, political leanings, news
agency service, and Sunday magazine if there is one.
Other features include a listing of new dailies, suspensions, mergers, and frequency changes; a listing of and
information about weeklies, black newspapers, college and
university newspapers, principal foreign-language newspapers, and a variety of professional, business, and
special service dailies; groups of dailies under common
ownership; action/hot line editors; a geographic listing
of principal newspapers published in foreign countries,
with brief information about each; various newspaper
services--news and syndicate, mechanical equipment,
supplies; clipping bureaus; films about newspapers;
advertising clubs; other clubs and associations; the
membership roster of the American Newspaper Publishers
Association; foreign press and radio-TV correspondents
in the U.S., members of the United Nations Correspondents
Association; a directory of the Foreign Press Association
membership; newsprint statistics; schools and departments
of journalism; award winners; representatives of newspapers in foreign countries; and even more similar information.

665. Eisenstein, Elizabeth L. The Printing Press as an Agent
    of Change: Communications and Cultural Transformations
    in Early-Modern Europe. 2 vols. New York: Cambridge
    University Press, 1979. 794p.

In this scholarly and detailed work Eisenstein focuses
on the shift from script to print in Western Europe. In
the first volume she deals with the main features of the
communications revolution and the relationship between
these changes and other developments conventionally associated with the transition from medieval to early modern
times. In the second volume she views familiar developments "from a new angle of vision." Concentration is on
cultural and intellectual movements rather than on political ones, which she says she will take up in another
book. Her primary concern is with the effects of printing
on written records and on the transmission of views from

one already literate culture to another (rather than from
an oral to a literate culture). Contains footnotes, a
detailed bibliography, and an index.

666. Emery, Edwin, and Michael Emery. The Press and American
An Interpretative History of the Mass Media. 4th ed.
Englewood Cliffs, N.J.: Prentice-Hall, 1978. 574p.

In this chronological history of American journalism
which has become a standard text, the aim of the authors
is to emphasize the correlation of journalism history with
political, economic, and social trends, showing the interaction between the press and the course of events in the
U.S.--how history has been influenced by the press and
conversely has done some influencing. In accomplishing
this they have stressed the roles of personalities
involved. The portion covering the modern period deals
with electronic as well as print media. At the end of
each chapter is an annotated bibliography. Indexed.

Encyclomedia. Newspapers. (See No. 1103.)

667. Epstein, Edward Jay. News from Nowhere: Television and
the News. New York: Random House, 1973. 321p.

Epstein studies the effect of the processes of a news
organization on the news product, using the three major
networks, with emphasis on NBC. Among topics he examines:
the relation of the news to reality; the structure imposed
on network news by government regulations, affiliates,
parent networks, and economic realities; the effect of
internal procedures and structure; and finally, a com-
posite picture of American society as depicted on network
news over a three-month period. Source notes, bibliography, and index.

668. Epstein, Laurily Keir, ed. Women and the News. New York:
Hastings House, 1978. 144p.

An examination of various aspects of the status of
women vis à vis the news in terms of three concepts in
news media research: agenda setting, access to the
media, and definitions of the news.

669. Facts about the IOJ. Prague: International Organization
of Journalists, 11001 Praha 1, Parizska, 1973. 95p.

Gives the purpose and activities of the International
Organization of Journalists, including its centers of
professional education, publicity, statutes, executive
committees, and the composition of its membership.

670. Feuereisen, Fritz, and Ernst Schmacke, comps. Die Presse
     in Afrika: Ein Handbuch für Wirtschaft und Werbung.
     The Press in Africa: A Handbook for Economics and
     Advertising. 2d ed. Pullach/Munich: Verlag Dokumen-
     tation, 1973. 280p.
     _____. Die Presse in Lateinamerika: Ein Handbuch für
     Wirtschaft und Werbung. The Press in Latin America:
     A Handbook for Economics and Advertising. 2d ed.
     Pullach/Munich: Verlag Documentation, 1973. 268p.
     _____. Die Presse in Asien und Ozeanien: Ein Handbuch
     für Wirtschaft und Werbung. The Press in Asia and
     Oceania: A Handbook for Economics and Advertising.
     2d ed. Pullach/Munich: Verlag Documentation, 1973.
     376p.
     _____. Die Presse in Europa: Ein Handbuch für
     Wirtschaft und Werbung. The Press in Europe: A Hand-
     book for Economics and Advertising. Pullach/Munich:
     Verlag Dokumentation; New York: Bowker, 1971. 328p.

     A bilingual series in English and German, limited to
     general and trade newspapers, and intended for business
     and advertising. Arrangement is by country and informa-
     tion is in tabular form. For each publication it includes
     political trends, address, circulation, language, fre-
     quency of issue, kinds of readers (usually given in one
     word or phrase, as industry, engineers, all kinds), pages,
     size, column, printing method, screen of pictures, price,
     and closing date before publication. There is a final
     section on the international press. A nine- to twelve-
     line demographic summary precedes each section on the
     countries, giving size, type of government, composition
     of population, religions, and exports and imports.
     Indexed.

671. Fielding, Raymond. The American Newsreel, 1911-1967.
     Norman: University of Oklahoma Press, 1972. 392p.

     History of a vanished genre. The author appraises the
     newsreel critically and indicts it for having failed to
     live up to its potential. Contains illustrations, notes,
     a bibliography, and an index.

672. Filler, Louis. The Muckrakers. New and enl. ed. Univer-
     sity Park: Pennsylvania State University Press, 1976.
     456p.

     This classic history of the muckraking era, first pub-
     lished in 1939 covering the years 1902-14, was expanded
     in 1968 under the present title to cover the New Deal,
     and has now been brought up to date to include Nadar, the
     women's liberation movement, and the Watergate era, with

muckraking now called investigative reporting. Contains
a chronology, a bibliographic essay, and an index.

673. Films about Newspapers: A Listing of Films, Filmstrips
     and Slide Presentations about the Newspaper Business.
     Washington: American Newspaper Publishers Association
     Foundation, Box 17407, Dulles International Airport,
     and International Newspaper Promotion Association,
     Box 17422, 1974. Unpaged.

     A slim pamphlet listing films, filmstrips, and slide
     presentations. Under the headings "Freedom of the Press,"
     "The Newspaper and Its Community," "Career," and "Produc-
     tion," it gives a physical description of each film--16mm
     or 35mm, color or black and white, with or without sound,
     etc.--and date of production. Following this is the com-
     mittee's evaluation of audiences most appropriate to the
     particular film and comments describing it and its value
     for the audience. Finally, there is information regard-
     ing the source, availability, and cost if any.

674. Finkle, Lee. Forum for Protest: The Black Press during
     World War II. Rutherford, N.J.: Fairleigh Dickinson
     University Press, 1975. 249p.

     An analysis of the response of the black press to the
     wartime emergency, based upon the opinion and news it
     disseminated. Emphasis is on news content, editorials,
     and columnists. Preceding this is a forty-page section
     giving a brief history of the black press in the U.S.
     Contains a bibliography and an index.

Francis-Williams, Edward. See Williams, Francis.

675. Gans, Herbert J. Deciding What's News: A Study of CBS
     Evening News, NBC Nightly News, Newsweek and Time.
     New York: Pantheon, 1979. 393p.

     Result of a ten-year study in which Gans sat in on
     the day-to-day life of the studios and the newsrooms,
     witnessing the decision-making process. He examines the
     values of the journalists and the values in the news
     itself, and finds definite "enduring values" built into
     it which support a certain social order. While it thinks
     of itself as non-ideological and impartial, it is actually
     defending implicitly a conservative, although reformist,
     vision of America. Notes, bibliography, and index.

676. Gardner, Mary A. The Press of Guatemala. Association for
     Education in Journalism, 1971. 48p. (Journalism Mono-
     graphs No. 18.) (Obtain from AEJ Headquarters.)

". . . in most Latin American countries, the basic historical and descriptive research concerning the role of
the press, its problems, and the journalists who work
within it, has yet to be done. The study which follows is
an attempt to look at the press from inside out, largely
from the viewpoint of the working journalist. No attempt
is made to evaluate the effect or impact the press may
have on the people of Guatemala or to suggest what it
should be doing, but rather to describe what journalism
in Guatemala is, how it got that way and why."-Introduc-
tion. Footnotes.

677. Gelfman, Judith S. Women in Television News. New York:
Columbia University Press, 1976. 186p.

The author has based her findings on interviews and
on-the-job observation of thirty women who have succeeded
in television news. Among topics discussed are: breaking
ground, background for a career, dimensions and expecta-
tions of a career, being a woman in television news,
double tokenism, career versus home life, career guidance
and advice. Bibliography and index.

678. Glessing, Robert J. The Underground Press in America.
Bloomington: Indiana University Press, 1970.
207p.

Covering fifteen years of the underground press from
its beginning through the sixties, Glessing traces its
history and shows how it influenced American lifestyle
by changing music, clothing, hair styles, sexual mores,
politics, advertising, and so on. There are illustrations of writings from the press, a bibliography of
sources, a directory of underground newspapers, and an
index.

679. Gormley, William T., Jr. The Effects of Newspaper-
Television Cross Ownership on News Homogeneity. Chapel
Hill: University of North Carolina Publications,
Institute for Research in Social Science, Manning Hall,
1976. 276p.

A study which provides a detailed examination of the
results of cross-ownership of newspapers and broadcast
stations in the same market, based on a study of ten
markets of different sizes. The author examines effects
in three likely situations: when station and newspaper
are located in the same building, when both use the same
reporters, and when the station uses the stories from the
newspaper. There are tables, footnotes, and a bibliography.

680. Great Britain. Central Office of Information. Reference
     Division. The British Press. 2d ed. London: Her
     Majesty's Stationery Office, 1974. 43p.

A survey which includes the following on a basic level:
historical background, British newspapers today, the
periodical press, ownership and policy, pay and training
of journalists, press institutions, and the press and the
law. An appendix gives a list of press organizations, and
there is a reading list.

681. Great Britain. Royal Commission on the Press. Memoranda
     on Evidence Submitted to the Royal Commission on the
     Press, 1947-48. 5 vols. London: Her Majesty's Sta-
     tionery Office, 1978.
682. _____ . _____ . Minutes of Evidence Taken before the
     Royal Commission on the Press. 38 vols. and Index.
     1948.
683. _____ . _____ . Report, 1962. Lord Shawncross, Chair-
     man. 238p. (Command Paper 1811.)
684. _____ . _____ . Documentary Evidence . . . 1962.
     6 vols.
685. _____ . _____ . Minutes of Oral Evidence. 1962.
     3 vols. and Index. (Command Papers 1812, 1812-1,
     1812-2.)
686. _____ . _____ . Interim Report: The National News-
     paper Industry. O. R. McGregor, Chairman. 1976.
     (Command Paper 6433.)
687. _____ . _____ . Final Report, 1977. Appendices.
     2 vols. (Command Papers 6810, 6810-1.)

For decades Great Britain has had an ongoing appraisal
of its press by the Royal Commission on the Press. It
examines factors affecting the maintenance of independence,
diversity, and editorial standards of newspapers and periodicals, and the public's freedom of choice to obtain them
on national, regional, and local levels. Among issues
analyzed are economics and distribution; management and
labor practices; conditions of employment; concentration of
ownership and ownership by conglomorates; and the responsibilities, constitution, and functioning of the Press Council. The publications listed above contain findings from
documentary and oral evidence and the Commission reports
incorporating them. These are not only informative within
themselves, but are a good source for bibliographic references and statistics.

688. Great Britain. Royal Commission on the Press. O. R.
     McGregor, Chairman. Analysis of Newspaper Content: A
     Report by Professor Denis McQuail. London: Her

Majesty's Stationery Office, 1977. 364p. (Research
Series 4.) (Command Paper 6810-4.)

Brings together the reports of five separate studies
carried out for the Royal Commission on the Press. These
reports consist of several descriptive surveys of the
main kinds of newspapers in Britain, focusing in greater
depth on selected areas of content. Categories for news
about Britain include political, social, and economic; law
and police; accidents; and personalities (including sports).
Categories for external news, both international and Commonwealth, follow much the same lines. There are also
categories for financial, scientific, and technical, and
miscellaneous news; features of all kinds; editorials;
correspondence; cartoons and comic strips; fiction; puz-
zles; regular information about radio and TV programming,
etc.; advertisements; parliamentary debates; and picture
content. There are many tables in the main body of the
report and the appendices. Descriptions of the methodology are also in an appendix.

689. Gustafsson, Karl Erik, and Stig Hadenius. Swedish Press
Policy. S-103 82 Stockholm 7: The Swedish Institute,
P.O. Box 7072, 1977. 127p.

In Sweden, perhaps more than in any other country, the
state has actively intervened to maintain diversity in the
press through a program of subsidies. The authors, who
both served on the 1972 Parliamentary Commission on the
Press, describe the structure of the press policy and its
effects since its introduction ten years ago. They also
summarize press history, newspaper economy, and newspaper
market. An appendix lists Swedish newspapers since 1975.
There is a bibliography of references in both English and
Swedish.

690. Hale, Oran J. The Captive Press in the Third Reich.
Princeton, N.J.: Princeton University Press, 1964.
353p.

A thoroughgoing examination of the way in which the
Nazis gained possession of the German press and the way
in which they maintained it and used it for their own
purposes. There are charts on the organization of the
Reich Press Chamber and the organization of the Eher
Verlag in 1944. Contains notes on records, interviews,
and books, a bibliography, and an index.

691. Handbook of News Agencies. Oldrich Bures and Jaroslav
First, comps. Prague: International Organization of
Journalists, General Secretariat, Publications Depart-
ment, Parizska 9, 1969. Looseleaf.

A survey of about sixty international and national
agencies from all parts of the world. Information for
each varies, but gives such facts as address, telephone
number, branches at home and abroad, size of staff, frequency of publication, number of subscribers, special
services, external news sources, character of agency
(whether private or government owned), and name of owner.

692. Harrison, Stanley. Poor Men's Guardians: A Record of
the Struggles for a Democratic Newspaper Press, 1763–
1973. London: Lawrence and Wishart, 1974. 256p.

Traces the story of the radical and working-class press
in Britain from the time of John Wilkes and the "Wilkes
and Liberty" agitation in the eighteenth century to the
present. The author surveys the struggle for press freedom between the haves and the havenots, the conflicts of
definitions of freedom that marked it from the beginning,
and the tremendous stakes in the outcome of these struggles for the labor and progressive movement over the last
200 years. The story is told in terms of the newspapers
which led the fight for progress. Contains a bibliography, an index to the newspapers mentioned, and a general index.

693. Hausman, Linda Weiner. Criticism of the Press in U.S.
Periodicals, 1900–1939: An Annotated Bibliography.
Association for Education in Journalism, 1967. 49p.
(Journalism Monograph #4.) (Obtain from AEJ Head-
quarters.)

Articles are presented under "The Press in General,"
"The Press as a Social Institution," "The Press as Busi-
ness," "The Newspaper," "The Periodical Press," "The News
Services," and "Press Personalities." Name-subject index.

694. Hepple, Alex. Press under Apartheid. London EC1A 7AP:
Information Department, International Defence and Aid
Fund, 104 Newgate St., 1974. 67p.

An analysis of freedom of the press in South Africa,
including the long war against the free press, the laws
that restrain and control it, relations with the police,
press ownership, and the role of the press in an apartheid
society. Appendices give circulation figures and group
ownership.

695. Holden, W. Sprague. Australia Goes to Press. Detroit,
Mich.: Wayne State University Press, 1961. 297p.

An overview of Australian newspaper journalism--how it
works, press law, the Australian Journalists' Association,

training for journalism, advertising, circulation, and promotion. Appendices give brief historical sketches of fifteen leading newspapers; a very brief survey of radio and TV structure; a discussion of professional associations, trade services, and publications; and the authorized news agent system. There is a selected bibliography and an index.

696. Hopkins, Mark W. Mass Media in the Soviet Union. New York: Pegasus, 1970. 384p.

"The focus of this book is on the Soviet newspaper press, which has throughout Soviet history been dominant in the mass media. Most of what is said about newspapers and the work of Soviet newspaper journalists applies also to the Soviet magazine press and to radio and television. Yet the latter especially deserve increasing separate attention for the changes they are effecting in Soviet society." – Preface.

As the Milwaukee Journal's Soviet affairs specialist since 1964, the author has spent much time in Russia and has attended Leningrad University. He possesses insights into what are in his opinion the good and bad elements of the Soviet system, which he frequently compares with the good and bad elements of our own. Contains detailed footnotes and an excellent bibliography as well as maps, lists, tables, and an index.

697. Hudson's Washington News Media Contacts Directory. Howard Penn Hudson and Mary Elizabeth Hudson, eds. Washington: National Directories, Inc., 2626 Pennsylvania Ave., N.W., annual. (1967--.)

An organized listing of the Washington news media, giving in the present edition approximately 2,500 news outlets and 2,800 correspondents and editors. Coverage includes general news services; Washington news bureaus; Washington correspondents; foreign-language newspapers; special news services and syndicates; syndicated columnists and features; specialized newspapers; Washington newspapers; foreign newspapers and news services; radio-TV networks, with listing of their news bureaus and guest interview and discussion programs; freelance writers; foreign magazines; specialized magazines, newsletters, and periodicals. This latter section has a classified subject index. There is also a straight alphabetical index and an assignment locator to enable the user to find quickly the correspondents who have special beats and assignments. Revisions are provided three times a year.

698. Hynds, Ernest C. <u>American Newspapers in the 1970s.</u> New
York: Hastings House, 1975. 349p.

In this ambitious book the author explains that his
aim is: "(1) to help individuals make more effective use
of their newspapers by discussing what newspapers are and
should be and how they operate, and (2) to help all newspapers realize more of their potential by describing what
many newspapers are doing successfully in the 1970s." He
surveys roles and responsibilities, history, types of
newspapers, the newspaper as a business institution, news
and opinions, the right to know and to publish, and the
new technology. He ends with thumbnail sketches of some
of the country's leading newspapers. Contains chapter
notes, a bibliography, and an index.

<u>IENS Press Handbook.</u> (<u>See</u> No. 1113.)

699. <u>ILPA Directory of Member Publications.</u> Washington 20006:
International Labor Press Association, 615 16th St.,
N.W. (1955--.)

Lists newsletters, newspapers, magazines, and pamphlets
published by AFL-CIO-affiliated organizations in the U.S.
and by CLC (Canadian Labour Congress). Entries include
all or some of the following information: name, sponsor-
ing union or organization, owner, address, telephone,
editor, frequency, and circulation.

<u>INFA Press and Advertisers Year Book.</u> (<u>See</u> No. 1114.)

700. <u>In the Public Interest: A Report by the National News
Council, 1973-1975.</u> New York 10023: National News
Council, One Lincoln Plaza, 1975. 163p.

A discussion of the problems the council has dealt with
since its inception and the principles involved. It
includes a list of the council's members, advisers, and
staff; its history; an analysis of complaints handled; its
fellowship program; its bylaws and rules of procedure; how
to make complaints; and similar pertinent information about
what it has accomplished and its manner of operation.

701. <u>The Japanese Press.</u> Tokyo: The Japan Newspaper Publishers
and Editors Association (Nihon Shinbun Kyokai), Nippon
Press Center Bldg., 2-2-1, Uchisaiwa--cho, Chiyoda-Ku,
annual. (1949--.)

The first part of this annual is devoted mainly to
trends in the newspaper press, although advertising and
broadcasting are dealt with briefly in one article each.
The second part is a directory of newspapers, news

agencies, broadcasting stations, TV newsreel agencies, Japanese correspondents overseas, and foreign press personnel in Japan. There is an index to statistical data.

702. Johnson, Michael L. *The New Journalism: The Underground Press, the Artists of Nonfiction, and Changes in the Established Media.* Lawrence: University Press of Kansas, 1971. 171p.

The author believes that the new journalism is a new journalistic genre. The first two chapters are devoted to the underground press from its beginnings to the mid-1960s. Next is a critical survey of the new journalism as an evolving literary form. Following this the author discusses its effect on the established press. Notes and an index.

703. Johnstone, John W. C., Edward J. Slawski, and William W. Bowman. *The News People: A Sociological Portrait of American Journalists and Their Work.* Urbana: University of Illinois Press, 1976. 257p.

In this, the first systematic treatment of newsmen at large, based on extensive interviews with more than 1,300 practicing journalists, the authors say that their main concern is "to present a representative overview of the nature of newsmen and newswork in contemporary America." "News people" is interpreted broadly to include those who work in radio and TV, wire services and syndicates, news magazines, daily and weekly newspapers, as well as some of the journalists in the alternative media. Data is analyzed to show social characteristics, education and training, career patterns, political affiliations, division of labor, the ways in which news men and women perceive their journalistic responsibility, and the rewards and satisfactions they find in their work. Finally, the authors draw their conclusions as to *who* and *where* the news-gathers are and how this affects the quantity and quality of their work. Extensive appendices give charts and tables of data. Bibliography and person-subject index. Winner of the National Association of Public Broadcasters' Award in 1977.

704. Jones, William H., and Laird Anderson. *The Newspaper Business.* Washington: *Washington Post*, 1977. Unpaged.

A twelve-part series which appeared in the *Washington Post*. It discusses concentration in general and specific important newspapers and chains in particular. Interspersed are short general articles on such topics as the future of newspapers, the possible fate of independents, antitrust suits, and so on.

705. Journalism Scholarship Guide and Directory of College Journalism Programs. Princeton, N.J.: Newspaper Fund, Inc., P.O. Box 300, annual. (1961--.)

Contains a rundown of universities, colleges, newspapers, professional societies, and journalism-related organizations, all of which offer more than $2 million in financial aid. For colleges and universities it gives, in addition to scholarships, sequences, name of head, telephone number, degree or degrees awarded, and average yearly costs. For other sources, it describes scholarships and tells to whom to direct inquiries. Another section, "Other Journalism Scholarships," names institutions with minority scholarships, miscellaneous sources, and sources of continuing education for news people and teachers. Contains a bibliography and an index.

706. Kaplan, Frank L. Winter into Spring: The Czechoslovak Press and the Reform Movement, 1963-1968. Boulder, Colo.: East European Quarterly, 1977. 208p. (Distributed by Columbia University Press.)

During its brief existence as an independent state, Czechoslovakia has been subjected to distinctly different forms of political ideology and government. Focusing on a critical four-year period, Kaplan has analyzed the role played by a traditionally Western-oriented and pluralistic press in a society which becomes Communist-oriented. Appendices give numerous facts and figures about the press, including a list of daily and weekly newspapers and periodicals (as of 1968). There are copious footnotes, an extensive bibliography, and an index. Kaplan's fifty-four-page monograph, The Czech and Slovak Press: The First 100 Years, also appeared in 1977 as Journalism Monograph 47 (Association for Education in Journalism).

707. Kent, Ruth K. The Language of Journalism: A Glossary of Print-Communications Terms. Ohio: Kent State University Press, 1971. 186p.

A dictionary of journalistic and many printing terms, preceded by a discussion of the meaning and origins of such associated words as muckraker, tabloid, yellow journalism, and so on, and followed by a list of abbreviations, a list of proofreaders' marks, footnotes, sources consulted, and a bibliography. Although the author says that she does not attempt to present a complete journalism glossary, her scope is extensive. Emphasis is mainly on editorial

journalism, with a scattering of entries having to do with
paper, book production, the electronic media, statistical
research, law of the press, and photography.

708. Kesterton, Wilfred H. A History of Journalism in Canada.
    Toronto: McClelland and Stewart, 1967. 304p.

    A critical and analytical account of the growth of the
    Canadian press from the 1750s to the present. Chapter
    headings indicate content and scope: "The First Press
    Period: The Transplant, 1752 to 1807"; "The Second Press
    Period: Thickening Growth, 1807 to 1858"; "The Third
    Press Period: The Western Transplant and Spreading Growth,
    1858 to 1900"; "The Fourth Press Period: The Mutation";
    "Journals and Journalism"; "Qualitative Developments: How
    the Daily Newspapers Changed During the Twentieth Century";
    "Twentieth-Century Newspaper Content"; "The Development of
    Radio and Television"; "Canadian Press Freedom in the
    Twentieth Century." Contains footnotes and an extensive
    index.

709. King, Frank H. H., and Prescott Clarke, eds. A Research
    Guide to China-Coast Newspapers, 1822-1911. Cambridge,
    Mass.: Harvard University Press, 1965. 235p.

    "This research guide is designed primarily to facilitate
    the use of Western-language newspapers published in China,
    including Hong Kong and Macao, during the late Ch'ing per-
    iod. It contains information on several related topics,
    including those newspapers published in London concerned
    with news of China, and certain Chinese-language sheets
    published as an integral part of or in close connection
    with the Western-language newspapers. There is also an
    appendix listing Japanese-language newspapers published
    in China during the period through 1911." - Introduction.
    Contains a bibliography.

710. Kirsch, Donald. Financial and Economic Journalism: Analy-
    sis, Interpretation and Reporting. New York: New York
    University Press, 1978. 343p.
711. _____. Documentary Supplement to Financial and Economic
    Journalism: Analysis, Interpretation and Reporting.
    New York: New York University Press, 1978. 242p.

    Although these are intended for classroom use, they are
    included here because of the scarcity of information on
    the structure of business journalism and will give the
    novice or layman an excellent idea of what is involved.
    Two sections of the Documentary Supplement, one a list of
    periodicals and books of interest to the business journal-
    ist and the other a glossary and reference source, are
    especially valuable.

712. Kobre, Sidney. The Development of the Colonial News-
        paper. Pittsburgh, Pa. 13191: Colonial Press,
        620 Second Ave., 1944. 188p.

    Takes the American newspaper from 1690 through 1783,
    tracing its social development and discussing various
    newspapers. Contains a number of charts and tables, an
    appendix giving a chronological account of newspapers in
    other colonies, a list of newspapers within the period,
    and a bibliography.

713. La Brie, Henry C., ed. Perspectives of the Black Press:
        1974. Kennebunkport, Maine: Mercer House, 1974.
        231p.

    An anthology which gives an eclectic overview of the
    black press as seen by black--and some white--journalists
    and journalism educators. Its articles touch on a num-
    ber of topics: the role of the black press in the past
    and speculations about its role in the future; experiences
    of practitioners who have "made it"; pressure groups;
    testimony before Congress; successful examples of news-
    papers; the black press as an outlet for poets and fiction
    writers. Contains a name index and a subject-title index.

714. Lee, Alfred McClung. The Daily Newspaper in America: The
        Evolution of a Social Instrument. New York: Macmillan,
        1937. 797p.

    Forty or more years have not outdated this sociological,
    or in Lee's words, "natural," history of the daily news-
    paper in which he has brought together many of the inter-
    related forces that shaped it. Organization is topical,
    with such headings as the newspaper in society; the pre-
    daily paper; the physical basis of the newspaper; labor,
    ownership, and management; chains and associations; adver-
    tising; weekly and Sunday issues; propaganda and public
    relations tie-ins; the gathering of world news; feature
    syndicates; the editorial staff; crusades; invasion of
    privacy, and others. His approach and Mott's chronological
    one (No. 729) offer interesting contrasts.

715. Lent, John A., ed. The Asian Newspapers' Reluctant Revolu-
        tion. Ames: Iowa State University Press, 1971. 373p.

    History and contemporary description of the newspaper
    presses of fifteen Asian nations, written by eighteen
    authors who include editors, publishers, professors, and
    media specialists, both Asian and American. Emphasis is
    on patterns of development within individual countries.
    Contains notes, a bibliography, and an index.

716. LeRoy, David J., and Christopher H. Sterling, eds. Mass News: Practices, Controversies, and Alternatives. Englewood Cliffs, N.J.: Prentice-Hall, 1973. 334p.

This anthology, intended as a supplemental text for undergraduates, deals almost exclusively with the three major sources of public news--the wire services, newspapers, and TV--assessing their strengths and their weaknesses. There is an excellent bibliography and an author-subject index.

Levin, Harvey J. Broadcast Regulation and Joint Ownership of Media. (See No. 480.)

717. Lewis, Roger. Outlaws of America; The Underground Press and Its Context: Notes on a Cultural Revolution. Harmondsworth, England: Penguin, 1972. 204p.

The author, an Englishman who attended an American university, traveled across the U.S. gathering his material. He has identified the main groups and tied in their publications with various of the counter-culture movements. One chapter discusses the underground press in England. There is a listing, "Underground Press Syndicate--Members and Friends, June, 1971," and a name and subject index.

718. Liu, Alan P. L. The Press and Journals in Communist China. Cambridge, Mass.: Massachusetts Institute of Technology, Center for International Studies, Research Program on Problems of International Security, 1966. 121p. (Distributed by Clearinghouse of Federal Scientific and Technical Information, U.S. Dept. of Commerce, National Bureau of Standards, Institute for Applied Technology.)

Succinct analysis of the background, structure, function, and content of news and news reporting, newspaper reading patterns, and periodicals, with a concluding chapter on the effectiveness of the press. The author has documented his study (necessarily from secondhand sources) with extensive footnotes and a bibliography.

719. McGregor, O. R. See Great Britain. Royal Commission on the Press. Interim Report. The National Newspaper Industry. (No. 686) and Great Britain. Royal Commission on the Press. Analysis of Newspaper Content. (No. 688.)

720. McQuail, Denis. Review of Sociological Writing on the Press. London: Her Majesty's Stationery Office, 1976. 86p. (Great Britain. Royal Commission on the Press. Working Paper No. 2.)

A bibliographic essay in which the author's aim has
been to show the main themes of sociological work on the
press and to summarize part of the evidence and interpretation which has accumulated. Various sections take up
the social theory of the press, the press as a social
institution, press content, the press and its readers,
press effects, and functions of the press. Works mentioned throughout are brought together in a full bibliography.

McQuail, Denis. See also Great Britain. Royal Commission on
the Press. Analysis of Newspaper Content. (No. 688.)

721. Marbut, F. B. News from the Capital: The Story of Washington Reporting. Carbondale: Southern Illinois
University, 1971. 304p.

A history of governmental reporting in the U.S. from
the early 1800s to the mid-1960s. Contains bibliographical
notes and an index.

722. Marty, Martin E., and others. The Religious Press in America. New York: Holt, Rinehart & Winston, 1963. 184p.

The aim of the authors is to familiarize readers of
denominational publications, both newspapers and magazines,
with the ways in which these publications interpret the
world in terms of religious commitments. In chapters both
descriptive and broadly analytical, they discuss the Protestant, Catholic, and Jewish presses and the secular uses
of the religious press. Footnotes.

723. Marzio, Peter C. The Men and Machines of American Journalism: A Pictorial Essay from the Henry R. Luce Hall of
News Reporting. Washington: National Museum of History
and Technology, Smithsonian Institution, 1973. 144p.

"The history of journalism, as pursued until now, has
been unimaginative. Too many works follow a simplistic,
chronological, newspaper-by-newspaper approach which omits
the need for a thesis, fails to illuminate the need for
the larger issues. Boredom reigns." So says the author
in his introduction. And it would be difficult to be bored
with his illustrated history clustered around topics, with
the main theme the effect of mechanical inventions. Illustrations play as large or an even larger part than text.
The time span encompasses the period from the post rider
to the present communication satellites. Contains a bibliography and an index.

724. Marzolf, Marion. Up from the Footnote: A History of Women
Journalists. New York: Hastings House, 1977. 310p.

The story of women journalists from colonial widow-
printer to TV anchorwoman. The author discusses pioneers
and latter-day figures in their many roles--reporters,
printers, editors, publishers, foreign correspondents,
researchers, columnists, news directors, and teachers,
with sections on the feminist press then and now and on
the situation in Europe. There is a bibliography at the
end of each chapter and an index.

725. Mayer, Henry. The Press in Australia. Melbourne: Lans-
     downe, 1964. 281p.

     "This book attempts three main tasks: First, to give
the basic facts about the history, structure and content
of the Australian press; second, to argue that newspapers,
given the technical and business conditions under which
they work, and granted my view about why they are read,
are bound to be much as they are; third--and this is my
major interest--to analyze common attitudes toward the
Press and criticize the assumptions made both by its
critics and its defenders." - Preface.
     The author further states that he is not aiming to
bring out the special flavor of the Australian press or
to compare it with the press of other countries. He
deals only with capital-city dailies and gives considerable information about content and readership. Although
there is no bibliography, there are detailed footnotes at
the end of each chapter. Indexed.

726. Meetings of Experts on the Development of News Agencies
     in Africa, Tunis, 1963. Paris: UNESCO, 1963. 225p.

     An examination of measures to promote the development
of existing news agencies, the establishment of agencies
in areas not yet possessing them, and the flow of news
within the region, as well as in other regions of the
world.

727. Merrill, John C., Carter E. Bryan, and Marvin Alisky.
     The Foreign Press: A Survey of the World's Journalism.
     2d ed. Baton Rouge: Louisiana State University Press,
     1970. 365p.

     The authors' aim is "to present a panoramic picture of
the world's press systems with a minimum of distortion
and to bring to the student who desires a more intensive
study many excellent sources of investigation." Using an
overview of the U.S. press as a point of departure, they
give sketches of national press systems in Europe,
including the Communist block, Latin America, the Far
East and Southeast Asia, Africa, Canada, Australia, and
New Zealand. Emphasis is on the newspaper press and to

some extent the magazine press, with briefer data on radio
and TV. Developments within the last decade have outdated
some of the material, particularly in Africa and Asia.
The bibliographical section is lengthy, with notes and
selected readings

728. Merrill, John C., and Harold A. Fisher. The World's Great-
     est Dailies: Profiles of Fifty Elite Newspapers. New
     York: Hastings House, 1979. 350p.

     This book, an outgrowth of Merrill's Elite Press (Pit-
     man, 1968), is a completely rewritten and expanded version.
     The present volume presents fifty separate profiles of out-
     standing dailies of the world, ten more than appeared in
     the earlier book. Some of the new U.S. dailies in the
     present volume are the Wall Street Journal, the Washington
     Post, and the Miami Herald. A few of the new foreign
     dailies are the Statesman of India, El Pais of Spain, the
     Suddeutsche Zeitung of West Germany, and the Straits Times
     of Singapore. This book makes no attempt to rank the
     dailies as was done in the 1968 book. Bibliography and
     index.

Moment of Truth. (See No. 630.)

729. Mott, Frank Luther. American Journalism: A History, 1690-
     1960. 3d ed. New York: Macmillan, 1962. 901p.

     In spite of its age this history of journalism, like
     Lee's Daily Newspaper in America (No. 714), remains stan-
     dard. Mott states that his purpose is "to provide a com-
     prehensive work in which historical narrative is combined
     with some of the characteristics of a reference book."
     Arrangement is chronological, with much attention to indi-
     vidual newspapers as well as to such broad trends as the
     party press of the pre-Civil War period, yellow journalism,
     and so on. Footnotes, bibliographic notes, and an index.

730. Murphy, Sharon. Other Voices: Black, Chicano, and Ameri-
     can Indian Press. Dayton, Ohio: Pflaum/Standard, 1974.
     132p.

     Surveys these three minority presses, with brief his-
     tories and extensive use of quotes from personnel and pro-
     minent personalities from the minorities. Lists newspapers
     and other existing media, briefly analyzes treatment of
     minorities in some of the standard histories of journalism,
     and suggests further readings.
     Sharon Murphy, with James E. Murphy and Neva S. Lehde-
     White, has also compiled the Directory of American Indian
     Print and Broadcast Media (University of Wisconsin-
     Milwaukee, Box 67, 1978[?]), which lists by states the

215

names, addresses, and frequency of currently publishing
Indian newspapers and magazines, as well as the call let-
ters and addresses of radio stations which broadcast
Indian programs.

731. Murthy, Nadig Krishna. Indian Journalism: Origin, Growth
and Development of Indian Journalism from Asoka to
Nehru. Mysore, India: "Presaranga," University of
Mysore, 1966. 506p.

Traces the development of India's press against the
background of her history, with special emphasis upon the
problem of the country's various languages and its
struggle for independence from England. Contents include
an overall introduction; the history of English daily newspapers; journalism in Indian languages; periodicals; and a
general section including government publicity, news
agencies and syndicates, newsprint and technical problems,
teaching of journalism, professional organizations, press
laws, and the Indian Press Commission. A bibliography
and appendices give tables of facts and figures.

732. Nafziger, Ralph O., comp. International News and the
Press: Communication, Organization of News Gathering,
International Affairs, and the Foreign Press--An
Annotated Bibliography. New York: Arno, c1940, 1972.
193p.

Nafziger has examined thousands of books, articles,
proceedings, documents, memoirs, occasional papers, and
various fragmentary and episodic bits and made them into
a topical bibliography which covers the U.S. and foreign
news gathering from the turn of the century to World War
II. Name index.

733. Natarajan, Swaminath. A History of the Press in India.
New York: Asia Publishing House, 1962. 425p.

A social history, sponsored by the Audit Bureau of
Circulation, designed to show the press as a medium both
for news dissemination and for advertising. Appendices
include press legislation, the press and the Registration of Books Act, leading newspapers, and wages of
journalists. There is a bibliography and an index.

734. National Directory of Weekly Newspapers. Washington:
National Newspaper Association and Publishers Auxiliary, 1627 K St., N.W., annual. (1920--.)

Weekly, semiweekly, and triweekly newspapers in the
U.S., listed alphabetically by state and city. For
each is given circulation, publisher, address, phone

number, information about advertising, day of publication, and characteristics of area--i.e., agricultural,
suburban, industrial, resort, mining, fishing, oil,
lumber, etc. A brief introduction contains trends and
statistics.

735. News Agencies: Their Structure and Operation. New York:
     UNESCO Publications Center, 1953. 208p.

A detailed and thorough analysis of news agencies
throughout the world. Gives a historical review, discusses legal organization and international regulation,
and describes their relationship with radio newscasting
and their use of telegraph and telecommunication. Also
contains an alphabetical list of telegraphic news agencies.

Newspaper Rates and Data. (See No. 1143.)

736. Newsprint Data: Statistics of World Demand and Supply.
     Montreal PQ H3B 2X9: Canadian Pulp and Paper Associa-
     tion, 2300 Sun Life Bldg., annual. (1930--.)

Statistical tables show, country by country for approximately forty countries, newsprint capacity, production,
exports, imports, and demand.

737. Norland, Rod. Names and Numbers: A Journalist's Guide
     to the Most Needed Information Sources and Contacts.
     New York: Wiley-Interscience, 1978. 560p.

Intended as "a directory of news makers for the benefit of the news media," this contains more than 20,000
listings in annotated form, with contact information for
government, businesses, institutions, organizations, and
people. It gives names and numbers of people whom journalists may need to reach; sources of specialized information, comment, and background; and outlets for documents,
records, and advice. Part I, "Useful Logistics," provides
practical, often hard-to-find information on the logistics
of getting around; Part II, "Information Sources and Contacts," which constitutes the bulk of the book, lists services available at various levels of government, and
through colleges and universities and various specialized
agencies--police, emergency, business, consumers, labor,
education, science and technology, religion, politics,
sports, art and entertainment, recreation, weather, and
worldwide. Part III, "The Media," lists media organizations, networks, daily newspapers, all-news radio stations,
wire services, public relations firms and wire services,
national journalism awards, and press clubs. It is

217

minutely indexed and is a welcome addition to the reference
literature for journalists and, coincidentally, for librarians.

738. Oey, Hong Lee. Indonesian Government and Press during
Guided Democracy. Zug, Switzerland: Inter Documentation Company, 1971. 401p. (Hull Monograph on Southeast Asia No. 4.)

Traces the development of the Indonesian press in
relation to politics from the beginning of the Dutch
period in 1594 through the regime of President Sukarno.
Emphasis is on the newspaper press during Sukarno's
period of "guided democracy." Contains a bibliography
and a brief index.

739. Olson, Kenneth E. The History Makers: The Press of
Europe from Its Beginnings through 1965. Baton Rouge:
Louisiana State University Press, 1966. 471p.

The growth of the press in twenty-four nations of
Europe, with an evaluation of the European press today.
Contains a list of papers for each country and a compre-
hensive bibliography.

740. One Hundred Years of the Yiddish Press in America, 1870-
1970: Catalogue of the Exhibition. Z. Szajkowski,
comp. New York 10028: YIVO Institute for Jewish
Research, 1048 Fifth Ave., 1970. 20p.

This listing of items, with notes about each, forms
an outline history of the Yiddish press in the U.S.--its
weeklies and dailies, including the labor press, its
writers, compositors, newsdealers, readers, advertisements, and its social role. It is not limited to the
past; one section gives dailies appearing in 1970. There
is also a section on the Yiddish press of various cities
and various groups. All items are available at the YIVO
Institute.

741. Overseas Press Club of America and American Correspondents
Overseas, 1975 Membership Directory. New York 10017:
Overseas Press Club of America, 420 Lexington Ave.,
1975. 125p.

Although we have one biography concerned exclusively
with living American journalists (No. 631), one with dead
American journalists (No. 780), and general biographical
directories like Contemporary Biography, Who's Who in
America, and Contemporary Authors (No. 42), which include
some prominent journalists, the field of communications
has no official biographical directory. This roster of

members of the Overseas Press Club of America does not
quite fill the gap, but it comes closer than anything
else. Its membership, by no means limited to overseas
correspondents, is wide and varied, and information on
a great number of newspaper reporters, editors and publishers, magazine and free-lance journalists, and
broadcasters can be found here, along with a smaller
number of educators, public relations practitioners,
and men and women in the business end of the industry.
Most of the entries contain the "who's who" type of
data, but some only give name and address. There are
considerable supplementary features: the history of the
Overseas Press Club; a survey of foreign correspondents--
"A Vanishing Species--the American Newsman Abroad"; a
table of the top ten countries with American correspondents; the Overseas Press Club Awards 1940-74; and a
comprehensive listing of U.S. correspondents abroad.
Updated at irregular intervals.

742. Penn, I. Garland. The Afro-American Press and Its
      Editors. New York: Arno Press/New York Times,
      c1891, 1969. 569p.

    Reprint of a book originally published in 1891. To
quote from the introduction to the new edition: "The
first part takes all of the Afro-American newspapers and
magazines, from Freedom's Journal (1827) to 1891. The
second part, which is very long, consists of many sketches
of editors and newspapers, opinions of eminent Negro men
on the Afro-American press, its editors' mission, and
other chapters on the relation of the Negro press to the
white press (including Negroes who write for white newspapers and magazines), the Afro-American League, and the
Associated Correspondents of Race Newspapers. There are
scores of photographs." Magazines as well as newspapers
are included. Indexed.

The Politics of Broadcasting, 1971-1972. (See No. 630.)

743. Potter, Elaine. The Press as Opposition: The Political
      Role of South African Newspapers. London: Chatto and
      Windus, 1975. 228p.

    The author, a South African living in England, explains
how the newspaper press, both Afrikaans and English, has
to this point preserved a degree of openness and freedom,
and how and why she feels that this is threatened. The
book, however, is full of other useful information in
addition to the issue of politics and the press; there
are sections on the history and ownership structure of

the press and the result of readership surveys. Contains
a lengthy bibliography and an index.

744. Press and Advertisers Year Book. New Delhi: INFA Publica-
     tions, Jeevah Deep, Parliament St., annual. (1961--.)

Subtitled "India's Leading Press and Media Guide," this
yearbook emphasizes newspapers, magazines, and advertising.
One of its most useful features is a listing of newspapers
and magazines which carry advertising, with address, telephone number, circulation, and details about rates. A
substantial portion is devoted to government information
services and press law. Among other features, it lists
trade and professional associations, journalism courses,
press correspondents, news agencies, a "who's who" in the
press and another in advertising and public relations,
and statistics on the cinema.

745. Press Councils and Press Codes. 4th ed. Zurich 8001:
     International Press Institute, Munstergasse 9, 1966.
     134p.

Summary prepared by the IPI Research Service on the
basis of texts published in IPI Report and other documents.
Part I gives eighty-eight pages of background information
on press codes and councils in Austria, Belgium, Canada,
Denmark, Germany, India, Israel, Italy, the Netherlands,
Norway, Pakistan, the Philippines, South Africa, South
Korea, Sweden, Switzerland, Turkey, the United Kingdom,
and the U.S. Part II gives texts of international codes
for the United Nations and the Inter-American Press Asso-
ciation, and texts of national codes for Australia, Bel-
gium, Canada, Chile, Denmark, France, Germany, India,
Israel, Italy, Nigeria, Norway, Pakistan, South Africa,
South Korea, Sweden, Turkey, the United Kingdom, and the
U.S.

746. Press in India. Report of the Registrar of Newspapers for
     India under the Press and Registration of Books Act.
     Pts. I-II. New Dehli: Minister of Information and
     Broadcasting, annual. (1956--.)

Annual report of the Registrar of Newspapers for India
under the Press and Registration of Books Act. Part I
contains general review and general statistics; this is
followed by data on circulation, ownership, the daily
press, the periodical press, the press in Indian dialects,
the press in the various states, non-included categories
and foreign mission publications, the administration and
working of the Press and Registration of Books Act, newsprint, and verification of circulation claims. Much of

the information is in statistical form. Appendices give
such data as newspaper-population ratio, circulation of
dailies per thousand inhabitants, and so on. Part II is
a listing of all newspapers and periodicals on the record
of the Registrar, arranged by state, with a title index.
Particulars for each newspaper include address and place
of publication, name of publisher, name of printer, name
of editor, retail selling price, name of printing press,
name of owner, circulation, and classification according
to content.

747. Price, Warren C. The Literature of Journalism: An
     Annotated Bibliography. Minneapolis: University of
     Minnesota Press, 1959. 489p.
748. _____ and Calder Pickett. An Annotated Journalism Bib-
     liography, 1958-1968. Minneapolis: University of
     Minnesota Press, 1970. 285p.

     The first title is a valuable bibliography of 3,147
books. Emphasis is on newspapers and magazines rather
than on advertising and broadcasting, although these
receive brief attention. It deals at considerable length
with history, biography, anthologies, freedom and ethics
of the press, public opinion, and propaganda.
     After Price's death this was updated by Pickett with
An Annotated Journalism Bibliography, whose scope was
broadened to include new developments in the field.
Entries total 2,172. Unlike the earlier edition, which
was arranged by categories, this is alphabetical with a
subject index.

Public Perceptions of Television and Other Media: A Twenty-
     Year Review, 1959-1978. (See No. 539.)

749. Rafferty, Keen. That's What They Said about the Press.
     New York: Vantage, 1975. 137p.

     This is a collection of more than 500 quotations about
the press made by "the famous, the infamous and the non-
descript," a wide range which includes such strange bed-
fellows as Lord Acton, Cicero, Jane Austin, Turner
Catledge, Erasmus, Shana Alexander, Stalin, Shakespeare,
Oscar Wilde, and so on ad infinitum (well, not quite).
Apart from the fact that it is fun, it provides a handy
reference tool when occasions call for such quotes.
Arrangement is topical, with an author index.

750. Rajan, S. P. Thiaga. History of Indian Journalism.
     Thanjavur, India: Columbia House, Gandhigi Rd., 1966.
     138p.

Collection of talks by the author in which he discusses
aspects of the Indian newspaper press. Among his topics
are the Press Commission, the Press Council, Reuters and
India, a free press, parliamentary immunities, the press
in developing countries, and training for journalism.

751. Reilly, Mary Lonan. A History of the Catholic Press Asso-
      cation, 1911-1968. Metuchen, N.J.: Scarecrow, 1971.
      350p.

      Tells how the Catholic Press Association came into
      being, its changing interests over the years, the evolu-
      tion of the organizational structure, and cooperative
      efforts with other groups. Appendices include membership
      statistics, convention dates and sites, and prominent
      officials. There is a lengthy bibliography which also
      includes archival material. Indexed.

Rich News, Poor News. (See No. 630.)

752. Righter, Rosemary. Whose News? Politics, the Press and
      the Third World. Times Books, 1978. 272p.

      An analysis of the struggle between the Western con-
      cept of the press as a means through which the public is
      freely informed about those in authority so that it can
      form judgments and act accordingly, and the Third World
      concept that the press should be a national voice func-
      tioning to make a better life for the people in terms of
      such things as nutrition and literacy. Bibliographical
      notes and index.

753. Robinson, Gertrude Joch. Tito's Maverick Media: The
      Politics of Mass Communication in Yugoslavia. Urbana:
      University of Illinois Press, 1977. 263p.

      Against the background of the sociopolitical factors
      that have shaped this multinational, multilingual Com-
      munist state, the author discusses the development and
      operation of the press and broadcasting. She details the
      history of communications from 1945 to 1975; analyzes the
      national news agency, Tanjug; examines the way in which
      characteristic news values have evolved; and describes
      the role of the media in nation-building in a country
      with widely diverse ethnic groups. In conclusion she
      explores the composition of readers, listeners, and
      viewers. Appendices give the journalism code, the con-
      tent of three geographical foreign policy registers
      (1964), and a comparison of overlapping subject matter
      in Tanjug and the Associated Press. There are footnotes
      and a bibliography.

754. Romano, Frank J. How to Build a Profitable Newspaper: Printing Impressions. Philadelphia 19108: North American Publishing Co., 401 North Broad, 1973. 220p.

This is not the kind of "how to" book one might suspect from the title. Rather, it is a Whole Earth Catalog type of book which tells you in a clear and specific way not only what to do but also how to get what you need. Although it does not go deeply into the editorial aspects, it does give some rather casual and pleasant instructions. But its value lies primarily in its clear explanations and information about sources of supplies, which are scattered through the text. There are also a bibliography and a glossary.

755. Rosengarten, Frank. The Italian Anti-Fascist Press (1919-1945). Cleveland, Ohio: Press of Case Western Reserve University, 1968. 263p.

Traces the development from the legal opposition press to the underground newspapers of World War II, which were carried on with considerable success by the resistance forces. An appendix gives some key aspects of the laws and principles governing the exercise of freedom of the press in Italy after fascism, and there is a detailed bibliography, most of which is in Italian. Indexed.

756. Rosewater, Victor. History of Cooperative Newsgathering in the United States. Norwood, N.J.: Johnson Reprint, c1930, 1971. 430p.

A definitive history of U.S. news agencies from their beginnings in the early 1800s to 1930. Appendices give "Regulation of the General News Association of the City of New York, 1856" and "By-laws of the Associated Press of New York." Bibliography and index.

757. Rosse, James N., Bruce M. Owen, and David L. Grey. Economic Issues in the Joint Ownership of Newspaper and Television Media: Comments in Response to "Further Notice of Proposed Rule-Making," Federal Communications Commission, Docket 18110. Stanford, Cal.: Stanford University, Research Center in Economic Growth, 408 Encina Hall West, 1970. 24p.

An investigation by three economists, who deal with the following points: effects of joint ownership on advertising prices and on the marketplace of ideas; the issue of cross-subsidization; the effects of divestiture; a definition of the market for newspapers; alternative policies to increase diversity. Tables contain hard facts and figures; there is a bibliography and footnotes;

and an appendix gives "A Proposed Test for the Effect of Newspaper Ownership on TV Programming Quality."

758. Rutland, Robert A. The Newsmongers: Journalism in the Life of the Nation, 1690-1972. New York: Dial, 1973. 430p.

A history of American newspaper journalism which interprets as well as chronicles. Rutland shows the way the press has dealt with some of the important national issues, the influence it has wielded or failed to wield, and the economic forces which affect it. On the whole it is an astute and somewhat disenchanted survey. Chapter notes showing sources of data may serve as a partial bibliography. There is a comprehensive index.

759. Sarkar, Chanchal. Challenge and Stagnation: The Indian Mass Media. New Delhi, India: Vikas Publications, 1969. 116p.

The author, director of the Press Institute of India, surveys his country's mass media and that of other parts of Asia as well. He discusses critically both the government-owned and private sectors. Much emphasis is on newspapers, perhaps because they play a major role. Contains a bibliography, only a small portion of which concerns India, and an index.

760. Schudson, Michael. Discovering the News. New York: Basic Books, 1978. 228p.

An outstanding analytical history of American journalism which deals with it in terms of the concept of objectivity-- its origin and development. In carrying out this aim, the author has examined the relationship between the institutionalization of modern journalism and the general currents in economic, political, social, and cultural life. Contains extensive notes and an index.

761. Schulte, Henry F. The Spanish Press 1470-1966: Print, Power, and Politics. Urbana: University of Illinois Press, 1968. 280p.

An analysis of the Spanish newspaper press, especially with relation to censorship, which places it in historical perspective. Contains an extensive bibliography and an index.

Shawncross Report. See Great Britain. Royal Commission on the Press. Report, 1962. (No. 683.)

762. Skornia, Harry J. _Television and the News_. Palo Alto,
Cal.: Pacific Books, 1968. 232p.

"In this book," says Skornia, "symptoms are examined
which tell us that citizens of the world are too often
not getting the news they need, and that all is not well
in the areas of broadcast news, public affairs, and
related practices." He hopes these "diagnostic" essays
can help correct the situation and makes some modest
proposals. Chapter notes and index.

Smith, Anthony. _The Politics of Information: Problems of
Policy in the Modern Media_. (_See_ No. 191.)

763. Smith, Anthony, comp. _The British Press since the War:
Sources for Contemporary Issues_. Totowa, N.J.: Row-
man and Littlefield, 1974. 320p.

An anthology in which the articles, charts, documents,
and other materials show the evolution of the continuing
newspaper crisis in Britain since the end of World War II.
Deals with newspaper finance, amalgamation, and production;
social and governmental restraints; and the changing relationships between owner, editor, journalist, and reading
public. Indexed.

764. Sommerlad, Ernest Lloyd. _The Press in Developing Coun-
tries_. Sidney, Australia: Sidney University Press,
1966. 189p.

A broad survey, devoted entirely to newspapers. Arrangement is by topics—patterns of development, role, problems,
training, production, news agencies, and so on—rather than
by specific countries. Contains a bibliography, footnotes,
and an index.

765. _Speaking of a Free Press: A Collection of Notable Quotations about Newspapers and a Free Press_. Washington
20041: American Newspaper Publishers Association
Foundation, Box 17407, Dulles International Airport,
1974. 24p.

A slim and inexpensive pamphlet with emphasis on "quotes
which have met the test of time and on those contemporary
quotes which seem particularly insightful." Among the
seventy or so authors included are Learned Hand, John
Adams, Thomas (not Tom) Wolfe, Heywood Broun, Napoleon,
James Madison, de Toqueville, Artemus Ward, both Theodore
and Franklin Roosevelt, Carl Rowan.

766. Special Commission on the Student Press. _The Student Newspaper: Report . . . to the President of the University_

of California. Washington: American Council on Education, 1970. 58p.

A report of the Special Commission on the Student Press to the President of the University of California in which the commission attempts to answer such broad questions as the following: How effective are campus newspapers in meeting student needs? How should they be financed and supervised? What is obscene language and how should its use in college publications be viewed? Is the student paper an "official" publication of the university? Journalists, ranging from editors of student publications themselves to journalism professors and reporters, have contributed chapters. In conclusion are the commission's recommendations. The commission consisted of Norman Isaacs, vice-president and executive editor of the Courier-Journal and Louisville Times; William B. Arthur, former editor of Look; and Edward W. Barrett, Director of the Communications Institute, Academy for Educational Development, and former Dean of Columbia's Graduate School of Journalism.

767. Steinby, Torsten. In Quest of Freedom: Finland's Press, 1771-1971. Fred A. Fewster, tr. Helsinki: Government Printing Centre, 1971. 163p.

An historical survey concentrating on the newspaper press—its regulations, the emergence of a party press, its struggles with Russia, its national background, and its present status. An appendix gives a list of Finnish newspapers in 1971.

Stokke, Olav, ed. Reporting Africa. (See No. 196.)

Survey of Broadcast Journalism. See Alfred I. DuPont-Columbia University Survey of Broadcast Journalism. (No. 630.)

768. Sussman, Leonard R. Mass News Media and the Third World Challenge. Beverly Hills, Cal.: Sage, 1977. 80p. (The Washington Papers, 5:56.)

No matter how disparate their ideologies, developing countries agree on the charge that in reporting about them, Western news services primarily advance the economic, political, and cultural interests of their own countries by concentrating mainly on the adverse events, both natural and man-made, but rarely on the progress achieved or even on a constructive analysis of development problems, says Sussman. He analyzes these accusations and shows how Western media may respond to the challenge, including educational and technical recommendations. Lists references.

769. Swain, Bruce M. Reporters' Ethics. Ames: Iowa State
     University Press, 1978. 153p.

     Some sixty-seven reporters of widely varying levels of
experience on sixteen metropolitan dailies in ten cities
talk about questions of ethics they have faced, from
freebies to conflicts of interest. Appendices give codes
for the American Society of Newspaper Editors, the Associated Press Managing Editors Association, the Society of
Professional Journalists (Sigma Delta Chi), and seven
newspapers. Notes, bibliography, and index.

770. Taylor, Henry A. The British Press: A Critical Survey.
     London: Arthur Barker Ltd., 1961. 176p.

     Survey of English journalism, reviewing its history
but dwelling chiefly on the report of the Royal Commission on the Press in 1949.

771. Tebbel, John. The Compact History of the American News-
     paper. 2d ed. New York: Hawthorn Press, 1963. 286p.

     Survey extending from colonial times to the present and
examining the role of the newspaper--first as propaganda,
next as a personal instrument, and currently as a business
institution. Contains a list of suggested readings.

772. Todorov, Dafin. Freedom Press: Development of the Pro-
     gressive Press in Western Europe and the U.S.A. Pra-
     gue 1: International Organization of Journalists,
     Parizska 9, 1978(?). 97p.

     A Communist journalist discusses the origins, develop-
ment, and present state of the working-class press in
four major capitalist countries from its beginnings in the
1830s to the present. Todorov categorizes and describes
the various newspapers and magazines that played, or play,
a part. Bibliography.

773. Udell, Jon G., and contributing authors. The Economics
     of the American Newspaper. New York: Hastings House,
     1978. 160p.

     The authors' purpose is to show through economic analy-
sis a picture of the daily newspaper and how it functions,
to explore its problems and opportunities, and to examine
the role that business and economic considerations play
in attempting to maintain press freedom. They discuss
the economic status of American newspapers, the marketing
concept, profit, quality, price, planning, production,
revenues, costs and control, employee relationships, and
the newspaper of the next decade. Most of the contributing authors are in the newspaper business. The book is

aimed at journalism and communication students and a wide
variety of newspaper employees--publishers excepted. The
picture of newspaper economics it presents is in breadth
rather than in depth. Some of the chapters have notes.
Indexed.

The Underground and Alternative Press in Great Britain. (See
    No. 1067.)

774. Underground Press Directory. William D. Lutz, comp. 7th
        ed. New York 10014: Alternative Press Syndicate,
        Box 26, Village Station, 1973.

    Alphabetical list with addresses, but no descriptions,
    of about 800 publications which originated and were part
    of the alternative or counter culture that existed within
    the U.S. and around the world in the mid and late 1960s.
    Titles range from "establishment" underground like the
    Berkeley Barb and East Village Other to the lesser known,
    more ephemeral, and more highly specialized such as the
    Marijuana Review. Obviously, the latter type predominates.
    (See also No. 634.).

775. U.S. Library of Congress. Slavic and Central European
        Division. Reference Department. Newspapers of East
        Central and Southeastern Europe in the Library of
        Congress. Robert G. Carlton, ed. Washington: Gov-
        ernment Printing Office, 1965. 204p.

    Lists holdings of newspapers issued during the period
    from 1918 to 1965 within the territorial boundaries of
    Albania, Bulgaria, and Czechoslovakia, and those issued
    in Estonia, Latvia, and Lithuania from 1917 to 1940.
    Contains a language index and an index to titles.

776. Walker, R. B. The Newspaper Press in New South Wales,
        1803-1920. Sydney, Australia: Sydney University
        Press, 1976. 272p.

    A history which places the press in a social and polit-
    ical context and relates it to overseas development,
    particularly in Britain. Footnotes and index.

777. Weiner, Richard, ed. News Bureaus in the United States.
        3d ed. New York 10019: Richard Weiner, Inc., 888
        Seventh Ave., 1974. 143p.

    A listing of news bureaus by geographical location,
    giving telephone number, address, editor, and, for
    larger syndicates, their columnists (or some of them).
    It also enables users to find the bureau for which spe-
    cific columnists write, although it obviously cannot list
    specific newspapers and magazines in which their columns

appear. Covers newspaper, news magazine, and wire services syndicates, as well as a few major business and trade publications and consumer magazines that maintain syndicates. Indexed by bureaus, newspapers, and magazines.

778. Weiner, Richard. <u>Syndicated Columnists</u>. New York 10019: Richard Weiner, Inc., 888 Seventh Ave., 1974. 143p.

Briefly discusses thirteen of the largest syndicates and lists about 700 columnists alphabetically within his or her subject category, giving for each the title of the column, the syndicate, the address, and telephone number except when requested not to. The thirteen syndicates covered in some depth are King Features, United Features Syndicate, Los Angeles Times, the Chicago Tribune-News, Field Newspaper Syndicate, New York Times, Newspaper Enterprise Association, Des Moines Register and Des Moines Tribune, San Francisco Chronicle, McNaught Syndicate, Columbia Features, Universal Press Syndicate, and National Newspaper Syndicate. Somewhat marred by the author's too frequent anecdotes.

779. Whatmore, Geoffrey. <u>The Modern News Library: Documentation of Current Affairs in Newspaper and Broadcasting Libraries</u>. London WCIE 7AE: 7 Ridgmount St., 1978. 202p.

A practicing librarian discusses the organization and management of the news information library--the term <u>news</u> covering newspaper, radio, and television. He takes up the various kinds of materials to be collected, the organization, the equipment, the new technology, and other aspects. Indexed.

White, Llewellyn, and Robert D. Leigh. <u>Peoples Speaking to Peoples: A Report on International Mass Communication from the Commission of Freedom of the Press</u>. (<u>See</u> No. 212.)

780. <u>Who Was Who in Journalism</u>. Detroit, Mich.: Gale, c1925, c1928, 1978. 664p.

"A consolidation of all material appearing in the 1928 edition of <u>Who's Who in Journalism</u>, with unduplicated biographical entries from the 1925 edition of <u>Who's Who in Journalism</u>," is the subtitle of this reprint, which will be of interest to anyone concerned with the history of American journalism and journalism education in the earlier part of the twentieth century. It contains approximately 4,000 biographical sketches of editors, reporters, managers and publishers of newspapers and magazines, syndicate writers, and journalism teachers. Other features include a listing of news and feature syndicates,

teaching staffs and courses and other pertinent features
about journalism schools in their formative years, newspaper clubs and associations' foreign news agencies and
foreign newspapers in the U.S. and foreign correspondents,
the Code of Ethics, a bibliography, and classified directories of journalists both by position and geographical
area.

781. Wilcox, Dennis L. English Language Newspapers Abroad: A
Guide to Daily Newspapers in Non-English-Speaking
Countries. Detroit, Mich.: Gale Research Co., 1967.
243p.

For fifty-six countries--Aden through Zambia--gives
names of newspapers, including for each circulation, founding date, readership, circulation patterns, advertising
ratio, news emphasis, wire services, and editorial policy,
other languages used, and a brief description of physical
appearance. Also contains a short bibliography of articles,
books, and reports, and a newspaper microfilm list.

782. Williams, Francis. Dangerous Estate: The Anatomy of Newspapers. London: Longmans, 1957. 504p.
783. _____. The Right to Know: The Rise of the World Press.
London: Longmans, 1969. 336p.
784. _____. Transmitting World News: A Study of Telecommunications and the Press. New York: Arno, 1972. 95p.

In these studies of various aspects of the press,
Williams always places it in a broad context.
Dangerous Estate shows the social role of newspapers,
past and present, with press history woven around the
issues of society as they affect and are affected by the
papers of the time and by the men responsible for them.
The Right to Know treats the media as barometers of
time and geography, assuming various shapes in various
countries. Here Williams shows the switch from political
control to business orientation in certain parts of the
world; the growth of radio; the place of TV; the press in
the new nations; and public interest and commercial ownership.
Transmitting World News investigates the system of
rates and priorities as well as other technical factors
affecting the dispatch of press messages. Although
Williams discusses the physical means of news transmission, he goes beyond this to show the human elements:
the competence, integrity, and judgment of those who collect and distribute news, and the readiness of governments
and peoples to allow or forbid objective reporting. He
also takes cost factors and availability of newsprint into
account.

785. Willing's Press Guide. West Sussex RH16 3BS: Thomas
     Skinner Directories, Stuart House, 41-43 Perrymount
     Rd., Haywards Heath, annual. (1874--.)

   A country-by-country listing of newspapers, general
   and specialized periodicals, and even some annual publications which are published in the United Kingdom and
   twenty-eight other countries, giving for each the year
   established, frequency, price, and publisher's name and
   address. Publications by the United Nations are also
   included. Among other features are a list of some leading periodical publishers with their periodicals and a
   list of reporting, news, and press cutting agencies.

786. Wittke, Carl. The German-Language Press in America.
     Lexington: University of Kentucky Press, 1957. 311p.

   A history of America's German-language press, from
   1732 to the present, with emphasis primarily upon the
   role it played in American social, political, and economic history rather than upon individual papers. Footnotes, but no bibliography. Indexed.

787. Wolseley, Roland E. The Black Press, U.S.A. Ames: Iowa
     State University Press, 1971. 362p.

   The author first discusses the validity of the concept
   of a black press (there is such a thing, he concludes),
   then relates its history, examines today's newspapers and
   magazines, describes its present and past prominent
   reporters and editors, considers its problems, and goes
   into several other areas such as circulation, advertising,
   syndicates, and public relations. Black radio is also
   treated briefly. There is a bibliography, notes on
   sources, and an index.

Woodworth, Anne, comp. The "Alternative" Press in Canada: A
Checklist of Underground, Revolutionary, Radical and Other
Alternative Serials from 1960. (See No. 1073.)

788. The Working Press of the Nation: Newspaper and Allied
     Services Directory. Vol. I. Burlington, Iowa 52601:
     National Research Bureau, 424 N. Third St., annual.
     (1947--.)

   Contains a name entry for every daily newspaper in the
   U.S. and Canada, with address and editor and managing
   editor, and a more detailed entry for daily newspapers
   located in cities of 50,000 or over, which gives address,
   phone number, publishing company, circulation, wire services, politics, deadlines, and key personnel. Other
   features include a listing of editors and writers assigned

231

to specific subjects, principal U.S. weeklies, special-interest newspapers, black newspapers, religious weeklies, principal foreign-language newspapers, Sunday magazine supplements and their personnel, daily newspapers which publish a weekend supplement or section, news services and news pictures and their personnel, and newsreel companies and their personnel.

789. Wynar, Lubomyr, and Anna T. Wynar. Encyclopedic Directory of Ethnic Newspapers and Periodicals in the United States. 2d ed. Littleton, Col. 80160: Libraries Unlimited, Inc., P.O. Box 263, 1976. 248p.

"The main objective of this directory is to identify the newspapers and periodicals published by various ethnic groups in the United States and to describe their content and bibliographical features," say the authors. Covers sixty-one ethnic groups, with a separate section giving multi-ethnic publications. Certain groups are purposely excluded: the American Indian press and the black American press because the editors feel that sufficient information exists in other sources which they cite; non-English professional and trade publications which are not intended primarily as ethnic reading; and newspapers and periodicals that did not return the questionnaire on which information is based and for which additional information could not be found in secondary sources. Data for each publication includes date founded, address and telephone number, name of editor and sponsor, language, circulation, frequency, and cost of subscription. A preliminary section gives the historical development, role, and status of the ethnic press, with numerous tables of statistics of various kinds. An appendix presents alphabetically arranged statistical analyses of individual ethnic press groups. An index lists individual publications.

V
Film

790. Allan, Angela, and Elkan Allan. The Sunday TIMES Guide to
     Movies on Television. London: Times Newspapers, 1973.
     398p.

   An annotated listing of American and British films from
the 1950s and 1960s which have been rerun on British TV.
Annotations are pithy and subjective, and each film is
rated under six headings: "Cancel All Other Engagements";
"Catch It If You Can"; "If You've Nothing Better to Do";
"Find Something Better to Do"; "Don't Waste Your Time";
"Ring Up and Complain." Other information includes whether
the film is in color or black and white, the date, and the
leading members of the cast. There is an index of alternative titles—particularly necessary in this case because
there are often title changes for British films shown in
the U.S. and vice versa.

791. Allen, Nancy. Film Study Collections: A Guide to Their
     Development and Use. New York: Ungar, 1979. 194p.

   A comprehensive guide to film study resources, intended
for librarians and scholars, which covers such aspects as
the relationship between university film study programs
and supporting libraries; a descriptive list of major U.S.
collections of film study documentation; information on
publishers who specialize in film books and other materials; and film reference services, including recommendations on building a basic collection, the impact of
computer technologies on film services, and a list of
accessible data bases. Special features are a survey of
some 100 university libraries, detailing size and description of their film study collection, especially unpublished
filmscripts, and a cataloguing/classification scheme for
film-related materials by Michael Gorman. There is also a
bibliography of 100 important books and an index.

792. The American Film Institute. Guide to College Courses in Film and Television. 6th ed. Princeton, N.J.: Peterson's Guides, 1978. 420p.

A detailed listing of courses and programs offered in 1,067 institutions (all that responded to the American Film Institute Survey). The name of each institution is followed by a brief paragraph providing information about the type of institution, its accreditation, location, campus size, total enrollment, faculty size, calendar, and grading system. In some cases this paragraph is followed by a note about special features such as consortium membership or an unusual interdisciplinary arrangement. Institutions are classified by type into two-year, four-year, upper-level, professional, and university. It provides an excellent overall profile of each institution, and there is a separate section for foreign film and TV schools. Other features include a statistical summary of film and TV courses on campus, facts about careers, a list of student film/video festivals and awards, and useful film/TV opportunities. Appendices list schools separately by degrees offered, schools with animation courses, schools with intern/apprentice programs, schools with screen-writing courses, and schools with teacher training. Indexed.

793. The American Film Institute Catalog of Motion Pictures Produced in the United States. Part I. Feature Films, 1921-1930. Kenneth W. Munden, ed. New York: Bowker, 1971. 936p.
_____. Part II. Credit and Subject Indexes. 1,653p.
794. The American Film Institute Catalog of Motion Pictures: Feature Films, 1961-1970. Richard P. Krafaur, ed. New York: Bowker, 1976. 1,268p.
_____. Part II. Feature Films, 1961-1970: Indexes. 976p.

First volumes of a projected series which pinpoints credits for the films of the decades involved in detail as complete as possible, and gives a synopsis, source when known, and information as to the production company, dates, and length. Part I, 1921-1930 limits itself to films produced in the U.S., but in the 1961-70 volume the editors found this too limiting because of the growing internationalism of film. The index volumes for 1921-30 lead back to the persons receiving credits in the main volume and classify all films by subject. The index volume of 1961-70 has, in addition to the credit index and subject index, a literary and dramatic source index and a national production index. Future volumes will deal with film beginnings, short films, and newsreels.

234

795. Armes, Roy. <u>A Critical History of the British Cinema</u>.
     New York: Oxford, 1978. 374p.

     "The primary aim of this present history--in addition
     to providing a synthesis of the available knowledge--is
     . . . to provide a genuinely critical perspective on
     eighty years of British film making," says Armes, who
     uses a chronological framework to illustrate the economic
     and cultural factors which have shaped the British film,
     both entertainment and documentary, over this period. He
     relates its social functions, defined largely in terms of
     economic structure, and the artistic achievements of its
     individual filmmakers (colored by their personal beliefs
     and values) to the enormous technological changes that
     have taken place and the particular formal pattern of
     communication which has become dominant--the narrative
     structure of the ninety-minute feature film. Notes, bib-
     liography, and index.

796. Armes, Roy. <u>French Cinema since 1946</u>. Vol. I. <u>The Great
     Tradition</u>; Vol. II. <u>The Personal Style</u>. New York:
     Barnes, 1966.

     A critical survey centered around the creative role of
     the director and of the film as a narrative medium like
     novels and plays, rather than strictly visual. Contains
     filmographies, with credits for directors and a biblio-
     graphy for each. Both volumes are indexed.

797. Aros, Andrew A., comp. <u>An Actor Guide to the Talkies</u>,
     <u>1965 through 1974</u> (as conceived by Richard B. Dimmitt).
     Metuchen, N.J.: Scarecrow, 1977. 771p.
798. _____. <u>A Title Guide to the Talkies, 1964 through 1974</u>
     (as conceived by Richard B. Dimmitt). Metuchen, N.J.:
     Scarecrow, 1977. 336p.

     Updates of two earlier books by Dimmitt, <u>An Actor Guide
     to the Talkies: A Comprehensive Listing of 8,000 Feature-
     Length Films from January, 1949, until December, 1964</u> and
     <u>A Title Guide to the Talkies: A Comprehensive Listing of
     16,000 Feature-Length Films from October, 1927, until
     December, 1963</u>.
     The new <u>Actor Guide</u> follows Dimmitt's format, listing
     films alphabetically by title and giving producer, date,
     and full cast, followed by an extensive name index through
     which the user can put together the film career of an
     actor. Coverage is foreign and domestic.
     The new <u>Title Guide</u> has changed the format somewhat and
     expanded the information. The primary purpose remains the
     same: to give the origins of the screenplay from which
     the talkie was derived. In the new edition, novels writ-
     ten from screenplays are also identified. Among other

235

changes, foreign films exhibited in this country have been
included, and in addition to distribution company, year
of general release, and pagination, Aros has added the
director's name. He has, however, dropped the producer's
credit. Sources of reviews are given. There is an index
of names.

799. Atkins, Dick, ed. Method to the Madness: (Hollywood
      Explained). Livingston, N.J.: Prince Publishers,
      1975. 207p.

   For the uninitiated who don't know how Hollywood works
and its relation to TV, this guide will tell some of the
"what's" and "why's." Gives "a few random definitions";
major film studios, TV networks, and independents; a long
chapter on writers, directors, bosses, stars, creators,
technicians, and agents; the new media; and the three
magazines which report on the industry. The author's
style is often on the cute side, but some of the chapters
are written by authorities in special fields, and the
book's organization presents an overview of the industry.
There are a number of illustrations, although this type
of guide does not seem to call for them.

800. Babitsky, Paul, and John Rimberg. The Soviet Film Indus-
      try. New York: Praeger, 1955. 377p.

   Shows the principal steps by which the Communist party
consolidated its power over the Soviet motion picture
industry; gives the economic base and central administration; discusses scenarios and writers, imports and exports,
and production under the five-year plan; and makes a quantitative content analysis of heroes and villains in Soviet
films, 1923-50.

801. Baechlin, Peter, and Maurice Muller-Strauss. Newsreels
      across the World. New York: UNESCO Publications
      Center, 1952. 100p.

   "This book seeks to present an objective, worldwide
survey of news films as they are today, and the problems
they raise--from the production of the actual newsreels
to their projection on the cinema. It deals both with
international organization for production and exhibition
of newsreels and with the machinery for exchange of newsreels between countries. It was also considered useful
to include an analysis of the impact of television and
certain types of documentary films upon the newsreel
industry." - Preface. Its thoroughness, its international
scope, and the scarcity of other materials on the subject
make it extremely valuable for this aspect of communication.
Contains a bibliography and an index.

802. Baer, D. Richard, ed. The Film Buff's Bible of Motion
     Pictures, 1915-1922. Hollywood, Cal. 90069: Hollywood
     Film Archive, 8344 Melrose Ave., 1972. 771p.
803. _____ . The Film Buff's Checklist of Motion Pictures,
     1912-1979. Hollywood Film Archive, 8344 Melrose Ave.,
     1979. approx. 300p.

     Both of these are intended to supplement TV logs but
have reference uses as well. The 1972 volume gives tabular information on 13,000 motion pictures, including short
as well as long features and those made especially for TV.
Information, much of it in code, includes title, alternate
title, release date, running length, award notations, and
critical ratings as expressed by Steven Scheuer in his TV
Key Movie Guide (now Movies on TV, No. 954) and Leonard
Maltin's TV Movies, distributor, and occasional comments
by the editor.
     The Checklist has between 18,000 and 19,000 titles and
more alternate titles and information on each film, but
without critical ratings and award notations. Added features are a selected guide to producers and a brief outline of what happened to significant companies which are
now out of business.
     A new Film Buff's Bible, now in process, will use the
Bible and the Checklist as the beginning for a much larger
book.

804. Balio, Tino, ed. The American Film Industry. Madison:
     University of Wisconsin Press, 1976. 499p.

     This anthology of original and previously published
papers is designed primarily as a collateral text for
undergraduate film courses. The editor has designed a
systematic survey of the history of the industry to show
the ways in which its economics, legal restraints, technological advances, studio organizations and procedures,
financing, distribution trade practices, and exhibiting
practices have influenced form and content. Some of the
pieces were written years ago by stars, producers, and
others involved with the movies; some are by scholars;
one is an analysis of the prospectus of an investment
firm. Their dates range from the early days of the
industry to the present; their authors include Gordon
Hendricks, Carl Laemmle, Mae Huettig, the staff of
Fortune, John Cogley, Thomas Guback, and Michael Conant,
among others. There is a bibliography, an index to movie
titles, and a name-subject index.

805. Balshofer, Fred J., and Arthur C. Miller. One Reel a
     Week. Berkeley and Los Angeles: University of Cal-
     ifornia Press, 1967. 218p.

As source material on the early days of movie-making,
this is an important book. The authors, veteran film
makers who each give their accounts in alternate chapters, tell of the power structure and the struggle for
power--the commercial piracy which was taken for granted,
the attempt of a small group of men to monopolize the
making of pictures, and the methods used by the independent companies to survive.

806. Barbour, Alan G. <u>Cliffhanger: A Pictorial History of</u>
<u>the Motion Picture Serial</u>. New York: A & W Publishers,
1977. 248p.

Although intended primarily for the nostalgia market,
this chronological picture story of the movie serial also
has reference possibilities which are increased by an
appendix listing sound serials chronologically by audio
and by the person/title index.

807. Bardeche, Maurice, and Robert Brasillach. <u>The History of</u>
<u>Motion Pictures</u>. Iris Barry, ed. and trans. New York:
Norton and Museum of Modern Art, 1938. 412p.

This book "attempts to survey the entire history of
film making in Europe and in America and to describe the
exchange of influences to which the film as a whole has
been subject. That it surveys the field from a European
angle, even from a distinctly French angle, rather than
from our own native viewpoint, makes it a useful check
on other accounts of this art-industry." - John E. Abbott,
director of the Museum of Modern Art Film Library. Beginning in 1895, the book encompasses prewar and World War I
films; the emergence of film as an art (1919-23); the
silent film (1923-29); the talking film (1929-35); the
film as a world industry; and, in conclusion, a summary
of forty years of film, "The Music of Images." There is
also an editorial postscript for the years 1935-38, an
index to film titles, and a general index.

808. Barnes, John. <u>The Beginnings of Cinema in England</u>. New
York: Barnes & Noble, 1976. 240p.

Combining information gathered from the literature of
the time with that obtained by direct examination of sur-
viving apparatus and films, Barnes has pieced together
the two years from October 1894 to the end of 1896, when
film grew from a single Kinetoscope parlor in London into
a main attraction in major music halls of Great Britain.
There are detailed discussions with illustrations of the
early technology and its inventors. Appendices include
a catalog of news, nonfiction, and fiction films made

during the two-year period, again with illustrations; a
chronology; notes; an index of films; and a general index.

809. Barnouw, Erik. Documentary: A History of the Non-fiction
     Film. New York. Oxford University Press, 1974. 332p.

   Traces the documentary in the leading centers where it
is made (twenty in all, excepting China and Cuba) from the
time of the Lumiere brothers to the Vietnam war documentaries. The author discusses its various forms such as
direct cinema, cinema verité, and the TV documentary; its
well-known creators; and its subject matter--exploration,
animals, aspects of war, human behavior, social problems,
propaganda. There is special stress on the attempts of
governments and large corporations to influence and control content. Contains source notes, an extensive bibliography, and an index.

810. Barnouw, Erik, and Subrahmanyam Krishnaswamy. Indian Film.
     New York: Columbia University Press, 1963. 301p.

   Development of the motion picture industry in India--
its economic structure, its censorship problems, its content.

811. Barsam, Richard M. Nonfiction Film: A Critical History.
     New York: Dutton, 1973. 332p.

   Traces the development of the documentary and factual
film from 1920 to 1970 in the U.S. and Great Britain.
Appendices contain "Production Facts on Major Films" and
"Major Nonfiction and Documentary Awards." Footnotes, a
bibliography, and a detailed index.

812. Bawden, Liz-Ann, ed. The Oxford Companion to Film. New
     York: Oxford University Press, 1976. 767p.

   A wide-ranging directory of the film, in which the
author's aim is to include selectively all aspects--
individuals who have played a leading role in the industry, trends, technical processes, associations and
societies, production companies, outstanding motion
pictures, etc. A few entries chosen at random give some
idea of the breadth of scope: abstract film, Federation
Internationale des Archives de Film (FIAF), Kwaiden (a
Japanese film), Great Britain, Melina Mercouri, propaganda, Satyajit Ray, dolly system, censorship, John
Cassavetes, copyright, Eric Ambler, and so on. A work of
this scope will obviously have a number of omissions,
many intentional, but overall it contains so much that
the average user is more likely than not to find what is
needed. The writing is excellent and often entertaining.

The editor says that her aim is "to answer any query which may occur to the amateur of film in the course of reading or film going, and to lead him on to topics of related interest." In this she has succeeded well. Abundant cross-referencing makes an index unnecessary.

813. Baxter, John. The Gangster Film. New York: Barnes, 1970. 160p.

Lists actors, directors, and others engaged in the production of "gangster" films (defined by the author as "films that deal, even in a general way, with organized as opposed to conventional crime"), giving a "who's who" type of information and filmographies where pertinent, along with some subject information—e.g., Private Detectives, Saint Valentine's Day Massacre. Indexed.

814. Beattie, Eleanor. A Handbook of Canadian Films. Toronto: Peter Martin, 1973. 280p.

The author describes this as "an attempt to bring together and to make accessible all information about film and filmmaking in Canada." It is in essence a directory, but with a lengthy introduction which gives a history and analysis. About half of the contents is taken up with information about Canadian filmmakers—a brief biography, a filmography, and a bibliography. Following are sections on writing and writers; actors; music in films; film people; emerging filmmakers; professional associations; film societies; film study centers; media and film courses; children's films; video and community film; film festivals and competitions; cooperative distribution and production; technical equipment and services; technical information and assistance; film and photography archives; educational material; film collectives; trade journals and periodicals; directories and film catalogs; addresses; a bibliography; and an index of films.

815. Behind the Scenes: Equal Employment Opportunity in the Motion Picture Industry. Washington 20425: U.S. Commission on Civil Rights, 1121 Vermont Ave., N.W., 1978. 48p.

A report, prepared by the California Advisory Committee, which explains the background of the film industry in terms of the work force, unions, and the hiring process; discusses the Equal Employment Opportunity Commission Hearings in 1969; analyzes the major studios in terms of affirmative action and the effort being made by the federal government to enforce it; and concludes

with findings and recommendations. Appendices list pro-
ducers of TV primetime shows in 1977 and give a table,
"Contract Services Administration Trust Fund, Industry
Experience Rosters, February 1977."

816. Berton, Pierre. Hollywood's Canada: The Americanization
of Our National Image. Toronto: McClelland and
Stewart, 1975. 303p.

A well-known Canadian writer has documented and analyzed the 575 films Hollywood has set, although not necessarily made, in Canada and has found them to be stereotyped,
distorted, and narrow in their focus upon the North Woods
and Mounted Police almost exclusively. His conclusion is
that Canada has been exploited financially and culturally.
An appendix lists "Hollywood Movies about Canada." Includes
notes and a name-title index.

817. Betts, Ernest. The Film Business: A History of British
Cinema, 1896-1972. New York: Pitman, 1973. 349p.

A factual survey of the British film in which the author
criticizes important films, gives character studies of the
men who built the industry, and examines its political and
economic structure, emphasizing the relationship with the
American film industry.

818. Birkos, Alexander S., comp. Soviet Cinema: Directors and
Films. Hamden, Conn.: Archon, 1976. 344p.

On one level this book may be regarded as a reference
guide to films and careers of Russian filmmakers from 1918
to the mid-seventies; on another level the abstracts of
the films give insight into the Russian political thought
and value system. In two alphabetical sections: the first
lists films released during the period covered and describes
content, critical reception, and often political manifestations; the second lists all directors by name and gives
brief career histories and titles of their films. Many
cross references bring both sections together. A fourteen-
page introduction surveys the history of Soviet film after
1918. Contains a list of Soviet film studios and a selected
annotated bibliography.

819. Bluem, A. William, and Jason E. Squire, eds. The Movie
Business: American Film Industry Practice. New York:
Hastings House, 1972. 368p.

Although this anthology is concerned primarily with
techniques, it nevertheless provides the layman an idea
of the structure of the film industry. Sections include:
developing the story and screenplay; financing and

budgeting films; film company management; the prelimi-
naries and creative functions of production; distribution
and exhibition; promotion; the new technology. Appendices
include "Notes on a Sponsored Film" and "Basic Elements of
Craft and Guide Contracts." Indexed.

820. Bogle, Donald. Toms, Coons, Mulattoes, Mammies and Bucks:
An Interpretative History of Blacks in American Films.
New York: Viking, 1973. 260p.

The author, himself black, has screened and researched
every film he could find in which black actors appeared
from 1905 to the early 1970s. His purpose is not only to
ferret out facts but also to appraise the performances
they gave, and he concludes that "the essence of black
film history is not found in the stereotyped role but in
what certain talented actors have done for the stereotype,
showing how they progressed from jester and servants to
militants." There are many illustrations and a name-title
index.

821. Bohn, Thomas W., and Richard L. Stomgren. Light and Shadows: A History of Motion Pictures. 2d ed. Sherman
Oaks, Cal.: Alfred Publishing Co., 1978. 479p.

The authors interpret their history according to the
interaction of the factors they feel have shaped it--the
industrial, technological, social, aesthetic, and personal.
Thus, rather than emphasizing the chronological, they have
presented an "integrated story of those experiences which
influenced artistic expression (cultural, economic, political) and those which have influenced the advancement of
an industry (technological, management, distribution)."
Contains a subject bibliography and name, film, and general
indexes. The second edition has added a film distributor
key to the film index.

822. British Film and TV Yearbook. London: British and American Film Holdings Ltd., annual. (1946--.)

The greater portion of this yearbook is an extensive
"who's who" in British film and television. Among other
features are lists of film production companies, distributors, British film studios, preview theaters, trade
organizations, agents, press representatives, leading
cinema circuits, companies making TV commercials, and the
various radio and TV networks--BBC, ITV, and regional systems in the British Isles, with addresses and leading
personnel. A special feature is a guide to production and
distribution services and studio facilities in Europe.

823. The British National Film Catalogue. Michael Moulds, ed.
      London: British Industrial and Scientific Film Asso-
      ciation, bi-monthly with annual cumulations. (1963--.)

      Includes all nonfiction and short films generally
   available in Britain for hire, loan, or sale; films available to specialized or limited audiences only; fiction and
   nonfiction TV programs available in film for nontheatrical
   release for loan or hire; film magazines and certain nonfiction shorts which, though made for theatrical release,
   frequently become available on 16mm at a later date;
   British films distributed abroad through British Information Services and the British Council. Straight advertising, home movies and features covered by the Monthly
   Film Bulletin, and newsreels are excluded.
      The catalogue lists entries by subject, with a subject-
   title and a production index. For each title information
   is given on distribution, date, production company and
   sponsor, technical data, language version, credits, length,
   and a synopsis. (See also Denis Gifford's The British Film
   Catalogue, 1895-1970, No. 863.)

824. Brosnan, John. The Cinema of Science Fiction: Future
      Tense. New York: St. Martin's Press, 1978. 320p.

      A social history of the science fiction genre in film,
   which is also a history of the genre in literature as
   Brosnan covers the difference between written and filmed
   versions. The approach is sociological and the arrangement chronological, with analyses of specific films. An
   appendix gives a chronological listing of science fiction
   on TV and summarizes each show. There is also a bibliography and an index.

825. Brownlow, Kevin. The Parade's Gone By. New York: Knopf,
      1968. 577p.

      History of the silent film based upon interviews with
   those who worked with them in one capacity or another,
   profusely illustrated with stills. Indexed.

826. Bucher, Felix. Germany. New York: Barnes, 1970. 298p.

      Directory of actors, actresses, and others important
   in German films, with preference given to those made
   before 1945 because Bucher believes most of the important
   films were before that time. Gives brief biographical
   data and a filmography. Some of the leading movements in
   film--e.g., "avant-garde"--are discussed. There is a
   detailed index to names and films.

827. Butler, Ivan. <u>The War Film</u>. Cranbury, N.J.: A. S. Barnes, 1974. 191p.

"This book is a study of the main trends in the treatment of war by the fictional cinema. It is not intended as a sociological or political treatise--though such aspects are of course inseparable from such a theme; neither does it touch on film aesthetics. . . ." Thus the author describes his aim and scope. Because of the great number of war films, the author has been selective, although he has attempted to include all major productions. Arrangement is by war, with a chronological listing of the seven most-filmed wars and a final brief section, "The Atomic Threat." Indexed.

828. Cameron, Ian, and Elisabeth Cameron. <u>Dames</u>. New York: Praeger, 1969. 144p.
829. _____. <u>The Heavies</u>. New York: Praeger, 1969. 143p.

Twenty-five year's worth (from the mid-1940s to the 1970s) of Hollywood actresses who have portrayed dolls, molls, floozies, and other disreputable ladies, and Hollywood actors who have portrayed gunmen, cattle rustlers, racketeers, and other dastardly types. In the latter volume the authors have omitted big names about whom much material exists in favor of middle-bracket players. Biographical information is as complete as possible, including a list of films with dates. There are also photographs.

830. Casty, Alan. <u>Development of the Film: An Interpretive History</u>. New York: Harcourt Brace Jovanovich, 1973. 425p.

An interpretation of the progress of film as an art form. Arrangement is chronological; scope is international. Casty treats both people and movements--i.e., the emergence of a film style, D. W. Griffith, the Russians and epic montage, realism, comedy, genres and stars, sound, Orson Welles, Renoir, Antonioni, France's New Wave, Britain's "angry young men," and so on. Indexed by person and films.

831. Champlin, Charles. <u>The Flicks, or Whatever Became of Andy Hardy</u>? Pasadena, Cal.: Ward Ritchie, 1977. 277p.

Champlin's aim has been to write about commercial films--Hollywood and abroad--in greater depth than the host of nostalgic and worshipful fan books achieve, yet with a broader approach than the scholarly works on film history and analysis usually have. Taking off with the movies made during the height of the popularity of the Andy Hardy series, he traces various trends in subject matter and philosophy which have characterized them from their depiction of the positive, optimistic world of the forties to today's less reassuring world.

832. Cinematographic Institutions: A Report by the International Film and Television Council (IFTC). Paris: UNESCO, 1973. 98p. (Reports and Papers on Mass Communication No. 68.)

Primarily "a study of institutions of the public or public utility character whose purpose is to promote the art and technique of the cinema and their applications in education, science and culture." Thus, film and trade associations and trade union types of associations are not dealt with. It uses as examples detailed descriptions and charts of organizations in Britain, India, Sweden, and Poland, with an annex giving names and addresses of national branches of the International Council for Educational Media (ICEM) and the International Scientific Film Association (ISFA) throughout the world. There is also a list of the membership of the International Newsreel Association (INA).

Communications and the United States Congress: A Selectively Annotated Bibliography of Committee Hearings, 1870-1976. (See No. 385.)

833. Conant, Michael. Antitrust in the Motion Picture Industry: Economic and Legal Analysis. Berkeley and Los Angeles: University of California Press, 1960. 240p. (Publications of the Bureau of Business and Economic Research.)

Analyzes and evaluates the impact of antitrust actions on the structure, behavior, and performance of the industry. Updates Huettig (No. 885) and is updated by about five years by Jobes (No. 896). Contains a bibliography, an index of cases, and an index.

834. Cowie, Peter, ed. A Concise History of the Cinema. Vol. I. Before 1940. Vol. II. Since 1940. Cranbury, N.J.: A. S. Barnes, 1971.

Paperback original which briefly surveys film in certain selected countries: U.S., Britain, France, Italy, Germany and Austria, Scandinavia, Eastern Europe, Japan, India, Brazil, Spain, Canada, Cuba, Switzerland, and Greece. Chapters also discuss documentary and animated films, economic trends, and technical developments. There is an index to film titles.

835. Cowie, Peter. Eighty Years of Cinema. Cranbury, N.J.: A. S. Barnes, 1977. 323p.

"This book does not pretend to be a comprehensive history of the cinema. Instead, it offers certain signposts
to the significant developments in film art and entertainment. The 280 reviews pay tribute to the films responsible
for such trends; to the movies that, either at the time of
their release or later, have opened new paths or set a
standard for others to follow," says Cowie in his introduction. Arrangement is chronological, from 1895 through
1975. For each year he discusses at length what he
believes to be the several outstanding films, giving credits, running time, and an analytical commentary which
often involves reviews as well as his own opinions. Other
feature films he considers important he lists briefly,
with names of producer and director, and five to ten lines
of commentary. There is a similar section on short films
and documentaries, and another giving "Facts of Interest."
Index to films reviewed or listed.

836. Cowie, Peter. Finnish Cinema. Cranbury, N.J.: A. S.
Barnes, 1976. 128p.

Although Finnish film production has been small, some
of the pictures produced have been outstanding. Cowie
discusses these in terms of themes and people involved.
Over sixty photographs, eighteen filmographies, a brief
bibliography, and an index of films.

837. Cowie, Peter, ed. World Filmography, 1967. Cranbury,
N.J.: A. S. Barnes, 1977. 688p.
_____. World Filmography, 1968. Cranbury, N.J.:
A. S. Barnes, 1977. 723p.

Lists alphabetically by country feature films of 1,000
or more metres (approximately thirty-six minutes) from
forty-five countries in the volume covering films released
in 1967, and forty-nine in the volume covering films
released in 1968. Extensive credits, as complete as possible, are given for each film, along with release date,
length in minutes, and a brief synopsis. The countries
selected were those were Cowie could find reliable correspondents. He plans future volumes which will move back-
ward in time and will then cover from 1969 to the present
"if the venture proves commercially viable." Indexes list
directors and film titles.

838. Cowie, Peter, in collaboration with Arne Svensson. Sweden.
Vols. I-II. Cranbury, N.J.: A. S. Barnes, 1970.

Vol. I contains biographical material about leading
directors, players, technicians, and other important figures in the Swedish cinema, and gives credits and plot
outlines of seventy well-known films. It contains an

index to titles mentioned--about 1,000 in all. Vol. II
assesses certain themes, trends, and directors prominent
in Swedish film. Bibliography.

Cowie is currently at work on a series, Films in Sweden
(Barnes, 1977--), of which three volumes have been published so far: New Directors (1977. 128p.), Stars and
Players (1978. 128p.), and Ingmar Bergman and Society
(1979. 128p.).

839. Cripps, Thomas. Slow Fade to Black: The Negro in American Film, 1900-1942. New York: Oxford University
Press, 1977. 447p.
840. _____. Black Film as Genre. Bloomington: Indiana
University Press, 1978. 184p.

Slow Fade to Black is a social history which chronicles,
against the background of the times, the slow impact of
Afro-American films on American ones in terms of those who
act in or take part in them in other ways. Footnotes and
subject and title indexes.

In Black Film as Genre Cripps defines "black film" and
gives its history from the 1890s to the present, with an
analysis of six well-known examples. In conclusion he discusses the state of criticism and scholarship. Contains a
bibliography, a filmography, and an index.

841. Curtis, David. Experimental Cinema. New York: Universe
Books, 1971. 168p.

Traces the development of cinema experimentation from
pioneer efforts in the early years of the century to the
underground filmmakers of the 1960s. Bibliography and
index of names.

842. Dickinson, Thorold, and Catherine De La Roche. Soviet
Cinema. London: Falcon Press, 1948. 136p.

An analysis of the Soviet film, beginning shortly before
the revolution and ending in the mid-1940s. Discusses
techniques, specific pictures and producers, and the interplay between government and filmmakers.

843. Directors Guild of America, Inc. Directory of Members.
Hollywood, Cal. 90046: 7950 Sunset Blvd., annual.
(1967-68--.)

The 1976-77 edition lists more than 4,500 members with
varying information about each. In most cases this
includes home and/or business address, telephone number,
title, and film or TV credits. Types of directors and
their locations range widely, although many are centered
around Hollywood and New York and most but not all are in

247

commercial film and TV. Other information: National Board of Directors, bylaw provisions; a brief chronological history of the organization; a geographic breakdown by name of members in each area, which includes fifteen foreign countries as well; DGA award winners for television and theatrical direction; recipients of the D. W. Griffith Award and the Critics Award; honorary life members; and an index of agents, attorneys, and business managers.

844. Drabinsky, Garth H. Motion Pictures and the Arts in Canada: The Business and the Law. Toronto: McGraw-Hill Ryerson, 1976. 201p.

A comprehensive treatment of Canadian law as it applies to film production. It explains each stage of the production process, outlines the differences between Canadian and American copyright law, and deals in detail with the various kinds of contractual agreements required. The author, a lawyer, has also been a film producer and publisher. Bibliography and index.

845. Druxman, Michael B. Make It Again, Sam: A Survey of Movie Remakes. Cranbury, N.J.: A. S. Barnes, 1975. 285p.

For reference purposes the most valuable part of this book is a lengthy compendium which lists more than 500 remakes (by no means all, says Druxman), with year of release, producer, distributor, stars (if known, as they often were not in early films), and country of origin if other than the U.S. The main portion, however, consists of a fascinating analysis of thirty-three of the most famous remakes--An American Tragedy, Les Miserables, Wuthering Heights, Stagecoach, for example--with commentary on the various versions, a synopsis, and quotes from reviews.

846. Durgnat, Raymond. A Mirror for England: British Movies from Austerity to Affluence. New York: Praeger, 1971. 336p.

The author reviews British films from the twenty-five years between the mid-1940s to the late 1960s, contending that they have reflected national predicaments, trends, and moods. Contains a bibliography, filmographies to 662 films, and indexes for British film artists and foreign film artists and films.

847. Dwoskin, Stephen. Film Is . . . .: The International Free Cinema. London: Owen, 1975. 268p.

Something of a history of the underground film, something of a contemporary survey, and something of the
author's reminiscences of his own experiences as an independent filmmaker. The range of his recollections includes
a number of countries and goes back in time to the beginnings of the movement. Over 700 films are discussed, many
for the first time. Includes a bibliography, "Books and
Magazines Consulted"; an index of films; a list of illustrations, and a general index.

848. Enser, A. G. S. Filmed Books and Plays: A List of Books
     and Plays from Which Films Have Been Made, 1928-1974.
     London: Deutsch, 1975. 549p.

Consists of three indexes: the film title index,
which lists under title the name of the maker or distributing company, the year the film was registered, the
author, the publisher, and any change of title; the
author index; and a change-of-original-title index.

849. Everson, William K. American Silent Film. New York:
     Oxford University Press, 1978. 387p.

A scholarly reassessment of the film industry during
its formative decades from the era of the nickelodeon to
sound. Everson analyzes the history in terms of its
actors and actresses, its producers and directors, its
genres, its technological changes, its influences from
Europe. From today's perspective he views the place and
influence of women before sound came and other topical
areas. Contains an appendix: "The State of Film Scholarship in America: The Silent Film--Books, Films, Archives,
and other Reference Tools," and a chronology: "The Movies
in America: Art and Industry--a Chronological Survey of
Highlights of the Silent Period." Indexed.

850. Fadiman, William. Hollywood Now. New York: Liveright,
     1972. 174p.

This book is a far cry from the pseudo-glamorous
exposés that characterize so much of the literature about
Hollywood. The author, who has worked for RKO, MGM,
Columbia, Seven Arts, and Warner Brothers, gives a
straight and lucid account of its working structure,
beginning with an overview of the industry and following
with chapters on the star, the writer, the producer, and
the future. Bibliography and index.

851. Feinstein, Peter, ed. The Independent Film Community: A
     Report on the Status of Independent Film in the United
     States. New York, N.Y. 10012: Anthology of Film

Archives, Committee on Film and Television Resources
and Services, 1977. 97p.

The result of four years of study based on conferences
and contributions by a number of authorities across the
country and sponsored by the John and Mary Markle Foundation, the Rockefeller Foundation, and the National Endow-
ment for the Arts, this small book is packed with information on a subject where too little of it exists. It
discusses the nontheatrical film in terms of the filmmaker,
distribution, funding, exhibition, preservation, and
places where it may be studied. There are conclusions and
recommendations.

852. Fenin, George N., and William K. Everson. The Western:
From Silents to the Seventies. New and expanded ed.
New York: Penguin, 1977. 396p.

The authors say that in this, as in their first edition
(Grossman, 1973), they have attempted a detailed history
of the Western which will show the aesthetic and industrial
growth of the genre, along with a critical analysis.
Fenin has added two final chapters to the second edition.
Several chapter headings from the contents give an idea of
its range and scope: "Western History and the Hollywood
Version," "Contents and Moral Influence of the Western,"
"The Primitives: Edward S. Porter and Broncho Billy
Anderson," "William Surrey Hart and Surrealism," "Tom Mix
and Showmanship," "Stuntman and Second Unit Director,"
"The Western's International Audience and the International
Western," "Spaghetti Western and the Western 'Made in
Japan.'" Index.

Fielding, Raymond. The American Newsreel, 1911-1967. (See No.
671.)

853. Film Canadiana: The Canadian Film Institute Yearbook of
Canadian Cinema. Marg Clarkson, ed. Ottawa: Canadian
Film Institute, quarterly with annual cumulations.
(1969--.)

A national bilingual yearbook which includes a report
of the Canadian film industry. It consists of four main
divisions: Filmography, Bibliography, Organizations, and
Festivals and Awards. The filmography section documents
alphabetically Canadian film production during the year,
lists by year all feature films from 1970 to the current
year, lists the names of individuals and companies
involved in the production and programs for the current
year, and contains a subject index. The bibliography section lists books on Canadian cinema published in Canada
during the year and major periodical articles, with short
descriptions of the contents of each article. It also

250

contains a list of Canadian film and TV periodicals with
addresses and descriptive information. The organization
section includes federal and provincial agencies, cultural
organizations, associations, guilds and unions, and production and distribution companies. The festivals and
awards section tells which films participated in foreign
and domestic film festivals, along with awards won. It
also contains a list of Canadian film festivals with
descriptive information, dates, and addresses.

854. Filmfacts. Los Angeles 90069: Southern California Uni-
        versity, P.O. Box 69610, West Station, semimonthly.
        (1958--.)

    Each issue deals at length with about a dozen films,
giving complete credits, a full synopsis, a critique, and
excerpts from reviews. Current issues stay a year or more
behind, so it is not good for strictly up-to-date films.
Published by Southern California University's Division of
Cinema.

855. Film Review Digest Annual. David M. Brownstone and Irene
        M. Franck, eds. Millwood, N.Y.: KTO Press, quarterly
        with annual cumulations. (1976--.)

    Excerpts of film reviews of approximately 300 films for
1977 taken from twenty-four American, British, and Canadian
publications. Preceding the excerpts is information about
the film: cast and crew listings, country and year of
origin, producer, U.S. running time, original name of film
when available (for foreign films), and Motion Picture
Association of America ratings when appropriate. Contains
a general index of titles and individuals concerned with
the film, and a separate index of reviewers.

856. Film Vocabulary. London S.W.1: Western European Union,
        9 Grosvenor Pl., 1958. 224p.

    Multilingual vocabulary of some 900 cinema terms in com-
mon use among those who work in the fields of cultural and
educational film and audiovisual education. In cases where
a word in one language has no equivalent in the other languages, a short description in the other language is given.

857. The First Ten Years. Washington 20566: American Film
        Institute, John F. Kennedy Center for the Performing
        Arts, 1978. 96p.

    A report of the American Film Institute's organization,
services, and program from its inception in 1967 through
1977.

858. French, Philip. <u>Westerns: Aspects of a Movie Genre</u>. 2d
     ed. New York: Oxford University Press, 1977. 208p.

     In this book, which deals with the Western since 1950,
     the author says that his approach is largely "social,
     aesthetic and moral." Setting the genre against this
     background, he discusses, among other topics, politics,
     heroes and villains, women and children, Indians and
     blacks, landscape, violence, and poker. There is a
     final chapter on the post-Western. Contains a brief
     filmography of the directors mentioned and a bibliography.

859. Fulton, Albert R. <u>Motion Pictures: The Development of
     an Art from Silent Films to the Age of Television</u>.
     Norman: University of Oklahoma Press, 1960. 320p.

     A history and analysis tracing the development and
     techniques of the film. Emphasis is on its art (or art
     entertainment) aspects rather than on its entertainment
     function alone.

860. Garbicz, Adam, and Jacek Klinowski. <u>Cinema, the Magic
     Vehicle: A Guide to Its Achievement. Journey One:
     The Cinema through 1949</u>. Metuchen, N.J.: Scarecrow,
     1975. 551p.

     "The purpose of this book is to give a panoramic view
     of the achievement of the cinema through the 'film by
     film' approach," say the co-authors, who have attempted
     to include all films they feel that anyone seriously
     interested in the cinema would consider worth seeing.
     Scope is international; the main concern is with aesthe-
     tic standards. Arrangement is chronological, with title,
     running time, credits, and a critique. Index of direc-
     tors and an index of films.

861. Gerlach, John C., and Lana Gerlach, comps. <u>The Critical
     Index: A Bibliography of Articles of Film in English,
     1946-1973, Arranged by Names and Topics</u>. New York:
     Teachers College Press, 1974. 726p.

     ". . . a guide to articles about directors, producers,
     actors, critics, screenwriters, cinematographers, specific
     films, and 175 topics dealing with the history, aesthetics
     and economics of film, the relation of film to society,
     and the various genres of film." There are in all 5,000
     items from twenty-two British, U.S., and Canadian period-
     icals and more than sixty general ones. Contains an
     author and a film index.

862. Gifford, Denis. <u>British Cinema: An Illustrated Guide</u>.
     Cranbury, N.J.: A. S. Barnes, 1968. 176p.

"This book is the first attempt to put between handy
covers at a handy price the complete story of British
films in factual form. It is a kind of All Time Who's
Who of stars and directors, 546 of them, selected for
their contribution to the overall seventy year scene."
So says the author in his introduction. His description
is accurate except for the use of the word complete. As
he later states, he has dealt with stars and directors
who have a substantial body of work in film rather than
with bit players or minor directors. For each entry he
gives a filmography. Writers and producers are generally
omitted. Contains a title index.

863. Gifford, Denis. The British Film Catalogue, 1895-1970:
   A Reference Guide. New York: McGraw-Hill, 1973.
   (Catalog numbers of film in chronological order serve
   for film pagination.)

   The author says that this is "the first complete catalogue of every British film produced for public entertainment since the invention of cinematography." Films
   excluded are those made specifically for television; news
   films; documentaries; films made for the purposes of
   advertising, education, information, propaganda, and
   travel; and animated films without a live actor. Information about each includes as many of the following items as
   pertinent: date, catalogue number, title, length, censor's
   certificate, silent or sound, color systems, screen ratio,
   stereoscopy, production, distribution companies, reissue,
   producer, director, story source, screenplay, narrator,
   cast and characters, subject, summary, awards, series and
   serials, and any additional information available.
   Arrangement is by date, so that the whole presents a chronological history of the British entertainment film. An
   index lists films in alphabetical order. (See also the
   British National Film Catalogue, No. 823.)

864. Gifford, Denis. Movie Monsters. London: Studio Vista,
   1969. 158p.

   Paperback history of the monster from 1896 to the present. The author has gathered film monsters into twelve
   classifications and discusses some of the leading examples,
   illustrating with numerous stills. Pictures predominate
   over text. At the end is a chronological filmography of
   every known monster in each of the twelve categories.

865. Gottesman, Ronald, and Harry Geduld. Guidebook to Film:
   An Eleven-in-One-Reference. New York: Holt, Rinehart
   & Winston, 1972. 230p.

This excellent reference book begins with a comprehensive annotated bibliography broken down by subject: reference works, history, theory, criticism and reviews, genre studies (including documentary), adaptation, film and society, film techniques, screenplays, film personalities, Hollywood novels, film magazines, special series, and teaching materials. There are also the following miscellaneous listings: theses and dissertations about film; museums and archives in the U.S., Canada, Central and South America, Europe, (including Great Britain and the U.S.S.R.), the Middle East, Asia, and Australia; film schools in the U.S. and other countries; equipment and supplies; distributors; bookstores, publishers, and sources for stills (the latter two in the U.S. only); film organizations and services; festivals and contests in the U.S. and other countries; awards; and terminology. In the past it has been necessary to dig out this kind of material from a variety of books; this one accumulates it succintly.

866. Graham, Peter. A Dictionary of the Cinema. Rev. ed. 1968. 175p.

Hundreds of short biographical listings of international film actors and actresses, directors, script writers, and others prominent in films, with a list of their films and dates. Also discusses certain of the terms which describe cinema trends--neo-realism, new cinema, nouvelle vague, expressionism, for example--in fact-packed prose reminiscent of "who's who" entries. There is a two-page "Guide to Technical Terms." Scope is international.

867. Great Britain. House of Commons. Monopolies Commission. Films: A Report on the Supply of Films for Exhibition in Cinemas. London: Her Majesty's Stationery Office, 1966. 120p.

An investigation into monopoly in Britain's film industry, with recommendations to Parliament and an appendix filled with statistics and documents on the industry.

868. Griffith, Mrs. D. W. (Linda). When the Movies Were Young. New York: Dutton, c1925, 1965. 266p.

". . . one of the earliest volumes containing eyewitness testimony to the conditions under which early motion pictures were made." - Introduction to the Dover reprint edition, 1969. Indexed.

869. Griffith, Richard. The Movie Stars. New York: Doubleday, 1970. 498p.

A mammoth, coffee-table-type book which attempts to
analyze the factors which constitute "star appeal," using
past and present examples and many photographs. Beginning with "Early Fanfare" and going into "The Heydey of
the Stars," it concludes with "Death and Transfiguration,"
the diminution of the system. The author does more than
tell a story; he delves into the reasons for the rise and
fall of the institution of stardom. Indexed.

870. Griffith, Richard, and Arthur Mayer. The Movies. Rev.
     ed. New York: Simon & Schuster, 1970. 494p.

     The authors contend that the beginning of motion pic-
tures coincided with a high degree of industrialization
which the movies have mirrored and in turn affected.
Briefly and chronologically they touch upon trends, with
profuse illustrations. Good for an overview and for
entertainment. Lack of space prevented the authors from
dealing with cartoons (including Walt Disney) and documentaries. Indexed.

871. Guback, Thomas H. The International Film Industry: West-
     ern Europe and America since 1945. Bloomington:
     Indiana University Press, 1969. 244p.

     "The object of this study is to uncover and analyze
relationships between the American and European film
industries, keeping in mind the financial stake American
companies have in Europe." - Introduction. To accomplish
his aim, the author penetrates economic, sociological,
and cultural factors which have a bearing.
     Contains a bibliography of books, monographs, pamphlets,
documents, reports, and articles. Also has a particularly
useful index with a minute subject breakdown.

872. A Guide to Film and Television Courses in Canada, 1978-79.
     Un Guide des Cours de Cinéma et de Télévision Offerts
     au Canada, 1978-79. Marie-Claude Hecquet and David
     McNicoll, eds. and comps. Ottawa K1P 5E7, Canadian
     Film Institute/Institut Canadien du Film, 75 Albert
     St., Suite 1105, 1978. 167p.

     Contains information from more than seventy univer-
sities, colleges, and CEGEPS. Information for each
includes program head, address, and telephone, with program and/or course descriptions when available.

873. Halliwell, Leslie. Halliwell's Film Guide: A Survey of
     8000 English-Language Movies. London: Hart-Davis,
     MacGibbon, 1977. 897p.
874. _____. Filmgoer's Companion. 6th ed. London: Hart-
     Davis, MacGibbon/Granada, 1977. 825p.

The _Guide_ is a delightful and scholarly reference book
in which Halliwell gives a great deal of information about
films ninety minutes or over in length, including title; a
rating system within its genre by means of stars; country
of origin; year of release; whether black and white or in
color; a brief synopsis; a brief appraisal; the writer or
other original source; director; photographer; composer
of music scores; other credits as available and applicable;
the principal cast, with comments about them; and brief
quotes from well-known critics (for about a fifth of the
titles). Pithy and pertinent comments add flavor to the
facts. For example, he sums up _A Fistful of Dollars_: "An
avenging stranger, violent and mysterious, cleans up a
Mexican border town. A film with much to answer for: it
began the craze for 'spaghetti westerns,' took its director
to Hollywood, and made a TV cowboy into a world star. In
itself it is simple, noisy, brutish and actionful."
Halliwell ends with an essay, "The Decline and Fall of the
Movie." There is an alphabetical list of alternative
titles.

The aim of the sixth edition of _Companion_ is the same
as that of the first: "to bring all available sources
(about film and filmmaking) together while at the same
time excluding inessential or dated information." Halliwell calls it "potted" rather than comprehensive, but in
spite of its electicism, it covers a large territory. "I
have continued to seek, digest and present information
about producers, small part actors, silent stars, cinema-
tographers, art directors, composers, original authors,
screenwriters, and indeed anyone who has had a creative
role to play in the history of the cinema. Trade matters
are virtually ignored." Interesting features are the
mini-essays on general topics, themes, and subjects movies
frequently employ. An example: "_abortion_, unmentionable
on the screen for many years save in continental dramas
like _Carnet De Bal_, 37, and officially ostracized exploitation pictures like _Amok_, 38, was first permitted as a
Hollywood plot in _Detective Story_, 51. . . ." Under
"amnesia" he lists all actors who have suffered from this
affliction on film and the names of the films in which
they did so. He has continued the practice of including
descriptions of a selected number of films from the _Guide_
in cases where they underline trends or are especially
significant in cinema history. The main text contains a
special list of these. Another list gives fictional
screen characters and series, like _Fu Manchu_ and _The Thin
Man_. Themes explored--i.e., abortions, concentration
camps, religion, private eye--are listed, and so are title
changes. Finally come Halliwell's "Recommended Books" and
his 100 favorite films.

875. Hampton, Benjamin B. History of the American Film Indus-
     try from Its Beginnings to 1931. New York: Dover,
     c1931, 1970. 456p.

     Reprint of a book written in the late twenties and very
     early thirties, formerly titled A History of the Movies,
     with a new introduction by Richard Griffith. Hampton,
     whose book preceded Jacobs's The Rise of the American Film
     (No. 893) by almost a decade, takes a much more sanguine
     view of the economics of the motion picture industry in
     the U.S. than did Jacobs. He discusses the early days
     when a new form of theater came into being, the question
     of quantity versus quality, the star system, feature pic-
     tures, the change in content and structure brought about
     by Mary Pickford, the rise of the giant film companies,
     the battle for theaters, Hollywood scandals and censor-
     ship, the apex of the silent film and the beginning of
     talkies, American films abroad. Contains an index but
     no bibliography or footnotes. Read in conjunction with
     Ramsaye (No. 979) and Jacobs, it gives an excellent
     insight into film history in this country up to the first
     years of the talkies, as seen from different viewpoints
     by three film historians of the period.

876. Hardy, Forsythe. Scandinavian Film. London: Falcon
     Press, 1962. 62p.

     As the author points out, Sweden and Denmark have made
     a contribution to world cinema all out of proportion to
     their size. He traces the development of their film
     industry, stressing the influences that have made its pro-
     ducts different from those of other countries.

877. Harmon, Jim, and Donald F. Glut. The Great Movie Serials:
     Their Sound and Fury. New York: Doubleday, 1972.
     384p.

     Informal social history of the serial, 1930-60. Serials
     are analyzed by categories--science fiction, jungle stories,
     aviation, detective thrillers, Westerns, etc.--and the
     authors give casts, story synopses, and evaluations. Jim
     Harmon is a special consultant on old-time radio to the
     Hollywood Museum and the Canadian Broadcasting Co.; Donald
     Glut is a professional free-lance writer. Both live in
     Hollywood, where they researched the book, drawing from
     scripts, anecdotes, interviews, and photographs. Indexed.

878. Hendricks, Gordon. The Edison Motion Picture Myth.
         Berkeley: University of California Press, 1961. 216p.
879. _____. Beginnings of the Biograph: The Story of the
         Invention of the Mutoscope and the Biograph and Their
         Supplying Camera. New York 10011: The Beginning of

257

the American Film, GPO Box 2552, 1964. 11, 78p.
880. _____ . The Kinetoscope: America's First Commercially
      Successful Motion Picture Exhibitor. New York 10011:
      The Beginning of the American Film, GPO Box 2552, 1966.
      182p.

   This series of three monographs is intended to throw
light on the early technological history of the motion
picture and to clear up some misconceptions. The author
in his preface hopes that they will be a "beginning of
the task of cleaning up the morass of well-embroidered
legend with which the beginning of the American film is
permeated." Much of it centers around W. K. L. Dickson,
an employee of Thomas Edison, who Hendricks feels has
not been given sufficient credit, and other employees of
the early days. His beliefs are well documented; some of
the evidence is included in the appendices. All three
volumes are indexed.

881. Hibben, Nina. Eastern Europe: An Illustrated Guide.
     Cranbury, N.J.: A. S. Barnes, 1969. 239p.

   Brief factual information about the postwar work of
film directors, players, and technicians in Albania,
Bulgaria, Czechoslovakia, East Germany, Hungary, Poland,
Romania, the Soviet Union, and Yugoslavia. Since the
territory is large, considerable selection was required.
A criterion was the knowledge of the personalities and
films in the West. There is also emphasis on the specialities of each country--for example, the high propor-
tion of animators in the Yugoslav section and of documentation in the German section. In dealing with the
U.S.S.R., the compiler omitted information available in
Peter Graham's A Dictionary of the Cinema (No. 866).
Data on each country precedes the discussions of its
films and personalities. There is an index to film
titles.

882. Higham, Charles. Hollywood at Sunset. New York: Satur-
     day Review Press, 1972. 181p.
883. _____ . The Art of the American Film, 1900-1971. New
      York: Doubleday, 1973. 322p.

   Higham's theme in both books is Hollywood's struggle
to maintain artistic integrity. In Hollywood at Sunset
he presents his answer to those who wonder what has
caused its decline. He analyzes the events that have
taken place and forces that were at work from the peak
years of 1946 to the seventies--the government antitrust
actions which resulted in the consent decree, the House
Un-American Activities investigation of alleged Commun-
ists in the film industry, the advent of TV, and other

258

lesser-known factors he deems disastrous. Higham meant
this for an interesting bit of reading rather than a
depth study, but it nevertheless gives good background on
social aspects of the film industry.

In The Art of the American Film his approach is different but his interest is the same. "Since this book is
concerned with the art of the American film, an art which
has survived the businessmen who run it, I have been
chiefly concerned with their enemies, the men who have
fought them to achieve a measure of personal expression,"
he says. He has written about Hollywood films in terms
of certain traditions--the pastoral tradition as exemplified by Griffith, King Vidor, and others; the epic
Belasco-like tradition of DeMille and Ince; the Viennese-
Berliner sophisticated boudoir-comedy tradition introduced by Lubitsch; the emergence of entirely new traditions. There are many stills and an index.

884. Hillier, Jim, ed. Cinema in Finland. London WlV 6AA:
     British Film Institute, 81 Dean St., 1975. 67p.

     Designed to serve as an introduction--the first in
English--to the traditions, history, and achievements of
the Finnish cinema in general, emphasizing social, political, and economic factors. The final section provides a
guide to most of the films in the Finnish Film Archive.

885. Huettig, Mae D. Economic Control of the Motion Picture
     Industry: A Study in Industrial Organization. Phila-
     delphia: University of Pennsylvania Press, 1944.
     163p.

     Probably the first study to approach the American film
strictly from the economic angle. Gives a thorough analysis of the financial structure, including exhibition and
distribution, up to about 1944. Contains a bibliography.
Conant (No. 833) is useful for information up to 1960.
Jobes (No. 896) takes the subject to 1966.

886. Hull, David Steward. Film in the Third Reich: A Study
     of the German Cinema, 1933-1945. Berkeley and Los
     Angeles: University of California Press, 1969. 291p.

     Carefully documented study based on years of research
during which the author tracked down and screened virtually all important films of the period. Arranged
chronologically beginning with 1933, it shows the take-
over of the film industry by Goebbels as he abolished
critics and absorbed the industry, and the trends in
German films, such as war, escapism, and antisemitism.
Several useful sections are the prologue, which reviews

the literature on the subject, the notes, the bibliography, and the index.

887. Hurst, Walter E., and William Storm Hale. Motion Picture Distribution (Business and/or Racket?!?). Hollywood, Cal.: Seven Arts Press, 1975. 158p. (Entertainment Industry Series Vol. X.)

A rough-and-ready rundown of do's, don'ts, and how-to's intended as a guide to newcomers in the distribution end of the industry "both in its business aspects and its unfortunate unethical and illegal practices."

888. Inglis, Ruth A. Freedom of the Movies: A Report on Self-Regulation from the Commission on Freedom of the Press. Chicago: University of Chicago Press, 1947. 241p.

". . . the movies can realize their full promise only by unremitting effort from all concerned: the government, the industry and the public—each in his own sphere." Thus Inglis summarizes her rosy view stressing self-regulation, which has not worked out. As background, she discusses the social role of film, the history and economics, attempts to control, the evolution of self-regulation, and self-regulation in action—largely through the Production Code Administration. An appendix gives the production code. Source notes and index.

889. The International Encyclopedia of Film. Roger Manvell, ed. New York: Crown, 1972. 574p.

The major portion of this work consists of over 1,000 alphabetical entries giving biographies, national film histories, general topics, and technical terms. Preceding this is a chronological outline of film history, indicating selected events year by year. Films are not entered separately but can be easily found through an index. There are two other indexes—one to names and one to principal title changes. The bibliography is broken down by subject. Contributors include such well-known film writers as Lewis Jacobs, David Robinson, Jay Leyda, and a number of others, who treat the subject both as an art and as an industry. Although there are numerous illustrations, this is primarily a reference rather than a picture book. Nonetheless it would make excellent coffee-table reading.

890. International Film Guide. Peter Cowie, ed. Cranbury, N.J.: A. S. Barnes, annual. (1964—.)

Each year the content of this estimable and hardy annual varies somewhat, especially in the notables it

treats, but its basic structure remains much the same.
Partial contents include essays on prominent film personalities, with a number of directors and their filmographies; academy awards; book reviews; film bookshops;
film magazines; preview theaters; film music. But its
chief feature is its world survey of individual countries,
which in the 1978 edition number fifty. For each country
it gives a summary of the year's principal events and a
selected list of recent and forthcoming films, with commentary. In addition some countries provide statistics,
lists of associations, and distributors, etc.

891. International Motion Picture Almanac. New York 11019:
     Quigley Publishing Co., 159 West 53d St., annual.
     (1929--.)

     This is a companion volume to the International Tele-
vision Almanac, (No. 449). There is duplication of material in both, notably in the lengthy "Who's Who in Motion
Pictures and Television," "Credit for Feature Films" of
the year, "Film Distributors in Key Cities," "Services
for Producers," "Feature Films from 1955" to the current
year. Also the term International used in both titles is
misleading; except for a relatively few pages at the end
of the book--"The World Market," "The Industry in Great
Britain and Ireland," and "International Film Festivals,"
emphasis is on the U.S. and Canada. This is not to put
down the usefulness of these yearbooks, for both of them
contain much that is not readily available elsewhere, but
to forewarn the user.
     The "Who's Who" section is broad, including, in addi-
tion to actors and actresses, directors, writers, executives, set designers, and other categories of workers in
film and broadcasting. Among other features are various
kinds of statistics; awards and award winners; distributors; talent and literary agents (duplicated); motion
picture corporations, giving structure, organization,
executive personnel; government film bureaus; theater
circuits in the U.S. and Canada; a list of drive-in
theaters with locations, owners, and capacity; the film
press, including trade publications, newspapers with
film departments, and fan magazines; and the motion picture code.

892. Jacobs, Lewis, comp. The Documentary Tradition, from
     Nanook to Woodstock. New York: Hopkins & Blake, 1971.
     530p.

Examines fifty years of documentaries through discussions by ninety filmmakers and critics and eighty illustrations. Arrangement is chronological and coverage is international. Selected bibliography and index.

893. Jacobs, Lewis. The Rise of the American Film: A Critical History with an Essay, "Experimental Cinema in America, 1921-1947." New York: Teachers College Press, c1939, 1948, 1967. 585p.

894. Jacobs, Lewis, ed. The Emergence of Film Art: The Evolution and Development of the Motion Picture as an Art, from 1900 to the Present. New York: Hopkinson & Blake, 1969. 453p.

The first title tells the story of the motion picture in the U.S. from its beginning at the turn of the century to 1947. Although the author's main stress is on the film as entertainment and as art, with discussions of individual directors and pictures that have helped shape its history, he has also placed considerable emphasis on its economic development. Contains an extensive bibliography and picture, name, and general indexes. The original edition and the 1948 printing are published by Harcourt, Brace. "Experimental Cinema in America, 1921-1947" has been added to the 1967 edition.

"The purpose of this book is two-fold," says Mr. Jacobs of the second title. "First, to provide insight into creative film expression, and second, to present an historical overview of the medium's artistic development." It is divided into three sections--the silent film, the sound and color film, the creative process--with each part consisting of essays by eminent filmmakers, critics, and historians, and an introduction by Mr. Jacobs. The scope is international. Contains an index to names and titles.

895. Jarvie, Ian C. Movies and Society. New York: Basic Books, 1970. 394p.

"An essay, no more, toward a sociology of the cinema," says Jarvie. "What I attempt here," he continues, "is to sift and put together some of the innumerable snippets of information that are to be found scattered throughout the very large literature on the cinema" and construct them around "a tenatative sociological framework" which will explain or make sense of the facts, pose questions and indicate answers, and reveal gaps. In addition to published information, he has drawn upon his own experience and has included trash as well as art, for his aim is not aesthetic. In fitting all this to his framework he has divided the problem into four main areas--the making, viewing, experiencing and evaluating of film.

Although Jarvie's data have been used mainly to contrast Great Britain and America, he has included facts about the film industry in a number of other countries—France, Germany, India, Italy, Japan, Russia, Poland, Hong Kong, Singapore, Taiwan, and Thailand. Contains an appendix, "Film and Communication of Values," a bibliography, and an index of subjects, names, and films.

Published in Great Britain as Toward a Sociology of the Cinema.

896. Jobes, Gertrude. <u>Motion Picture Empire</u>. Hamden, Conn.: Archon, Shoe String Press, 1966. 398p.

Economics-based history, coupling careful research with firsthand knowledge. Contains an index of names and a bibliography. For other useful studies of the economics of film see Huettig (No. 885) and Conant (No. 833).

897. Jowett, Garth S. <u>Film: The Democratic Art</u>. Boston: Little, Brown, 1976. 518p.

A social history packed with both facts and ideas, which the author describes as "an attempt to chronicle and analyze some of the ways in which the motion picture affected the lives of the American people, and those forces, both positive and negative, which shaped the final product seen on the screen." Jowett has grouped film around broad topics—recreation, censorship and control, for example—beginning with the very late nineteenth century. His concern is with the accommodation between films and the American people—the obstacles that have slowed the process, and the social, political, and cultural adjustments that have been required. The book ends with a chapter, "The Uncertain Future," dealing with the present. A lengthy section of appendices contain valuable reference material: the industry codes in 1921, 1924, 1927, and 1930-34; box office receipts from 1929 to 1973 in relation to personal consumption expenditures; the growth of attendance from 1922 to 1965; profits from 1932 to 1972 by individual companies; a great deal of information about audiences; and various other useful facts and statistics. There are chapter notes, a bibliography of books, articles, and other materials of major significance, and a comprehensive index.

898. Kardish, Laurence. <u>Reel Plastic Magic: A History of Films and Filmmaking in America</u>. Boston: Little, Brown, 1972. 297p.

Histories of Hollywood are numerous. This differs from
others in that it emphasizes technical aspects and does
not concentrate on Hollywood, although it gives it a fair
share of attention. One chapter, "Another Cinema," deals
with the underground film. There is a brief and, in the
author's words, highly selective prose bibliography, a
list of 100 programs illustrating the growth and scope of
the American film, a list of distributors of 16mm films,
and a film index and a general index.

899. Kauffmann, Stanley, with Bruce Henstell, eds. American
Film Criticism from the Beginnings to "Citizen Kane":
Reviews of Significant Films at the Time They First
Appeared. New York: Liveright, 1972. 443p.

This chronological anthology of skillfully selected
reviews gives insight into the development of an art and
an industry. Kauffmann has preceded each review with
editorial notes, usually brief. There is a bibliography
in the form of the books and articles cited and an index.

900. Kelly, Terence. A Competitive Cinema. London SW1P 32B:
Institute of Economic Affairs, 2 Lord North St., 1966.
204p.

Study of the economics, structure, and institutions of
the British cinema industry, ranging from the financing
of production to the exhibition of the film in theaters
throughout the country. Contains a bibliography.

901. Klein, Walter J. The Sponsored Film. New York: Hastings
House, 1976. 210p.

Little has been written on sponsored films--those special kinds of motion pictures backed by industry, government,
organizations, and religious orders, which are being made
by the tens of thousands for public relations purposes.
Here a producer describes the industry: its definition;
how sponsored films are created, marketed, and distributed;
how the business is managed; trade associations; government
and legal regulations; personal ethics; associations;
awards; career possibilities. Appendices give a standard
contract, motion picture specifications outline, a list of
distribution centers, and the membership rosters of Infor-
film and of the International Quorum of Motion Picture
Producers. Indexed.

902. Klingender, F. D., and Stuart Legg. Money behind the
Screen: A Report Prepared on Behalf of the Film Council.
New York: Arno, c1937, 1978. 79p.

A detailed analysis of British film finances filled
with facts and figures, useful to show the economic state
of the industry in pre-World War II days. Because of the
important role of American film companies in British
cinema, an appendix gives "A Summary of American Film
Finances." Originally published in England by Lawrence &
Wishart.

903. Knight, Arthur. The Liveliest Art: A Panoramic History
of the Movies. New York: Macmillan, 1957. 383p.

A film history, international in scope and aesthetic
in emphasis. In his own words, Knight has "centered this
book on what I consider to be key films, pictures that
are important not only in themselves but also that seem
to summarize a whole style or movement in film history."
Contains a bibliography of "100 Best Books on Film," an
index to film titles, and a general index.

904. Knight, Derrick, and Vincent Porter. A Long Long Look at
Short Films: An A.C.T.T. Report on the Short Entertainment and Factual Film. New York: Pergamon Press
and the Association of Cinematograph, Television and
Allied Technicians, 1967. 185p.

Factual report, written for a British trade union, the
Association of Cinematography, Television and Allied
Technicians, which documents both the social and aesthetic
need for short films and their present plight. Contains
many facts and figures, both in the main body and in the
appendices. Bibliography and index.

905. Kobal, John, comp. and ed. Fifty Years of Movie Posters.
New York: Bounty Books, 1973. 175p. (Distributed by
Crown.)

A big book reproducing in all their glory posters from
Hollywood's early days to its heyday in the 1950s. David
Robinson has written an introduction in which he details
the economic importance of the posters. There is an
index to movie titles represented.

906. Kowalski, Rosemary Ribich. Women and Film: A Bibliography. Metuchen, N.J.: Scarecrow Press, 1976. 278p.

Divided into four major sections: women as performers,
women as filmmakers, images of women presented on the
screen, and women as columnists and critics. Many entries
are annotated, especially when necessary to convey contents.
Subject and name index.

907. Kracauer, Siegfried. From Caligari to Hitler: A Psycho-
     logical History of the German Film. Princeton, N.J.:
     Princeton University Press, c1947, 1966. 361p.

     Although the author says that he is not concerned with
German films merely for their own sake but rather as a
means to increase knowledge of pre-Hitler Germany in a
specific way, this book nevertheless gives a great deal
of information about structure and content of the motion
picture in Germany as well as about individual films.
     Includes as a supplement "Propaganda and the Nazi War
Film," which with a few changes is a reprint of the
author's pamphlet of the same title issued in 1942 by
the Museum of Modern Art Film Library. There is also a
structural analysis giving specific examples of the ways
in which propaganda is used, an excellent bibliography,
and a name-subject index.

908. Kracauer, Siegfried. Theory of Film: The Redemption of
     Physical Reality. New York: Oxford University Press,
     1960. 364p.

     An aesthetic theory of film in which the author's
approach is through medium (photography) and content. He
discusses types, characteristics, highlights, and history.
Has notes, a bibliography, and an author-title-subject
index.

909. Lahue, Kalton C. Continued Next Week: A History of the
     Moving Picture Serial. Norman: University of Oklahoma
     Press, 1964. 203p.

     A chronological story of the old-time serial. Follow-
ing the text, a 123-page appendix traces chronologically
various serials from 1912 to 1930, giving for each the
director, cast, release date, company, and chapter titles.
There is an index.
     In 1968 the author brought out a similar book, Bound
and Gagged: The Story of the Silent Serials (Barnes).
Profusely illustrated, it is designed primarily to enter-
tain all ages and to promote nostalgia in those old enough
to remember the heydey of the serial.

910. Lahue, Kalton C. Worlds of Laughter: The Motion Picture
     Comedy Short, 1910-1930. Norman: University of Okla-
     homa Press, 1966. 240p.

     Account of the major films, firms, actors, and directors
of short comedy up to the advent of sound. An appendix
lists by date the films of selected major comedians in this
genre. There is a very brief bibliography and a name-title
index.

266

911. Leab, Daniel J. From Sambo to Superspade: The Black
     Experience in Motion Pictures. Boston: Houghton-
     Mifflin, 1975. 301p.

     A history and interpretation of the black in American
     motion pictures which presents a bleak and well-documented
     picture. Illustrations, footnotes, bibliography, and
     index.

912. LeGrice, Malcolm. Abstract Film and Beyond. Cambridge,
     Mass.: MIT Press, 1977. 160p.

     A theoretical and historical account of the trends in
     abstract filmmaking which covers not only nonrepresenta-
     tional forms, but also experiments into film's manipula-
     tion into time. Beginning with a discussion of Cezanne,
     whom LeGrice considers influential because of his pre-
     occupation with pictorial space, LeGrice discusses the
     Futurists' cinema; the early abstract film experiments
     in Germany, France, and the U.S. in the 1920s; post-World
     War II experimental film, and finally the present. There
     are many illustrations, footnotes, a list of catalogues,
     and an index.

913. Leiser, Erwin. Na i Cinema. Gertrud Mander and David
     Wilson, tr. Ne York: Macmillan, 1975. 179p.

     The author exami ; notorious and forgotten German
     films to show how Hitler's Minister of Popular Enlighten-
     ment converted German cinema into a highly efficient cog
     in the Nazi propaganda machine to help sell the German
     people on his government and its policies. Contains a
     bibliography, a selected filmography, and an index of
     names.

914. Lejeune, Caroline A. Cinema. London: Alexander Macle-
     hose, 1931. 255p.

     Even the contemporary portions of these perceptive
     essays have now become history, and as history they are
     excellent. Most of the essays are about film personal-
     ities--actors, actresses, directors, producers--and about
     types of film, such as war, travel, the soil, experimental,
     and so on, grouped into three sections--American, European,
     and miscellany--in which latter category Lejeune has placed
     the various genres. Contains a bibliography and an index.

915. Leprohon, Pierre. The Italian Cinema. Tr. from the
     French by Roger Greaves and Oliver Stallybrass. New
     York: Praeger, 1972. 256p.

     Traces Italian film from its beginnings in 1895, rela-
     ting its directions to the social, cultural, and political

crises in Italy, and ending with the year 1969. Arrangement is chronological. There is a three-page section, "Notes and References," a lengthy biographical dictionary, and an index to people and film.

916. Leyda, Jay. Dianying: An Account of Films and the Film Audience in China. Cambridge, Mass.: MIT Press, 1972. 515p.

The author traces Chinese films and filmmaking chronologically, tying it in with history. Within this framework he discusses important films and their casts. He includes both the films made with the endorsement of the political party and those made by the underground forces, and attempts to show the influence of politics and the reactions of the Chinese audiences. There are a number of appendices: "Contributors to the Art and History of Chinese Film," "Important Chinese Films Made by Chinese and Foreign Groups from 1897 to 1966," "A Counter-Revolutionary Record Aimed at the Restoration of Capitalism." Contains a list of sources and a detailed index.

917. Leyda, Jay. Kino: A History of the Russian and Soviet Film. New York: Macmillan, 1960. 493p.

Gives an intensive treatment of the background, personalities, political interests, industrial growth, and artistic development. Concludes with the death of Eisenstein in 1948. Has five appendices, one of the most useful of which is "Fifty Years of Russian and Soviet Films 1908-1958, a Select List." The list of sources for each chapter forms a bibliography, and there is an index.

918. Liehm, Mira, and Antonin Liehm. The Most Important Art: East European Film after 1945. Berkeley: University of California Press, 1977. 467p.

What effect does the nationalization of an art have upon it? Surveying films and filmmakers of Bulgaria, Czechoslovakia, the German Democratic Republic, Poland, Romania, the U.S.S.R., and Yugoslavia, this comparative study shows how the history of their film industries has been one of conflict between the potentialities of a publicly supported art (not dependent on box office) and the limitations and interests of the political forces controlling state support. Films discussed include lesser-known ones which did not achieve foreign notice as well as the better-known which circulated through much of the world. Contains many illustrations, a bibliography, and an index.

919. Limbacher, James L. Feature Films on 8mm, 16mm, and Video-
      tape: A Directory of Feature Films Available for Rental,
      Sale, and Lease in the U.S. and Canada. 6th ed. New
      York: Bowker, 1979. 447p.

      Lists more than 20,000 feature films, of which some
      1,500 are available on videotape. Information for each
      gives releasing company or country of origin for foreign
      films; release date; running time; whether black and white
      or color; whether sound or silent; principal cast; direc-
      tor; current distributors; and whether available for ren-
      tal, sale, or lease. Includes documentaries, educational
      features, animated and experimental films as well as those
      primarily for theaters. Contains an index of directors
      and their films, a distributor index of names and
      addresses, a geographical index to distributors, and a
      selective listing of film reference works.

920. Limbacher, James L. Haven't I Seen You Somewhere Before?
      Remakes, Sequels and Series in Motion Pictures and
      Television, 1896-1978. Ann Arbor, Mich. 48106:
      Pierian Press, P.O. Box 1808, 1979. 295p.

      It comes as a surprise to many of us to know that a
      film called Up in Desdemona's Room is a remake of Othello;
      I Married a Doctor, a remake of Arrowsmith; and
      Le Cheminlau, The Price of a Soul, The Galley Slave, and
      twenty-one other titles are all remakes of Les Miserables.
      After twelve years of research Limbacher has unearthed
      thousands of remakes covering a period of over eighty
      years, giving for each entry the distributor and year of
      release and, when available, the source of the production--
      book, original screenplay, comic book, play, etc. The
      last portion lists series and sequels by year of release.

921. Limbacher, James L., comp. and ed. Film Music: From
      Violin to Video. Metuchen, N.J.: Scarecrow, 1974.
      835p.

      Part I consists of articles commenting on the history,
      theory, and techniques of film music, treating the general
      aspects and the scoring of various genres. Part II is
      strictly for reference, with a list of film titles and
      dates, two other lists linking films and composers, and a
      discography of recorded musical scores. Part I is indexed.

922. Lindsay, Vachel. The Art of the Motion Picture. New York:
      Macmillan, 1915. 324p.

      A delightful, informally written book about the early
      days of movies by the famous poet who wrote of them con-
      temporarily. His aim is to supply viewers with a social

269

and aesthetic way of regarding them. One chapter, "California and America," deserves special mention, for in it he makes the prophecy that California, "as the natural moving picture playground, has the possibility of developing a unique cultural leverage upon America."

923. Liu, Alan P. L. The Film Industry in Communist China. Cambridge, Mass.: Massachusetts Institute of Technology, 1965. (Distributed by the Clearinghouse for Federal Scientific and Technical Information, U.S. Department of Commerce, National Bureau of Standards, Institute for Applied Technology.) 92p.

Report, based almost exclusively on Chinese publications, which seeks to update the data on the subject and to analyze the dynamics of the film industry. Deals briefly with Chinese films in the pre-Communist era and discusses at length the development, production, and audience under the later government, as well as the role of foreign film in the country. An appendix charts the distribution of the Film Copy System, and a bibliography lists Communist Chinese books, Chinese books from Hong Kong and Taiwan, articles in Western journals, and Western books on China.

924. London, Mel. Getting into Film. New York: Ballantine, 1977. 178p.

Intended as "the first complete career guide to the film industry," London's survey provides succinct information on most aspects of filmmaking. Contents include: the many kinds of films which comprise the industry; production; writing for film; cinematography; the editor; music; sound; animation, art, and graphics; actors and models; "the unsung heroes and heroines" who handle special effects, sales and syndication, equipment technicians, business management, etc.; directors; advertising agencies; film unions; film versus tape; schools and training programs; film grants; film festivals; women in film; the free-lance market; and a practical look at job-hunting. The author has included book titles within the text from time to time rather than in a bibliography, and in a final page mentions the leading trade publications and the three bookstores which specialize in film collections.

925. Low, Rachael. The History of the British Film. 4 vols. London: Allen & Unwin, 1948--.

A multivolumed project, with four volumes completed, covering thus far the period from 1896 through 1929. Roger Manvell collaborated with Miss Low on Vol. I.

The series has been published under the auspices of the British Film Institute and includes production, distribution, and exhibition information as well as discussions of specific films and an excellent selection of stills. Each volume is indexed, and Vol. IV contains a comprehensive film list of the 1920s, together with a general index of fifty-eight pages for that volume. Vols. V and VI have been scheduled for September 1979.

926. MacCann, Richard Dyer. The People's Films: A Political History of U.S. Government Motion Pictures. New York: Hastings House, 1973. 238p.

In his preface the author says: "I am concerned . . . with the questions: What factual motion pictures have been produced by the United States Government? When? How? But I am also concerned with the question: Why? What pressures and personalities produced the decisions which produced these films? And beyond this, it is important to make some attempt at criticism of the 'why.'" The author stresses the public relations and propaganda aspect of government films, and devotes a chapter to the documentary in Canada and England. The USIA, too, comes up for discussion in connection with films and foreign policy. Person, film, and subject index.

927. McCarthy, Todd, and Charles Flynn, eds. Kings of the Bs: Working within the Hollywood System: An Anthology of Film History and Criticism. New York: Dutton, 1975. 561p.

The editors of this anthology believe that American B (and C and Z) movies are as necessary to the economics of the Hollywood system as the works of master directors. With this in mind they tour the slums of U.S. filmmaking, digging out figures and facts as well as making observations. Contains filmographies for 325 directors hard to find elsewhere, seventy-five illustrations, and an index.

928. McClure, Arthur F., comp. and ed. The Movies, an American Idiom: Readings in the Social History of the American Motion Picture. Rutherford, N.J.: Fairleigh Dickinson University Press, 1971. 435p.

Collection of articles, drawn from the writings of journalists, critics, historians, sociologists, and humorists, which describe the historical relationship between the American motion picture and the environment of the twentieth century. Articles are arranged chronologically in three parts: "Admission and Ascendancy, 1900-1949"; "Retrenchment and Renewal, 1950-1969"; and

271

"Whither Hollywood?" Among the contributors are Foster
Rhea Dulles, Terry Ramsaye, Richard Schickel, Lewis
Jacobs, Siegfried Kracauer, Richard Dyer McCann, Hollis
Alpert, Arthur Mayer, Paul Reynolds, Ben Hecht, John
Cassavetes, Bosley Crowther, Arthur Knight, and Olivia
de Havilland.

929. Macgowan, Kenneth. Behind the Screen: The History and
Techniques of the Motion Picture. New York: Dela-
corte, 1965. 528p.

Detailed history, with technical background, of the
invention and development of the motion picture as a
major industry. Emphasis is American, although brief
sections are devoted to the German, Scandinavian, and
Russian film.

930. Maltin, Leonard. Movie Comedy Teams. New York: New
American Library, 1970. 352p.

Intended for both nostalgia reading and historical
research, this film history centers around famous comedy
teams--the Marx Brothers, Burns and Allen, Abbott and
Costello, the Three Stooges, and many others. The
author gives a picture of the old Hollywood through
biographies of the teams, peppered with anecdotes. There
are also synopses of major films by comedy teams, along
with painstaking filmographies and over 200 still photographs.

931. Manvell, Roger. Films and the Second World War. Cranbury, N.J.: A. S. Barnes, 1974. 388p.

"The purpose of this book is to discuss and illustrate
a cross-section of films about the Second World War, both
fiction films and factual films--the picture of war and
its motivation from the popular viewpoint as it was (and
sometimes still is) presented to the public of the
principal nations involved, both during and after the
actual years of fighting. The few films that anticipated
the coming struggle for power are also discussed in a
preliminary chapter." - Preface. Notes, a bibliography,
and indexes of films and of titles.

932. Manvell, Roger. New Cinema in Europe. New York: Dutton,
1966. 60p. (Vista Paperback.)
933. _____. New Cinema in the USA: The Feature Film since
1946. New York: Dutton, 1968. 160p. (Vista Paperback.)

The first of these two books deals with film in Europe
after World War II, with emphasis on the realistic and

naturalistic approach of major filmmakers. Among nations
included are Italy, Britain, France, Russia, and Poland.
Indexed.

The second contrasts American film with that in other
parts of the world and fills in the 1950s background of
U.S. films. It then discusses films and directors in
terms of traditionalism and experimentation, and has a
chapter on the musical. Indexed.

934. Manvell, Roger, ed. Experiment in the Film. New York:
     Arno, 1948, c1970. 273p.

An anthology in which contributors take stock of the
achievements of the experimental and in some cases the
genre film during the first five decades of the century
in France, the U.S., the U.S.S.R., Germany and Austria,
and Britain. A final short essay deals with the contributions of film to science. Indexes to titles and to
novels.

935. Manvell, Roger, and Heinrich Fraenkel. The German Cinema.
     New York: Praeger, 1971. 159p.

This first survey of German movies to be published in
English analyzes films from their origins in 1895 through
the 1960s, discussing the trends and developments, detailing the Nazis' use of the film as propaganda and subsequent "deNazification" of the industry, and examining the
post-World War II cinema. There is also a survey of
younger German directors. Bibliography and index.

936. Manvell, Roger, and Peter Day. The Technique of Film
     Music. 2d ed. New York: Hastings House, 1975. 310p.

Addressed to filmmakers and musicians, this traces the
development and function of all kinds of music in the
silent and sound film up to about 1955. After that date
an analytical approach stressing contemporary achievement
is substituted for the historical one. Further chapters
discuss the music director and sound recordist, and give
the composer's view. Appendices include "An Outline History of Film Music," "Film Music Criticism," and a bibliography. Indexed.

937. Mapp, Edward. Blacks in American Films: Today and Yester-
     day. Metuchen, N.J.: Scarecrow Press, 1972. 278p.

After a brief history of the Negro in motion pictures
from the earliest appearances through 1961, the author
examines the content of Negro portrayals in films of each
year from 1962 through 1970, comparing old and new stereotypes and changing screen images. Bibliography and index.

938. Martin, Marcel. _France: An Illustrated Guide to 400 Key Figures in the French Cinema_. Cranbury, N.J.: A. S. Barnes, 1971. 191p.

Thumbnail sketches of French actors, directors, and others connected with the film industry, along with short descriptions of principal trends. Identification for individuals usually consists of a summary paragraph capsuling their careers and a list of their works. Contains title index to feature films made in France.

939. Mast, Gerald. _A Short History of the Movies_. Indianapolis: Bobbs-Merrill, 1976. 575p.

Focuses on the key elements in the major films of directors who have made significant contributions in this country and in western Europe. A beginning section tells of the birth of the motion picture and the commercial development of the narrative film. An appendix contains a bibliography of books and films. Indexed.

940. Mayer, Michael F. _The Film Industries: Practical Business/ Legal Problems in Production, Distribution and Exhibition_. 2d ed. New York: Hastings House, 1978. 230p.

While teaching a course in film industry management, Mayer, a theatrical lawyer, wrote the first edition of this book as a text to chart the way for students and any other interested laymen through the complicated processes of production, distribution, and exhibition. Among the numerous aspects he discusses are contracts, financing agreements, markets abroad and at home, non-theatrical as well as theatrical film, conglomerates, antitrust, copyright, and problems of context. An excellent guide for the novice.

941. Mehr, Linda Harris. _Motion Pictures, Television and Radio: A Union Catalogue of Manuscripts and Special Collections in the Western United States_. Boston: G. K. Hall, 1977. 201p. (Sponsored by Film and Television Study Center, Inc.)

This is the first effort to collect a checklist of sources of archival materials in these relatively new media. It locates, identifies, and describes research collections currently available for use in established institutions, libraries, museums, and historical societies in Arizona, California, Colorado, Idaho, Montana, Nevada, New Mexico, Oregon, Utah, Washington, and Wyoming. There is a general index and an index by the occupations of the individuals represented in the collections. The other thirty-nine states should be covered by similar projects.

942. Mellen, Joan. The Waves at Genji's Door: Japan through
        Its Cinema. New York: Pantheon, 1976. 436p.
943. _____. Voices from the Japanese Cinema. New York:
        Liveright, 1975. 295p.

    In both books Mellen's desire is to introduce Wester-
ners to the Japanese film. Believing that they have been
intimidated by the degree to which it is concerned with a
national history which seems unfamiliar and even unappeal-
ing to the West, she has written The Waves at Genji's
Door "in the hope of dispelling the myth of inaccessibil-
ity which has denied the Japanese film its due." Within
this framework she discusses films, centering upon various aspects of national history from medieval times to
the present, as well as more specific aspects like the
role of women and the family today and yesterday. There
are footnotes and an index.
    In Voices from the Japanese Cinema she presents an
inside view of films, directors, and actors, with emphasis
upon the cultural factors which shape Japanese filmmaking.

944. Monaco, James. American Film Now: The People, the Power,
        the Money, the Movies. New York: Oxford University
        Press, 1979. 540p.

    "Anthologists unearthing Jaws, Heaven Can Wait, Grease,
Close Encounters of the Third Kind, and other popular
films of the seventies a thousand years from now will be
hard-pressed to divine from this evidence just what the
1970s were all about," says Monaco in this critical but
loving analysis of the American entertainment cinema of
the seventies--its subject matter, its producers, its
directors, its players. One of the most revealing portions is his analysis of Hollywood's economic structure,
which he feels dominates its aesthetics. In addition,
American Film Now has features that make it a valuable
reference book. A section, "The Data," contains a discussion of film critics and their choices, ten major filmographies of important directors, a long and detailed subject bibliography, chapter references, and a lengthy "Who's
Who in American Film Now." Indexed.

945. Monaco, James, and Susan Schenker. Books about Film: A
        Bibliographical Booklist. 3d ed. New York 10003: New
        York Zoetrope, 1976. 48p.
946. _____. Film, How and Where to Find Out What You Want
        to Know: A Comprehensive Guide to Reference Materials
        (Indexes, Encyclopediae, Checklists, Periodicals).
        Montreal H3B 23L3: Take One, 1975, 8p.

    Two reference books--the first, a selective bibliography
in thirteen sections, each with a brief introductory note

about the literature and occasional annotations; the second,
a compact guide to source material, with brief, to-the-point
comments.

947. Monaco, Paul. <u>Cinema and Society: France and Germany dur-
     ing the Twenties</u>. New York: Elsevier, 1976. 194p.

   An analysis of the social function of the cinema in a
particular historical setting--France in the period between
World Wars I and II, and Germany in the same period during
the Weimar Republic. Emphasis is cultural, historical,
and economic rather than aesthetic. Chapters include the
film as big business; film and governmental policy; film as
national folklore; popular cinema as reflection of the
group process in France, 1919-29; and German movies and the
obsessions of a nation. The goal is to interpret compara-
tively the mass, public meaning of the most popular French
and German films of the decade. Appendices list the films
studied, their directors, and the year each premiered. An
excellent bibliography breaks sources down into primary
and secondary. There is an index.

948. Montgomery, John. <u>Comedy Films, 1894-1954</u>. 2d ed. Lon-
     don: Allen & Unwin, 1968. 286p.

   Factual history of comedy film in the U.S. and England.

949. Morin, Edgar. <u>The Stars</u>. Richard Howard, tr. New York:
     Grove Press, 1960. 189p.

   Study of stardom as an institution in which the author,
using famous film personalities as examples, discusses
the sociology of stardom. There is a table of chronological landmarks.

950. <u>The Motion Picture Industry</u>. Gordon S. Watkins, ed.
     Philadelphia: American Academy of Political and Social
     Science, 1947. (Annals of the American Academy of
     Political and Social Science, Vol. 254.)

   Compilation of articles about film in the mid-forties--
some by people within the industry and the majority by
social scientists--on the development of the motion picture, its business and financial aspects, the sources and
production of motion pictures, the possible effects,
motion pictures and the public, censorship and self-
regulation, and suggestions for further research.

951. <u>The Motion Picture in Its Economic and Social Aspects</u>.
     Clyde L. King and Frank A. Tichenor, eds. Philadelphia:
     American Academy of Political and Social Science, 1926.
     (Annals of the American Academy of Political and Social
     Science, Vol. 128.)

Compilation of articles, almost entirely by business
and professional men unconnected with the film industry
or universities, which show the way things were in the
mid-twenties and earlier. Emphasis is on financial,
technical, and educational factors, with a final section
on censorship, both voluntary and involuntary.

952. Motion Picture Market Place. Tom Costner, ed. Boston:
     Little, Brown, annual. (1976/77--.)

   Surveys in directory format aspects of doing business
in the theatrical and TV film community in the U.S. Concentrates on films produced for motion picture and TV exhibition, with industrial films and educational audiovisual
markets covered only incidentally. Includes more than
seventy categories of information, beginning with "Advertising Agencies" and ending with "Wardrobes." Among the
many "in-betweens" are literary and talent agents, festivals, film libraries, distributors (including those for
x-rated films), costumes, manuscript services, film commissions, guilds and unions, casting agencies and consultants, set design, recording studios, props, producers
and production companies, stunts, translations. Information given for most items includes name, address, and
telephone number; others, like festivals, get a fuller,
although still brief, treatment because of their nature.

953. Motion Pictures, 1894-1912, Identified from the Records
     of the United States Copyright Office. Howard Lamarr
     Walls, ed. Washington: Library of Congress, Copy-
     right Office, 1953. 92p.
     Motion Pictures, 1912-1939. Washington: Library of Con-
     gress, Copyright Office, 1951. 1,256p.
     Motion Pictures, 1940-1949. Washington: Library of Con-
     gress, Copyright Office, 1953. 595p.
     Motion Pictures, 1950-1959. Washington: Library of Con-
     gress, Copyright Office, 1960. 495p.
     Motion Pictures, 1960-1969. Washington: Library of Con-
     gress, Copyright Office, 1971. 744p.

   These five catalogues of copyright registration of fiction and nonfiction films list a total of over 135,000
motion pictures registered since the beginning of the
motion picture industry. The first volume, covering 1894-
1912, is in two parts: one an alphabetical list under
title, giving name of claimant, date, and registration
number, and the second an index of claimants, listing
under each the films copyrighted. The next four volumes
are in three sections: an alphabetical list under title,
giving date, length, credits, producer, original source
when adapted from a printed work, and in some cases a

brief summary of content; an index listing names of persons and organizations associated with the productions and of the authors if based on a printed work; and the series contained in the main entries. Kept up to date by semi-annual additions.

954. <u>Movies on TV, 1978–79</u>. Steven H. Scheuer, ed. 8th ed. New York: Bantam, 1977. 816p.

Brief, literate appraisals of thousands of films, intended to guide the discriminating viewer. Lists each film alphabetically by title and gives date, cast, a rating by asterisks, and succinct annotations which capture plot, mood, and quality. Emphasis in this edition is on motion pictures from the 1960s and 1970s which have been recently released for telecasting, although many go back as far as the 1930s.

955. Murray, James P. <u>To Find an Image: Black Films from Uncle Tom to Superfly</u>. Indianapolis: Bobbs-Merril, 1973. 205p.

The film editor of <u>Black Creation</u> magazine surveys the treatment of blacks in film from the earliest days of Oscar Michaux and other black filmmakers of the 1920s through Stepin Fetchit, Sidney Poitier, and Shaft. He includes films made by both white and black production companies. An appendix lists the "establishment," labor unions, black films from 1905 to the present (produced by both black and white companies), and representative black producers, directors, screenwriters, scorers, and production companies. Indexed.

956. Nachbar, John G. <u>Western Films: An Annotated Critical Bibliography</u>. New York: Garland, 1975. 98p.

The author's aim is, through his bibliography, "to sum up what has been discovered about Western films and their relationship to their culture," and more important, to provide a tool for research. In his introduction he surveys the evolution of the genre through various popular culture forms, narrative dramas, and spectacles that came together in the early 1900s in the Western film. In the bibliography that follows, articles and books are listed under ten categories: reference sources, pre-1950 criticism, specific films, specific performers, specific producers, Western film history, the audience, comparative studies, and Westerns in the classroom. Author and subject indexes.

957. <u>National Film Archive Catalogue</u>. Part I. <u>Silent News Films, 1895–1933</u>, 2d ed.; Part II. <u>Silent Non-Fiction</u>

Films, 1895-1934; Part III. Silent Fiction Films,
1895-1930. 3 vols. London, W. 1: British Film
Institute, 81 Dean St., 1960-66.

Each film is arranged chronologically and annotated.
Part I contains a subject index so that the films may
be approached by historical event; Part II, an index
to titles; and Part III, fiction films--an index to
films, persons, and companies. Thus far sound films
have not been catalogued. To quote the curator: "The
complete published catalogue of the Archive is . . .
gradually taking shape, but far too slowly owing to
our restricted resources. It will have taken nearly
twenty years to cover only our silent films, and the
accurate cataloguing of our larger collection of sound
films still stretches before us."

958. New York Times Film Reviews. New York: The New York
Times Library Service and Information Division, 1970--.

The five-volume 1970 set contains over 18,000 film
reviews going back fifty-six years, reproduced exactly
as they appeared in the Times. This set is accompanied
by a sixth volume, a 1,100-entry computer-generated
index arranged three ways: by film title; by producing
and distributing company; and by names of all actors,
actresses, directors, and others listed in the credits.
Four further volumes carry the collection through 1976.
New compilations appear periodically. Each update carries the same computer-based index as accompanies the
1970 set.

959. The New York Times Guide to Movies on TV. Howard Thompson,
ed. Chicago: Quadrangle, 1970. 223p.

Thumbnail summaries of over 2,000 films, with well-
written capsule evaluations. For example, about The Car-
petbaggers: "Sow's purse from a sow's ear." Or The
Cardinal: "The spirit is willing but the film is weak."
Less subjective information includes names of producer,
director, and cast; date; color or black and white;
source, if from a novel. A still shot accompanies each
entry.

960. Niver, Kemp R. The First Twenty Years: A Segment of
Film History. Los Angeles 90046: Locare Research
Group, Box 46505, 1968. 176p.

"This book concerns over one hundred motion pictures
selected from the more than 3,000 films restored from
the Library of Congress as proof of copyright application

prior to ratification in 1912 of a motion picture copyright law. Each film described was selected because, in
the author's opinion, it contributed something of value
to the progress of communication through the new medium
of moving photography." Most of the films chosen for
restoration were 16mm. Contains a list of film titles
in alphabetical order.

961. Noble, Peter. The Negro in Films. London: Skelton
     Robinson, 1948. 288p.

     Some years before the treatment of blacks in the enter-
tainment world became the issue it is today, their status
was undergoing examination in Britain. This book examines
portrayals of and by Negroes on the stage beginning with
the Federal period, and moves on to the silent and then
the sound film. It takes up the Negro in song and dance
roles, in independent and government films, and in European films; discusses some of the leading Negro players;
and assays what the future may hold. Appendices give a
brief historical background of the American Negro, a
bibliography, a list of films featuring Negroes or containing important racial themes--American, British, and
continental--and a defense of The Birth of a Nation made
by D. W. Griffith. Indexed.

962. Oakley, Charles Allen. Where We Came In: Seventy Years
     of the British Film Industry. London: Allen & Unwin,
     1964. 245p.

     A chronological history told largely in terms of films
and the people connected with them, set against the background of the times. Oakley never loses sight of the
economics of the industry. Documentary as well as theatrical films are included. Contains a twelve-page
chronology, "The Sequence of Events," many illustrations,
and an index.

963. Parish, James Robert, and Michael R. Pitts. Film Direc-
     tors: A Guide to Their American Films. Metuchen,
     N.J.: Scarecrow, 1974. 436p.
964. _____. Film Directors Guide: Western Europe.
     Metuchen, N.J.: Scarecrow, 1976. 292p.

     The first of these "directors" series is intended to
provide in a single volume a checklist of domestic and
international motion picture directors who have contributed feature-length films to the U.S. cinema. Selection
"covers a wide spectrum of professionals who have been
employed at major or poverty row studios in grade A or Z
features, serials, or documentaries, and in the silent
and sound eras."

The second volume is the first of a projected series
that intends eventually to cover Eastern Europe including the U.S.S.R. and Asia, Africa, and Australia. Sweden
they omit, intending to place it among the Eastern European countries.

Each volume lists under the director's name his dates,
birthplace, and films, with production company, distributor, and release given in the cases in which this information was available.

965. Parish, James Robert, and Michael R. Pitts. The Great
     Gangster Pictures. Metuchen, N.J.: Scarecrow, 1976.
     431p.
966. _____. The Great Science Fiction Pictures. Metuchen,
     N.J.: Scarecrow, 1977. 382p.
967. _____. The Great Spy Pictures. Metuchen, N.J.:
     Scarecrow, 1974. 585p.
968. _____. The Great Western Pictures. Metuchen, N.J.:
     Scarecrow, 1976. 455p.

The main portion of each of these volumes consists of
an alphabetical list of motion pictures which the authors
consider best within the genre. Each film is discussed,
with date, running time, credits, a synopsis, and comments. This is preceded by an introduction and followed
by lists of radio and TV series, and a selected bibliography. The volumes might have been more substantial if
Parish and Pitts had used a chronological, rather than an
alphabetical, arrangement, which would have better traced
the development of the genre, and if they had provided
indexes.

969. Patterson, Lindsay, comp. Black Films and Film-Makers:
     A Comprehensive Anthology from Stereotype to Superhero.
     New York: Dodd, Mead, 1975. 298p.

Approximately thirty articles divided into six sections
moving from early criticism of the black as a caricature
and the controversy over Birth of a Nation to an examination of black movies of the 1970s. Emphasis is on the
place of black films in the black culture and on the blacks
who have acted in or produced the films. Contains a filmography and a bibliography.

970. The Payne Fund Studies. Motion Pictures and Youth. W. W.
     Charters, Chairman. New York: Macmillan, c1933, 1935.
     (Reprinted by Arno.)

This series of empirical studies is the first major
undertaking on the effects of film on youth--in this case
the youth of the 1930s. It has historical value both for

its findings and because it is seminal. Charters, Dale,
Blumer, and others of the authors were among the best-
known early researchers in this field. A list of individual volumes--in some cases, two titles are combined
in one book--are:

Blumer, Herbert. Movies and Conduct, 1933.
Blumer, Herbert, and Philip M. Hauser. Movies, Delin-
    quency, and Crime, 1934.
Charters, W. W. Motion Pictures and Youth: A Summary,
    1933, together with Holday, P. W., and George D.
    Stoddard. Getting Ideas from the Movies, 1933.
Cressey, Paul G., and Frederick M. Thrasher. Boys,
    Movies, and City Streets. 1934.
Dale, Edgar. Content of Motion Pictures, together with
    Edgar Dale. Children's Attendance at Motion Pictures,
    1935.
Dale, Edgar. How to Appreciate Motion Pictures, 1934.
Dysinger, W. S., and Christian A. Ruckmick. The Emotional
    Responses of Children to the Motion Picture Situation,
    1933, together with Charles C. Peters. Motion Pictures
    and Standards of Morality, 1933.
Forman, Henry James. Our Movie-Made Children, 1933.
Peterson, Ruth C., and L. L. Thurstone. Motion Pictures
    and Social Attitudes of Children, 1933, together with
    Frank K. Shuttleworth and Mark A. May. The Social Con-
    duct and Attitude of Movie Fans.
Renshaw, Samuel, Vernon L. Miller, and Dorothy Marquis.
    Children's Sleep, 1933.

971. Perlmutter, Tom. War Movies. New York: Hamlyn, 1974.
     156p.

     From World War I propagandistic war films to bitterly
realistic ones, some of which were made quite early, this
book examines and illustrates trends. Newsreels, documentaries, and anti-war films are also included. The format
is very large--18-by-11-inches--and illustrations outweigh
texts, but both work well together and the text is analytical. Title/name index.

972. Perry, George. The Great British Picture Show from the
     Nineties to the Seventies. New York: Hill & Wang, 1974.
     367p.

     A history of the British film in which the author
searches to find the characteristics and contributions
which differentiate it from the film of other national-
ities, discussing specific films, directors, and players.
In his introduction he tells the reasons that he feels
lie behind "its failure to achieve an independent status."

"A Biographical Guide to the British Cinema" gives data on leading actors, actresses, and directors, including film credits. Bibliography and index.

973. Pichard, R. A. E. Dictionary of 1,000 Best Films. New York: Association Press, 1971. 406p.

Although Pichard says that his selection of 1,000 titles is obviously personal, he has tried to include as many of the generally accepted masterpieces as possible, taking 1903 as a starting date. The films are international in scope, covering the U.S., Britain, Spain, France, Italy, Germany, Sweden, and Denmark, with emphasis on the U.S. Brief story synopses and highlights are accompanied by comprehensive production credits--i.e., producer, director, screenwriter and story source, cameraman, composer, art director, editor, and leading players. These detailed credits are probably the most important part of the dictionary, for full production credits are difficult to find. The lack of indexes is somewhat compensated for by these detailed credits.

Poteet, G. Howard. Published Radio, Television, and Film Scripts: A Bibliography. (See No. 533.)

974. Powers, Anne, comp. Blacks in American Movies: A Selected Bibliography. Metuchen, N.J.: Scarecrow Press, 1974. 157p.

References, including indexes, general reference works, bibliographies, periodical articles, dissertations, biographies and autobiographies, and other general books, with a subject listing of periodical citations; a chronological listing; a filmography of features by and about blacks, 1904-30; and an author and subject index. There are brief annotations where necessary for clarification.

975. Pratt, George C. Spellbound in Darkness: A History of the Silent Film. Rev. ed. New York Graphic Society, 1973. 548p.

A compilation of original readings about the silent film from 1896 to 1929, collected from contemporary sources and bound together by the compiler's commentary. Scope is both American and foreign. Though most are reviews, there are also articles, particularly in the early portion.

Press and Advertisers Year Book. (See No. 744.)

Press, Film, Radio. (See No. 160.)

976. Quigley, Martin, Jr. <u>Magic Shadows: The Story of the</u>
     <u>Origin of Motion Pictures</u>. New York: Biblo & Tannen,
     c1960, 1969. 191p.

     A pre-history of the motion picture, from ancient times
     through the kinetoscope. Contains a chronology from 6000
     B.C. through 1896, a bibliography, and an index.

977. Quinn, James. <u>The Film and Television as an Aspect of</u>
     <u>European Culture</u>. Leyden: A. W. Sijthoff, 1968. 168p.

     Survey of the educational and cultural significance of
     film and television, commissioned by the Council for Cul-
     tural Co-operation of the Council of Europe. Gives dif-
     ferent forms of governmental support, steps taken by
     educational bodies in various countries to develop film
     and television studies, use of film and television in
     education, attitudes of the church and the public, and
     attitude of film industries of different countries toward
     the film as art.

978. Ragan, David. <u>Who's Who in Hollywood, 1900-1976</u>. New
     Rochelle, N.Y.: Arlington, 1976. 864p.

     This worshipful biographical directory reads like a
     fan magazine or a gossip column, with heavy emphasis on
     private lives, especially the marital and financial
     aspects. It is included because some users may want this
     kind of information and also because coverage is good,
     with a great number of TV and motion picture performers,
     some of whom are little known. Arrangement is alphabet-
     ical, with the quick divided from the dead--i.e., "Living
     Players"; "Later Players (1900-1974)"; and "Players Who
     Died in 1975 and 1976."

979. Ramsaye, Terry. <u>A Million and One Nights: A History of</u>
     <u>the Motion Picture</u>. New York: Simon & Schuster,
     c1926, 1964. 868p.

     First published in 1926, at a time when many of the
     founders of the film were alive, this book goes into
     detail about the history of the motion picture in the
     U.S. from its inception to 1926. The author, first con-
     nected with the industry in 1913 as a journalist, used
     original sources whenever possible and interviewed
     every person then living whom he mentioned. Contains
     an index but no bibliography or footnotes. Over the
     years certain historical inaccuracies have been found
     in Ramsaye, but it is still a useful and interesting
     source.

980. Rehrauer, George. <u>Cinema Booklist</u>. Metuchen, N.J.:
    Scarecrow Press, 1972. 473.
    _____. _____. <u>Supplement One</u>. 1974. 405p.
    _____. _____. <u>Supplement Two</u>. 1977. 470p.

    Intended for a large general audience interested in
    film and for the librarian rather than for the scholar,
    this bibliography is called by its author "an attempt
    to sample the entire spectrum of books on film, ranging
    from the trashy original paperback through souvenir pro-
    gram books to the commercialized doctoral dissertation."
    Published scripts are also included. Annotations are
    comprehensive and evaluative. This latter is quite a
    feat, considering that the three volumes cover 3,999
    titles. There are author, subject, and film script
    indexes, cumulative in the case of the supplements.
    Because of the scope of the work, the subject indexes
    are of necessity selective rather than cumulative.

981. Renan, Sheldon. <u>An Introduction to the American Under-
    ground Film</u>. New York: Dutton Paperback, 1968. 318p.

    Renan's work is substantial. Beginning with a lengthy
    definition of the underground film in its many aspects,
    he then gives its history in the U.S. and its earlier
    European background and a gallery of its chief filmmakers,
    its stars, and its "establishment"; and finally he dis-
    cusses "expanded cinema," which he defines as a spirit of
    inquiry leading in many directions.
    An appendix lists the 400 to 500 films mentioned, tell-
    ing their length, whether in color or black and white,
    silent or sound, and availability for sales or rental,
    with sources from which they may be obtained. Contains a
    bibliography and an index.

982. Rhode, Eric. <u>A History of the Cinema: From Its Origins
    to 1970</u>. New York: Hill & Wang, 1976. 674p.

    A history of the film in major countries of the world
    where the industry has developed, with stress on Europe
    and the U.S. Rhode has systematically attempted to relate
    movies to the societies from which they emerge, and he
    treats them in a social, economic, and artistic context,
    with much attention to individual directors and films and
    an analysis of the techniques used. Contains footnotes
    and a bibliography for each chapter, and a name-title
    index, but unfortunately none for subject.

983. Richards, Jeffrey. <u>Swordsmen of the Screen: From Douglas
    Fairbanks to Michael York</u>. London/Boston: Routledge
    & Kegan Paul, 1977. 296p.

An analysis of a genre which no longer seems to fit
today's style. Richards examines its values; possible
reasons for its popularity; and its place in the long
tradition of folklore entertainment. Almost half of the
book consists of illustrations. Contains a bibliography,
a general index, and an index of film titles.

984. Richie, Donald. Japanese Cinema: Film Style and
     National Character. London: Secker & Warburg, 1972.
     250p.

In many ways Japanese cinema is unique. In this succinct history, which traces it from its beginning around
1869 through 1971, Ritchie has attempted to place it
within the setting of Japanese culture by relating it to
other art forms and to national traditions and attitudes.
He deals with art as well as popular entertainment films.
Although based upon Japanese Movies, published in 1961 by
the Japan Travel Bureau and now out of print, this is an
almost completely new book, treating a later time period
and providing later thoughts and insights, as well as
different stills. Contains an index.

985. Robinson, David. The Great Funnies: A History of Film
     Comedy. New York: Dutton, 1969. 156p.

"This essay pretends to be no more than a bird's-eye
view, only lingering from time to time over a figure of
particular importance or special attention," says the
author with too much modesty. For, building his history
around various well-known comedians, he packs in a great
deal of material in a succinct and interesting fashion.
The scope is international. Indexed.

986. Robinson, David. The History of World Cinema. New York:
     Stein & Day, 1973. 440p.

A history encompassing seventy-five years of world
cinema must of necessity be fact-packed and concise. As
the author puts it: "What I hope I have achieved is . . .
an outline of film history--a skeletal chart, with a few
landmarks dotted in. . . ." Events are structured in
relation to four elements: the aesthetic, the technological, the economic, and the audience. Arrangement is
chronological. There are many illustrations and three
appendices: "A Note on Animated Films"; "Selected Filmographies"; and "Bibliography." It contains three separate
indexes--subject, film, and name.

987. Rodney, James C. Film as a National Art: NFB of Canada
     and the Film Board Idea. New York: Arno, 1977. 760p.

"I have tried to analyze the NFB [National Film Board] not merely in terms of the films it produced, but as an organic entity--one that is continually evolving and functioning in a number of varied contexts--historical, political, social, economic, bureaucratic, and cinematic, on both national and international levels," says the author. Beginning with a discussion of the information film in Canada, 1896-1939, which preceded the NFB, he then traces the NFB in terms of its people, its policies, and its productions, including nonfilm materials. Appendices include "Grierson Report to Establish NFB," "An Act to Create a National Film Board," "Principal Recommendations of the Woods and Gordon Report," "An Act Respecting the National Film Board." Contains bibliography, name index, film index, and general index.

988. Rosnow, Eugene. Born to Lose: The Gangster Film in America. New York: Oxford University Press, 1978. 422p.

"The recurring characters, stories, themes, motifs, and iconography of gangster movies represent a superstructure of values and ideas that make up a self-image of America's advanced capitalist society," says Rosnow about this analysis of the genre, which puts it in the framework of popular culture in the broad sense of the term. His treatment is chronological. There are notes, a bibliography, an annotated filmography, and an index.

989. Rosten, Leo C. Hollywood: The Movie Colony; the Movie Makers. New York: Harcourt, Brace & World, 1941. 436p.

"This book is primarily concerned with putting Hollywood under the microscopes of social science. For Hollywood is an index to our society and our culture." - Preface. The result is a systematic analysis by the author and a staff of social scientists, who combine statistical documentation with perception. Appendices contain data on such items as: the movies and Los Angeles; production costs, analysis of movie companies, comparison with other industries; annual earnings, weekly salaries, and spending patterns; social data; marriage and divorce data; comments and preferences of movie makers; dogs, yachts, resorts; fan mail. Useful both historically and for certain eternal verities. Reference notes form a bibliography, and there is an index of subjects.

990. Rotha, Paul. Documentary Film. 3d ed. London: Faber & Faber, 1952. 412p.

Subtitled "The use of the film medium to interpret creatively and in social terms the life of the people as it exists in reality," this is an intensive study.

Limiting himself to no one country, the author first
gives a general introduction to the cinema, then treats
the following aspects of documentary film: its evolution;
certain basic principles; techniques; developments,
policies, purposes; and a history from 1939 to the early
1950s. Three appendices include the use of films by the
U.S. Armed Forces, 100 important documentary films, and a
select bibliography. Fully indexed. Sinclair Road and
Richard Griffith collaborated with Mr. Rotha.

991. Rotha, Paul. The Film till Now: A Survey of World Cinema.
     3d ed. New York: Twayne, 1960. 820p.

     A history and analysis of the motion picture, worldwide
in scope, and treating both its factual and theoretical
backgrounds. Part I, "The Actual," discusses its development, its various forms, and its growth and characteristics
in the U.S., U.S.S.R., Germany, France, Britain, and other
countries. Part II, "The Theoretical," discusses its aims
and influence of form upon dramatic content. Part III, by
Richard Griffith, brings the first edition up to 1948. An
epilogue in the third edition goes to 1958 and covers about
thirty-five western and eastern countries.

992. Sadoul, Georges. The Cinema in the Arab Countries. Beirut,
     Lebanon: Interarab Centre of Cinema & Television, P.O.
     Box 3434, 1966. 290p.

     Anthology, prepared for UNESCO, which provides the first
general view of the cinema in the Arab world. It is divided
into six sections: the cinema and Arab culture, history of
the Arab cinema, geography of the Arab cinema, problems and
future development, recommendations, film lists and statistics.

993. Sadoul, Georges. Dictionary of Film Makers. Tr., ed., and
     updated by Peter Morris. Berkeley: University of Cal-
     ifornia Press, 1972. 288p.
994. _____. Dictionary of Films. Tr., ed., and updated by
     Peter Morris. Berkeley: University of California Press,
     1972. 432p.

     Film Makers provides compact biographical information on
some 1,000 directors, writers, editors, animators, composers,
art directors, and cameramen, giving country of citizenship,
birth and, where appropriate, death dates, biography, filmography, and assessment of role. This is a valuable reference book because data on behind-the-scenes film workers can
be hard to find.
     Films covers more than 1,000 films produced in fifty
countries over a seventy-year period. Information includes
title, country of origin, year, major credits, a brief

288

synopsis, and a brief discussion of the film's role in cinema history. The two volumes are designed to be used together.

995. Salmane, Hala, Simon Hartog, and David Wilson, eds. Algerian Cinema. London W1V 6AA: British Film Institute, 81 Dean St., 1976. 58p.

Declaring that this is not intended as a comprehensive study of Algerian cinema, the editors state their aims: to provide basic information on a national cinema little known outside of French-speaking countries and to assess it in the context of Algerian history. In a still broader context this small book throws light on the effects of colonialism on national film.

996. Sampson, Henry T. Blacks in Black and White: A Source Book on Black Films. Metuchen, N.J.: Scarecrow, 1977. 333p.

Presents relatively little-known facts concerning films with all-black casts independently produced between 1910 and 1950. Contains a historical overview, a discussion of two important black companies and of white and black independents, a synopsis of some of the black films produced between 1910 and 1950, and biographies of leading actors and filmmakers. Appendices list all-black films by independent film producers between 1904 and 1950, a partial list of individuals and corporations organized to produce black-cast films in the years 1910-50, and film credits for featured players in black-cast films, 1910-50. Indexed.

997. Sarris, Andrew. The American Cinema: Directors and Directions, 1929-1968. New York: Dutton, 1968. 383p.

A brief but pointed examination of 200 American film directors. The author, a film critic, rates his directors in categories ranging from "pantheon" to "strained seriousness," "less than meets the eye," and "oddities, one-shots, and newcomers," and gives sound judgments as well as facts. Taken as a whole, the book constitutes an excellent survey of the American sound film. Special features are a directional chronology of the most important films of each year from 1929 through 1967 and an alphabetical list of over 600 films with year of release and director.

998. Schmidt, Georg, and others. The Film: Its Economic, Social, and Artistic Problems. London: Falcon Press, 1948. [124p.]

A study of the contemporary film, limited to what the authors term the fiction film rather than the documentary,

289

the newsreel, or the advertising film, and showing its
present function, its technical and artistic means, and
the nature of its economic and social structure. Some
history is also given as background.

999. Screen World. New York: Crown, annual. (1946--.)

Lists domestic and foreign films released during the
year, with credits and shots. Among other features:
Academy Award winners of current and previous years,
and obituaries.

1000. Shale, Richard, comp. Academy Awards: An Unger Reference Index. New York: Ungar, 1978. 615p.

A study of the Oscar awards given annually by the
Academy of Motion Picture Arts and Sciences over the
past fifty years. "Those who examine motion pictures
through the achievements of the Academy will literally
find a story with a cast of thousands, and this index
has been compiled to make more accessible the names of
those performers, craftsmen, and scientists--all artists
in their respective fields--and the films they created,"
says Shale. After a beginning chapter on the history of
the Academy, he lists 1927-77 awards by their various
categories--best picture, best actors and actresses, best
writing, best musical scores and songs, best costuming,
and so on. Following this is a chronological list for
the same fifty years. Appendices include names of the
Academy founders, presidents, and the directors of the
best pictures. Finally there is an index of films and
people.

1001. Shales, Tom, Kevin Brownlow, and others. The American
Film Heritage: Impressions from the American Film
Institute Archives. Washington: Acropolis Books,
1972. 134p.

Not a history of the American Film Institute, but as
the title suggests, an assessment of certain of its
aspects, made by more than a dozen film specialists.
They have tackled stars, directors, individual films,
and topics--"Mary Pickford at Biograph," "Thomas Ince,"
"Warners Musicals," "American Films, 1907-1914," "Miss
Lulu Bett," "The RKO Shorts," "Hal Roach Shorts," and
about twenty-five others. Each article is illustrated.
Contains an index of film titles and filmmakers.

1002. Sitney, P. Adams. Visionary Film: The American Avant-
Garde, 1943-1978. 2d ed. New York: Oxford University Press, 1979. 463p.

A survey of the avant-garde film tradition in the U.S. As a taking-off point the author has interviewed twenty-four filmmakers and analyzed their films, from which he has devised a theory. He relates the avant-garde tradition to the larger film content, which he connects to the subjective European films of the 1920s. There are sixty-six still photographs, footnotes for each chapter, and a name-subject index.

1003. Sklar, Robert. Movie-Made America: A Social History of American Movies. New York: Random House, 1975. 340p.

"The advent of the movies on the American cultural scene . . . clearly posed a challenge to existing cultural policies and institutions," says the author, who examines, among other topics, the invention of motion picture technology; the nature and evolution of the audience; the organization and business tactics of the movie trade; the design and economics of theaters; the social and professional lives of movie workers; government policies toward movies, and the attitudes and strategies of censorship groups; and the cultural influence of movies at home and overseas. Contains chapter notes and an index.

1004. Skvorecky, Josef. All the Bright Young Men and Women: A Personal History of the Czech Cinema. Michael Schonberg, tr. Toronto: Peter R. Martin Associates, 1971. 280p. (Take One Film Book Series.)

"It is not a scholarly work, just a personal remembrance," says the author. Nonetheless, it is a fascinating account of the flowering of an art under considerable odds for all too brief a period, and of the young men and women who made it possible. In spite of the author's statement that the history is not scholarly, he has referred to the writings of the Czech film critics and historians for background facts, although he has not documented the sources. There are almost 200 photographs--many of them never before seen in the West and available nowhere outside the book. A chronological list, of "The Most Interesting Czech Feature Films, 1898-1970," follows the text. Indexed.

1005. Slide, Anthony. Early American Cinema. Cranbury, N.J.: A. S. Barnes, 1970. 192p.
1006. _____. Aspects of American Film History prior to 1920. Metuchen, N.J.: Scarecrow, 1978. 161p.
1007. _____. Early Women Directors. Cranbury, N.J.: A. S. Barnes, 1977. 119p.

Early American Cinema is a brief history from 1900 to about 1915, constructed around the people and companies

291

who helped create it. There is a useful bibliography and
an index. Aspects of American Film History prior to 1920
covers much the same ground but from a different vantage
point. An eclectic series of essays, its subjects
include the evolution of the star, child stars, forgotten
directors, film magazines, the first motion picture bibliography, certain companies (including Kalem, the first
to shoot films on location abroad), and a fascinating
three-page vignette of Katherine Anne Porter's brief
employment with the motion picture industry. Appendices
include bibliographies on nine of the companies and a
list of source material on American film production during the period. Contains an index.

In Early Women Directors Slide contends that in this
early period the film industry was controlled by women.
The importance of women stars, some of whom had their own
production organizations, is well known, but not so the
importance of women directors, of whom there were more
than thirty. Slide tells about their lives and works,
some in much greater detail than others. Bibliography.

1008. Smith, John M., and Tim Cawkwell. The World Encyclopedia
      of the Film. New York: World Publishing Co., 1972.
      444p.

      "From Hollywood and the great national cinemas to docu-
      mentary and the 'Underground' every aspect of the film is
      covered through its creators--the directors, actors,
      writers, cameramen, set designers and many others are all
      represented," say the co-authors. The book takes the form
      of a biographical dictionary with pertinent facts about
      careers and listings of credits with dates. An index sec-
      tion, which constitutes a reference work in itself, includes
      all films mentioned in the biographical section, with dates,
      main credits, technical specifications, releasing organiza-
      tions (in most cases), and alternative titles.

1009. Smith, Paul, ed. The Historian and Film. New York: Cam-
      bridge University Press, 1976. 208p.

      Eleven contributors from Britain, France, Holland, and
      the U.S. discuss the uses to which historians may put films
      of various types, from newsreel to feature. Among subjects
      examined are resources, preservation and archives, evalua-
      tion as to historical evidence, and value in the interpre-
      tation and teaching of history. Contains a select biblio-
      graphy, a list of addresses of organizations involved with
      film and history, and an index.

1010. Smith, Sharon. Women Who Make Movies. New York: Hopkin-
      son & Blake, 1975. 307p.

A survey which shows that women have contributed sub-
stantially to filmmaking in its early years, both in this
country and abroad, and again in the 1960s with the
increased use of 16mm films. The author identifies individuals and describes their role. Contains a directory
of women filmmakers throughout the U.S., a listing of
organizations to which most of them belong, and a bibliography and index of names.

1011. Spehr, Paul C. The Movies Begin: Making Movies in New
       Jersey, 1887-1920. Newark, N.J.: The Newark Museum
       and Morgan & Morgan, 1977. 190p.

       The roots of the Hollywood movie industry were in New
       Jersey. This book, which grew out of an exhibit at the
       Newark Museum, examines the movies from their beginnings
       in Edison's day until 1920, when the extensive studio
       facilities built in the state began to shut down. Much
       space is devoted to Edison's contribution. Chapters
       include the pre-cinema, invention of the motion picture
       and its early development, early filmmaking in New Jersey,
       the studios, the personalities. Many illustrations, a
       bibliography, and an index.

1012. Spraos, John. The Decline of the Cinema: An Economist's
       Report. London: Allen & Unwin, 1962. 168p.

       One of the best economic studies of the film industry
       in Britain, which the author contends is declining--a con-
       tention he bolsters with facts and figures. He then pro-
       ceeds to give the reasons, some of which directly pertain
       to the American film industry. Indexed.

1013. Stanley, Robert. The Celluloid Empire: A History of the
       American Motion Picture Industry. New York: Hastings
       House, 1978. 328p.

       Emphasis is on the business side of motion picture pro-
       duction--the development, the corporate structure, and the
       managerial control of the major companies, and the person-
       alities involved. There is also a lengthy discussion of
       censorship. Appendices give the Motion Picture Code and
       the Advertising Code for Motion Pictures. Contains a bib-
       liography of books, periodicals, unpublished materials,
       government documents, U.S. Supreme Court cases, and lower
       court decisions. Indexed.

1014. Stedman, Raymond William. The Serial: Suspense and Drama
       by Installment. 2d ed. Norman: University of Okla-
       homa Press, 1977. 574p.

From <u>What Happened to Mary</u> in 1912 through <u>The Adams Chronicles</u> in 1976, Stedman chronicles the births, deaths, and intervening developments of an infinite variety of movie, radio, and TV serials covering a number of genres. In a concluding chapter he summarizes his own observations. This makes a good reference source to pinpoint popular serials over a period of years. Appendix A lists daytime network serials on radio, with sponsor, writer, cast, dates, and sometimes musical theme; Appendix B lists by birth date daytime network serials on TV. A bibliography contains books, pamphlets, magazine and newspaper articles, and unpublished sources on the subject. There is a general index and a title index.

1015. Stewart, John. <u>Filmarama</u>. 2 vols. Metuchen, N.J.: Scarecrow, 1975, 1977. 398, 733p. (Vol. I. <u>The Formidable Years, 1893-1919</u>; Vol. II. <u>The Flaming Years, 1920-1929.</u>)

Lists screen and stage credits for motion picture actors and actresses, along with such other information as is available about these early players--for example, birth and death dates, dates of production of films, roles played. A title index follows the name index in each volume. Stewart plans to continue the series with three more volumes extending to 1969.

1016. Stoil, Michael Jon. <u>Cinema beyond the Danube: The Camera and Politics</u>. Metuchen, N.J.: Scarecrow Press, 1974. 198p.

A combination of film criticism with political and social analysis written primarily for those with little or no knowledge of the history of filmmaking in Eastern Europe. Emphasis is on the social significance of film. Countries considered are the U.S.S.R., Poland, Czechoslovakia, Hungary, Yugoslavia, Bulgaria, Romania, and Albania. Contains an "Index to Eastern European Films," a bibliography, and a scant general index.

1017. Sussex, Elizabeth. <u>The Rise and Fall of British Documentary: The Story of the Film Movement Founded by John Grierson</u>. Berkeley: University of California Press, 1976. 219p.

Using a kind of documentary method herself, the author has talked with important living figures who have created film history and skillfully edited the material into a chronological story of the documentary movement in England which poses issues, past and present.

1018. Svenska Filminstitutet; the Swedish Film Institute. Stock-
      holm: Ab Svensk Film Industri, Kungsgatan, 36, 1964.
      20p.

      Pamphlet packed with facts about the Swedish film
      reform of 1963, giving economic and legal status of the
      industry and the effect upon quality. In both French and
      English languages.

1019. Svensson, Arne. Japan. Cranbury, N.J.: A. S. Barnes,
      1971. 189p. (Screen series.)

      Guide to the work of the major directors, players,
      technicians, and other key figures in the Japanese cinema.
      Filmographies are given as completely as possible. Com-
      plete careers of directors have been covered, but it was
      more difficult, the author states, to do so in cases of
      actors and actresses, where information about the early
      stages of their careers was not always known. He also
      would have liked to have included more technicians and
      scriptwriters, but again had difficulty acquiring relevant
      information. Filmographies list those connected with the
      film and give plot, comments, and an illustration. There
      is an index of 2,000 titles, and in the introduction, a
      list of materials on the Japanese film used in the compil-
      ation.

1020. Thomas, David Bowen. The First Colour Motion Pictures.
      London: Her Majesty's Stationery Office, 1969. 44p.

      A brief history of the early days of color cinemato-
      graphy in Britain, with especial emphasis on Kinemacolor,
      invented in 1920 by G. A. Smith and marketed widely by
      Charles Urban.

1021. Thomson, David. A Biographical Dictionary of Film. New
      York: Morrow, 1976. 629p.

      ". . . a Personal, Opinionated and Obsessive Biograph-
      ical Dictionary of the Cinema," is how Thomson character-
      izes his lively but nonetheless serious account of the
      directors, actors, actresses, and producers who seem to
      him most central to the history and theory of the cinema.
      In some ways it is a conventional reference tool. It is
      alphabetical; it has place and date of birth and certain
      other relevant facts about the lives of those selected,
      including, of course, their films; it has bibliographical
      and cross references. But in other ways it is not so
      conventional. It represents Thomson's personal taste; it
      contains jokes, digressions, insults, and eulogies.
      Emphasis is on the last two decades, and animated and
      underground films are omitted.

295

1022. Thorp, Margaret Farrand. America at the Movies. New
      Haven, Conn.: Yale University Press, 1939. 313p.

      A perceptive series of articles on the social influ-
      ence of the motion picture in America which the author
      wrote during the years before TV, when movies were at
      their peak. Indexed.

1023. Truitt, Evelyn Mack. Who Was Who on the Screen. 2d ed.
      New York: Bowker, 1977. 505p.

      Covers over 6,000 screen personalities, primarily
      American, British, and French. Among those included are
      some who appeared briefly on the screen but are better
      known for their achievements in other fields: Senator
      Everett Dirkson, author Somerset Maugham, newscaster
      Edward R. Murrow, for example. Rin Tin Tin (Sr. and Jr.)
      are also in, along with a few other animals who made it
      in the movies. Each entry is comprised of a brief bio-
      graphical sketch, giving birth, death, and marriage
      information, together with a complete list of screen
      credits when available. Emphasis is British and American.
      Contains a bibliography of biographical sources.

1024. Tucker, Richard. Japan: Film Image. London: Studio
      Vista, 1973. 144p.

      An examination of the Japanese film industry from a
      social and aesthetic viewpoint. After a historical sur-
      vey noting important changes and key films, there follows
      the major portion in which Tucker groups Japanese films
      by types and examines the social attitudes underlying
      the groupings and the prominent filmmakers involved. The
      last section deals with recent major changes. Contains a
      bibliography.

1025. Tudor, Andrew. Image and Influence: Studies in the
      Sociology of Film. New York: St. Martins, 1975. 260p.

      Attempting to avoid "the scientism and objectivism
      which has so long characterized media research," Tudor
      has produced a general text which explores the relation-
      ship between the cinema and society through abstract dis-
      cussion and empirical detail drawn from examples like the
      workings of the Hollywood community, the German silent
      film, the star system, and similar characteristics and
      manifestations. Bibliography and index.

1026. Tuska, Jon. The Detective in Hollywood. New York:
      Doubleday, 1978. 436p.

      "The Detective in Hollywood has to do with three dif-
      ferent aspects of the same phenomenon: the popular

296

detectives and the authors who created them; how those detectives changed what they brought to the screen; and the lives and personalities of those who played in detective films, or adapted them for the screen, or directed them," explains Tuska. Within this framework he discusses famous fictional detectives from Sherlock Holmes, with whom the filmed genre began, to contemporary examples like Chinatown. Many illustrations and a name-title index. This is the second volume of a projected trilogy, of which the Filming of the West was the first.

1027. Tuska, Jon. The Filming of the West. New York: Doubleday, 1976. 588p.

In this history of the making of Westerns from 1903 to the 1970s, Tuska focuses on 100 key films, analyzing the development of the genre and the economic factors which played a large part in the trends. Data is drawn mainly from the films themselves and from interviews. There is a name-title index.

1028. Tyler, Parker. Underground Film: A Critical History. New York: Grove Press, 1969. 249p.

Intended as a definitive history of the experimental film movement. The author, a prominent film critic, assesses the work of the leading directors, discusses specific films, and shows the variety of current aims and techniques, tracing the origins. Contains a filmography.

1029. Vallance, Tom. The American Musical. Cranbury, N.J.: A. S. Barnes, 1970. 192p.

". . . a guide to the artists who gave Hollywood supremacy in the form of the musical. It lists their musical credits with a small amount of biographical material and comment. Though complete objectivity is probably impossible, I have generally tried to keep any controversial views in check and have given what are mainly widely held judgments and opinions on the artists involved." - Introduction.
Not all the entries are under performers. Some deal briefly with subject--e.g., "Animation in the Musical," "Band Leaders," "Ghosting," "Composers on the Screen." Choreographers, directors, composers, and various others connected with the musical are listed along with the actors. Indexed.

1030. Vronskaya, Jeanne. Young Soviet Film Makers. London: Allen & Unwin, 1972. 127p.

297

Much has been written about the giant Russian filmmakers of a generation or more ago, but less about the strictly contemporary ones. Jeanne Vronskaya, a Soviet film critic living since 1969 in London, deals with the filmmakers who began their work in the 1950s. She gives a short history of the Russian film and tells of its departure from social realism in the 1960s, illustrating her point by a discussion of some of the leading directors. The latter part of the book takes up the cinema of national minorities. Appendices list Soviet film studies and main films, and give filmographies of directors. Bibliography and index.

1031. Waldron, Gloria. The Information Film. New York: Columbia University Press, 1949. 281p. (A Report of the Public Library Inquiry.)

"This survey is concerned primarily with film as an instrument for adult eduction and culture. It is necessarily concerned, too, with the institutions--particularly the public library--that are making films an educational force," says the author. She investigates production, distribution, and possibilities and finds that possibilities far exceed production and distribution, which had many problems to overcome. A comprehensive and critical overview which has now become historical. Contains appendices, a glossary, a bibliography, and an index.

1032. Walker, Alexander. Hollywood, UK: The British Film Industry in the Sixties. New York: Stein & Day, 1974. 493p.

"To be an Englishman in the film industry is to know what it's like to be colonized," said Tony Garnett, a prominent English director. As the author discusses the social revolution in Britain and the forms it took on the screen, he relates it to the effect of American power operating on British talent. Thus the book is useful on two levels--to show the power of American dollars on the English film industry, and to show the renaissance of British filmmaking in an exciting period of cultural change. Perhaps a third level should be included: that of straight, chronological film history. There is an appendix, "An Industry Chronology," and title index.

1033. Walker, Alexander. Stardom: The Hollywood Phenomenon. New York: Stein & Day, 1970. 392p.

The author, film critic for the London Evening Standard, examines stardom and its implications, illustrating, with case studies of past and present Hollywood stars, how they

are made and broken, often at the expense of their talent.
Contains a bibliography and an index.

1034. Weaver, John T., comp. Twenty Years of Silents, 1908-1928.
    Metuchen, N.J.: Scarecrow Press, 1971. 514p.
1035. _____. Forty Years of Screen Credits, 1929-1969.
    2 vols. Metuchen, N.J.: Scarecrow Press, 1970. 1458p.

Twenty Years of Silents lists actors, actresses, directors, and producers with birth and death dates and the
films in which they appeared or which they made, with
dates. Other features include listings of names of individuals in some of the popular series shows, such as the
Keystone Kops, the Sennett Bathing Beauties, the original
Our Gang kids, the Wampus Babies. There is also a list
of silent film studio corporations and distributors.
Forty Years of Screen Credits lists approximately 4,800
players with birth or birth and death dates and screen
credits. Other features are Oscar and special awards winners, and the names of the children in series or a group
context such as the Dead End Kids.

1036. Weiss, Ken, and Ed Goodgold. To Be Continued. . . . New
    York: Crown, 1972. 341p.

A chronological guide to 231 motion picture serials
from 1929 through 1956, giving for each serial a brief
synopsis, the number of episodes, the director, the cast,
and some stills. Indexed.

1037. White, David Manning, and Richard Averson. The Celluloid
    Weapon: Social Comment in the American Film. Boston:
    Beacon Press, 1972. 271p.

The purpose of the authors is "to present an overview
of the origins and development of social comment in the
American film by describing the range of problems and
issues explored, by identifying those filmmakers whose
careers reveal a continuing concern for using film as a
celluloid weapon, and by noting any relevant sociological
'climate' that may have influenced the content of certain
message films." The films examined span seventy years
and a wide range of topics which in themselves identify
American concerns and preoccupations. Documentaries are
not included, and films are chosen for their propagandis-
tic rather than their aesthetic value. Contains numerous
illustrations, notes, an index of film titles and an
index of names, and a bibliography.

1038. Who Wrote the Movie and What Else Did He Write? An Index
    to Screen Writers and Their Film Works, 1936-1969.

Los Angeles 90069: Academy of Motion Picture Arts and
Sciences, 9038 Melrose Ave.; Los Angeles 90048:
Writers Guild of America, West, 8955 Beverly Blvd.,
1970. 401p.

Two organizations concerned with screen writing have
collaborated on this reference book which identifies
authors of film scripts. It is composed of three indexes--
the "Writers Index," listing approximately 2,000 authors
with titles of motion pictures they wrote or were in some
way involved in, followed by other data about their
careers; "Film Title Index," with approximately 13,000
listings, each giving producing or distributing company,
year of release, and any other titles by which the film
may have been known; and the "Awards Index," including
films which either were nominated for writing awards or
won other honors, with date.

1039. Wright, Basil. <u>The Long View</u>. New York: Knopf, 1974.
      709p.

"This is neither a history of the film nor a technical
study. It is, rather, the record of a love affair with
the film medium which began in 1913 when my grandmother
took me to the cinema for the first time," begins the
author in his preface to this informal and insightful history of the film in this and other countries. As he goes
on to explain, his approach is eclectic, governed somewhat
by his likes and dislikes. His arrangement indicates the
individuality of this method. Each chapter is designated
as a signpost for a given year: "Signpost--1895: The
Year of the Lumiere Brothers," followed by "Signpost--1915:
The Year of 'Birth of a Nation,'" and so on through eight
chapters, which brings us up to 1970. Wright is one of the
pioneering documentary filmmakers. Contains a bibliography,
an index of films and of names, and a general index.

VI
Magazines

APS Directory. (See No. 634.)

Arndt, Karl J. R., and May E. Olsen. German American Newspapers and Periodicals, 1732-1955. (See No. 635.)

1040. The Associated Church Press. Directory. Geneva, Ill.
   60134: The Associated Church Press, P.O. Box 306,
   annual. (1951--.)

   Lists Protestant religious periodicals in the U.S. and
   Canada belonging to the Associated Church Press. For
   each periodical, gives address, personnel, frequency,
   circulation, and advertising policy and rates.

Ayer Directory of Publications. (See No. 636.)

Benn's Press Directory. (See No. 640.)

Bertrand, Claude Jean, comp. The British Press, an Historical
   Survey: An Anthology. (See No. 641.)

1041. Bush, Alfred L., and Robert S. Fraser. American Indian
   Periodicals in the Princeton University Library: A
   Preliminary List. Princeton, N.J.: Princeton Uni-
   versity Library, 1970. 78p.

   Periodicals produced by or for the American Indians,
   ranging from newspapers published by a tribe to scholarly journals intended primarily for a non-Indian
   audience but whose content is of interest and value to
   the larger Indian community. Only periodicals represented at Princeton by at least one issue have been
   included. Skeletal descriptions give individual,
   organization, or institution which acts as publisher
   and the place of publication.

Business Publication Rates and Data. (See No. 1143.)

1042. Canada. Royal Commission on Publications. <u>Report</u>.
    Ottawa: Queen's Printer, 1961. 263p.

    Report by a commission "appointed to investigate
every aspect of the Canadian periodical publishing
industry with a view to insuring its place in Canada's
way of life." The <u>Report</u> has three parts: "The Situation," analyzing Canadian media in general and periodicals in particular; "The Problem," analyzing the
various kinds of publications--i.e., consumer magazines,
business publications, and cultural and little magazines,
with discussions of advertising and the social role of
periodicals; and "Recommendations" on advertising and
circulation. In conclusion, overall recommendations are
summarized. More than 150 pages of appendices include
such valuable information as "The Periodical Press in
Foreign Countries," "Report of Technological Developments," "Report of the Financial Consultant," "Economic
Implications of Overflow Advertising," and "Statistics."
Index.

<u>Catholic Press Directory</u>. (<u>See</u> No. 649.)

1043. Conlin, Joseph R., ed. <u>The American Radical Press</u>,
    <u>1880-1960</u>. 2 vols. Westport, Conn.: Greenwood
    Press, 1974.

    Essays on various periodicals, many written as intro-
ductions for Greenwood Press's Radical Reprints series.
Headings include: "Early Radical Periodicals," "The
Socialist Party Press, 1900-1919," "Wobbley Papers,"
"Journals of the Bolshevik Crisis," "Publications of the
Socialists," "The Communist Press," "Periodicals of the
Sect and Splinter Groups," "Anarchist Publications,"
"Independent and Ad Hoc Journals," "Theoretical Journals,
Little Magazines and the Arts," "Personal Journalism,"
"Postwar Periodicals."

<u>Consumer Magazine and Farm Publication Rates and Data</u>. (<u>See</u>
    No. 1143.)

1044. <u>Directory, American Society of Journalists and Authors:</u>
    <u>A Listing of Professional and Free-Lance Writers</u>.
    New York: ASJA, 1501 Broadway, Suite 1907, annual.
    (1952--.)

    This listing of professional nonfiction writers who
have met the ASJA's exacting standards gives home and
office addresses, present occupation and former connection, books written and periodicals contributed to,
subject specialties, areas of expertise (i.e., editing,

cartooning, ghostwriting, advertising, lecturing, etc.),
and other categories, such as awards and memberships,
when pertinent. There are also listings by geographical
locations, by subject specialties, and by areas of expertise. Contains their Code of Ethics and Fair Practices
and further guidelines, "On 'Work for Hire': A Statement
of Position." This is especially useful for public relations purposes because the writers have been so well
screened before being admitted to membership. The current edition contains more than 500 names.

1045. <u>Directory of Publishing Opportunities</u>. 3d ed. Chicago:
     Marquis Academic Media, 1977. 850p.

      Intended as a marketplace guide for writers, this
      lists more than 2,600 trade and scholarly journals;
      professional magazines; technical journals; and publi-
      cations produced by business firms, unions, or associa-
      tions, arranged alphabetically within sixty-nine
      specific fields. In addition to name and address, each
      entry includes subscription data, publisher or sponsor,
      editorial description, and comprehensive information
      about the submission of manuscripts. Indexed by period-
      ical, by subject, by sponsor, by publisher, and by
      editor.

1046. <u>Directory of Small Magazine/Press Editors and Publishers</u>.
     Len Fulton and Ellen Ferber, eds. Paradise, Cal.
     95969: Dustbooks, P.O. Box 100, annual. (1970--.)

      An alphabetical listing by name of all the editors
      and publishers of small presses and magazines in its
      companion volume, the <u>International Directory of Little</u>
      <u>Magazines and Small Presses</u> (No. 1052). Information
      for each entry includes the press or publication with
      which the individual is associated, with address and
      phone number.

<u>Directory of the College Student Press in America, 1977-78</u>.
     (<u>See</u> No. 660.)

<u>Editor and Publisher Annual Directory and Syndicated Services</u>.
     (<u>See</u> No. 663.)

<u>Encyclomedia</u>. <u>Consumer Magazines</u>. (<u>See</u> No. 1103.)

1047. Evans, James F., and Rudolfo N. Salcedo. <u>Communications</u>
     <u>in Agriculture: The American Farm Press</u>. Ames:
     Iowa State University Press, 1974. 264p.

      ". . . focuses upon a knowledge-moving system that
      helps American farmers provide food for more than 600

million meals a day in this nation. . . . In particular,
it deals with one of the nation's most powerful instruments of agricultural communication: commercial farm
periodicals, the subscription and/or advertising journals directed to farmers." - Preface. Treatment is
chronological from 1880 to 1970, ending with a ninety-
year perspective. Following the 115 pages of text are
another 100 pages of tables and charts giving the data
on which the authors have founded their facts. Footnotes
and bibliography.

Filler, Louis. The Muckrakers. (See No. 672.)

1048. First National Directory of "Rightist" Groups, Publica-
      tions and Some Individuals in the United States (and
      Some Foreign Countries). 6th ed. Los Angeles 90005:
      Noontide Press, P.O. Box 76062, 1968. 128p.
      Supplement. 1974. 62p.

      Alphabetical listing of several thousand educational,
      social, and religious organizations and their publica-
      tions where they exist--all of which represent a protest
      of some sort against prevailing "leftist" political or
      social trends. Information for each item includes name
      and address. Every publication has a separate entry and
      is entered again under the name of the organization.
      Compiled by the Alert Americans Association.

Gebbie House Magazine Directory. See Working Press of the
      Nation. Internal Publications Directory. (No. 1075.)

1049. Goldwater, Walter. Radical Periodicals in America, 1890-
      1950: A Bibliography with Brief Notes. Rev. ed.
      New Haven, Conn.: Yale University Library, 1966.
      51p.

      Consists of a listing of 321 periodicals with a
      genealogical chart and a concise lexicon of the parties
      and groups which issued each. Every entry has a brief
      annotation giving contributors and character. Contains
      a bibliography, "A Short List of Useful Books."

1050. Goulart, Ron. Cheap Thrills: An Informal History of the
      Pulp Magazines. New Rochelle, N.Y.: Arlington, 1972.
      192p.

      In less than 200 pages nothing definitive can be said
      about the pulps, which the author admits on page 1. So
      he concentrates on giving a general outline of the his-
      tory of the genre and a more detailed account of one
      specific and important period between about 1920 and

1940, with various types treated briefly by subject.
Obviously this is meant for entertainment rather than
for research, but it can provide a beginning. Unfor-
tunately for this purpose, there is no index.

Great Britain. Central Office of Information. Reference
Division. The British Press. (See No. 680.)

Great Britain. Royal Commission on the Press. (See Nos.
681-87.)

1051. Great Britain. Royal Commission on the Press. Per-
iodicals and the Alternative Press. London: Her
Majesty's Stationery Office, 1977. 73p. (Research
Series 6) (Command Paper 6910-6.)

Part I describes the periodical press and shows the
range of titles, their circulation and readership, and
their ownership. It also summarizes the finances of
periodicals and examines ease of entry into the industry. Part II records the findings of a sample survey
undertaken on the alternative press. It shows something of its scope, opportunities for starting such
papers, and problems involved in successful publication.
Appendices list the alternative press questionnaire, the
publications which responded, and an extract from the
evidence submitted by Gay News.

Hoggart, Richard. The Uses of Literacy: Aspects of Working-
Class Life with Special Reference to Publications and
Entertainment. (See No. 93.)

Hudson's Washington News Media Contacts Directory. (See No.
697.)

ILPA Directory of Member Publications. (See No. 699.)

1052. International Directory of Little Magazines and Small
Presses. Len Fulton, ed. Paradise, Cal.: Dustbooks,
Box 1056, annual. (1965--.)

This directory is essential for anyone interested in
the status of alternative publishing in the U.S. and
Canada. Although its primary use is for writers search-
ing out a market and for libraries verifying subscriptions, it is also a fine source of knowledge about what's
happening in the little magazine/small press world. And
much is happening, as editor Len Fulton tells us in his
introduction. The body of the directory lists publications alphabetically, with varying information about each
according to whether magazine or press. Typical entries

305

give name, address, editor(s), price, circulation, frequency, type of material used, payment rates, rights
purchased, discount schedules, size, personal statement
of editors, number of issues/titles published in previous year and projected for coming year, and membership in small press or magazine organizations. A
subject index and a regional index of U.S. publications
document Fulton's introduction. There is also a list
of distributors and of organization acronyms. One warning in using the directory: the word <u>international</u> in
the title is misleading. Entries are limited to the
English language and are confined largely to this continent. And only U.S. publications (not even Canadian)
are included in the geographic index. The <u>Directory of
Small Magazine/Press Editors and Publishers</u> (No. 1046)
serves as a name index.

Johnson, Michael L. <u>The New Journalism: The Underground Press,
the Artists of Nonfiction, and Changes in the Established
Media.</u> (<u>See</u> No. 702.)

Johnstone, John W. C., Edward J. Slawski, and William W. Bowman.
<u>The News People.</u> (<u>See</u> No. 703.)

Kaplan, Frank L. <u>Winter into Spring: The Czechoslovak Press
and the Reform Movement, 1963-1968.</u> (<u>See</u> No. 706.)

1053. Kimbrough, Marvin. <u>Black Magazines: An Exploratory
Study.</u> Austin: University of Texas, School of Communication, Center for Communication Research, 1973.
78p.

This project identifies 421 black magazines, with
varying degrees of information about each, and includes
a few which are no longer extant. The second part of
the study is a two-part bibliography, one section of
which is material about individual magazines and the
other about black magazines in general.

1054. Kronick, David A. <u>A History of Scientific and Technical
Periodicals: The Origin and Development of the
Scientific Press, 1665-1790.</u> 2d ed. Metuchen, N.J.:
Scarecrow, 1976. 336p.

In addition to examining the origins and development
of scientific journalism, Kronick also makes a statistical analysis of the forms which the periodical literature assumed between the years covered. He discusses
original publications (substantive journals and proceedings of societies), derivative ones (abstracts, reviews,
collections), almanacs and annuals, and scientific

journals. Scope is international. There is a lengthy
bibliography and subject, title, and name indexes.

1055. The Little Magazine in America, a Modern Documentary
      History: Essays, Memoirs, Photo-Documents. An
      Annotated Bibliography. Elliott Anderson and
      Michael York, eds. Yonkers, N.Y.: Pushcart Book
      Press, 1979. 770p. (Also constitutes the Fall
      1978 issue of TriQuarterly.)

   Since 1946, when Frederick J. Hoffman, Charles Allen,
and Carolyn F. Ulrich published The Little Magazine: A
History and a Bibliography (Princeton University Press),
there has until now been no one single source for the
history of little magazines in the U.S. and for bibliographic data on specific titles. The Little Magazine
in America, a Modern Documentary History is a successor
and companion volume, although with a different approach.
The earlier book was a history of the various movements,
themes, causes, and types of little magazines; the later
book is an anthology of essay-memoirs by prominent and
representative little magazine editors, publishers, and
contributors, with a large selection of photo-documents
and an annotated bibliography of eighty-four important
magazines of the period. The editors explain why they
chose a different structure: "Although such a documentary project inevitably lacks the integration of more
conventional histories, our basic concern has been for
the phenomenon of little magazines--for the curious and
oftentimes eccentric processes of the field--not for one
or another interpretation of their collective merit,
however congenial. The field today is so large, the
kinds of magazines and attitudes of their editors so
diverse, that no literary historian could hope to offer
more than a gloss." Not all of the essays center around
specific magazines; there are "A Living Belfry and Ram-
part: On American Literary Magazines since 1950,"
"Academia and the Little Magazine," "Felix Pollak: An
Interview on Little Magazines," "The Little Magazine in
Its Place: Literary Culture and Anarchy" and others,
including one on Afro-American magazines. Nor is the
scope entirely limited to the little magazine. There
is a discussion of its connection with the small press,
and stories about Pushcart Press and the Fiction Collective. The annotated bibliography of eighty-four
little magazines is almost 100 pages long.

Liu, Alan P. L. The Press and Journals in Communist China.
   (See No. 718.)

1056. Madden, Lionel, and Diana Dixon, comps. The Nineteenth-
Century Periodical Press in Britain: A Bibliography
of Modern Studies, 1901-1971. Toronto: Victorian
Periodicals Newsletter, 1975. 76p.

". . . concentrates upon general studies of the press
and upon studies of individual periodicals and newspapers
of general interest rather than those designed for a
specialized or professional audience. The work lists
technical studies of journalism, advertising and finance
as well as autobiographical memoirs and reminiscences and
biographies and studies of individual proprietors,
editors, journalists and regular contributors of periodicals." Historical development of periodical literature
is included, but not studies whose primary significance
is in the field of literary history. Types of materials
included are books, portions of books, periodical
articles, and theses. Arrangement is in four sections--
bibliographical materials, history, studies of individual
periodicals and newspapers, and studies and memoirs,
linked together by an author index.

1057. Magazine Circulation and Rate Trends, 1940-1976. New
York 10017: Association of National Advertisers,
155 E. 44th St., 1978. 114p.

Latest in a series of trend compilations of circulation data, rates, and costs per thousand for seventy-
three ABC-audited consumer magazines, covering selected
years from 1940 to 1967 and every year thereafter through
1976, and useful for analysis of individual magazines as
well as for comparision among them. With each edition
the list of magazines changes because of additions, dis-
continuations, mergers, etc. In this edition categories
include general weeklies and biweeklies; business and
news; general monthlies; men and boys' magazines; out-
doors and sports; women's fashion and home; motor,
mechanics, and science; movie and romance. The category
of farm magazines has been dropped. Detailed source
references are listed in the appendix.

1058. Magazine Profiles: Studies of a Dozen Contemporary Magazine Groupings. Medill School of Journalism, North-
western University, 1974. 194p.

Collection of a dozen papers written by graduate students in a Magazine Publishing Seminar at Medill. Magazines are discussed by types: entertainment like Oui,
Penthouse, and Playboy; black consumer magazines;
establishment underground like Rolling Stone and Village
Voice; house organs; photography magazines; regional

magazines; homemaking magazines; religious magazines;
sports magazines; career-oriented women's magazines;
journals of opinion; and general--the Atlantic, Esquire,
the New Yorker, Ladies Home Journal, McCalls, Redbook.
Slim footnotes and a slim bibliography.

Marty, Martin E. The Religious Press in America. (See No.
    722.)

Merrill, John C., Carter E. Bryan, and Marvin Alisky. The
    Foreign Press: A Survey of the World's Journalism.
    (See No. 727.)

1059. Mott, Frank Luther. A History of American Magazines.
    5 vols. Cambridge, Mass.: Harvard University Press,
    1930-68. (Vol. I, 1741-1850; Vol. II, 1850-65; Vol.
    III, 1865-85; Vol. IV, 1885-1905; Vol. V, 1885-1905.)

A thorough and comprehensive history of the American
magazine from pre-Revolutionary times to 1900. Arrangement is chronological. Vol. V, published posthumously
and edited by the author's daughter, Mildred Mott Wedel,
assisted by Theodore Peterson and John T. Frederick, is
somewhat different, consisting of a series of sketches
of twenty-five of the most prominent magazines of the
period.
    The appendices of the first four volumes contain a
chronological list of magazines covered, with dates of
establishment and demise (except in the rare cases where
they are extant). Vol. V indexes the entire series.
For the period from 1900 on see Peterson's Magazines in
the Twentieth Century (No. 1061).

1060. Muller, Robert H., Theodore Jurgen Spahn, and Janet M.
    Spahn. From Radical Left to Extreme Right: A Bib-
    liography of Current Periodicals of Protest, Contro-
    versy, Advocacy, or Dissent, with Dispassionate
    Content-Summaries to Aid Librarians and Other
    Educators through the Polemic Fringe. 2 vols. 3d ed.
    Vol. I. Ann Arbor, Mich. 48108: Campus Publishers,
    711 N. University Ave. Vol. II. Metuchen, N.J.:
    Scarecrow Press, 1970-72. 1,000p.

A bibliography of alternative press periodicals of
the 1960s. The authors have tried to keep bias out of
their evaluations by letting the longer-than-usual
content-summaries speak for themselves and by making
sure that the many editors of the periodicals included
considered the content-summaries fair. An incidental
by-product of the bibliography is the overview it gives
of the intellectual climate of the period covered.

Information for each periodical includes address, frequency, founding date, circulation, format, and the excellent content-summaries. Detailed index by subject as well as by name.

Murphy, Sharon. Other Voices: Black, Chicano, and American Indian Press. (See No. 730.)

Penn, I. Garland. The Afro-American Press and Its Editors. (See No. 742.)

1061. Peterson, Theodore. Magazines in the Twentieth Century. 2d ed. Urbana: University of Illinois Press, 1964. 484p.

The best single source for detailed information on trends in consumer magazines for the first sixty years of the century and for the history of specific ones. The author deals with special-interest as well as big-name magazines, tracing their development and placing them in historical and economic context. Arrangement is broadly by aspects of magazine publishing and types of magazines--for example, "Advertising: Its Growth and Effects," "The Economic Structure of the Industry," "The Old Leaders That Died," "The New Leaders That Survived," "New Leaders: The Missionaries," "New Leaders: The Merchants," "Success by Compression," "Magazines for Cultural Minorities." The first edition (1956) contained a lengthy bibliography which has been omitted from the second. However, footnotes somewhat replace it. There is an index.

Press and Advertisers Yearbook. (See No. 744.)

Price, Warren C. The Literature of Journalism. (See No. 747.)
_____ and Calder Pickett. An Annotated Journalism Bibliography. (See No. 748.)

1062. Schacht, John A. A Bibliography for the Study of Magazines. 4th ed. Urbana 61801: University of Illinois, Institute of Communications Research, 222B Armory, 1979. 95p.

A selective list of periodical articles, arranged by subject. Categories include bibliographies, general, directories, history, editorial research and its use, law, magazine advertising, circulation, editors and editing, classes of magazines, individual editors and magazines, layout and production, and foreign magazines and publishers. Entries are annotated when necessary to indicate contents.

1063. Shaffer, Harry G. Periodicals on the Socialist Coun-
     tries and on Marxism: A New Annotated Index of
     English-Language Publications. New York: Praeger,
     1977. 134p.

     Over 450 periodicals in sixteen countries that "con-
     centrate on subject matter of concern to students of
     communism whose interest lies in the social sciences,
     in the humanities, or in related fields." Technical
     periodicals and statistical yearbooks are omitted. The
     following information is given for each: title, pub-
     lisher, a brief description of focus, the publisher's
     declared purpose, special section, sample titles of
     representative articles, number of pages, frequency,
     address, and price. Countries represented: Albania,
     Bulgaria, Cambodia, China, Cuba, Czechoslovakia, German
     Democratic Republic, Hungary, Laos, Mongolia, North
     Korea, Poland, Romania, U.S.S.R., Vietnam, and
     Yugoslavia. Contains a geographic reference index and
     the names of selected bookstores and agencies in the
     U.S. handling subscriptions.

1064. Standard Periodical Directory, 1979–80. 6th ed. New
     York: Oxbridge, 1978. 168p.

     The Directory's subtitle, The Most Complete Guide to
     U.S. and Canadian Periodicals . . . Information on More
     Than 65,000 Publications, is not boastful. (Actually,
     there are 68,520 publications.) "Periodical" is defined
     as any publication having a frequency of issue of at
     least one every two years. Types of periodicals included
     are consumer magazines; trade journals; news letters;
     government publications; house organs; directories;
     transactions and proceedings of scientific societies;
     yearbooks; museum, religious, ethnic, literary, and
     social group publications, etc.
     Information for each title varies, including all, or
     in most cases some, of the following: title, publisher,
     address, telephone number, editor and several other key
     personnel, capsule descriptions of editorial content,
     indexing/abstracting information, year established,
     frequency, subscription rate yearly or by individual
     copy, circulation, advertising/auditing information, dis-
     tribution of readership (national or international),
     advertising rates, format, uses of regional editions and/
     or split runs, catalogue numbers of government publica-
     tions. Arrangement is by subject, with an alphabetical
     index.

1065. Tebbel, John. The American Magazine: A Compact History.
     New York: Hawthorn Press, 1969. 279p.

The author has described his book perfectly: "What
I am offering here is a narrative history that necessarily depends in large part on the scholarship of others,
but does what the others were of course not intending to
do, that is, to tell the story of the magazine business
in America from 1749 to the present, within the scope of
a single volume, in terms the general reader, and especially the preprofessional reader, will find helpful in
his study and understanding." Contains a short list of
recommended readings and an index.

Todorov, Dafin. *Freedom Press: Development of the Progressive Press in Western Europe and the U.S.A.* (See No.
772.)

1066. *Ulrich's International Periodical Directory: A Classified Guide to Current Periodicals, Foreign and
Domestic.* New York: Bowker, biennial. (1932--.)

The 1977-78 edition includes 60,000 periodicals published throughout the world and currently in print,
arranged by subject classification, with an alphabetical
index. Each entry contains basic information about
title, frequency, publisher's name and address, classification code, and Dewey Decimal number. Additional
information is given when available and pertinent as to
editor, format, circulation, advertising, inclusion of
book reviews, availability on microform, and whether or
not it has an index. It also tells which, if any, of
the periodical indexes analyze its contents. *Ulrich's
Quarterly*, which began in March 1977, brings up-to-date
information on new serial titles, title changes, and
cessations.

1067. *The Underground and Alternative Press in Great Britain.*
Sussex, England: Harvester Press, 2 Stanford Terrace,
Hassocks, Nr. Brighton, annual. (1972--.)

An index to the Harvester Press's collection of micro-
fische and microfilm underground and alternative publications in itself constitutes a bibliography. For each
entry is given date of founding and often, too--for small
publications have a high death rate--of ending; address;
and a full descriptive annotation about contents and
slant. The 1972 volume contains an essay on the underground and alternative press in Great Britain by John
Spiers.

Underground Press Directory. (See No. 774.)

1068. Union List of Serials in Libraries of the United States
      and Canada. Edna Brown Titus, ed. 3d ed. 5 vols.
      New York: Wilson, 1965.

   Listing of over 156,000 periodicals available in
libraries in the U.S. and Canada. In addition to telling where they may be found, it gives dates and changes
in titles.
   Among some of the types of publications omitted are:
government publications (except periodicals and monograph series issued by governments); United Nations
publications; administrative reports of various sorts;
almanacs; law reports and digests; house organs;
reports of national and international conferences and
congresses, etc.; and various types of publications
having limited or emphemeral value.
   This third edition carries periodicals up to 1949.
After that date new periodicals appear in New Serials
Titles (monthly with annual cumulations). A section
at the back of each cumulation, "Changes in Serials,"
notes titles, cessations, suspensions, resumptions,
etc.

1069. U.S. Library of Congress. Slavic and Central European
      Division. The U.S.S.R. and Eastern Europe: Period-
      icals in Western Languages. Paul L. Horecky and
      Robert G. Carlton, comps. 3d ed. Washington:
      Superintendent of Documents, 1967. 89p.

   A selective inventory covering Albania, Estonia,
Latvia, Lithuania, Bulgaria, Czechoslovakia, Hungary,
Poland, Romania, the Soviet Union, and Yugoslavia.
English-language material gets the widest coverage;
among other Western languages French and German are
most extensively represented. A highly selective list
of periodicals no longer in existance but of continuing research value has been added to this edition.
Entries have been arranged by country and for each is
given as much of the following information as is ascer-
tainable: name, founding date, editor and publisher,
address, price. In most cases a brief annotation
indicates nature and scope.

1070. White, Cynthia Leslie. Women's Magazines, 1963-1968.
      London: Michael Joseph, 1971. 348p.

   A sociological study of women's magazines in Britain,
tracing their growth as an industry and relating their
character and function to economic change. A final
chapter of twenty-five pages is devoted to the women's
press in the U.S. The major part of the text is taken
from the author's doctoral thesis at the University of

313

London. Contains a number of appendices giving circulation charts and graphs. There is a bibliography and an
index.

Who Was Who in Journalism. (See No. 780.)

Willing's Press Guide. (See No. 785.)

1071. Wolseley, Roland E. The Changing Magazine: Trends in
Readership and Management. New York: Hastings House,
1973. 146p.

Analyzes the state of consumer magazines in the last
few years of the sixties and the first few of the seventies; discusses their problems, such as spiraling postal
rates, rising labor costs, and increasing competition
from other media; and predicts their possible future
role. There are statistical appendices, a bibliography,
and an index.

Wolseley, Roland E. The Black Press, U.S.A. (See No. 787.)

1072. Wood, James Playsted. Magazines in the United States.
3d ed. New York: Ronald Press, 1971. 476p.

In five volumes, Mott (No. 1059) covers the magazine
in America from its beginnings to the twentieth century;
Peterson (No. 1061) picks up with the twentieth century.
In one 500-page volume, Wood spans both periods in
breadth rather than in depth. This third edition is
completely updated and reorganized. There is a bibliography and an index, but practically no footnotes.

1073. Woodsworth, Anne, comp. The "Alternative" Press in
Canada: A Checklist of Underground, Revolutionary,
Radical and Other Alternative Serials from 1960.
Toronto: University of Toronto Press, 1972. 74p.

Defining "alternative" as any newspaper or magazine
that appears serially and expresses views which disagree
with present governmental policies and social mores, the
compiler has listed 388 such periodicals, giving for
each name in full, address, frequency, price, and date
of first issue. Following this is a list (title only)
by subject and another which is geographic. There is
also a bibliography.

1074. Working Press of the Nation: Feature Writer, Photographer and Syndicate Directory. Vol. IV. Burlington, Iowa 52601: National Research Bureau, 424 N.
Third St., annual. (1947--.)

314

Lists writers and photographers both alphabetically
and by subject specialty, with addresses, telephone
numbers, subject specialties, and other pertinent information under the alphabetical listing. Includes for
writers the names of the magazines in which they publish.
The section on photographers contains a list of sources
for pictures. Syndicates, too, are in alphabetical order
with address, chief personnel, and names of their features, followed by a listing of individual features with
parent syndicates. Although intended for publicists,
this directory could be useful to writers and photographers looking for markets.

1075. Working Press of the Nation: Internal Publications
      Directory. Milton Paule, ed. Vol. V. Burlington,
      Iowa 52601: The National Research Bureau, Inc.,
      424 N. Third St., annual. (1977--.)

      Gives detailed information about internal and exter-
      nal "house organs" of more than 3,500 companies, clubs,
      government agencies, and other groups throughout the
      U.S. and Canada. Each entry contains name and address
      of sponsor, house magazine title, name of editor, year
      publication was established, frequency of issue, number
      of pages, page size, printing method used and name of
      printer, circulation, and editorial policy. Other
      information includes a geographic list of house maga-
      zines by state and city, with street addresses and
      house magazine titles published by each sponsor, an
      alphabetical list of titles, a listing of house maga-
      zine sponsors arranged by industry classification, a
      circulation breakdown by title, type of editorial mate-
      rial used, and the commercial printing firms together
      with the title of the house magazines they print arranged
      in alphabetical order by state and city. (Formerly Geb-
      bie House Magazine Directory: A Public Relations and
      Free-Lance Guide to the Nation's Leading House Magazines.)

1076. The Working Press of the Nation: Magazine and Editorial
      Directory. Vol. II. Burlington, Iowa 52601: National
      Research Bureau, 424 N. Third St., annual. (1947--.)

      The purpose of this volume is to list those magazines
      of importance to public relations officials and to give
      pertinent facts about each. The main sections list ser-
      vice, trade, professional, industrial, farm and agricul-
      tural, and consumer publications, with such detailed
      information as name, address, phone number, personnel in
      some detail, deadlines, circulation, subscription rates,
      and both an editorial and a circulation analysis, along
      with an indication by the editor of the general types of

editorial and departmental features of interest to them. There is also a subject classification index and an alphabetical index. The latest edition contains over 4,700 publications in the U.S. and Canada.

1077. Writer's Market. Cincinnati, Ohio 45242: Writer's Digest Books, 9933 Alliance Rd., annual. (1930--.)

A comprehensive guide to the editorial requirements of consumer magazines, trade journals, play producers, greeting card companies, book publishers, newspapers, and syndicates in the U.S. and Canada. Magazines are arranged by subject in two groups--"Consumer Publications" and "Trade, Technical, and Professional Journals." Other markets are listed alphabetically. Preceding this market section, which is the main portion of the book, is a series of articles giving tips and commenting on events of the year of special interest to writers. Following the market section are listings of agents and literary services; contests and awards; government information sources; picture sources; and writers' clubs, colonies, conferences, and organizations. Canada is included. There is also a glossary and an index.

This is a directory for paying markets, although a few prestigeous ones which do not pay are included, and so are subsidy publishers, but with words of warning.

Wynar, Lubomyr, and Anna T. Wynar. Encyclopedic Directory of Ethnic Newspapers and Periodicals in the United States. (See No. 789.)

316

VII
Advertising and Public Relations

1078. Aaron, Dorothy. <u>About Face: Toward a Positive Image of Women in Advertising.</u> Toronto M5G 1Z6: Ontario Status of Women Council, 801 Bay St., 1975. 30p.

Summarizes the results of a province-wide study. It is designed not so much to yield statistical data as to provide insight into the sorts of things women find objectionable in advertising and the most common sources and subjects of offensive ads. This is the second in a series of reports. (See also <u>Toward a Positive Image of Women in Textbooks</u> No. 224.)

<u>Action for Children's Television: The First National Symposium on the Effect of Television Programming and Advertising on Children.</u> (See No. 320.)

1079. <u>Advertisers' Annual: An Annual Directory for All Engaged in Advertising and Selling.</u> Kingston upon Thames, Surrey, England KT1 1BX: Kelly's Directories Ltd., annual. (1925--.)

Includes lists of daily, weekly, and local (provincial) newspapers; consumer publications classified by subject, with data about each; information about outdoor advertising, commercial radio, and television; advertising agencies and public relations companies; services and suppliers; and British advertisers in England, Wales, Scotland, the Channel Islands, and the Isle of Man, with information about each. There is a lengthy "who's who" section and a geographic overseas section.

1080. <u>The Advertising Agency Business around the World: Reports from Advertising Agency Associations and Agency Leaders in Fifty-one Countries.</u> 7th ed. New York 10017: American Association of Advertising Agencies, Pan Am Bldg., 200 Park Ave., 1975. 244p.

Information about each country varies, with most of
them including expenditure by media and product classification. Australia, for example, gives brief economic
background; expenditure as a whole and by media and
industrial classification; amount of agency-placed advertising; agency statistics; recognition (accreditation)
and compensation; cash discount; acceptance of foreign
commercials; taxes on advertising; and restrictions;
government relations; self-regulation; liability for payment; major problems; total expenditure broken down by
media and product. Developing countries obviously give
less information and sometimes dwell on demography and
plans. All reflect to a greater or lesser degree their
economic and governmental concerns. Useful not only for
the facts about individual countries but also to show
the development of advertising on a world scale.

1081. Advertising and Press Annual of Southern Africa: The
Blue Book of Advertising in Southern Africa. New
York 10016: International Publications Service,
Collings, Inc., 114 E. 32d St., annual. (1968?--.)

Includes a map and statistics of the South African
market; a classified directory of newspapers and magazines, including trade and specialized ones, with advertising and subscription rates and production information;
press, radio, cinema, and outdoor advertising expenditures; advertising agencies and leading advertisers; code
of the South African Press Council and laws and regulations; the Trade Practices Act; conference facilities;
postal information; who's who in advertising and publishing.

1082. Advertising Expenditure. London SWIV INJ: Advertising
Association, Abford House, 15 Wilton Rd., annual.
(1948--.)

Detailed analysis of British advertising statistics,
formerly published approximately every four years and
now published annually, with the latest issue cumulated
to cover 1960-76. Statistics initially appear in the
Advertising Association's quarterly journal, Advertising,
previously entitled Advertising Quarterly.

1083. Attitudes of Canadians toward Advertising on Television.
Prepared by Armin Lazar & Associates, Ltd., for the
Research Branch of the Canadian Radio-Television &
Telecommunications Commission. Ottawa, 1978. 55p.
(Available from Printing and Publishing Supply and
Services, Hull, Quebec, Canada R1A 059.)

A study based on the results of a survey-sample composed of 3,060 respondents representing a cross-section
of the Canadian population. Three primary attitudinal
areas were investigated: attitudes toward advertising
as an economic and commercial activity, attitudes toward
television as a medium, and attitudes toward advertising
on television specifically.

1084. Ayer Glossary of Advertising and Related Terms. 2d ed.
        Philadelphia: Ayer Press, 1977. 219p.

        Half of the book is given over to general terms used
in advertising. The other half includes terms used in
television and radio, printing, photography and graphic
arts, computer and data-processing research in advertising media and in marketing, associations, unions, government bureaus, and similar allied areas.

1085. Bacon's International Publicity Checker: Guide to
        Western European PR Markets. Chicago 60604: Bacon's
        Clipping Bureau, 14 E. Jackson Blvd., annual. (1975--.)

        Lists under sixty-four subject headings trade and tech-
nical publications for Western European countries. For
each listing the following information is given: title,
correct mailing address for press releases, telephone
number, Telex number, frequency, circulation, editor's
name, and a code indicating the types of publicity
releases accepted and used by publication. There is also
brief general information in the introductory material
about time differences and overseas telephone, telegraph,
and mail rates. Upon request, Bacon's supplies lists of
translators for the countries represented.

1086. Bacon's Newspaper Directory: Dailies, Weeklies. Chicago
        60604: Bacon's Clipping Bureau, 14 E. Jackson Blvd.,
        annual. (1975--.)

        Like Bacon's Publicity Checker (No. 1087), this is
intended primarily for public relations purposes, but
its information has a variety of other uses. It gives
daily newspapers by state and city, with address, telephone number, circulation, and a detailed list of personnel including editors in the following areas: automotive, book review, business and financial, editorial
page, education, environmental and ecology, farm, fashion,
food, home and garden, radio and television, real estate,
science, sports, travel. It also includes editors of
women's news, managing editors, and city editors. In
addition, it lists by name dailies with over 50,000 circulation, dailies serving the top 100 metropolitan

319

markets, black daily and weekly newspapers, weekly and
semi-weekly newspapers, and within the final section,
"Bacon's Publicity Placement Guide," the eleven public
relations news wire services in the U.S.

1087. Bacon's Publicity Checker: Magazines, Newspapers.
Chicago 60604: Bacon's Clipping Bureau, 14 E. Jack-
son Blvd., annual. (1933--.)

Although intended primarily as a public relations
aid, this analysis of the publicity requirements of
3,920 business, trade, farm, and consumer magazines in
the U.S. and Canada, 694 daily newspapers, and forty-
six news services and feature syndicates has other
reference uses. In particular its extensive list of
magazines by subject classification is valuable. For
each entry it gives address, editor, frequency, circulation, publisher, and telephone number, as well as
coded information pertinent for public relations--for
example, whether it uses publicity photographs, whether
articles are staff-written, whether it carries book
reviews, and similar details about content and regulations. Less information is given for newspapers, perhaps because it is readily available elsewhere (See
No. 1086). For news services and syndicates, address
and telephone number, and occasionally the name of the
editor are included. In conclusion there is a list of
all publishers of two or more of the publications
listed, with names of publications.

Barcus, F. Earle, with Rachel Wolkin. Children's Television:
An Analysis of Programming and Advertising. (See No.
332.)

1088. Barnes, Michael, ed. The Three Faces of Advertising.
London SWIV INJ: The Advertising Association,
Abford House, 15 Wilton Rd., 1975. 277p.

A series of articles, extracts, and lectures, embrac-
ing both "pro" and "anti" views of advertising and span-
ning the years 1950-73. Part I discusses ethics; Part
II, economics; and Part III, effects. Among contributors are Raymond Williams, Richard Crossman, Nicholas
Kaldor, and Julian L. Simon.

1089. Barnouw, Erik. The Sponsor: Notes on a Modern Potentate.
New York: Oxford University Press, 1978. 220p.

In this penetrating study of an important and neglected
aspect of advertising history, one of broadcasting's
finest historians analyzes the pervasive influence of the
advertiser on commercial network programming. He sketches

the rise of the sponsor on radio and television; examines
the sponsor's impact on TV programming; and assesses the
dominant role broadcast advertising has played in terms of
its influence on society, mores, and institutions. Public
TV is not exempt: he discusses the sponsor as an instrument of power in this area as well. Contains notes and an
index.

1090. Bishop, Robert L., comp. Public Relations, a comprehensive Bibliography: Articles and Books on Public Relations, Communication Theory, Public Opinion, and
Propaganda, 1964-1974. Ann Arbor, Mich.: A. G. Leigh-
James, 1974. 212p. (Obtain from Publications Distribution Service.)

A wide-ranging list, comprised of over 4,000 entries
from dissertations, surveys, and an assortment of other
sources in addition to books and periodicals. Entries
are grouped under about 1,800 headings, with numerous
cross entries and an author index. There are annotations when needed. Updated by two supplements in Public
Relations Review--Vol. I:4 (1975-76) covering 1973-74,
and Vol. III:2 (1977) covering 1975.

1091. Borden, Neil H. The Economic Effects of Advertising.
Homewood, Ill.: Richard D. Irwin, 1944. 988p.

A classic factual analysis of the economics of advertising, which, though decades old, has not lost any of
its value. It contains background information about the
development and use of advertising by businessmen, gives
its relation to price and pricing practices, and discusses its effect on the range and quality of products
and on investment and volume of income. It also takes
up ethical aspects. Appendices and index.

1092. The British Code of Advertising Practice. 5th ed. London WC1E 7AW: Advertising Standards Authority, Code
of Advertising Practice Committee, 15-17 Ridgmount
St., 1974. 67p.

Lays down criteria for professional conduct for those
in advertising and indicates to the general public the
industry's self-imposed regulations. A second printing
of this edition has incorporated amendments to July 1977.

Canada. Senate. Report on the Mass Media. Vol. II. (See
No. 29.)

1093. Brozen, Yale, ed. Advertising and Society. New York:
New York University Press, 1974. 189p.

This series of lectures on the impact of advertising, delivered in 1973 at the Graduate School of Business at the University of Chicago, comes out with a vigorous defense of advertising as a social force for good. Among aspects dealt with are: its place in American civilization (here Daniel Boorstein tells us how "outrageous over-statements" by enterprising advertisers helped entice settlers to America), advertising and the consumer, economic values, advertising in an affluent society, institutional advertising by nonprofit organizations (Philip Kotler believes that they pose a threat), brand loyalties, advertising and the law. Some of the articles are footnoted.

1094. Circulation: The Annual Geographic Penetration Analysis of Major Print Media. Northfield, Ill. 60093: American Newspaper Markets, Inc., annual. (1962--.)

"A comprehensive print analysis showing circulation and penetration in every U.S. county, in every U.S. metro area, in television viewing areas for every U.S. daily newspaper, every U.S. Sunday paper, all regional sales groups, five leading national supplements, twenty-four leading magazines." In addition to circulation figures, it also gives demographic information for all areas.

1095. Cohen, Dorothy. Advertising. New York: Wiley, 1972. 689p.

Using the systems approach, the author explains the processes that constitute advertising, the elements of which they are composed, and the inter-relationships existing between them. The book is divided into six sections: the nature of advertising, advertising as a social and economic process, advertising as an administrative process, advertising as a creative process, the communication process, and the integration process. Thus, part is theoretical, part practical. Each of the thirty chapters contains a bibliography, and there is an index.

1096. Commercial Radio in Africa. 53 Bonn, Federal Republic of Germany: German Africa Society/Deutsche Afrika-Gesellschaft e. V., Markt 10-12, 1970. 307p.

Although the title mentions only radio, TV services are also included in this handbook of broadcasting stations throughout Africa, intended primarily for advertisers and marketers. Arrangement is alphabetical by country. Data for each station includes official address; name; language or languages in which commercials are broadcast; coverage; transmitting power and wave

length; times of transmission for commercial programs;
time classification; advertising rates; special regulations and services. Alphabetical index of stations.

1097. Cook, Harvey R. Selecting Advertising Media: A Guide
for Small Business. 2d ed. Washington: U.S. Small
Business Administration, Office of Management Information and Training, 1977. 133p. (Small Business
Management Series No. 34.)

A concise rundown on the various media which points
out the advantages and disadvantages of each medium and
suggests ways to judge probable usefulness to small businesses and to laymen in general. There are also discussions of advertising agencies and advertising budgets; a
section on "Advertising Terms and What They Mean"; and
one on "Where to Get More Information," which includes
media directories, associations, postal service publications, FTC guides, Small Business Administration publications, and books and booklets.

1098. Critchley, R. A. Television and Media Effect: A Review
of the Relevant Research. London WIN 7DG: British
Bureau of Television Advertising, Knighton House,
52-66 Mortimer St., 1974. 134p. (BBTA Occasional
Papers No. 9.)

In his preface Critchley calls this ". . . essentially
a pulling together of the main information--already published in UK and elsewhere--which seems to be relevant"
to the knowledge about the effectiveness of TV communication with special reference to advertising. Various
theories are discussed, as are the findings from
empirical data. In conclusion there is a three-page summary of facts that have been ascertained and a lengthy
bibliography.

1099. Critchley, R. A. U.K. Advertising Statistics: A Review
of the Principal Sources and Figures. London SW1V
INJ: The Advertising Association, Abford House, 15
Wilton Rd., 1973. 50p.

A monograph which brings together readership and circulation figures for the press, audience data for television, as much information as is available for other
media, and data about advertising billings and employment.
Part I gives U.K. advertising expenditure; Part II, advertising rates and audiences; and Part III, advertising
agency data. Sources for all figures are included, along
with a great deal of explanatory text. Appendix I is
"Bibliography and Sources"; Appendix II, "Control Systems
in Advertising Practice," or codes.

1100. Cutlip, Scott M., comp. A Public Relations Bibliography.
      2d ed. Madison: University of Wisconsin Press, 1965.
      305p.

   "Books, articles and other related material written
   about public relations since it first emerged as an
   identifiable vocation in the early 1900s are classified
   under seventy-four subject categories," says Marketing
   Information Guide. Public relations is interpreted
   broadly to include theory as well as practice and includes
   such allied fields as communications and opinion change.
   The second edition reflects changes in attitude toward the
   profession, with more attention paid to substantive issues
   and to self-justification, tools, and research. Indexed.

Davis, Anthony. Television: The First Forty Years. (See No.
   393.)

1101. A Design for Public Relations Education: The Report of
      the Commission on Public Relations Education. 1976?
      20p.

   Co-sponsored by the Public Relations Division of the
   Association for Education in Journalism and the Public
   Relations Society of America, this pamphlet recommends
   curriculum on the undergraduate, master's, and doctoral
   level; discusses the role of the educator and his relation with practitioners; and goes briefly into research,
   and the transition from campus to practice. No address
   is given, but it can probably be obtained from either of
   the co-sponsors.

Directory, American Society of Journalists and Authors: A
   Listing of Professional Free-Lance Writers. (See No.
   1044.)

1102. Elliott, Blanche B. A History of English Advertising.
      London: Business Publications Ltd., 1962. 231p.

   The author traces English advertising from its beginning in the late sixteenth century to the present, with
   most of the emphasis on pre-twentieth century. Her concern is basically with facts rather than with ethical
   pros and cons. Much of her information comes from
   original sources, notably the Burney Collection and the
   Thomason Tracts in the British Museum. Brief bibliography of monographs and an index.

1103. Encyclomedia. New York 10017: Decision Publications,
      342 Madison Ave., quarterly. (1978--.)

A series designed to assist in media planning by
presenting a wide assortment of pertinent facts and
figures. At this point three volumes have been published: Newspapers (1977--), Consumer Magazines
(1978--), and Radio (1978--) Television is in process and two others are planned, Business Publications
and Outdoor Advertising. Information about each medium
obviously varies, but for those published thus far it
is comprehensive. Newspapers, for instance, contains
dimensions in terms of dollar volume; readership reports;
circulation trends; ad agency billings; generalized
newspaper costs; circulation and coverage data for market-
by-market plannings; estimates of newspaper audience cost-
per-1,000s for eight important population segments; reach
and frequency; supplements and comics; characteristics of
eleven major national newspapers, their circulations, and
where to write for more information; costs of inserts and
preprints; audience and market studies made available by
individual newspapers; suburban groups in principal markets. Much is in tabular form. Singly or together these
are valuable tools for planning campaigns, for teaching
advertising or marketing, and for obtaining facts and
figures about the economics and reach of the media in general.

1104. Ewen, Stuart. Captains of Consciousness: Advertising
      and the Social Roots of the Consumer Culture. New
      York: McGraw-Hill, 1976. 261p.

      Placing modern advertising within the social structure,
Ewen theorizes that it is a conditioning process designed
by industry to structure a value system suitable to its
purposes--to create buyers and consumers. He traces the
ways in which this has been done back to its historical
roots in the early twentieth century, particularly in
the 1920s. Notes, a bibliography, and an author-title-
subject index.

Feureissen, Fritz, and Ernst Schmacke, comps. Die Presse in
      Afrika: Ein Handbuch für Wirtschaft und Werbung. The
      Press in Africa: A Handbook for Economics and Advertis-
      ing. (See No. 670.)
      _____. Die Presse in Lateinamerika. The Press in Latin
      America. (See No. 670.)
      _____. Die Presse in Asien und Ozeanien. The Press in Asia
      and Oceania. (See No. 670.)
      _____. Die Presse in Europa. The Press in Europe. (See
      No. 670.)

1105. Firestone, O. J. The Public Persuader: Government
      Advertising. Toronto: Methuen, 1970. 258p.

A Canadian study, made independently and later used as
a significant portion of the Report of the Canadian Task
Force on Government Information, which was tabled in 1969.
The author examines in detail the particular methods used
by the Canadian government and evaluates their effectiveness, gives details on amounts spent, discusses political
patronage in relation to government advertising, and
examines the role of advertising agencies. The book ends
with recommendations. There are several appendices, two
of which discuss government advertising in Britain and
the U.S. Indexed.

1106. Gardner, Herbert S., Jr. The Advertising Agency Business.
      Chicago: Crain Books, 1976. 211p.

"It is not intended that this book make the reader an
advertising man but, rather, that it make him an advertising business man." Gardner goes into many aspects of
agencies: the philosophy of success, economic facts, getting started, detailed financial operations, organization,
prospects and presentations, the place of psychology in
advertising, agencies in a recession. This book is an
outgrowth of a 1964 publication which was basically a compilation and amplification of the various "Agencies Ask
Us" columns written by Kenneth Groesbeck for Advertising
Age over a period of years. Indexed.

1107. Goffman, Erving. Gender Advertisements. Cambridge, Mass.:
      Harvard University Press, 1979. 84p.

Goffman presents 507 photographs taken from commercials
which he analyzes to show the unnatural symbols and rituals
which, all too often in the eyes of society and invariably
in the eyes of advertisers, surround the male/female relationship. Chapter references. This first appeared as a
monograph in the Fall 1976 issue of Studies in the Anthro-
pology of Visual Communication.

1108. Graham, Irvin. Encyclopedia of Advertising. 2d ed. New
      York: Fairchild, 1969. 324p.

Defines more than 1,100 entries relating to advertising,
marketing, publishing, law, research, public relations,
publicity, and the graphic arts. Section I, which is the
main body of the book, is devoted to terminology; Section
II groups the terms according to subject matter to form a
sort of index; Section III is a directory of associations.

Great Britain. Royal Commission on the Press. Documentary Evi-
      dence . . . 1962. (See Nos. 683-84.)

Great Britain. Royal Commission on the Press. <u>Minutes of</u>
   <u>Oral Evidence. . . .</u> (<u>See</u> No. 685.)

1109. Hanson, Philip. <u>Advertising and Socialism: The Nature</u>
   <u>and Extent of Consumer Advertising in the Soviet</u>
   <u>Union, Poland, Hungary and Yugoslavia</u>. White Plains,
   N.Y.: International Arts and Sciences Press, 1974.
   171p.

   Theoretically, advertising and communism are not com-
   patible, but Hanson explains why this is not necessarily
   the case. In Part I he treats the Soviet Union, in Part
   II, Eastern Europe, showing in both parts organization
   and function and highlighting similarities and differences. Much of the information in Part II comes from a
   survey in which nationals responded to a questionnaire.
   A bibliography in the appendix accompanies Part I. The
   study was originally published in 1971 and 1972 as two
   separate monographs in the (British) Advertising Association's Research Studies in Advertising series.

1110. Hill and Knowlton Executives. <u>Critical Issues in Public</u>
   <u>Relations</u>. Englewood Cliffs, N.J.: Prentice-Hall,
   1975. 234p.

   This anthology, in which contributors are practitioners in the large public relations firm of Hill and
   Knowlton, Inc., is something of a "how to" book, but it
   is also an excellent source of information on the structure and operation of public relations. Although
   obviously very much for it, contributors also discuss
   arguments against it. Among topics are financial and
   government relations, public interest issues, advertising, and international aspects. Max Ways, a <u>Fortune</u>
   editor and the one non-member of the firm, presents an
   overview, and the conclusion is an article about the role
   of public relations in society. Indexed.

1111. Hill and Knowlton International. <u>Handbook on Inter-</u>
   <u>national Public Relations</u>. 2 vols. New York:
   Praeger, 1967, 1968.

   Although concerned with the "how to" aspect of public
   relations, this handbook also contains a country-by-
   country discussion of such facts as media, audience,
   and government regulations. Specialists in each country
   contribute articles, each covering slightly different
   aspects. Vol. I treats Belgium, France, Italy, the
   Netherlands, Scandinavia, Spain, Switzerland, the United
   Kingdom, and West Germany. Vol. II treats Australia,
   Hong Kong, India, Japan, Latin America, Malaysia, New
   Zealand, and Singapore.

1112. Howard, John A., and James Hulbert. <u>Advertising and the</u>
<u>Public Interest: A Staff Report to the Federal Trade</u>
<u>Commission</u>. Chicago: Crain Books, 1973. 96p.

Based mainly upon the transcript of the commission's
hearings on modern advertising practices. The hearings
are chiefly concerned with helping to insure that regulation is conducted for the benefit of consumers and competitors; to determine more precisely what constitutes
"unfair" and "deceptive" advertising; and to understand
more clearly the mechanisms by which advertising works.
To these ends they examine the structure and process of
advertising; its role in marketing strategy; models of
advertising communication; an evaluation of techniques;
regulation and control. At the end of the report are
recommendations.

<u>Hudson's Washington News Media Contacts Directory</u>. (<u>See</u> No.
697.)

1113. <u>IENS Press Handbook</u>. New Delhi 11001: Indian & Eastern
Newspaper Society, IENS Bldgs., Rafi Marg, annual.
(1940/41--.)

Intended primarily as an aid for media space buyers,
this annual contains pertinent data about the 300 or
more IENS member publications and the almost 150 advertising agencies accredited by IENS; the larger newspaper
agencies in India and some abroad; representatives of
foreign newspapers and news agencies in India and those
of Indian newspapers and news agencies stationed abroad;
universities and other institutions which train in
journalism; information and public relations directors
of state and central governments; public relations managers and officers in leading commercial concerns; newsprint dealers and agents and printing equipment manufacturers and their agents in India; texts of important
rulings on advertising; and the government's newsprint
import policy.

1114. <u>INFA Press and Advertisers Year Book</u>. New Delhi 11001:
INFA Publications, Jeevan Deep, Parliament St., annual.
(1962--.)

Published by the India News and Feature Alliance,
this gives detailed general information about the structure and policies of the newspaper press; its information
services; a who's who in both areas and in advertising; a
general section on advertising; general census figures
and other information and a press circulation analysis to
be used in media planning; and rates and data for trade,
technical and professional publications, cinema theaters,

outdoor advertising, and radio and TV advertising. The
first section, "Press-General," contains a bibliography
of selected Indian books on mass media. This same section gives courses in journalism, and laws pertaining to
the media.

1115. Institute of Practitioners in Advertising. London SWIX
8QS: The Institute, 44 Belgrave Sq. (1971--.)

An on-going series which gives brief and basic facts
about such aspects of the countries involved as geography, demography, expenditures, chief media used,
research organizations, number of advertising agencies,
taxes, laws, regulations, and organizations.

Advertising Conditions in Austria. 1975. 16p.
Advertising Conditions in Belgium. 1971. 20p.
Advertising Conditions in Canada. 1975. 16p.
Advertising Conditions in Denmark. 1975. 16p.
Advertising Conditions in Finland. 1975. 20p.
Advertising Conditions in France. 1974. 20p.
Advertising Conditions in Germany (Federal Republic).
1976. 24p.
Advertising Conditions in Greece. 1975. 24p.
Advertising Conditions in Italy. 1975. 75p.
Advertising Conditions in Norway. 1925. 20p.
Advertising Conditions in the Netherlands. 1972. 24p.
Advertising Conditions in Poland. 1978. 24p.
Advertising Conditions in the Republic of Ireland. 1974.
16p.
Advertising Conditions in Spain. 1978. 24p.
Advertising Conditions in Sweden. 1976. 20p.
Advertising Conditions in Switzerland. 1975. 16p.
Advertising Conditions in the UK. 1976. 24p.

The Japanese Press. (See No. 701.)

1116. Lipstein, Benjamin, and William J. McGuire, comps. Evaluating Advertising: A Bibliography of the Communication Process. New York: Advertising Research Foundation, 1978. 362p.

The title is a misnomer. Actually, this 7,000-entry
bibliography is limited to an evaluation of periodicals
and various forms of monographs with findings applicable
to TV commercials, and does not include research on print
media. Nonetheless, it is a massive compilation. Entries,
which abstract the material, cover a range of literature
that has evolved from TV researchers as well as from professionals in related disciplines who are studying
effects--evaluation, comprehension, persuasion, learning,

behavior, and similar pertinent topics. The largest
portion consists of annotated author entries. There is
a topical index and an alphabetical list of access words.
Each compiler has written an essay--Lipstein on "Some
Observations about the Literature," and McGuire on
"Retrieving the Information from the Literature."

1117. Liu, Peter Yi-Chih. The Development of the Advertising
Industry in Japan and Taiwan: A Comparison, 1945-
1975. Taipei, Taiwan: International Advertising
Agency, P.O. Box 1705, 1975. 141p.

A comparison of the development and status of advertising in the two countries, taking into account the
similarities and differences of each. The author's conclusions are liberally bolstered by statistics and
regulatory documents. Footnotes, a bibliography, and
appendices containing pertinent laws and codes.

1118. Longman, Kenneth A. Advertising. New York: Harcourt
Brace Jovanovich, 1971. 425p.

In this textbook for advertising students, the
author's aim is to concentrate on the "whys" rather than
the "hows," with the manager's point of view salient.
Part I deals with the context of advertising; Part II,
the planning; Part III, the production. Among topics
discussed are history, structure, and economics; details
of planning a campaign; and finally the creation of the
advertisement itself. Footnotes and an index.

1119. Masson (Peter), and Partners. Television Advertising
Conditions in Europe. 4 vols. London WIN 7DG:
British Bureau of Television Advertising Ltd.,
Knighton House, 52-66 Mortimer St. (1973--.)

Discusses briefly, with accompanying tables, the following aspects for each of the countries covered: background, availability of advertising time, allocation
system, flexibility of system, rate card, advertising
restrictions, cancellations, TV research. A summary for
each follows. Vol. I includes Germany and France; Vol.
II, Austria, the Netherlands, Switzerland; Vol. III,
Finland, the Republic of Ireland, Spain; Vol. IV, Cyprus,
Greece, Italy.

1120. Measuring Payout: An Annotated Bibliography on the Dollar Effectiveness of Advertising. New York 10022:
Advertising Research Foundation, 3 E. 54th St., 1973.
39p.

One hundred and forty-three books, articles, and
speeches, arranged chronologically from 1965 to 1972,
with a separate section of the classics in the field.
There is an author and a subject index.

1121. The Media Book. New York 10022: Min-Mid Publishing,
156 E. 52nd St., annual. (1978--.)

Although intended primarily for advertisers, this
book will also be very useful for librarians, communications students, and practically anyone else who needs
concrete facts about the media, either separately or
placed in perspective. Its five sections analyze magazines, newspapers, Sunday supplements (and comics), and
radio and television, describing salient characteristics
and attributes of each. Each section gives a capsule
history of the medium and relevant trend data, indicating
growth in facilities, coverage, and revenues, and, in the
case of the broadcast media, their profit structures.
This is followed by an explanation of the most common
research methods used to measure the medium's audiences
and a demographic review. Whenever possible other pertinent aspects are described, such as time of day and
season that audiences are reached, and where they are
reached: at home, in a car, at work, etc. The qualitative characteristics of the various media are analyzed
as well, with each section presenting a description of
audience intensity or involvement, and defining the way
the medium communicates with its readers, viewers, or
listeners. Also included are measures of ad recall or
readership, with norms by type of ad and other relevant
comparisons. A further section compares media, showing
critical differences between them and strengths and
weaknesses of each. In this process the authors cite a
number of "landmark" studies on advertising effectiveness
to illustrate their point.

1122. Melody, William H. Children's Television: The Economics
of Exploitation. New Haven: Yale University Press,
1973. 164p.

Should children's television be declared an area that
requires the establishment of special protections for
children and positive responsibilities toward them? This
study, commissioned by Action for Children's Television,
examines the economic aspects of commercial children's
television and the relation to FCC public-policy options.
Melody analyzes the economic characteristics of advertising practices and the ways in which they affect programming, traces the history of children's programming from
TV's early years to the present, and suggests alternate

modes of financing it. Contains notes; an extensive
bibliography of articles, documents, and other materials;
and an appendix: "FCC News Release Announcing Its Notice
of Inquiry and Proposed Rulemaking into Commercial Children's Television."

1123. Morella, Joe, Edward Z. Epstein, and Eleanor Clark.
      Those Great Movie Ads. New Rochelle, N.Y.: Arling-
      ton House, 1972. 320p.

      Reproductions of film posters from the 1930s through
      the 1960s, divided into subdivisions to illustrate var-
      ious trends: "Stars," "Comic Strip Features," "Mislead-
      ing Ad Lines," "Movies from Other Media," "Logos," "Tie-
      ins and Endorsements," "Films from Other Lands,"
      "Classics," "Censorship and Advertising," and so on.
      Brief text precedes each section, and Judith Crist has
      written the introduction.

Natarajan, Swaminath. A History of the Press in India. (See
      No. 733.)

1124. National Rate Book and College Newspaper Directory.
      Chicago 60646: Cass Student Advertising, Inc.,
      6330 N. Pulaski Rd., annual. (1972--.)

      A geographic listing of college newspapers with infor-
      mation pertaining to each as an advertising medium: line
      rate; printing process; frequency; publishing date;
      enrollment broken down by men, women, and faculty; circu-
      lation; page size; inserts; second color; type of insti-
      tution, such as junior college, four-year college,
      parochial, private, or public, etc.; percentage of minor-
      ity and out-of-state students; cost of attendance; whether
      or not liquor ads are acceptable; and whether the student
      body is primarily residential or commuter. Canadian
      papers are also included, although less information is
      given. Other features are a two-page summary of the
      Belden Survey of student buying habits and media habits,
      and a two-page summary of college newspaper coverage of
      the college market.

1125. The New World of Advertising. Vernon Fryburger, ed.
      Chicago: Crain Books, 1973. 230p.

      On January 15, 1963, Advertising Age published The
      World of Advertising, an extra-thick issue devoted
      entirely to facts, figures, and articles designed to
      broaden the knowledge of practitioners and the general
      public about advertising. This proved a valuable refer-
      ence tool, but by the end of the 1960s was out of date
      except for historical purposes.

Ten years later, in its November 21, 1973, issue, Advertising Age brought out The New World of Advertising, designed "to put the changes of the past decade into perspective" and to attempt to show that advertising and marketing are necessary to the U.S. economy. In five parts, the first contains an introductory statement by the Council of Economic Advisers, a report on the state of the advertising business, and an essay defining advertising. The second part discusses the role of the advertiser, the agency, marketing research, advertising and regulatory associations, and the functions of the various media. The third tells the uses made of advertising by government, agricultural associations, labor unions, states and cities, and so on. It also defines the work of the Advertising Council. A fourth surveys aspects of international advertising, and the fifth debates pros and cons of advertising with Tom Dillon, president of BBD&O, pro, and Arnold Toynbee, con.

In 1975 a 129-page supplement appeared, also edited by Fryburger, with twenty selections from the 1973 edition, some of which are up-dated, and ten articles from more recent issues of Advertising Age.

1126. Nolte, Lawrence W. Fundamentals of Public Relations: Professional Guidelines, Concepts and Integrations. 2d ed. New York: Pergamon, 1979. 511p.

Although designed as a basic text for college students, with emphasis on techniques, this book nevertheless provides a synthesis of theory and practice which shows how public relations serves, whom it serves, and what it views as its function in society. Bibliography and index.

Norland, Rod. Names and Numbers: A Journalist's Guide to the Most Needed Information Sources and Contacts. (See No. 737.)

1127. Norton, Alice. Public Relations: Information Sources. Detroit: Gale Research Co., 1970. 153p.

An extensive annotated bibliography covering the study and practice of public relations. Divided into the following sections: "General Sources"; "Special Fields and Special Publics"; "Public Relations Tools"; "Public Relations Associations in the United States"; "Careers in Public Relations"; "International Public Relations." Author-title-subject index.

1128. O'Dwyer's Directory of Corporate Communications. New York 10016: J. R. O'Dwyer Co., 271 Madison Ave., annual. (1975--.)

The publisher states that the aim of this directory is to show "how America's largest companies and trade associations have defined, organized and staffed their public relations/communications operations." Among the 2,000 companies included are approximately 1,200 large industrial firms, as ranked by Fortune and Forbes magazines, and the fifty largest companies ranked by Fortune in the following six categories--commercial banking, life insurance, diversified-financial, retailing, transportation, and utilities. New entries in the 1977 edition include 550 companies listed on the New York Stock Exchange but not ranked by Fortune or Forbes. Information for each entry includes address, telephone number, amount of sales, person or persons involved in public relations (which is called by a variety of terms), and sometimes the budget. There is a geographical index to corporate headquarters. Following the list of corporations is a list of trade and professional associations, with address, telephone number, personnel, and budget.

1129. O'Dwyer's Directory of Public Relations Firms. New York 10016: J. R. O'Dwyer Co., 271 Madison Ave., annual. (1968--.)

Lists 719 public relations firms and public relations departments of advertising agencies, giving (in most cases) address, telephone number, number of employees, names of top officers, and the accounts they carry. Some also give their specialties. Foreign as well as U.S. firms are included. In addition there are breakdowns by specialized areas such as educational institutions, industrial/technical, beauty and fashion, financial/investor relations, foods and beverages, home furnishing, travel, political candidates, book publicity, and sports. Other features are a ranking of the forty largest U.S.-based public relations operations, both independent and agency-affiliated; the thirty-one largest independent public relations firms in the U.S.; and a geographical listing. Contains an index to client companies.

1130. Palek, David L., Robert E. Pearson, and Donald L. Willis. Politics in Public Service Advertising on Television. New York: Praeger, 1977. 123p.

The authors analyze public service advertising on television through interviews, questionnaires, telephone polls, and content analysis to show how akin it can be to advocacy and propaganda. They approach the analysis on two levels: the operation of production, distribution, and airing; and a more speculative discussion of

334

the values espoused in the spots and their political
relevance. Particular attention is given to the question
of selection. Since there is not nearly enough air space
for all the institutions, organizations, agencies, and
groups who request time, how are choices made? The
structure of the Advertising Council in particular is
examined. Footnotes and index.

1131. Polley, Richard W. Information Sources in Advertising
       History. Westport, Conn.: Greenwood, 1979. 312p.
       (approx.)

    This is a welcome addition to the literature of adver-
tising. It presents an exhaustive list of about 1,600
titles, arranged by subject and including reference books,
general histories, texts, and books on advertising psychology, criticism, and ethics. There is even some fiction.
It is particularly strong in representing primary sources,
many of them rare, from the pre-1940 era. All entries are
annotated.
    Preceding the bibliography are four essays, the first
outlining the state of the available literature and the
other three giving sources of economic data, commercial
sources of advertising data, and contributions of the
trade press to the literature. A special feature gives
directories to collections of advertising materials housed
in archives, museums, trade associations, and agencies
themselves. Indexed.

1132. Presbrey, Frank. The History and Development of Advertis-
       ing. New York: Doubleday, 1929. 642p.

    One of the best and fullest sources available for the
history of advertising from ancient days to the Depression.
Over 100 of its more than 600 pages are devoted to early
advertising outside the American colonies, and throughout
the book social and economic implications are stressed.
An appendix contains an address by President Coolidge on
the economic aspects of advertising. Indexed.

Press and Advertisers Year Book. (See No. 744.)

1133. Price, Jonathan. The Best Thing on TV: Commercials. New
       York: Viking/Penguin, 1978. 184p.

    "More fun than a gorilla with a suitcase, more explosive
than a camera that blows up, more entertaining than the
programs they interrupt, more informative than most network
news, commercials are often the best thing on TV. And the
best commercials outpace the programs they interrupt in at
least a dozen ways." After analyzing the commercial and its
environment, Price elaborates on the ways which, in his

opinion, commercials accomplish these feats. An unortho-
dox, entertaining, and illuminating book.

1134. Ramond, Charles. Advertising Research: The State of the
      Art. New York 10017: Association of National Adver-
      tisers, 155 E. 44th St., 1976. 148p.

      Designing his book for practitioners and students
      rather than for hard-core researchers, Ramond summarizes
      and appraises in layman's language studies in the field
      of advertising which give practical knowledge. Arrange-
      ment is topical under aim and scope: how advertising
      communicates; how it sells; how brand attributes and cor-
      porate images are arrived at and how they work; the
      selection of target audiences; copy, media, and budget
      research; studies of advertising frequency; and the
      future of advertising research. Appendices contain an
      annotated bibliography of reviews of advertising research
      and a twenty-page bibliography of the references cited.
      Indexed.

1135. Research on the Effects of Television Advertising on Child-
      ren. A Report prepared for the National Science Founda-
      tion, Research Directorate, and RANN--Research Applied
      to National Needs, Division of Advanced Productivity
      Research and Technology. Washington: Superintendent of
      Documents, 1977? 299p.

      A comprehensive review of existing research which sum-
      marizes the present state of knowledge about TV advertising
      and children, and recommends a plan of future research.
      The report has four components: identification of major
      policy issues; review of existing research organized around
      these issues; recommendations for future policy-relevant
      research; compilation of a national roster of researchers
      on TV advertising and children. Among the issues discussed
      at length are program-commercial separation, format and
      audio-visual techniques, source effects and self-concept
      appeals, premiums and unsafe acts, proprietary drug adver-
      tising, food advertising, volume and repetition, advertis-
      ing and consumer socialization, TV advertising and parent-
      child relations. A useful feature is an eight-page summary
      preceding the text. Appendices include a lengthy biblio-
      graphy, a research roster, and the NAB and NAD guidelines
      for children's advertising.

1136. Rosden, George Eric, and Peter Eric Rosden. The Law of
      Advertising. Vols. I-II. New York: Matthew Bender.
      (1973--.)

A multi-volume set by two Washington lawyers, of which
two volumes have thus far appeared. It goes comprehensively into the various legal aspects of advertising,
citing cases and decisions. Contents include: the law
governing the relationships between the originators of
advertising, constitutional problems, competitors' remedies, consumers' remedies, basic principles of the FTC
laws, laws regarding specific statements, procedure before
the FTC, judicial review, self-regulation, liabilities.
An appendix gives sample forms for advertising contracts
and a table of cases. Indexed.

1137. Rotzoll, Kim B., James E. Haefner, and Charles H. Sand-
      age. Advertising in Contemporary Society: Perspec-
      tives toward Understanding. Columbus, Ohio: Grid,
      1976. 151p.

      This is not a book of techniques, but rather one with
      a philosophical approach. It offers certain basic per-
      spectives and, with these in mind, discusses some of the
      fundamental issues. Among the perspectives are the
      classical liberal market, the neo-liberal market, and
      four institutional views of advertising: advertising as
      marketing information, the quest for market power, social
      control without social responsibility, and advertising's
      power to inform and persuade. The issues include adver-
      tising in relation to the firm, the individual, the
      economy, consumerism, and the press. A final portion,
      "Reflections," treats "the now and future of advertising."
      Each chapter has end notes and a bibliography.

1138. Sandage, Charles H., Vernon Fryburger, and Kim Rotzoll.
      Advertising Theory and Practice. 10th ed. Homewood,
      Ill.: Richard D. Irwin, 1979. 695p.

      Although much of this popular advertising textbook is
      concerned with techniques and market analysis, an almost
      equal part is given to an analysis of the place of adver-
      tising in our society--its evolution, its regulation, its
      possible effects, its possible future. Subject matter
      has been reorganized and where necessary updated, with
      account taken of new trends, strategies, and research.
      Footnotes, an index, and many well-chosen illustrations.

1139. Sandage, Charles H., and Vernon Fryburger, eds. The Role
      of Advertising: A Book of Readings. Homewood, Ill.:
      Richard D. Irwin, 1960. 499p.

      Discusses many pertinent facts and theories, such as
      advertising's place in society, its responsibility, its
      appeals, its function, and its impact. Includes a bib-
      liography at the end of each section and gives "Standards

of Practice of the American Association of Advertising
Agencies" and the Television Code. Since its orientation is theoretical, it has dated little.

1140. Simon, Morton J. Public Relations Law. New York:
       Appleton-Century-Crofts, 1969. 882p.

       "We have sought to produce for the PR practitioner a
       basic book which will also guide the layman when he
       ventures into the legal sectors of public relations,"
       says the author, a lawyer. Gives legal basics of such
       areas as copyright, privacy, libel, trademarks, photo-
       graphy, deception, contests, industrial espionage,
       government relations, lobbying, employee-employer rela-
       tions, and similar aspects, some of which have changed
       over the decade. Enough, however, remains the same to
       make the reference useful.

1141. Standard Directory of Advertisers. Skokie, Ill. 60077:
       National Register Publishing Co., 5201 Old Orchard
       Rd., annual with monthly cumulative supplements.
       (1917--.)
1142. Standard Directory of Advertising Agencies. Skokie, Ill.
       60077: National Register Publishing Co., 5201 Old
       Orchard Rd., three times a year, with monthly supple-
       ments between issues. (1917--.)

       Companion volumes. Advertisers tells which agency
       advertises a specific product; Advertising Agencies tells
       which accounts a specific agency carries.
       The Standard Directory of Advertisers lists 17,000
       corporations doing national and regional advertising,
       classified by type of product. Information about each
       corporation includes name, address, telephone number,
       heads of divisions, products and services, and not only
       the advertising agency employed but also the media used
       and, in some cases, the appropriation. There are several
       indexes--one by name of corporation, one by trade name,
       and two by classification--one by SIC (Standard Industrial
       Classification) code, and one by alphabetical order.
       There is also a small separate volume, The Geographical
       Index, which lists corporations by state and city.
       The Standard Directory of Advertising Agencies lists
       approximately 4,400 agencies, with address, telephone
       number, and some or all of the following information:
       year founded, number of employees, specialization, approx-
       imate annual billing and a breakdown of gross annual bill-
       ing by media, account executives, and accounts carried.
       Other features include a list of the twenty-five largest
       advertising agencies, ranked according to annual billing;

a list of foreign advertising agencies, many of which
are branches of U.S. agencies; a market index including
agencies specializing in advertising for blacks, in
marketing services, in media services, in the Spanish
market, and in financial, medical, and resort and
travel accounts.

1143. Standard Rate and Data Services, Inc. Skokie, Ill.
      60077: 5201 Old Orchard Rd., ca. 1919--.

      SRDS publishes a number of guides which bring
together comprehensive information on advertising rates
and specifications, as well as circulation figures from
auditing services for print media, demographic data,
and media maps for each of the fifty states in the U.S.
In the early years the service was limited to this
country, and the various types of media were included
in a single volume. Over the years the U.S. editions
have expanded into separate volumes for each of the
media, and coverage has extended to Canada and Europe,
with the media combined in one volume.

Domestic Publications:

Business Publication Rates and Data (monthly).
Community Publication Rates and Data (semiannual). For-
    merly Weekly Newspaper and Shopping Guide Rates and
    Data.
Consumer Magazine and Farm Publication Rates and Data
    (monthly).
Direct Mail List Rates and Data (semiannual).
Network Rates and Data (bimonthly).
Newspaper Rates and Data (monthly, including Part II of
    the August issue, Newspaper Circulation Analysis).
Print Media Production Data (quarterly).
Spot Radio Rates and Data (monthly).
Spot Radio Small Markets Edition (semiannual).
Spot Television Rates and Data (monthly).

Foreign Publications:

Canadian Advertising Rates and Data (monthly).
British Rates and Data (monthly).
Tarif Media (French language) (quarterly).
Dati e Tarriffe Pubblicitario (Italian language)
    (bimonthly).
Mexican Media Rates and Data (Spanish language)
    (quarterly).
Media Daten (German language) (bimonthly). West Germany.
Media Daten (German language) (semiannual). Austria.
Media Daten (German and French languages) (semiannual).
    Switzerland.

339

In addition to providing advertising information, these
rate and data services have other uses. Business Publication Rates and Data and Consumer Magazine and Farm Publication Rates and Data, with their classified arrangements
by subject and their editorial profiles of each publication, provide excellent information to non-fiction writers
who wish to determine the marketplace. Newspaper Rates
and Data lists national and daily newspapers, newspaper
comic sections, both independent and group-owned news-
paper-distributed magazines, and Afro-American newspapers.
Community Publications Rates and Data covers a fast-
growing segment of the communications industry--the
metropolitan area urban/suburban weekly, the independent
shopping guides, and the NAAP (National Association of
Advertising Publishers) member and free community newspapers, as well as non-metropolitan and religious weeklies.
Both Spot Radio and Spot Television Rates and Data contain thumbnail descriptions of programming by categories,
including time allotments for each category and target
audience. (Some of these profiles are much fuller than
others.) Spot Radio Rates and Data also presents a summary tabulation of radio stations regularly scheduling
farm programs, Afro-American programs, and foreign language programs. Newspaper Rates and Data and the two
broadcasting guides are in addition an excellent source
for lists of group ownerships.

1144. Statistical Trends in Broadcasting. New York 10022:
John Blair & Co., Blair Television & Blair Radio,
717 Fifth Ave., annual. (1964--.)

A compact source for a variety of valuable statistics
about television and radio, oriented toward the advertising community, but with many other uses. Section I gives
statistics on expenditures, both by themselves and in
relation to national figures and trends. Section II contains statistics on TV revenues, expenses, incomes, and
growth rates, with comparative figures as far back as
1954 and data on cable. Both network and non-network
data are included. Section III does the same for radio.
Sources of data are included--another useful feature.

1145. Stridsberg, Albert B. Effective Advertising Self-
Regulation: A Survey of Current World Practice and
Analysis of International Patterns. New York 10003:
International Advertising Association, Inc., 475 Fifth
Ave., 1974. 181p.

Study of the possibilities and problems of voluntary
self-regulation. The first part is general: basic
issues, how to organize, and future of self-regulation.

The second part gives profiles of what twenty-nine countries have done. There are four appendices: "International Code of Advertising Practice, 5th ed., 1973";
"International Code of Marketing Research Practice,
1971"; "International Code of Sales Promotion Practice,
1973"; "World Chart of Advertising Self-Regulation."

1146. Thompson (J. Walter) Co. <u>Advertising: An Annotated Bibliography, 1972</u>. London WIX 4BB: National Book
League, 7 Albemarle St., 1972. 35p.

A thirty-five-page pamphlet containing over 300
entries (all books), annotated and arranged by subject.
Emphasis is British.

1147. Urdang, Laurence, ed. <u>Dictionary of Advertising Terms</u>.
Chicago 60611: Tatham-Laird & Kudner, 625 N. Michigan
Ave., 1977. 209p.

Incorporates over 4,000 entries used in marketing planning, copywriting, art direction, graphic supply, print
production, commercial production, program production,
media planning, media research, media analysis, media
buying, marketing research, consumer research, field
interviewing, statistical analysis, merchandising and
promotion planning, public relations counseling, data
processing, and advertising finance.

1148. Williamson, Judith. <u>Decoding Advertisements: Ideology
and Meaning in Advertising</u>. London: Calder & Boyers,
1978. 180p.

A theoretical analysis of the way advertisements are
created and the way they work psychologically. In the
words of the author: "Advertisements . . . provide a
structure which is capable of transforming the language
of objects to that of people and <u>vice</u> <u>versa</u>. The first
part of this book attempts to analyze the way that
structure functions. The second part looks at some of
the actual systems and things that it transforms." She
uses specific ads as examples. Footnotes and brief
bibliography.

1149. Wilson, Alexander, ed. <u>Advertising and the Community</u>.
Manchester, England: Manchester University Press,
1968. 231p.

Essays about the social and economic effects of
advertising on British society, centering around the
question of advertising's present quality. Articles
discuss the need, if it exists, for advertising; the
public confidence in it; forms of control; responsibility

341

toward the consumer; and consumer safeguards. Contributors, who number both detractors and defenders, represent a variety of viewpoints--the media, consumer
organizations, the law, the advertising business, the
university professor. Appendices give the Independent
Television Authority's Advertising Code, a summary of
recommendations of the Advertising Inquiry Council,
and advertising statistics. Bibliography and index.

1150. Wood, James Playsted. The Story of Advertising. New
      York: Ronald Press, 1958. 512p.

     Five-hundred-page history in which the author dis-
cusses the good and bad points of advertising. Includes
a bibliography and an index.

1151. The Working Press of the Nation. 5 vols. Burlington,
      Iowa 52601: National Research Bureau, 424 N. Third
      St., annual. (1947--.)

     This series, which has grown from one volume, Working
Press of the Nation, into five, is intended primarily
for publicists, but includes detailed information pertinent to librarians and others engaged in various
aspects of communication. Individual volumes are:

Newspaper and Allied Services Directory. Vol. I. (See
     No. 788.)
Magazine and Editorial Directory. Vol. II. (See No.
     1076.)
Radio and Television Directory. Vol. III. (See No. 626.)
Feature Writer, Photographer and Syndicate Directory.
     Vol. IV. (See No. 1074.)
Internal Publications Directory. Vol. V. (See No. 1075.)

1152. World Advertising Expenditures: A Survey of World Adver-
      tising Expenditures in 1976. 13th ed. Mamoroneck,
      N.Y. 10543: Starch INRA Hooper, 566 E. Boston Post
      Rd., 1978. 56p.

     Latest in a series of biennial worldwide surveys of
advertising expenditures sponsored by the International
Advertising Association (IAA) and Starch INRA Hooper. As
in previous years, it provides estimates of expenditure
data in various media categories by country, and is
designed to enable comparisons to be made between countries and broad geographic regions. Estimates of advertising expenditures were obtained from eighty-six
countries, with distribution of expenditure by media
provided by seventy-two countries. A listing of sources,
by country, is shown at the end of the report. Among

data are: per capita advertising expenditures, advertising expenditures as a percent of gross national
product, print advertising, TV advertising, radio advertising. A table gives changes in expenditures in 1966,
1968, 1970, 1972, 1974, and 1976.

VIII
Indexes to Mass Communications Literature

by Frances Goins Wilhoit
Assistant Librarian and Head of the Journalism
Library, Indiana University Library

1153. <u>Abstracts of Popular Culture</u>. Bowling Green, Ohio:
Bowling Green University Popular Press, quarterly.
(1977--.)

Examines periodicals and conference papers for material about American culture which is not overly academic.
Topics germane to mass media are indexed under broad
terms such as film, TV, sports, music, and comics. It
indexes some journals (<u>Broadcasting</u>, <u>Journalism</u> Quarterly,
and <u>Columbia Journalism Review</u>) which are better indexed
elsewhere. The abstracts are not topically organized.
Because the subject headings are broad and cite only
accession numbers of the abstracts, the index is dis-
couraging to use. The publication of the abstracts is
about a year behind the publication of articles
abstracted.

1154. <u>Alternative Press Index</u>. Baltimore, Md.: Alternative
Press Centre, Inc., quarterly (irregular). (1969--.)

Indexes underground publications of Marxist, feminist,
and ethnic groups that are not generally indexed elsewhere. Publishing about two years behind the indexing
date, this one provides a unique access to periodical
literature on subcultures and the mass media (blacks and
the media, gays and the media, women and the media) and
complements <u>Abstracts of Popular Culture</u>.

1155. <u>Broadcasting Index</u>. Washington: Broadcasting Publications, Inc., annual. (1972--.)

An index to <u>Broadcasting</u> magazine, the weekly chronicle of the industry. The entire content of the magazine
is indexed, including personnel items and license
renewals. The articles are condensed, and entries for
personal and organization names are included. An article
about a FCC decision is indexed under the legal issues,
the call letters of the station involved, the station

owner's name, and the FCC, the latter entry being chronologically organized. The problem of a two-year publication lag is reduced by using the current Business Periodicals Index.

1156. Business Periodicals Index. New York: Wilson, monthly
      with annual cumulations. (1958--.)

      An index to current articles on business subjects
      including advertising, public relations, and communica-
      tions. The index is important because it covers three
      key trade journals--Advertising Age, Broadcasting, and
      Editor and Publisher.

1157. CBS News Index. Glen Rock, N.J.: Microfilm Corporation
      of America, quarterly with annual cumulations.
      (1975--.)

      A printed index to the four daily news broadcasts and
      public affairs programs on the Columbia Broadcasting Ser-
      vice network. Public affairs programs include presiden-
      tial press conferences and speeches, Face the Nation,
      and 60 Minutes. A descriptive phrase is assigned to each
      news item to provide the main thrust of the story. The
      transcripts of the news are published on microfilm. If
      the visual portion of the news is also needed, video cas-
      settes of the CBS news are available from the National
      Archive or the Vanderbilt Television News Archive.

1158. Communication Abstracts. Beverly Hills, Cal.: Sage
      Publications, with the School of Communications and
      Theater, Temple University, Philadelphia, quarterly.
      (1978--.)

      An international bibliographic service abstracting
      articles, reports, papers, and a limited number of mono-
      graphs. As communications is broadly defined, "media"
      is one of twenty-one subfields. Most of the abstracts
      under "media" are keyed to four journals: Journalism
      Quarterly, Journal of Communication, Journal of Broad-
      casting, and Communication Research. Selectively
      abstracts from two significant journals, Journalism
      History and Mass Comm Review, and also from the ANPA
      News Research Reports, not all of which are indexed
      elsewhere. Regularly searches over sixty communication
      journals and abstracts very thoroughly.

1159. Film Literature Index. Albany, N.Y.: Filmdex, Inc.,
      quarterly with annual cumulations. (1973--.)

      A thesaurus of 1,000 subject headings was carefully
      developed for this index, which arranges all entries--

subjects, titles, and persons--in a single alphabet. It
indexes a core of 124 film journals plus another 100
general periodicals which occasionally print film
articles. The depth of indexing, the selection of the
subject headings, and the large number of journals
searched make this an important index. The publication
lag time is almost two years.

1160. Humanities Index. New York: Wilson, quarterly with
      annual cumulations. (1974--.)

    Preceded by the International Index (1907-65) and the
Social Sciences and Humanities Index (1965-74), this
Wilson indexing service is a primary tool of almost any
literature search about print and broadcast journalism.
Topics include reporters and reporting, government and
the press, and television and politics. Three basic
journals--Columbia Journalism Review, Journal of Broadcasting, and Journalism Quarterly--are indexed. The
index's general focus is on the periodical literature of
history, performing arts, language, and literature.

1161. Index to Legal Periodicals. New York: Wilson, monthly
      with three-year cumulations. (1908--.)

    This index to the scholarly legal journals published
in the English language is essential for locating
articles on issues of communications law and public
policy for broadcasting. Pertinent subjects include
copyright, censorship, First Amendment rights of the
press, and governmental and legal decisions involving
telecommunications.
    To locate specific legal decisions and developments in
communications, the Media Law Reporter (1977--) is useful
because it indexes and prints the texts of decisions by
federal and state courts and selected administrative
agencies.

1162. The Information Bank. Parsippany, N.J.: New York Times
      Information Bank, weekly. (1973--.)

    A computer data base which includes articles published
in the New York Times and about seventy other newspapers
and periodicals. The Information Bank is current, indexing news published in the New York Times within the week.
As the data base is intended to be a "bank" of information rather than a traditional index to articles, only
selected articles are indexed and abstracted. It is most
useful as a resource for information about individuals
and organizations. At this time the expense of the
Information Bank has limited its availability to large
research and public libraries.

346

1163. <u>International Index to Film Periodicals</u>. New York: St.
     Martin's Press, annual. (1972--.)

    Begun by the International Federation of Film Archives,
the index covers more than eighty film periodicals and is
devoted to film research and scholarship. The annual
printed index is a cumulation of a card subscription service from London which issues 10,000 cards annually. In
1979 card service was extended to include forty TV journals. The card service is very expensive, and most
libraries elect to receive only the printed index, which
is issued about two years later. The entries are well
organized by broad film topics and are also indexed by
director, author, and detailed subject.

1164. <u>Journalism Abstracts</u>. Minneapolis: Association for
     Education in Journalism, University of Minnesota,
     annual. (1963--.)

    Abstracts of the masters' theses and doctoral disser-
tations on mass communications written in cooperating
schools and departments of U.S. colleges and universities.
The abstracts are presented alphabetically by author, and
titles are organized by subjects. Some attempt is made
to provide more than one subject listing per abstract.
<u>Journalism Abstracts</u> provides an efficient check on grad-
uate scholarship on mass communications, but <u>Dissertation
Abstracts International</u> should also be consulted for
relevant Ph.D. dissertations from academic departments
other than communications.

1165. <u>Journalism Quarterly Cumulative Index</u>. Minneapolis:
     Association for Education in Journalism, University
     of Minnesota.

    Three cumulative indexes to this primary journal of
mass communication research have been issued. The second
index to Vols. 1-40 (1924-63) incorporated the first
index to Vols. 1-25 (1924-48). The third index to Vols.
41-50 (1964-73) was published as a special supplement to
Vol. 51 of the journal. Both indexes are divided into
three sections: subject, author, and book reviews. The
excellent subject index is detailed and easy to use.

1166. <u>Language and Language Behavior Abstracts</u>. San Diego,
     Cal.: Sociological Abstracts, Inc., quarterly.
     (1967--.)

    The abstracts provide access to the scholarly litera-
ture of language. Articles from foreign journals not
indexed elsewhere, specifically German journals, appear

347

in the Communication Sciences section under the sub-
division "Mass Media."

1167. The (London) Times Index. Reading, England: London
      Times, monthly with annual cumulations. (1907--.)

   An excellent index to the Times and related publications: the Sunday Times and Magazine, the Times Literary Supplement, the Times Educational Supplement, and
the Times Higher Education Supplement. The subject
categories are not as broadly defined as in the New
York Times Index, and like the New York index, this
one is a reliable source for personal and organizational names.

1168. Newspaper Index. Wooster, Ohio: Bell & Howell, monthly
      with annual cumulations. (1972--.)

   Issued in four separate volumes: Chicago Tribune
Index, Los Angeles Times Index, (New Orleans) Times
Picayune Index, and Washington Post Index. The news
content of the microfilmed editions of the newspapers is
described and indexed'. The coverage includes syndicated
columns, reviews, and obituaries which appear as news
stories. Advertisements, classified obituaries, society
personals, routine sports events, food, and hobby stories
are omitted.

1169. The New York Times Index. New York: New York Times Com-
      pany, monthly with quarterly and annual cumulations.
      (1913--.)

   Because the New York Times is the national newspaper
of record and because the index abstracts each article
in detail, the index is frequently consulted to verify
names, dates, and events, and used as a guide to the contents of other newspapers. An index for the years 1851-
1912 has been issued, completing the indexing of the New
York Times. See also the notes on the Information Bank.

1170. Psychological Abstracts. Washington: The American
      Psychological Association, Inc., monthly. (1927--.)

   A major index for social science literature, Psychological Abstracts surveys about 950 journals. "Communication Systems" is one of sixteen divisions used to
group the abstracts. The subject index is excellent for
finding citations on specific research subjects such as
TV advertising, newspapers, radio, and magazines.

1171. Public Affairs Information Service (PAIS). New York:
      Public Affairs Information Service, Inc., annual
      cumulations. (1915--.)

      The unique value of this weekly indexing bulletin is
      that it selects material from a variety of published
      sources (in English)--books, periodicals, pamphlets, and
      government documents. The sources cited by PAIS gener-
      ally represent significant statements on the topic.
      Coverage is broadly defined as issues relating to eco-
      nomic and public affairs. Specific topics of interest
      to media scholars include press councils, CATV, TV
      broadcasting, advertising, and press law.

1172. The Readers' Guide to Periodical Literature. New
      York: Wilson, twice monthly with annual cumulations.
      (1901--.)

      An index to general literature in popular periodicals
      ranging in purpose from hobby magazines and weekly news
      magazines to scholarly publications. Journals indexed
      here which frequently carry articles on media topics are
      Atlantic, Commentary, Esquire, Harper's, the Nation, the
      New Yorker, and Publishers Weekly. Readers' Guide has
      recently extended its coverage to include Atlas World
      Press Review and the Center Magazine (Center for Study
      of Democratic Institutions).
      A competing service started in 1978, Magazine Index
      (Los Altos, Cal.), thoroughly indexes more than 370
      periodicals, including all of the 158 titles in Readers'
      Guide. This service is currently available in various
      forms: microfilm with printed supplements and via
      computer through Lockheed's data bases. TV Guide and
      Variety are indexed here.

1173. Resources in Education. Washington: Educational
      Resources Information Center (ERIC), U.S. Department
      of Health, Education, and Welfare, monthly, (1975--.)

      Previous title: Research in Education, 1966-1974.
      An abstract and guide to the reports in the ERIC sys-
      tem, a national program to disseminate papers related to
      education. Selected papers from the annual meeting of
      the Association for Education in Journalism and the pub-
      lications in the Journalism Monographs series are
      included in the system. The time lag is a problem; an
      abstract of a report of a 1976 Association for Education
      in Journalism plenary meeting appears in the November
      1978 issue of the index.

1174. Social Sciences Citation Index: An International Multi-
      disciplinary Index to the Literature of the Social,

Behavioral and Related Sciences. Philadelphia:
Institute for Scientific Information, three issues a
year. (1973--.)

This computer-based index is probably the broadest
in the social sciences in terms of inclusion and also
the most difficult to use, but well worth mastering.
It cites and analyzes thousands of journals, monographs,
and other types of print materials, among which are
letters, corrections, editorials, abstracts of meetings,
footnotes, book reviews, bibliographies, printed discussions of various sorts, and information about individuals,
such as obituaries, biographies, awards and tributes.
The citation of footnotes is particularly helpful. Its
primary use is as a tool for advanced scholars who may,
among other things, use it to track down the history of
a concept; a secondary and less scholarly use is to see
how often an individual is cited in footnotes. Needless
to say, many of its references pertain to communications.

1175. Social Sciences Index. New York: Wilson, quarterly with
      annual cumulations. (1974--.)

For a note on predecessors to this index, see the
entry for Humanities Index. One of five Wilson Company
indexes to periodical literature cited in this bibliography, the Social Sciences Index uses many of the same
subject headings, "Reporters and Reporting," for example,
as the others do. Because this index covers such journals as American Opinion, Public Opinion Quarterly, and
Economist, it is a useful guide to articles about public
opinion and newspaper publishing. It also cites a number of articles about news agencies and media performance
in foreign countries.

1176. Sociological Abstracts. San Diego, Cal.: American
      Sociological Association and other associations.
      (1952--.)

Abstracts articles selected from more than 1,000
international journals. The abstracts are presented
under broad topics, "Mass Phenomena" being the one of
interest to mass communications scholars. Three of the
categories in this section are "Public Opinion," "Communication," and "Mass Culture." The subject index
offers more specific terms, such as mass media, television, and advertising.

1177. Television News Index and Abstracts. Nashville, Tenn.:
      Vanderbilt Television News Archive, monthly with
      annual cumulations of the index only. (1972--.)

An index to a video archive of the TV network national
evening news as broadcast by ABC, CBS, and NBC. The
videotapes of the news programs may be borrowed from the
archive. The abstract of a news story includes the date,
time, and length of broadcast, the network, and the
reporter's name, as well as the specific news items in
the story. A retrospective index and abstract to the
archive's collection, which began in August 1967, has
been issued on microfilm. The archive also includes
tapes of major news events such as presidential speeches
and the Watergate and impeachment hearings.

1178. Topicator. Littleton, Colo.: Thompson Bureau, monthly
    with annual cumulations. (1965--.)

    Subtitled Classified Article Guide to the Advertis-
    ing/Communications/Marketing Periodical Press. Valued
    for its coverage of unique titles such as Media Decisions
    and Television/Radio Age. It also selectively indexes
    TV Guide and Variety. The value of this index to articles
    on advertising and marketing, areas in which recent infor-
    mation is usually desired, is diminished by the time lag
    in publication of more than a year.

1179. The Wall Street Journal. New York: Dow Jones, monthly
    with annual cumulations. (1958--.)

    The index is divided into two sections: "Corporation
    News" and "General News." A brief abstract of the news-
    paper articles is included. Like the New York Times Index,
    this index is as much a source of data, particularly for
    corporate statistics, as it is an index to the newspaper
    articles which frequently concern the media. The index
    has only a two-month lag time.

★ ★ ★ ★ ★

In the field of indexing, two trends are becoming increasingly apparent. One concerns newspapers and television programs;
the other, computer access to the literature.

Newspapers and Television Programs

Indexes to individual newspapers are becoming increasingly
available, either in printed form or as a computerized data base.
Unpublished indexes to individual newspapers in the United
States may be found at the newspaper's own library, at the local
public library, or at the local history archive. The newspaper
indexes cited in this bibliography are those which are available
in most libraries.

    The content of American television is not yet collected
by libraries as completely as libraries keep newspapers and
magazines. The Library of Congress is working on a project
to archive the informational and entertainment programs of
American national and public television networks. The private Museum of Broadcasting in New York City has begun to
selectively archive the entertainment programming of the
major networks. Television news programs have been archived
and indexed since 1968 at the Vanderbilt Television News
Archive and kept on a more limited basis at the National
Archives and Records Service in Washington, D.C., and the
regional archive branches.

Computer Access to the Literature

    A number of printed indexes annotated in the biblio-
graphy are also available via computer in research libraries
which subscribe to these data bases. The availability of
indexes "on line" is increasing as this valuable service is
expanded by commercial vendors. Language and Language
Behavior Abstracts, Psychological Abstracts, Public Affairs
Information Service, and Sociological Abstracts are examples
of indexes available through Lockheed's Dialog service, which
is a commonly purchased one. Bibliographic Retrieval Service,
System Development Corporation, and the New York Times Information Bank are also major vendors of reference data bases.

Subject Index

All references are to entry numbers,
not to page numbers.

ABC. See American Broadcasting Company
Abstract films. See Alternative films
Academy Awards, 890–91, 999–1000
Access to media, 338, 359, 363, 379, 414, 420, 429–30, 453–54,
    464, 482, 508, 539, 563, 566, 604, 613. See also Media
    action groups; Cable TV
Acronyms. See Terminology in communications
Adolescence: film, 970; television, 336, 434–35. See also
    Children
Adventure films, 983
Advertising, 159, 1091, 1093, 1095, 1118, 1121, 1125, 1137–
    39, 1148–49; Advertising Council, 1125–30; advertising
    agencies, 1106, 1125, 1127; agencies, directory, 1142;
    advertising and children, 320, 332 (see also Children,
    television); and consumerism, 1104; associations and
    organizations, 6, 353, 664, 1103, 1108, 1125, 1127; biblio-
    graphies, 1116, 1120, 1131, 1146; codes, 1138, 1145; com-
    mercials, 1089 (see also Advertising and children); Com-
    munist countries, 1109; directories, 21, 1079, 1103, 1121;
    economics, 1088, 1091, 1121, 1125; effects, 1086, 1088,
    1091, 1098, 1120–21, 1135; encyclopedia, 1108; ethics,
    1088 (see also Ethics and the media); expenditures, 195,
    1082, 1125, 1152; glossaries of terms, 1084, 1103, 1108,
    1147; government, 1105; history, 1102, 1132, 1150; history,
    bibliography, 1131; international, 1080, 1111, 1125, 1152;
    international, directory, 1085; law, 1136, 1140; outdoor,
    1103; rates, 1143; regulation, 1092, 1125, 1139, 1145;
    research, 1098, 1121, 1134–35; statistics, 1082, 1103, 1121,
    1144, 1152. See also specific place names, advertising;
    Public relations
Advocacy journalism. See Alternative journalism

Africa: advertising, 1081; book publishing, 226, 241, 249–51,
301; broadcasting, 409, 427, 439; broadcasting, directory,
1096; broadcasting, bibliography, 440; mass media, 52, 84,
104, 196, 202, 209, 213; mass media, bibliography, 84;
news agencies, 726; newspapers, directory, 670. See also
specific place names
Afro-Americans: film, 839–40, 996; film, bibliography, 974,
1053; film, portrayals, 820, 911, 937, 955, 961, 969; mass
media, directory, 17; periodicals, directory, 1053; press,
713, 730, 742, 787; press, directories, 636, 643, 664, 788;
press, history, 647, 657; press, World War II, 674; television, attitudes toward, 387; television, employment, 17
Agents. See Literary agents; Talent agents
Agricultural press, 1047; advertising rates, 1143; directories,
788, 1143
Albania: broadcasting, 524; film, 881, 1016; newspapers,
union list, 775; periodicals, directories, 1063, 1069
Algeria: broadcasting, 462; film, 995
Alternative book publishing, 255, 257, 267, 272; broadcasting,
50; directories, 1046, 1052; films, 841, 847, 851, 893, 898,
912, 981, 1002, 1028; journalism, 50, 678, 702, 734;
journalism, directories, 634, 774; periodicals, 1043, 1051,
1055; periodicals, directories, 1046, 1048–49, 1052, 1067,
1073
Alternative Press Syndicate, 634
American Booksellers Association, 232
American Broadcasting Company, 353, 593
American Film Institute, 857, 1001
American Newspaper Publishers Association: membership roster, 664
Annan Report, 324, 426
Anti-trusts: media industries. See Mass media, ownership;
specific media, ownership
Arab states: film, 992. See also United Arab Republic; spe-
cific place names
Archives: film, 791, 865, 941
Arts and the media, 83, 125; bibliography, 74; cable television, 321
Asia: book publishing, 242, 249, 291, 304–305; broadcasting,
427, 479; mass media, 104, 209; mass media bibliographies,
3, 121; mass media directory, 5; newspapers, 715; newspapers, directories, 664, 670; theses in communications,
2; training for communications, 3, 38
Associations and organizations: advertising, 6, 353, 664, 1103,
1125, 1127; authors, 287, 1077; book publishing, 6, 238,
252, 287; broadcasting, 6, 287, 353, 378, 407, 593; film,
6, 287, 865, 952; journalism, 6, 640, 664, 737; mass media,
6, 737; public relations, 6, 737; television (see Associations

and organizations, broadcasting). See also Professionalism in the media
Audience research. See Advertising research; Broadcasting,
research and rating services; Communication research
Australia: bookstores, 297; book trade, directory, 297;
broadcasting, 409, 427, 489; broadcasting, directory, 331;
newspapers, 725; newspapers, directory, 664; newspapers
(New South Wales), history, 776; popular culture, 8; television, 327
Austria: advertising, 1115, 1119; broadcasting, 409; film,
834; mass media, 176; mass media, bibliography, 189; press,
directory, 785
Authoritarian theory of the press, 188
Authors: directory, 1044
Authorship, 125, 217, 235, 238, 240, 287, 1038; directories
of marketplace, 1045, 1077; awards, 287, 1077
Avant garde film. See Alternative film
Awards: book publishing, 287; broadcasting, 70, 353, 449;
film, 70, 865, 890-91, 952, 1000; journalism, 70, 664,
737; literary, 70, 287, 1077; mass media, 70

Bahamas: press directory, 636
Bahrain: press directory, 785
BBC. See British Broadcasting Corporation
Belgium: access to media, 338; advertising, 1115; broadcast-
ing, 409; mass media, 19, 338; press directory, 336
Bestsellers, 278-79, 292
Biographies: broadcasting, 64, 449, 741, 822; communication,
42; communication, women, 64; film, 822, 826, 828-29, 843,
862, 866, 889, 891, 938, 993, 1008, 1021, 1023, 1034-35,
1038; film directors, 843, 963-64, 1007; (see also Filmographies); journalism, 42, 64, 631, 741, 780, 1044
Black media. See Africa; Afro-American
Book clubs, 195, 287. See also Book publishing
Book columnists and commentators, 287
Book publishers: firms, classified geographically, 287; classified by subject matter and type, 287; personnel, partial
listing, 287
Book publishing, 195, 234-35, 238, 252-53, 259, 261, 263, 269,
276-77, 313-15, 317; advertising and promotion, 238, 254,
287; associations and organizations, 6, 238, 252, 287;
awards, 287; children's book publishing, 267; cooperative,
255; courses (see Training for book publishing); developing
countries, 237-38, 280, 307-308; directories, 229-30, 246,
287; economics, 195, 254, 259, 261, 264, 316; employment,
195, 225; glossary of terms, 248, 311; government's role,
238, 287; history, 285-86, 288-89, 293-94, 299, 306, 310,
655; ownership of firms, 195, 238, 252, 287, 316; paperback, 309; research, need for, 264; reprint, 295; training

355

for, 225, 287, 305; wholesalers, directories, 229, 287.
See also Alternative book publishing; Authors; Authorship;
Fiction; International communications, book trade; Litera-
ture and media; Private presses; Scholarly book publishing;
University presses
Book readers: characteristics, statistics, 195
Book reviews and reviewers, 125, 235, 287
Books and printing: encyclopedia, 273; history, 260, 262,
270, 288-89, 310, 314, 665. See also Book publishing,
history
Bookselling, 125, 232, 235, 290
Books made into films: listing, 848
Bookstores: chains, 229; directory, 229; statistics, 195
Braille book publishers, 287
Brazil: broadcasting, 462; film, 833; mass media, 39
Britain: access to media, 338; advertising, 1082, 1092, 1097,
1099, 1102, 1115, 1143, 1149; alternative press, 1051; book
publishing, 233, 239, 284, 293, 299, 313; book publishing,
directories, 229, 256, 265; book stores, directory, 229;
broadcast journalism, 575, 650; broadcasting, 345, 393-94,
409, 415-16, 425-26, 522-23, 573-74, 590; broadcasting,
bibliographies, 347-48; editorial journalism, 641, 653-54,
680-88, 692, 763, 770; ·editorial journalism, directories,
640, 664, 1079; film, 795, 808, 817, 834, 846, 867, 900,
925, 932, 962, 972, 1012, 1032; film, directory, 822;
libraries and book trade, 233; mass media, 61, 79, 159, 187,
202; mass media, directory, 1143; mass media, research, 44;
newspapers (see Editorial journalism); periodicals, 1051,
1067; periodicals, bibliography, 19th century, 1056; popular
culture, 93; radio, 334, 519, 590; television, 545, 568-69,
589, 590; television, directory, 822
British Broadcasting Corporation, 335, 340, 431 (see also
Britain, broadcasting)
Broadcasting, 349-50, 353, 409, 440, 588; allocations, 377,
457, 518, 593, 595; associations and organizations, 6, 287,
353, 378, 407, 593; audiences and audience characteristics
(see Radio, audiences and audience characteristics; Television, audiences and audience characteristics); awards,
70, 353, 449; bibliographies, 325, 347-48, 353, 378, 385,
411, 483, 487, 533, 546, 567, 585, 592; biographies (see
Biographies, broadcasting); congressional hearings, bibliography, 385; criticism (see Criticism of media, broadcasting); dictionary, 407; directories, 353, 606, 626-27; documents, 399, 457, 459, 573; economics, 178, 329, 356, 480,
513, 515, 527-28, 557, 559, 757; effects (see Mass media,
effects; Radio, effects; Television, effects); employment,
statistics, 195, 204; glossaries of terms, 363, 407, 1103;
government, relationship with, 385, 408, 419, 465, 604,
609 (see also Broadcasting, regulation); history, 333, 345,

396, 399, 402, 428, 436, 443, 567, 586, 615; ownership, 174, 195, 353, 375, 450, 480, 528, 593, 595 (see also Broadcasting, regulation; Mass media, ownership); periodicals, list, 593 (see also Mass media, periodicals, lists); programs and programming (see Access to media; Cable TV, programs and programming; Radio, programs and programming; Television, programs and programming); ratings, 355, 1103; regulation, 174, 339, 346, 351, 353, 359, 381, 408, 410, 421, 450, 455, 457, 459, 469, 480, 504, 513, 550, 559, 620 (see also Press law); research and rating services, 353, 593; statistics, 195, 353, 593, 601. See also Cable TV; Radio; Television

Broadcast journalism, 195, 353, 394, 575, 625, 629–30, 664, 667, 675, 762; broadcast journalism, statistics, 195

Bulgaria: film, 881, 918, 1016; mass media, 139; newspapers, union list, 775; periodical directories, 1063, 1069

Cable TV, 350, 360, 373, 378, 421, 446, 471–72, 497, 550, 561–62, 576, 600; arts, 6, 321; associations and organizations (see Broadcasting, associations and organizations); bibliographies, 378, 420; community services (see Access to media); directories, 351, 377, 593; economics, 329, 363, 561; financial data, 351; franchise, 361–62, 550; municipal control, 362–63, 414, 452; ownership, 528 (see also Municipal control); pay TV, 351, 377, 504, 572; programs and programming, 508; regulation, 339, 346, 351, 359, 377–78, 550, 561; statistics, 195, 377. See also Europe, cable TV

Cambodia: periodicals directory, 1063

Canada: access to media, 338, 366, 420; advertising, 1083, 1105, 1115, 1143; alternative press, 1073; book publishing, 268; book publishing, directories, 229, 247, 278; broadcasting, 322, 364–66, 369–70, 373, 409, 427, 525–26, 603, 617; broadcasting, directories, 353, 368; cable TV, 421; cable TV, directory, 351; children and television, 581; film, 834–44; film, directories, 814, 853, 987; journalism, history, 708; mass media, 11, 29, 92, 151, 154, 190; mass media, bibliography, 30; mass media, directory, 1143; National Film Board, 987; newspapers, directories, 636, 664, 788; pay TV, 391; periodicals, directory, 636; periodicals, union list, 1068; portrayal of Canada in U.S. films, 816; press law, 628; satellites, 400; telecommunications, 329, 410, 447; television, directory, 593; training for film, 872; violence and media, 28, 372

Caribbean: mass media, 123; newspapers, directory, 664

Carnegie Commission reports on public broadcasting, 540–41

Catholic press, 722; directory, 649; history, 751

CBS. See Columbia Broadcasting System

Chicanos: access to media, 482; press, 730

357

Children: advertising, 21, 332, 1122, 1135; book publishing, 267; film, 970; handicapped children, 437; mass media, 159; media directory, 21; television, 320, 332, 381, 387, 401, 434, 437, 444–45, 464, 485, 503, 512, 535, 556, 560, 581, 583, 591–92, 624, 1122, 1135; television, bibliography, 592
China: book publishing, 296; broadcasting, 409; film industry, 916, 923; mass media, 35, 59, 126, 209; periodicals, directory, 1063; press, 718
Citizen participation in broadcasting. See Access to media; Criticism of media
Clipping bureaus, 664
Codes of ethics, 137, 353, 370, 378, 394, 409, 449, 459, 502, 547–48, 620, 647, 769, 780, 888, 891, 897, 1013, 1044, 1081, 1092, 1099, 1135, 1139, 1145, 1149
Colombia: mass media, 39
Columbia Broadcasting System, 353
Commercials. See Advertising, commercials
Communication, 14, 34, 40, 80, 101–104, 109, 111, 116, 125, 129–30, 133, 159, 162, 182; bibliography, 36; biography, 42, 64; concepts, taxonomy of, 18, 23; directory, 6; films about, 6; history, 101–103, 116, 665; research, 40, 43, 46, 75, 86, 114, 159, 162; research, bibliography, 44–45, 87; research, organizations, centers, etc., 6; theory, 34, 48, 55, 75, 88, 101–103, 109, 120, 127, 129–33, 182–83, 188, 219. See also International communications; Mass media
Communism and media, 43, 75, 139, 159, 202, 644, 669, 691, 706. See also Marxism and media; Socialism and media
Communist countries: advertising, 1109; broadcasting, 524; broadcast journalism, 644; education and media, 90; film, 881, 918, 1016; periodicals, directories, 1063, 1069; press in U.S., 1043; public opinion, 41. See also specific countries
Community broadcasting. See Access to media; Criticism of media
Community press: advertising rates, 1143; directory, 1143. See also Weekly newspapers
Concentration of media control. See Mass media, ownership; specific media, ownership
Consumer Electronics Industry: membership roster, 388
Contests. See Awards
Cooperative book publishing, 225, 1055
Corporation for Public Broadcasting, 353, 502, 593. See also Public broadcasting; Public television
Corporations: partial listing of those with advertising/ public relations operations, 1128, 1141
Costa Rica: mass media, 39
Credits. See Film, credits; Radio, credits; Television, credits

Crime and the media. See Violence and the media; Violence and
    television
Criticism of media: broadcasting, 379, 415, 504, 566, 574,
    577; film, 854-55, 899, 944, 958; mass media, 6, 50, 178-
    80, 191-92, 197, 464, 474-75; newspapers, 638, 654, 693
    (see also Press councils); periodicals, 693; radio, 474-75;
    television, 357, 428, 454, 499, 568-69, 571
Cuba: film, 834; mass media, 139; periodicals, directory, 1063
Cultural imperialism. See Media imperialism
Cypress: advertising, 1119; broadcasting, 462
Czechoslovakia: broadcasting, 524; film, 881, 918, 1004, 1016;
    mass media, 139; newspapers, union list, 775; periodicals,
    directory, 785; public opinion, 41

Daytime serials, 395, 405, 436, 579, 1014. See also Radio
    programs, listings; Television programs, listings
Delinquency and television, 435
Denmark: access to media, 338; advertising, 1115; broadcast-
    ing, 409; mass media, 308; press directory, 785
Detective films, 1026
Developing countries: book publishing, 237-38, 280, 307-308;
    broadcasting, 389, 431, 462, 495; mass media, 20, 43, 75,
    104, 145, 151, 158-59, 163-64, 167, 180, 202; press, 752,
    764, 768. See also Media imperialism; specific place names
Direct mail lists: directory, 1143
Directors. See Film directors
Directors Guild of America: membership roster, 843
Dissertations. See Theses and dissertations
Documentary film, 809, 811, 892, 904, 990, 1017
Drugs and media, 218

East Germany. See Germany (Democratic Republic)
Economic reporting, 710-11
Editorial journalism. See Alternative journalism; Broadcast
    journalism; Journalism; News; Newspapers; Periodicals;
    Press councils
Educational broadcasting: history, 443
Educational television, 424, 513
Education for mass media and specific media. See Training for
    mass media
Effects. See Mass media, effects; specific media, effects
Egypt: radio, 343
Employee publications, 664; directory, 1076
Estonia: newspapers, union list, 775; periodicals, direc-
    tory, 1069
Ethics and the media, 98-99, 147-48, 165, 181, 646, 796, 1088.
    See also Codes of ethics; Press councils
Ethnic press, 789. See also specific ethnic groups

359

Europe: book trade, directory, 247; broadcasting, 427; cable TV, 605; film, 932-33, 977; mass media, 151; newspapers, directories, 664, 670; press, history, 739; television, 977; trade and technical publications, directory, 1085
European Broadcasting Union, 344; membership roster, 409, 593
Experimental film: history, 841, 893, 934. See also Alternative film

Facsimile, 391
Farm press. See Agricultural press
Federal Communications Commission, 381; directory, 353. See also Broadcasting, regulation
Fiction, 43, 217, 313, 319
Film, 779, 804, 817, 819, 831, 870, 914, 922, 928, 940, 944, 950-51, 989, 991, 997-98, 1003, 1022, 1037, 1039; advertising, 952; aesthetics, 830, 859-60, 882-83, 903, 908, 922; archives, 791, 865, 941; associations and organizations, 6, 287, 865, 952; audience, 195, 897, 1003; awards, 70, 865, 890-91, 952, 1000; bibliographies, 861, 865, 945-46, 980; biographies (see Biographies, film); career guide, 924; color, 1020; congressional committee hearings, bibliography, 385; credits, 793-94, 797-98, 823, 891, 1015, 1034-35, 1038; criticism (see Criticism of media, film); directories, 822, 890-91, 952; directors, 843, 963-64, 997, 1007; documentary (see Documentary film); drive-ins, 891; economics, 833, 885, 893, 896, 900, 902, 927, 940, 944, 962, 1012; educational uses, 977, 1031; employment, 815, 924; encyclopedias, 812, 873-74, 889; experimental, 841; festivals, 70, 891, 952; finances, 195; history, 795, 805, 807-808, 817, 821, 825, 830, 834-35, 846, 849, 859, 868, 870, 875, 878-80, 889, 893-94, 896, 898, 903, 907, 915, 917, 925, 928-29, 935, 939, 962, 972, 975-76, 979, 982, 985-86, 991, 1003, 1005-1007, 1011, 1013, 1039; international (see International communications, film); libraries, 952; music, 890, 921, 935; ownership, 195, 833, 940; posters, 905, 1123; regulation, 888, 950; remakes, 845, 920; reruns on TV, 790, 802-803, 954, 959; reviews, 854, 859, 899, 944, 958; scripts, 533, 1038; serials, 806, 877, 909, 1014, 1036; shorts, 904, 910; star system, 869, 949; study resources, 791, 865, 941; title changes, 920, 1083; training (see Training for film). See also Alternative film; Documentary film; Genre film; Hollywood; Star system
Filmographies, 793-94, 796-98, 802-803, 814, 818, 823, 826, 837, 845-46, 855, 863, 873-74, 890-91, 919, 954, 957, 965-68, 973, 994, 997
Films made from books and plays: listing, 848
Financial reporting, 710-11
Finland: advertising, 1115, 1119; broadcasting, 409; film, 836, 884; newspapers, 767; press, directory, 785

Foreign correspondents from U.S., 741
Foreign correspondents in U.S.: listing, 664
Foreign-language newspapers in U.S.: listing, 664, 788
Foreign news coverage by U.S. and foreign newspapers: statistics, 195
Foundations: concerned with book publishing, 287; foundations, bibliography, 74; role in public broadcasting,
611
France: access to media, 338; advertising, 1115, 1119;
advertising media and rates, 1143; broadcasting, 392,
409, 574, 599; film, 796, 834, 932, 934, 939, 947; mass
media, 12, 56, 202; media directory, 1143; press directory, 785
Fraternal publications: directory, 363
Free-lance: editorial services, 387; marketplace, directory,
1045, 1077; writers, directory, 1044, 1047

Gallup poll, 71
Gangster films, 813, 965, 988
Genre film. See Adventure film; Afro-Americans, film;
Detective film; Gangster film; Monster film; Musicals;
Science fiction film; Shorts; Serials; Spy film; War
films; Western films
German-English dictionary of book publishing, 311
German-language press: of the Americas, directory, 635;
U.S.A., 786
German press and book trade in exile, 358
Germany: access to media, 338; advertising, 1115, 1119;
advertising media and rates, 1143; broadcasting, 409,
589; broadcast journalism, 575; film, 826, 834, 886, 907,
913, 934-35, 947; mass media, 202, 338; mass media, direc-
tory, 1143; press during Third Reich, 690. See also Germany (Democratic Republic); Germany (Federal Republic)
Germany (Democratic Republic): broadcasting, 524; film, 881,
918; mass media, 139, 176; periodicals, directory, 1063
Germany (Federal Republic): broadcasting, 622; mass media,
39, 57, 91, 176; press directory, 785
Gibralter: press directory, 785
Glossaries. See Terminology in communications; specific
media, glossaries
Government: advertising by, 1105; agencies connected with
book publishing, 238, 287; agencies connected with broadcasting, 353; agencies connected with cable TV, 378;
agencies connected with mass media, 6; broadcasting, role
in, 385, 408, 419, 465, 604, 609 (see also Broadcasting,
regulation); films produced for public relations and propaganda, 926; media activities abroad, 195; news reporting
of government, 721
Grants and media: bibliography, 74. See also Awards

361

Group ownership of media. See Mass media, ownership; specific
   media, ownership
Guatamala: journalism, 666
Guyana: broadcasting, 373

Handicapped children and television programming, 437
High school journalism, 651
Hollywood, 799, 850, 882-83, 927, 989
Hong Kong: mass media, bibliography, 3
House organs. See Employee publications
Humanities and cable TV, 321
Hungary: advertising, 1109; broadcasting, 409, 524; film,
   881, 1016; mass media, 39, 1039; periodicals, directories,
   1063, 1069; press, directory, 785; public opinion, 41

Iceland: broadcasting, 409; press directory, 785
ILPA. See International Labor Press Association
India: advertising directories, 744, 1113-14; book publish-
   ing, 227; broadcasting, 328, 409, 505; film, 810, 833;
   mass media, 33, 39, 202, 759; mass media, bibliography, 3;
   news agencies, 744; press, 642, 733, 746, 750; press,
   directories, 744, 1113-14; statistics, 746; training for
   journalism, 744
Indians: North American, 1, 730, 1041
Indonesia: broadcasting, 462; mass media, bibliography, 3;
   press, 738
Intelsat. See Satellites; Telecommunications
International Book Year, 231
International communications: advertising, 1080, 1152; book
   trade, 236, 238, 287; book trade, directories, 247, 282,
   300; broadcasting, 380, 389, 409, 451; broadcasting, bibliography, 484; film, 821, 890, 895, 903, 991; journalism, 212,
   656, 658, 727-28, 732, 783-84; law, 134, 151; mass media,
   63, 75, 111, 151, 158, 161, 164, 180, 209, 212, 409, 472,
   783, 784; mass media, bibliography, 119; mass media, directory, 221; news coverage, bibliography, 732; press systems,
   727; propaganda, 195, 431; public relations, 1111; telecommunications, 507, 607; telecommunications, bibliography,
   411. See also International communications, broadcasting;
   International communications, mass media; Telecommunications
International Council for Educational Media, 832
International Labor Press Association: directory, 699
International Newsreel Association, 832
International Organization of Journalists, 669
International Scientific Film Association, 832
I.O.J. See International Organization of Journalists
Iran: broadcasting, 462
Ireland: advertising, 1115, 1119; bookstores, directory, 229;
   broadcasting, 373, 409; mass media, 39, 271; press, direc-
   tories, 664, 785

Israel: mass media, 151
Italy: access to media, 338; advertising, 1115, 1119; adver-
    tising media and rates, 1143; anti-Fascist press, 755;
    broadcasting, 409; broadcast journalism, 575; film, 834,
    915, 932; mass media, 338

Japan: advertising, 1117; broadcasting, 373, 406, 409, 413,
    574, 613; educational television, 397; film, 833, 942-43,
    984, 1019, 1024; mass media, 39, 58, 108, 202; press, 710;
    press, directory, 636
Jewish press, 722; publications, directory, 636
Joint ownership of media. See Mass media, ownership; specific
    media, ownership
Journalism, 716, 720, 782-84; associations and organizations,
    6, 640, 664, 737; awards, 70, 664, 737; bibliographies,
    645, 747, 748; biographies (see Biographies, journalism);
    criticism review journals, 6, 50; glossary, 707; history,
    641, 653, 655, 666, 672, 692, 712, 714, 723, 729, 739, 758,
    760-61, 771; international (see International communications,
    journalism); muckraking, 672; libraries, 779; libraries,
    directories, 6, 659; quotations, 749, 765; resources, 6;
    training (see Training for mass media, journalism; scholar-
    ship). See also Alternative journalism; Broadcast journal-
    ism; News; Newspapers; Press councils; Periodicals

Korea: mass media, 39; mass media, bibliography, 3; period-
    icals, directory, 1063
Kuwait: press directory, 785

Labor groups, 353, 468, 593, 652, 952, 955; directory, 699;
    publications, directory, 788. See also Mass media, employ-
    ment
Laos: periodicals, directory, 1063
Latin America: book trade, directory, 247; broadcasting, 427,
    618; German-language press, 635; mass media, 144, 151, 175,
    202; newspapers, directories, 664, 670
Latvia: newspapers, union list, 775; periodicals, direc-
    tory, 1069
Law. See Advertising, regulation; Broadcasting, regulation;
    Press law; Public relations, law
Lending libraries. See Libraries, lending
Libertarian theory of the press, 25, 188
Libraries: and cable TV, 323, 508; and book trade, 233, 235,
    252; communications, listing, 6; news information, 779;
    news information, directory, 659; rental, 229
Literacy, 55, 93, 125, 446. See also Reading
Literary agents, 281, 287, 449, 891, 952, 1077. See also
    Talent agents
Literary awards, 70, 287, 1077

Literature and media, 125, 216-17, 269, 319
Lithuania: newspapers, union list, 775; periodicals, direc-
   tory, 1069
Little magazines, 1043, 1055; directories, 1046, 1052
Luxembourg: broadcasting, 409; press, directory, 785

Macao: mass media, bibliography, 3
Mailing list brokers, 287, 1143
Malaysia: broadcasting, 373; mass media, 77; mass media,
   bibliography, 3
Marxism and media, 43, 215; bibliography, 136. See also
   Communism and media; Communist countries; Socialism and
   media
Mass media, 7, 10, 14, 25, 31-32, 34, 37, 43, 47, 49, 51, 53,
   55, 62, 68, 79-80, 97, 99, 104, 125, 127-28, 148, 155, 159,
   177, 181, 186, 192-93, 198, 202, 209-11, 215, 222; associations and organizations, 6, 737 (see also Associations and
   organizations); audiences and audience characteristics, 7,
   14, 25, 125, 128, 148, 155, 157, 159, 181, 183, 185, 222,
   1103, 1121 (see also Radio, audiences and audience characteristics; Television, audience and audience characteristics); awards, 70; content, 14, 51, 62, 181, 183, 193,
   210-11, 215, 218, 222 (see also Media imperialism; Popular
   culture; Violence and the media; Violence and TV); criticism (see Criticism of media); directory (by country), 221;
   economics, 29, 51, 140, 145, 173, 178, 186, 193; economics,
   bibliographies, 153, 155, 206; economics, statistics, 195,
   204; effects, 14, 32, 43, 47, 62, 109, 113, 115, 133, 137,
   157, 159, 181-83, 186-87, 208, 211, 222, 432 (see also
   Advertising, effects; Radio, effects; Television, effects);
   effects, bibliography, 82; employment, statistics, 195,
   204; history, 81, 101-103, 116, 216-17; ownership, 9, 22,
   43, 54, 125, 174, 178; periodicals, listing, 6, 25, 217;
   regulation, 22, 37, 54, 65-67, 76, 134, 142, 149-50, 156,
   174, 223 (see also Advertising, regulation; Broadcasting,
   regulation; Press law; Public relations, law); regulation,
   bibliography, 206; research (see Communications, research);
   training (see Training for mass media); theory (see Communication, theory)
Media action groups: listing, 6. See also Access to media;
   Cable TV; Criticism of media
Media imperialism, 43, 104, 158, 162, 179-80, 389, 462, 514,
   596, 612, 618, 786
Mergers. See Book publishing, mergers; Mass media, ownership;
   specific media, ownership
Mexico: advertising media and rates, 1143; broadcasting, 409,
   427; broadcasting, directory, 627; trade, directory, 247
Middle East, 202; newspapers, directory, 664. See also Arab
   states; Israel; United Arab Republic

Minority presses in U.S., 789
Mongolia, 139; periodicals, directory, 1063
Monopoly in the media. See Mass media, ownership; specific
    media, ownership; Mass media, regulation; specific media,
    regulation
Monster films, 864
Motion pictures. See Film
Muckraking. See Journalism, muckraking
Musicals, 1029
Mutual Broadcasting System, 353, 593

Napal: mass media, bibliography, 3
National Association of Broadcasters, 353, 593
National Association of Educational Broadcasters: his-
    tory, 443
National Broadcasting Company, 353, 593
National Cable Television Association, 351, 377
National Film Board, 987. See also Canada, film
National News Council: report, 700. See also Press councils
National Public Radio, 353
Nazi: films (see Germany, film); press (see Germany, press
    during Third Reich)
NBC. See National Broadcasting Company
Netherlands: access to media, 338; advertising, 1115, 1119;
    broadcasting, 373, 409, 575; broadcast journalism, 575;
    mass media, 338; press, directory, 785
New Guinea: broadcasting, 492
"New" journalism, 50, 702
News: agencies, 104, 212, 221, 593, 664, 691, 716, 726, 735,
    756; bibliography, 693; content, 195, 629–30, 667, 675,
    688; councils (see Press councils); coverage, 212, 630,
    667, 675, 716, 758, 784; coverage, bibliography, 732;
    coverage of U.S. and foreign media, statistics, 195; dir-
    ectory, 353, 777; sources and contacts, 737
Newspapers, 652, 654, 698, 704, 728, 754, 782–83; advertising,
    652, 1103, 1143; audience characteristics (see Newspapers,
    readership characteristics); book review coverage, 287;
    chains (see Newspapers, ownership); circulation, 195, 636,
    652, 664, 1094, 1103, 1143, 1151; content (see News, con-
    tent); coverage (see News, coverage); directories, 636,
    640, 656, 664, 788, 1143 (see also College press); econom-
    ics, 652, 654, 757, 773; editors, classified by subjects
    or departments, 788; employment, 652, 703; employment,
    statistics, 195, 204; English-language newspapers in non-
    English-speaking countries, directory, 781; films about
    newspapers, 664, 673; finances, 195, 652, 1103; history
    (see Journalism, history); libraries (see Libraries);
    ownership, 195, 652, 664, 679, 704, 757; readership

characteristics, 195, 1094, 1103, 1121; regulation (see
Mass media, regulation; Press law); supplements, 788,
1103, 1121; training (see Training for media, journalism);
union lists, 632, 645. See also Journalism
Newsprint, 639, 652, 736
Newsreels, 671, 801; directory of companies, 788
New Zealand: book trade, directory, 247; broadcasting, 490,
511; newspapers, directory, 664; television, 456
Nigeria: book publishing, 302; broadcasting, 462, 491
Norway: advertising, 1115; broadcasting, 409; press, direc-
tory, 785
Novels. See Fiction
Novels made into films, 797-98, 848
NPR. See National Public Radio

Offshore radio, 438
Oman: press, directory, 785
Organizations in the media. See Associations and organiza-
tions
Overseas Press Club: membership roster and history, 741

Pacific Ocean territories: newspapers, directory, 664
Pakistan: book publishing, directory, 256; mass media, bibliography, 3
Panama: press, directory, 636
Paperbound books, 309. See also Book publishing
Pay TV, 351, 377, 503, 574
Periodicals, 1058, 1071, 1103; advertising, 1103, 1121; advertising rates, 1143; agricultural, 1047; agricultural,
directories, 636, 1076, 1143; associations and organizations,
6; audience and audience characteristics, 195, 1103, 1121;
bibliography, 1062; book review coverage, 287, 1087; circulation (see Periodicals, directories); classified by subject
and type, 287, 636, 1045, 1058, 1076-77, 1103; consumer
magazines, 1103, 1143; criticism of periodical press, bibliography, 693; directories, 636, 640, 1045, 1064, 1066,
1087, 1103; employment, 195, 204; finances, 195, 1103; glossary of advertising terms, 1103; history, 1058, 1061, 1065;
ownership, 195; statistics, 195, 204, 1103, 1121; union list,
1068; women's magazines, 1070
Peru: broadcasting, 462; mass media, 39
Personnel of media. See specific media, directories
Philippines: mass media, 122; mass media, bibliography, 3;
newspapers, directory, 636; periodicals, directory, 636
Pilkington Report, 425
Pirate radio stations, 438
Plays made into film: listing, 848
Poland: advertising, 1109, 1115; film, 881, 918, 932, 1016;
mass media, 139; periodicals, directories, 1063, 1069; press,
directory, 785; public opinion, 41

Politics and media, 96, 115, 120, 159, 168, 172, 178, 521, 575
Popular culture, 16, 24, 43, 73, 83, 85, 89, 93, 105, 125, 146,
    152, 169–70, 184–85, 211, 216–17, 228, 279, 292, 404, 509–
    10, 944
Portugal: press directory, 785
Precision journalism, 50
Press clubs, 738
Press councils, 637–38, 646, 700, 745, 750, 753
Press law, 65–67, 76, 134, 149–50, 156, 171; college publica-
    tions, 199, 223; courses offered, 6; dictionaries, 149, 407
Printing. See Books and printing; Private presses
Private presses, 257; directory, 266
Professionalism in the media, 43, 654, 703
Propaganda: bibliographies, 117–19, 159; radio, 431. See
    also Public opinion
Protestant press, 722
Public broadcasting, 353, 376, 419, 495, 502, 540–41, 611;
    Public Broadcasting Act of 1967, text, 457, 459, 495;
    finances, 195. See also National Public Radio; Public
    television
Public opinion, 14, 41, 71, 96, 124; bibliographies, 117–19,
    208. See also specific place names
Public relations, 1111, 1126; associations and organizations,
    6, 737; bibliographies, 1090, 1100; corporations with
    advertising/public relations programs, directory, 1128;
    firms, directory, 1129 (see also Advertising agencies);
    information sources, directories, 697, 737, 1127; law,
    1140; training, 1101. See also Publicity, directories
Public service advertising on television, 1130
Public television, 540–42; audience and audience character-
    istics, 556–57; economics, 534, 556; programs and program-
    ming, 195, 463; stations, 195. See also Educational
    television; Public broadcasting
Publicity directories, 636, 670, 788, 1074–75, 1079, 1085–87,
    1129, 1151
Publishers' Association (Britain), 284
Puerto Rico: press, directory, 636
Pulitzer Prize, 94. See also Awards
Pulp magazines, 1050

Qatar: press directory, 785
Quotations about journalism, 749, 765

Radical press, 1043; bibliography, 1060; directory, 1049
Radio, 476–78, 554, 570, 578, 615, 620; advertising rates,
    1143; advertising statistics, 1103; all-news stations,
    737; allocations, 353, 481; announcers, 532; audiences
    and audience characteristics, 195, 474–75, 1103, 1121;
    bibliographies, 487, 546, 582; book programs, 287;

campus-limited stations, 383; characters in radio dramas,
436, 564; credits, 564; developing countries, use in, 159;
directories, 353, 606, 626–27, 737, 1103, 1143; documents,
457, 459; effects, 474–75, 570; finances, 195, 1121; glossary, 1103; history, 396, 402, 426, 470, 484, 493, 615,
620; pirate stations, 438; programs and programming, 195,
358, 402, 436, 470, 474–75, 506, 619; programs available
for station use, 536; programs classified by subject and
type, 353; programs, listings, 358, 402, 549, 587; propaganda, 431; reading, relation to, 473; regulations, 481
(see also Broadcasting, regulation); scripts, 530, 533,
537; shows, 402, 470 (see also Radio characters; Radio
history); stations, 195, 1103; statistics, 195, 388, 1103,
1121, 1144. See also Broadcasting; Telecommunications
Radio Free Europe/Radio Liberty, 195, 353, 431
Rape: influenced by media, 218. See also Violence and media;
Violence and television
Ratings, television programs, 355, 562, 1103
Reading, 125, 195, 217, 228, 473. See also Literacy
Regulation. See Advertising regulation; Broadcasting regula-
tion; Federal Communication Commission; Mass media, regu-
lation; Press law; Public relations law
Religion and communication: history, 116, 125
Religious press, 722; directory, 1040; publications, 636,
788, 1103
Remakes. See Film, remakes
Rental films, 919; libraries, 229
Reprint publishing: scholarly, 295. See also Book publishing
Research. See Communication research
Research and rating services: broadcasting, 353, 593
Reviews. See Book reviews; Criticism of media, film; News-
papers, book review coverage; Periodicals, book review
coverage; Radio, book programs; Television, book programs
"Rightest" press: bibliography, 1060; directory, 1048
Romania: book publishing, 244; broadcasting, 524; film, 881,
918, 1016; mass media, 139; periodicals, directory, 1069;
press, directory, 785

Satellites, 145, 151, 158, 352–53, 377, 382, 390, 400, 465,
471–72, 488, 497–98, 501, 506, 527, 531, 544, 567, 579,
616; bibliography, 325
Saudi Arabia: press directory, 785
Scandinavia: film, 834, 876; mass media research, biblio-
graphy, 15
Scholarly book publishing, 295, 298. See also Book publish-
ing; University presses
Scholarship: journalism, 705
Science: presentation by media, 107
Science fiction: film, 417; filmography, 966; television, 417

Scientific press: history, 1054
Scripts: radio, television, film, listing, 533
Senegal: broadcasting, 462
Serials. See Daytime serials; Film, serials
Sex stereotyping in media, 69, 623, 1107
Short films, 904, 910
Silent films. See Film, history
Singapore: broadcasting, 462; mass media, 78; mass media,
   bibliography, 3
Sloan Commission on Cable Communication, 572
Soap operas. See Daytime serials
Socialism and media, 41, 75, 139, 215. See also Communism
   and media; Communist countries; Marxism and media; specific
   place names
Socialist press in U.S., 1043
Social responsibility theory of the press, 25, 68, 188
Society of Authors (Britain), 240
Sociology of media, 88, 125, 131-33, 203, 219, 222, 720,
   895, 1025
South Africa: book publishing, directory, 256; journalism,
   694, 743; newspapers, directory, 655
Spain: advertising, 1115, 1119; broadcasting, 409; film, 833;
   press, directory, 785; press, history, 761
Sponsored film, 901
Spy film: filmography, 967
Sri Lanka: mass media, 39; mass media, bibliography, 3
Star system: film, 869, 949, 1033. See also Hollywood
Statistics. See Mass media, statistics; specific media,
   statistics
Stereotyping in the media. See Sex stereotyping; Women in
   media, portrayal; specific groups
Student journalism. See College student press; High school
   journalism
Subsidized film, 901
Sweden: advertising, 1115; broadcasting, 373, 409; broad-
   cast journalism, 575; film, 838, 1018; mass media, 39;
   press, 689; press, directory, 785
Syndicated columnists, 788; services, 622, 1074

Taiwan: advertising, 1117; mass media, bibliography, 3;
   television, directory, 597
Talent agents, 353, 449, 891, 952, 1077. See also Literary
   agents
Talkies made from silent films: filmographies, 797-98
Tanzania: broadcasting, 462
Taxonomy of communication concepts, 18, 23
Telecommunications, 120, 220, 329, 352, 356, 386, 390, 410,
   447, 450, 455, 497, 501, 507, 552, 607, 609; bibliography,
   567; congressional committee hearings, bibliography, 385;

dictionary, 407; documents, 399; films about, available
for showing, 448. See also Broadcasting, history; Broadcasting, regulation; Cable TV; Radio; Satellites
Television, 374-75, 460, 499, 562, 564, 570, 578, 622;
advertising (see Advertising, television); allocations,
353, 518, 593; associations and organizations (see Broadcasting, associations and organizations); audience and
audience characteristics, 195, 341-42, 387, 423, 539, 543,
584, 592, 1103, 1121; bibliography, 487, 546; biographies
(see Biographies, television); book programs, 287; children, influenced by (see Children and television); commercials (see Advertising, commercials); credits, 516-17, 564;
delinquency and television, 218; directories, 353, 449,
593, 606, 626-27, 1103, 1121, 1143; documents, 457, 459;
economics, 356, 513, 515 (see also Broadcasting, economics);
educational uses, 977; effects, 341, 387, 428, 432-33, 444,
485, 521, 529, 543, 570, 583 (see also Advertising, effects);
encyclopedia, 355; films, interrelationship, 799; finances,
195, 601; glossaries, 407, 1103; history, 428, 484 (see also
Broadcasting, history); literacy, use to encourage, 496;
news (see Broadcast journalism); ownership of stations, 195,
353, 449, 593, 595, 679, 757; political influence (see
Politics and media); programs and programming, 321, 337,
349, 357, 418, 428, 463, 499, 500, 504, 508-509, 514-15,
555, 558-59, 612, 625; programs and programming, children,
320, 332, 418, 437, 445, 464, 581, 624; programs available
for station use, 537; programs, listings, 354, 422, 449,
594, 598, 602; ratings, 355, 1103; regulation (see Mass
media, regulation; Broadcasting, regulation); scripts, 533,
537, 941; statistics, 195, 388, 449, 593, 1103, 1121, 1144;
training for television (see Training for media, broadcasting); violence (see Violence and television). See also
Popular culture; Public broadcasting; Public television
Terminology in communications, 18, 23, 205, 311, 363, 378, 398,
407, 707, 856, 865, 1084, 1103, 1108, 1147
Terrorism and media, 141
Textbooks, 194, 224, 298
Thailand: broadcasting, 462; mass media, bibliography, 3
Theory. See Communication, theory
Thesaurus: mass media, 205
Theses and dissertations: broadcasting, 446; communications,
1164; film, 865; mass media, 2, 1164
Third world. See Developing nations
Title changes: films, 920, 1038
Trade publications: directories, 636, 664, 788, 1143
Training for media: book publishing, 225, 287, 305; broadcast-
ing, 353, 553, 593, 792; film, 553, 792, 832, 865, 872, 924;
journalism, 6, 195, 197, 633, 664, 705, 780; mass media, 6,

110, 143, 200, 201; public relations, 1101; television
    (see Training for media, broadcasting)
Turkey: broadcasting, 409; press, directory, 785

Underground films. See Alternative films; Experimental film,
    history
Underground press. See Alternative press
Underground Press Syndicate, 634
Union list of U.S. newspapers, 632
Unions in the media. See Labor groups
United Arab Emirates: press directory, 785
United Arab Republic, 104, 202, 209
United Kingdom: advertising, 1115; press, directory, 785.
    See also Britain
United Nations: press directory, 785
University presses, 283
U.S.: advertising, 1125, 1132, 1143; best sellers, 278–79,
    292; book publishing, 195, 238, 252–54, 259, 261, 263–64,
    283, 285–86, 289, 295, 306, 315; book publishing, direc-
    tories, 229–30, 246–47, 265, 282, 287; book publishing,
    training, 225, 287, 305; broadcasting, 180, 195, 202, 333,
    337, 341–42, 355, 375, 381, 399, 428, 440, 454, 459, 474–
    75, 484, 499, 504, 509–10, 513, 515, 521, 539, 565, 570–
    71, 574, 586–87, 591, 608; broadcasting, directories, 351,
    353, 359; broadcasting, training, 353, 593, 792; communi-
    cation research, 43, 114; film, 195, 804–805, 819, 833,
    849, 852, 858, 868, 870, 875, 877–80, 883, 888, 893–94, 896–
    98, 903, 926–28, 933, 940, 944, 950, 981, 988, 1001, 1003,
    1005–1007, 1011, 1013, 1026–27, 1037; film, catalogues,
    793–94, 953; film, directories, 891, 952; film, training,
    792, 924; foreign correspondents, 741; journalism, 630,
    638, 646–47, 651–52, 662, 666–67, 672, 677–79, 693, 698,
    700, 703–704, 712, 714, 716, 721, 723, 729–30, 742, 757–
    58, 762, 766, 771–73; journalism, directories, 634, 636,
    660, 664, 777, 788; journalism, training, 633, 705;
    journalism, union list of newspapers, 632, 645; mass media,
    7, 9, 25, 32, 37, 47–50, 53–54, 81, 89, 97, 137, 140, 152–
    53, 155, 163, 168, 173–74, 177–80, 192–93, 195, 198, 202,
    211; mass media, directory, 6; media, training, 6; period-
    icals, 195, 1043, 1047, 1049–50, 1055, 1057–59, 1061, 1065,
    1072; periodicals, directories, 636, 1015, 1074–77; radio
    (see U.S., broadcasting); television (see U.S., broadcast-
    ing)
USIA, 195, 926
U.S.S.R.: advertising, 1109; book publishing, 245, 275, 298,
    318; broadcasting, 403, 409, 459, 486, 524; broadcast jour-
    nalism, 661; education and media, 90; film, 800, 818, 842,
    881, 917–18, 932, 934, 1016, 1031; journalism, 696; mass
    media, 60, 95, 100, 135, 139, 209; periodicals, directories,

1063, 1069; public opinion, 41, 100; theory of the
press, 188

Videotape: rental, 899
Vietnam: periodicals, directory, 1063
Violence and media, 26, 137, 218. See also Canada, violence
and media
Violence and television, 195, 336, 372, 418, 441–42, 591–92,
608
Virgin Islands: press, directory, 636
Voice of America, 353, 431, 627
Voting and the media, 218

War films, 827, 931, 971
Washington, D.C.: news media, directory, 697
Weekly newspapers: directories, 336, 664, 734, 788. See also
Community publications
Western films, 852, 858, 1027; bibliography, 956; filmo-
graphy, 967
Wholesalers. See Book publishing, wholesalers
Wire services. See News agencies
Women in media: biography, 64; directories, 27, 106, 1010;
employment, 520, 623, 906; history, 13, 724; portrayal, 69,
112, 207, 224, 551, 623, 1078, 1107; portrayal, biblio-
graphy, 906; publishers, 106; status, 13, 668, 703, 1007,
1011; status, bibliography, 906
Women's magazines, 1070
Women's press, 106
World War II: damage to media, 160; films about, 903
Writers' conferences, 287, 1077

Yiddish press, 740
Yugoslavia: access to media, 338; advertising, 1109; book
publishing, 243, 298; broadcasting, 409, 524; film, 881,
1016; mass media, 39, 338, 753, 918; periodicals, directories, 1063, 1069

Author-Title Index

Aaron, Dorothy, 1078
About Face: Toward a More Positive Image of Women in Text-
    books, 224
About Face: Toward a Positive Image of Women in Advertis-
    ing, 1078
Abstract Film and Beyond, 912
Abstracts of Popular Culture, 1153
Academy Awards: An Unger Reference Index, 1000
Access: Some Western Modern Models of Community Media, 338
Access: Technology and Access to Communications Media, 614
The Accidental Profession: Education, Training, and the
    People of Publishing, 225
Action for Children's Television: The First National Symposium
    on the Effect of Television Programming and Advertising on
    Children, 320
An Actor Guide to the Talkies: A Comprehensive Listing of
    8,000 Feature-Length Films from January, 1949, until Decem-
    ber, 1964, 798
An Actor Guide to the Talkies, 1965 through 1974, 797
Actors' Television Credits, 516-17
Adam, G. Stuart, 628
Adams, William, 629
Adhikarya, Ronny, 373
Adler, Richard, 321, 374-75
Advertisers' Annual: An Annual Directory for All Engaged in
    Advertising and Selling, 1079
Advertising, 1095
Advertising, 1118
The Advertising Agency Business, 1106
The Advertising Agency Business around the World, 1080
Advertising and Press Annual of South Africa, 1081
Advertising and Socialism: The Nature and Extent of Consumer
    Advertising in the Soviet Union, Poland, Hungary and
    Yugoslavia, 1109
Advertising and Society, 1093

373

Advertising and the Community, 1149
Advertising and the Public Interest: A Staff Report to the
    Federal Trade Commission, 1112
Advertising Conditions in Austria, . . . in Belgium, . . . in
    Canada, . . . in Denmark, . . . in Finland, . . . in France,
    . . . in Germany (Federal Republic), . . . in Greece, . . .
    in Italy, . . . in Norway, . . . in Poland, . . . in Spain,
    . . . in Sweden, . . . in Switzerland, . . . in the Nether-
    lands, . . . in the Republic of Ireland, . . . in the
    U.K., 1115
Advertising Expenditure, 1082
Advertising in Contemporary Society, 1137
Advertising Research: The State of the Art, 1134
Advertising Theory and Practice, 1138
African Book Publishing Record: The African Book World and
    Press, 226
The Afro-American Press and Its Editors, 742
The Age of Television: A Study of Viewing Habits and the Impact
    of Television on American Life, 341
Alajmo, Alberto Carrizosa, 39
Alfred I. Dupont-Columbia University Survey of Broadcast
    Journalism, 630
Algerian Cinema, 995
Alisky, Marvin, 727
Allan, Angela and Elkan, 790
Allard, T. J., 322
Allen, Charles, 1055
Allen, Nancy, 791
All the Bright Young Men and Women: A Personal History of the
    Czech Cinema, 1004
Alphabetized Directory of American Journalists, 631
Altbach, Philip G., 227, 298
The "Alternative" Press in Canada, 1073
Alternative Press Index, 1154
Altick, Richard D., 228
Amateur Radio Operation in the Soviet Union, 403
America at the Movies, 1022
American Book Trade Directory, 229
American Broadcasting: A Source Book on the History of Radio
    and Television, 484
The American Cinema: Directors and Directions, 1929-1968, 997
American Film Criticism from the Beginnings to "Citizen Kane":
    Reviews of Significant Films at the Time They First
    Appeared, 899
The American Film Heritage: Impressions from the American
    Film Institute Archives, 1001
The American Film Industry, 804
The American Film Institute, Guide to College Courses in Film
    and Television, 792

The American Film Institute Catalog of Motion Pictures: Feature Films, 1961–1970, 794
The American Film Institute Catalog of Motion Pictures Produced in the United States: Feature Films, 1921–1930, 793
American Film Now: The People, the Power, the Money, the Movies, 944
American Indian Media Directory, 1
American Indian Periodicals in the Princeton University Library, 1041
American Journalism: A History, 1690–1960, 729
The American Magazine: A Compact History, 1065
American Mass Media: Industries and Issues, 7
The American Musical, 1029
American Newspapers, 1821–1936: A Union List of Files Available in the United States and Canada, 632
American Newspapers in the 1970s, 698
The American Newsreel, 1911–1967, 671
American Publisher's Directory, 230
The American Radical Press, 1880–1960, 1043
The American Radio: A Report on the Broadcasting Industry in the United States from the Commission on Freedom of the Press, 37, 620
American Silent Film, 849
America's Mass Media Merchants, 163
AMIC List of Theses: Studies on Mass Communication in Asia, 2
Analysis of Newspaper Content, 688
Anatomy of an International Year: Book Year--1972, 231
Anderson, Charles B., 232, 290
Anderson, Elliott, 1055
Anderson, Laird, 704
Anderson, Mike, 77–78
The Annan Report, 426
The Annan Report: An ITV View, 324
An Annotated Bibliography of UNESCO Publications and Documents Dealing with Space Communication, 1953–1977, 325
An Annotated Journalism Bibliography, 1958–1968, 748
Annual Directory of Religious Broadcasting, 326
ANPA Foundation, Education for Newspaper Journalism in the Seventies and Beyond, 633
Antitrust in the Motion Picture Industry, 833
Approaches to Popular Culture, 16
APS Directory, 634
Arboleda, Amadio Antonio, 304
Armes, Roy, 795–96
Armstrong, Ben, 326
Arndt, Karl J. R., 635
Aros, Andrew A., 797–98
Art and Changing Civilization, 125
The Art and Science of Book Publishing, 234

Art and Social Life, 125
The Art of the American Film, 1900-1971, 883
The Art of the Motion Picture, 922
The Arts and the World of Business: A Selected Bibliography, 74
Asian Mass Communication Bibliography Series, 3
Asian Mass Communication Institutions, Teaching, Training and
    Research: A Directory, 4
Asian Mass Communications: A Comprehensive Bibliography, 121
The Asian Newspapers' Reluctant Revolution, 715
Asian Press and Media Directory, 5
Aspects of American Film History prior to 1920, 1006
Aspen Handbook on the Media, 6
The Associated Church Press, Directory, 1040
Association for Education in Journalism, Education for News-
    paper Journalism in the Seventies and Beyond, 633
Astbury, Raymond, 233
Atkins, Dick, 799
Attitudes of Canadians toward Advertising on Television, 1083
Atwan, Robert, 7
Australia Goes to Press, 695
Australia National Commission for UNESCO, Entertainment and
    Society, 8
Australian Bookselling, 297
Australian Parliament, Joint Committee on the Broadcasting
    of Parliamentary Proceedings, Television Inquiry, 327
Authors by Profession: From the Introduction of Printing until
    the Copyright Act, 1911, 240
The Author's Empty Purse and the Rise of the Literary Agent, 281
Authorship, 125
Averson, Richard, 1037
Awasthy, G. C., 328
Ayer Directory of Publications, 636
Ayer Glossary of Advertising and Related Terms, 1084

Babe, Robert E., 329
Babitsky, Paul, 800
Back Talk: Press Councils in America, 637
Bacon's International Publicity Checker: Guide to Western Euro-
    pean PR Markets, 1085
Bacon's Newspaper Directory: Dailies, Weeklies, 1086
Bacon's Publicity Checker: Magazines, Newspapers, 1087
Baechlin, Peter, 801
Bae-Ho, Hahn, 39
Baer, D. Richard, 802-803
Baer, Walter S., 9, 321, 550
Bagdikian, Ben H., 10
Baggaley, Jon, 330
Bailey, Herbert S., Jr., 234
Baker, John, 235

Baker, Robert K., 137
Balio, Tino, 804
Balk, Alfred, 638
Ball-Rokeach, Sandra, 48
Balshofer, Fred J., 805
The B and T Yearbook, 331
Baran, Paul, 639
Barbour, Alan G., 806
Barcus, F. Earle, 332
Bardeche, Maurice, 807
Barker, Ronald E., 236-37, 269
Barkley, Jack, 631
Barnes, John, 808
Barnes, Michael, 1088
Barney, Ralph D., 147
Barnouw, Erik, 333, 809-10, 1089
Baron, Mike, 334
Barrett, Marvin, 630
Barron, Jerome A., 76, 223
Barry, Iris, 807
Barsam, Richard M., 811
Basic Issues in Canadian Mass Communication, 11
Bate, Michèle, 12
Bawden, Liz-Ann, 812
Baxter, John, 813
BBC Handbook: Incorporating the Annual Report and Accounts,
    1974-75, 335
Beasley, Maurine, 13
Beattie, Eleanor, 814
Beck, Lois, 439
Becker, Lee B., 127
Beebe, Jack H., 515
The Beginnings of Cinema in England, 808
Beginnings of the Biograph: The Story of the Invention of the
    Mutoscope and the Biograph and Their Supplying Camera, 879
Behind the Scenes: Equal Employment Opportunity in the Motion
    Picture Industry, 815
Behind the Screen: The History and Techniques of the Motion
    Picture, 929
Belson, William A., 336
Benjamin, Curtis G., 238
Bennett, H. S., 239
Benn's Press Directory, 640
Berelson, Bernard, 14
Berger, Arthur Asa, 337
Berna, Mary Ellen, 82
Berrigan, Frances J., 338
Berton, Pierre, 816
Bertrand, Claude Jean, 641

Bessie, Simon Michael, 251
The Best Thing on TV: Commercials, 1133
Betts, Ernest, 817
Beyond Babel: New Directions in Communications, 497
Beyond the Wasteland: The Criticism of Broadcasting, 577
Bhattacharjee, Arun, 642
The Bias of Communication, 102
Bibliocable, 363
Bibliography, Some Canadian Writings on the Mass Media, 30
A Bibliography for the Study of Magazines, 1062
The Bibliography of African Broadcasting: An Annotated
    Guide, 439
Bibliography of Austrian Mass Communication Literature, 1945–
    1975, 189
Bibliography of the History of Electronics, 567
A Bibliography of Theses and Dissertations in Broadcasting,
    1920–1973, 466
Bibliography of Works on Mass Communication Published by
    Scandinavian Scholars in English and List of Scandinavian
    Communication Researchers, 15
Bibliopola: Pictures and Texts about the Book Trade, 314
The Big Broadcast, 1920–1950, 358
Big Business and the Mass Media, 173
The Biggest Aspidistra in the World: A Personal Celebration
    of Fifty Years of the BBC, 340
Bigsby, C. W. E., 16
A Biographical Dictionary of Film, 1021
Birinyi, Anne E., 339
Birkos, Alexander S., 818
Bishop, Robert L., 1090
Bjelica, Mihailo, 39
Black, Peter, 340
Black, Sharon K., 605
Black Film as Genre, 840
Black Films and Film-Makers, 969
Black List: The Concise and Comprehensive Reference Guide to
    Black Journalism, Radio, and Television Educational and
    Cultural Organizations in the USA, Africa, and the Carib-
    bean, 17
Black Magazines: An Exploratory Study, 1053
The Black Press, U.S.A., 787
The Black Press (1828–1890): A Quest for National Iden-
    tity, 657
Black Press Handbook, 643
Blacks in American Films: Today and Yesterday, 937
Blacks in American Movies: A Selected Bibliography, 974
Blacks in Black and White: A Source Book on Black Films, 996
Blake, Reed H., 18
Blankenberg, William, 637

Bluem, A. William, 819
Blumstock, Robert, 41
Bogart, Lee, 341
Bogle, Donald, 820
Bohn, Thomas W., 821
Bol, Jean-Marie van, 19-20
Bonham-Carter, Victor, 240
The Book: The Story of Printing and Bookmaking, 288
The Book Business, 235
Book Development in Africa, 241
Book Development in Asia, 242
Book Distribution and Promotion Problems in South Asia, 303
The Book Hunger, 237
The Book in America: A History of the Making and Selling of
    Books in the United States, 286
The Book Industry in Transition: An Economic Study of Book
    Distribution and Marketing, 261
The Book Industry in Yugoslavia, 243
Book Industry Trends, 1977, 264
The Book in Multilingual Countries, 280
The Bookman's Glossary, 248
Book Publishers Directory, 246
Book Publishing: What It Is, What It Does, 263
Book Publishing and Distribution in Rumania, 244
The Book Publishing and Manufacturing Industry in Canada, 268
Book Publishing in America, 289
Book Publishing in the U.S.S.R., 245
The Book Revolution, 269
Books about Film: A Bibliographical Booklist, 945
Bookselling, Reviewing and Reading, 125
Bookselling in America and the World, 232
Books for All: A Study of International Book Trade, 236, 269
Books for the Developing Countries: Asia, Africa, 249
Books from Writer to Readers, 276
Books in East Africa, 250
Books in West Africa: Report and Recommendations, 251
The Book Trade of the World, 247
Borden, Neil H., 1091
Boretsky, R. A., 644
Born to Lose: The Gangster Film in America, 988
Bound and Gagged: The Story of the Silent Serials, 909
Bower, Robert T., 342
Bowker Annual of Library and Book Trade Information, 252
Bowker Lectures on Book Publishing, 253
Bowman, William W., 703
The Box in the Corner: Television and the Under-fives, 401
Boyd, Douglas A., 343
Boylan, James R., 47
Boyle, Deidre, 21

Brack, Hans, 344
Brandwein, Robert, 595
Branscomb, Anne W., 22
Brasillach, Robert, 807
Bretz, Rudolf, 23
Briggs, Asa, 24, 345
Brigham, Clarence S., 645
Brightbill, George D., 385
Brily, Sharon, 346
The British Book Trade from Caxton to the Present Day, 294
British Broadcasting, 573
British Broadcasting: A Bibliography, 347
British Broadcasting: Radio and Television in the United
   Kingdom, 522
British Broadcasting: A Selected Bibliography, 1922-1972, 348
British Broadcasting in Transition, 523
British Cinema: An Illustrated Guide, 862
The British Code of Advertising Practice, 1092
British Film and TV Yearbook, 822
The British Film Catalogue, 1895-1970: A Reference Guide, 863
The British National Film Catalogue, 823
The British Press, 680
The British Press: A Critical Survey, 770
The British Press, an Historical Survey: An Anthology, 641
The British Press: A Manifesto, 654
The British Press since the War: Sources for Contemporary
   Issues, 763
British Rates and Data, 1143
The Broadcast Communications Dictionary, 398
Broadcasting: The Critical Challenges, 349
Broadcasting: Its New Day, 554
Broadcasting and Bargaining: Labor Relations in Radio and
   Television, 468
Broadcasting and Cable Television, 350
Broadcasting and Democracy in France, 599
Broadcasting and Democracy in West Germany, 621
Broadcasting and Government: Responsibilities and Regula-
   tions, 408
Broadcasting and Mass Communications: A Survey Biblio-
   graphy, 585
Broadcasting and the Public, 588
Broadcasting Cable Sourcebook, 351
Broadcasting from Space, 352
Broadcasting from the High Seas: The History of Offshore
   Radio in Europe, 1958-1976, 438
Broadcasting in Africa, 439
Broadcasting in America, 440
Broadcasting in Asia and the Pacific, 479
Broadcasting in Australia, 489

Broadcasting in Canada, 373
Broadcasting Index, 1155
Broadcasting in Guyana, 373
Broadcasting in India, 328
Broadcasting in Ireland, 373
Broadcasting in Japan, 373
Broadcasting in New Zealand, 490
Broadcasting in Nigeria, 491
Broadcasting in Papua, New Guinea, 492
Broadcasting in Peninsular Malaysia, 373
Broadcasting in Sweden, 373
Broadcasting in the Netherlands, 373
Broadcasting in the Third World: Promise and Performance, 462
Broadcasting in the United States, 504
Broadcasting Stations around the World, 606
Broadcasting to the Soviet Union, 486
Broadcasting without Barriers, 380
Broadcasting Yearbook, 353
Broadcast Programmes and Research Branches, 366
Broadcast Regulation and Joint Ownership of Media, 480
Brooks, Jim, 354
Brosnan, John, 824
Brown, Charlene J., 25
Brown, Lee, 646
Brown, Les, 355
Brown, Roger L., 435
Brown, Ronald, 356
Brown, Trevor R., 25
Browne, Donald, 451, 483
Brownlow, Kevin, 825, 1001
Brownstone, David M., 855
Brozen, Yale, 1093
Bryan, Carter, 647, 727
Bucher, Felix, 826
Bunce, Kenneth, 58
Bunce, Richard, 357
Bures, Oldrich, 691
Burke, James Henry, 278
Burnet, Mary, 26
Bush, Alfred L., 1041
The Business of Publishing: A PW Anthology, 254
Business Periodicals Index, 1156
Business Publication Rates and Data, 1143
Butler, Ivan, 827
Butler-Paisley, Matilda, 27
Buxton, Frank, 358

Cable: A New Spectrum of Communications, 600
The Cable/Broadband Communications Book, 359
Cable Communications and the States, 360

Cable Economics, 363
Cable System Interconnection, 363
Cable Television: A Comprehensive Bibliography, 378
Cable Television: Developing Community Services, 550
Cable Television: Franchise Considerations, 550
Cable Television: Franchise Provisions for Schools, 361
Cable Television: A Guide to Federal Regulations, 550
Cable Television: A Handbook for Decision-Making, 550
Cable Television: Issues of Congressional Concern, 446
Cable Television and Telecommunications in Canada, 329
Cable Television for Europe, 605
Cable Television Information Center, Publications Service,
    How to Plan an Ordinance, 363; A Suggested Procedure:
    An Approach to Local Authorization of Cable Television,
    363; Technical Standards and Specifications, 363; The
    Use of Financial Analysis in Decision Making, 363
Cable Television in the Cities, 362
Cable Television State Regulation, 346
Cable Television U.S.A.: An Analysis of Government
    Policy, 561
The C.A.B. Story, 1926-1976: Private Broadcasting in
    Canada, 322
Cain, Michael Scott, 255
Califano, Joseph A., Jr., 140
Calvert, Stephen, 21
Cameron, Elisabeth, 828-29
Cameron, Ian, 828-29
The Campus Press: Freedom and Responsibility, 662
Canada, Committee on Broadcasting, Report, 364
Canada, Royal Commission on Broadcasting, Report, 365
Canada, Royal Commission on Publications, Report, 1042
Canada, Royal Commission on Violence in the Communication
    Industry, Report, 28
Canada, Senate, Report on the Mass Media, 29
Canadian Advertising Rates and Data, 1143
Canadian Broadcasting History Resources in English, 603
Canadian Ownership in Broadcasting: A Report on the Foreign
    Divestiture Process, 367
The Canadian Radio-Television Commission, 30, 366-72
The Canadian Radio-Television and Telecommunications Commis-
    sion, Report, 370; Report on Pay Television, 371
A Candid Critique of Book Publishing, 238
Cannon, Carl L., 648
Cantor, Muriel, 551
Cantril, Hadley, 71
Captains of Consciousness: Advertising and the Social Roots
    of the Consumer Culture, 1104
The Captive Press in the Third Reich, 690
Captive Voices, 651

Carey, James W., 114
Carlton, Robert G., 775, 1069
Carpenter, Edmund, 55
Carpenter-Huffman, Polly, 550
Cases and Materials on Electronic Mass Media, 457
Cases and Materials on Mass Media Law, 66
Case Studies on Broadcasting Systems, 373
Casey, Ralph D., 117-19
Cassan, Brent, 36
Cassell's Directory of Publishing in Great Britain, the Com-
     monwealth, Ireland, South Africa and Pakistan, 256
Casty, Alan, 31, 830
Catalogue of Films on Telecommunications, 1978-79, 448
Cater, Douglass, 374-76
Catholic Press Directory, 649
CATV and Its Implications for Libraries, 323
CATV and Station Coverage Atlas and Zone Maps, 377
Cave, Roderick, 257
Cavelli-Sforza, Francesco, 412
Cawkwell, Tim, 1008
Cazden, Robert E., 258
CBS News Index, 1157
The Celluloid Empire: A History of the American Motion Picture
     Industry, 1013
The Celluloid Weapon: Social Comment in the American Film, 1037
Chaffee, Steven H., 32, 387
Chaffee, Zechariah, Jr., 37
Challenge and Stagnation: The Indian Mass Media, 759
Champlin, Charles, 831
Chaney, D. C., 435
Changing Concepts of Time, 103
The Changing Magazine: Trends in Readership and Manage-
     ment, 1071
Chatterjee, Rama Krishna, 33
Cheap Thrills: An Informal History of the Pulp Magazines, 1050
Cheney, O. H., 259
Cherington, Paul W., 595
Cherry, Colin, 34
Chesman, Andres, 106
Children in Front of the Small Screen, 512
The Children's Literature Market, 1977-1982, 267
Children's Media Market Place, 21
Children's Television: An Analysis of Programming and Adver-
     tising, 332
Children's Television: The Economics of Exploitation, 1122
Children's Television Programming: Some Prior Considerations
     and Research Designs for Canadian Broadcasts, 581
Chin, Felix, 378
Chronological Tables of American Newspapers, 1690-1820, 645

A Chronology of Printing, 260
Chronology of State Cable Television Regulation, 1947–1978, 339
Chu, Godwin C., 35–36
Cinema, 914
Cinema, the Magic Vehicle: A Guide to Its Achievement, 860
Cinema and Society: France and Germany during the Twenties, 947
Cinema beyond the Danube: The Camera and Politics, 1016
Cinema Booklist, 980
Cinema in Finland, 884
The Cinema in the Arab Countries, 992
The Cinema of Science Fiction: Future Tense, 824
Cinematographic Institutions, 832
Circulation: The Annual Geographic Penetration Analysis of Major Print Media, 1094
Citizen Participation in Broadcast Licensing before the FCC, 429
Citizens' Groups and Broadcasting, 430
Citizen's Media Directory, 379
Clair, Colin, 260
Clark, Alden H., 250
Clark, Eleanor, 1123
Clarke, Prescott, 709
Clarkson, Marg, 853
Cliffhanger: A Pictorial History of the Motion Picture Serial, 806
Codding, George A., Jr., 380
Cohen, Dorothy, 1095
Cole, Barry, 381
Colino, Richard R., 382
College Carrier Current: A Survey of 208 Campus-Limited Radio Stations, 383
College Student Press Law, 199
Collins, N. A., 423
Collins, Richard, 650
Comargo, Nelly de, 39
Comedy Films, 1894–1954, 948
Comer, John, 208
The Coming of the Book: The Impact of Printing, 1450–1800, 270
Commercial Radio in Africa, 1096
Commission of Inquiry into High School Journalism, Captive Voices: The Report, 651
Commission on Freedom of the Press, Reports, 37, 68
Commonwealth Broadcasting Association, Handbook, 384
Communicating by Satellite: An International Discussion, 616
Communication, 133
Communication Abstracts, 1158

384

Communication and Cultural Domination, 180
Communication and Development: Critical Perspectives, 167
Communication by Satellite, 472
Communication/Journalism Education in Asia, 38
Communication Policies: The Case of Latin America, 175
Communication Policies in Brazil, . . . in Columbia, . . . in
  Costa Rica, . . . in the Federal Republic of Germany, . . .
  in Hungary, . . . in India, . . . in Ireland, . . . in
  Japan, . . . in Peru, . . . in Sri Lanka, . . . in Sweden,
  . . . in the Republic of Korea, . . . in Yugoslavia, 39
Communication Policy and Planning for Development, 161
Communication Yearbook, 40
Communications, 215
Communications and Media: Constructing a Cross-Discipline, 80
Communications and National Integration in Communist China, 126
Communications and the United States Congress, 385
Communications for Tomorrow: Policy Perspectives for the
  1980s, 166
Communications in Agriculture: The American Farm Press, 1047
Communications in Canadian Society, 190
Communications Research, 1948-1949, 478
The Communications Revolution: A History of Mass Media in the
  United States, 81
Communications Satellites in Political Orbit, 506
Communications Technology and Democratic Participation, 120
Communications Technology for Urban Improvement, 386
Communication via Satellite: A Vision in Retrospect, 576
Community Publication Rates and Data, 1143
The Compact History of the American Newspaper, 771
Compaine, Benjamin M., 261, 652
A Competitive Cinema, 900
Complete Directory to Prime Time Network TV Shows, 1946-
  Present, 354
The Complete Encyclopedia of Television Programs, 1947-
  1979, 598
A Computerized Bibliography of Mass Communication Research,
  1944-1964, 45
Comstock, George, 387, 591
Conant, Michael, 833
Concentration of Mass Media Ownership, 9
A Concise History of the Cinema, 834
Congress and Mass Communications: An Institutional Perspec-
  tive, 604
Conlin, Joseph R., 1043
Connell, Ian, 107
Connor, Walter D., 41
Consumer Electronics: Annual Review, 388
Consumer Magazine and Farm Publication Rates and Data, 1143
Contemporary Authors, 42

Content and Taste: Religion and Myth, 125
Continued Next Week: A History of the Moving Picture
    Serial, 909
Contreras, Eduardo, 389
Control of the Direct Broadcast Satellite: Values in Con-
    flict, 390
Cook, Harvey R., 1097
The Cool Fire: Television and How to Make It, 562
Co-op Publishing Handbook, 255
Corporation for Public Broadcasting, Office of Public
    Affairs, Mission and Goals, Tasks and Responsibilities, 502
Costigan, Daniel M., 391
Costner, Tom, 952
Cowie, Peter, 834-38, 890
Crane, Rhonda J., 392
Cranfield, G. A., 653
Crawford, Sheridan, 27
Cripps, Thomas, 839-40
Critchley, R. A., 1098-99
The Critical Factor: Criticism of the News Media in Journal-
    ism Education, 197
A Critical History of the British Cinema, 795
The Critical Index: A Bibliography of Articles on Film in
    English, 861
Critical Issues in Public Relations, 1110
Criticism of the Press in U.S. Periodicals, 1900-1939, 693
Cross-Cultural Broadcasting, 389
Crouch, Sunny, 157
The Crowd-Catchers: Introducing Television, 565
The Cultural Debate, 125
Culture and Mass Culture, 125
Culture and Society, 1780-1950, 216
Culture for the Millions? Mass Media in Modern Society, 105
Curran, James, 43, 654
Current British Research on Mass Media and Mass Communica-
    tion, 44
Current Perspectives in Mass Communication Research, 114
Current South African Newspapers, 655
Curtis, David, 841
Cutlip, Scott M., 1100
The Czech and Slovak Press: The First 100 Years, 706

Dahl, Svend, 262
The Daily Newspaper in America: The Evolution of a Social
    Instrument, 714
The Daily Press: A Survey of the World Situation in 1952, 656
Dames, 828
Dangerous Estate: The Anatomy of Newspapers, 782
Danielson, Wayne A., 45

Dann, Martin, 657
Dati e Tarriffee Pubblicitario, 1143
David, Nina, 602
Davidson, Emily S., 485
Davis, Anthony, 393–94
Davis, Dennis, 115
Davison, Peter, 125
Davison, Walter Phillips, 46–47
Day, Peter, 936
Daytime TV's Star Directory, 395
Deciding What's News: A Study of CBS Evening News, NBC Nightly
    News, Newsweek and Time, 675
The Decline of the Cinema: An Economist's Report, 1012
Decoding Advertisements: Ideology and Meaning in Advertis-
    ing, 1148
DeFleur, Melvin L., 48
De La Roche, Catherine, 842
Denis, Paul, 395
Dennis, Everette E., 49–51
Desai, M. V., 39
A Design for Public Relations Education, 1101
DeSilva, M. A., 39
Desmond, Robert W., 658
Dessauer, John P., 263–64
The Detective in Hollywood, 1026
Developing Information Media in Africa, 52
The Development of the Advertising Industry in Japan and
    Taiwan, 1117
The Development of the Colonial Newspaper, 712
Development of the Film: An Interpretive History, 830
The Development of Wireless to 1920, 396
DeVera, Jose Maria, 397
Deviance and Mass Media, 218
Diamant, Lincoln, 398
Dianying: An Account of Films and the Film Audience in
    China, 916
Dickerson, Donna L., 199
Dickinson, Thorold, 842
Dictionary of Advertising Terms, 1147
Dictionary of Book Publishing, 311
Dictionary of Film Makers, 993
Dictionary of Films, 994
Dictionary of 1,000 Best Films, 973
A Dictionary of the Cinema, 866
Dimmitt, Richard B., 797–98
Direct Broadcast Satellites and the United Nations, 544
Direct Mail List Rates and Data, 1143
Directors Guild of America, Inc., Directory of Members, 843
Directory, American Society of Journalists and Authors, 1044

387

Directory: Multilingual Broadcasting in Canada, 368
The Directory of American Book Publishing from Founding
    Fathers to Today's Conglomerates, 285
The Directory of American Indian Print and Broadcast
    Media, 730
Directory of British Publishers and Their Terms Including
    Agents for Overseas Publishers, 265
Directory of Newspaper Libraries in the U.S. and Canada, 659
The Directory of Private Presses and Letterpress Printers and
    Publishers, 266
Directory of Publishing Opportunities, 1045
Directory of Small Magazine/Press Editors and Publishers, 1046
Directory of the College Student Press in America, 1977-78, 660
Directory of Women and Minority Men in Academic Journalism/
    Communication, 27
Discovering the News, 760
Dissertation Abstracts International, 1164
Dixon, Diana, 1056
Documentary: A History of the Non-fiction Film, 809
Documentary Film, 990
Documentary Supplement to Financial and Economic Journalism, 711
The Documentary Tradition, from Nanook to Woodstock, 892
Documents for the Study of Communication Problems, 104
Documents in American Telecommunications Policy, 399
Documents of American Broadcasting, 459
Doebler, Paul D., 264
Domestic Satellite: An FCC Giant Step toward Competitive Tele-
    communications Policy, 498
Donati, Agnes, 412
Drabinsky, Garth H., 844
Draves, Pamela, 379
Drury, C. M., 400
Druxman, Michael B., 845
Duck, Steve, 330
Duke, Judith S., 267
Dunn, Gwen, 401
Dunning, John, 402
Durgnat, Raymond, 846
Durham, F. Gayle, 403, 661
Duscha, Julius, 662
Dwoskin, Stephen, 847
Dyer, Richard, 404
Dynamics of Television, 330

Early American Cinema, 1005
The Early Window: Effects of Television on Children and
    Youth, 485
Early Women Directors, 1007
Eastern Europe: An Illustrated Guide, 881

Economic and Policy Problems in Satellite Communications, 527
Economic Aspects of Television Regulation, 513
Economic Control of the Motion Picture Industry: A Study in
    Industrial Organization, 885
The Economic Effects of Advertising, 1091
Economic Issues in the Joint Ownership of Newspaper and Tele-
    vision Media, 757
Economics and Freedom of Expression: A Bibliography, 206
The Economics of Book Publishing in Developing Countries, 308
The Economics of Media Systems, 145
The Economics of the American Newspaper, 773
Economic Survey of the Book Industry, 1930-31, 259
The Edison Motion Picture Myth, 878
Editor and Publisher Annual Directory and Syndicated Ser-
    vices, 663
Editor and Publisher International Yearbook, 664
Edmondson, Madeleine, 405
Educational Television, 424
Educational Television in Japan, 397
Educational Use of Cable Television, 363
Education and the Mass Media in the Soviet Union and Eastern
    Europe, 90
Education for Newspaper Journalism in the Seventies and
    Beyond, 633
Effective Advertising Self-Regulation, 1145
The Effects of Mass Communication, 113
The Effects of Mass Communication on Political Behavior, 115
The Effects of Mass Communication with Special Reference to
    Television, 432
The Effects of Newspaper-Television Cross Ownership on News
    Homogeneity, 679
The Effects of Television, 433
The Effects of Television on Children and Adolescents, 560
Eguchi, H., 406
Egyptian Radio: Tool of Political and National Develop-
    ment, 343
Ehrenberg, A. S. C., 423
80 Years of Best Sellers, 1895-1975, 278
Eighty Years of Cinema, 835
Eisenstein, Elizabeth L., 665
The Electronic Box Office: Humanities and Arts on the
    Cable, 321
Elite Press, 728
Elliott, Blanche B., 1102
Elliott, P. R. C., 434
Ellis, Connie, 44
Ellmore, R. Terry, 407

The Emergence of Film Art: The Evolution and Development of
    the Motion Picture as an Art, 894
Emerson, Miles, 157, 529
Emery, Edwin, 666
Emery, Michael, 53, 666
Emery, Walter B., 408-409
Empire and Communication, 101
Encyclomedia, 1103
Encyclopedia of Advertising, 1108
Encyclopedia of the Book, 273
Encyclopedic Directory of Ethnic Newspapers and Periodicals
    in the United States, 789
Enduring Issues in Mass Communication, 51
English, Harry Edward, 410
English Books and Readers [1475-1640], 239
The English Book Trade, 299
The English Common Reader: A Social History of the Mass Read-
    ing Public, 1800-1900, 228
English Language Newspapers Abroad, 781
Enser, A. G. S., 848
Entertainment and Society, 8
Epstein, Edward Jay, 667
Epstein, Edward Z., 1123
Epstein, Laurily Keir, 668
Ernst, Morris L., 54
Ernst & Ernst, 268
Escarpit, Robert, 237, 269
Ethics and the Press: Readings in Mass Media Morality, 147
Evaluating Advertising, 1116
Evans, Hew, 412
Evans, James F., 1047
Everson, William K., 849, 852
The Evolution of the EBU through Its Statutes from 1950 to
    1976, 344
Ewen, Stuart, 1104
Experimental Cinema, 841
Experiment in the Film, 934
Explorations in Communication: An Anthology, 55
External Information and Cultural Relations Programs of
    France, 56; . . . of Japan, 58; . . . of the Federal Repub-
    lic of Germany, 58; . . . of the People's Republic of China,
    59; . . . of the Union of Soviet Socialist Republics, 60;
    . . . of the United Kingdom, 61
Eyck, F. Gunther, 57

Fackelman, Mary P., 411
Facts about the IOJ, 669
Fadiman, William, 850
Faenza, Roberto, 412

Fahkfakh, Abdelfattah, 20
The Family Guide to Children's Television, 464
Fantastic Television: A Pictorial History of Sci-Fi, the
    Unusual and the Fantastic, 417
Fax. The Principles and Practice of Facsimile Communica
    tion, 391
Feature Films on 8mm, 16mm, and Videotape: A Directory of
    Feature Films Available for Rental, Sale, and Lease in the
    U.S. and Canada, 919
Febvre, Lucien, 270
Federal Regulations Relevant to the Structural Development of
    Telecommunications Industries, 455
Feehan, John M., 271
Feinstein, Peter, 851
Felsenthal, Norman, 62
Fenin, George N., 852
Ferber, Ellen, 1046
Feuereisen, Fritz, 670
Fiction and the Fiction Industry, 313
Fielding, Raymond, 671
Fifty Years of Japanese Broadcasting, 413
Fifty Years of Movie Posters, 905
Filler, Louis, 672
Film: The Democratic Art, 897
Film, How and Where to Find Out What You Want to Know, 946
The Film: Its Economic, Social, and Artistic Problems, 998
The Film and Television as an Aspect of European Culture, 977
Filmarama, 1015
Film as a National Art: NFB of Canada and the Film Board
    Idea, 987
The Film Buff's Bible of Motion Pictures, 1915-1922, 802
The Film Buff's Checklist of Motion Pictures, 1912-1979, 803
The Film Business: A History of British Cinema, 1896-
    1972, 817
Film Canadiana, 853
Film Directors: A Guide to Their American Films, 963
Film Directors Guide: Western Films, 964
Filmed Books and Plays, 848
Filmfacts, 854
Filmgoer's Companion, 874
The Film Industries: Practical Business/Legal Problems in
    Production, Distribution and Exhibition, 940
The Film Industry in Communist China, 923
The Filming of the West, 1027
Film in the Third Reich, 886
Film Is . . .: The International Free Cinema, 847
Film Literature Index, 1159
Film Music: From Violin to Video, 921
Film Review Digest Annual, 855

Films: A Report on the Supply of Films for Exhibition in
    Cinemas, 867
Films about Newspapers, 673
Films and the Second World War, 931
Films in Sweden, 838
Film Study Collections: A Guide to Their Development and
    Use, 791
The Film till Now: A Survey of World Cinema, 991
Film Vocabulary, 856
Financial and Economic Journalism, 710
The Financing of Public Television, 557
Finkle, Lee, 674
Finnish Cinema, 836
Firestone, O. J., 1105
First, Jaroslav, 691
The First Amendment and the Fourth Estate: Communication Law
    for Undergraduates, 67
The First Amendment as a Shield or a Sword: An Integrated
    Look at Regulation of Multi-Media Ownership, 22
The First Colour Motion Pictures, 1020
The First Freedom, 54, 174
First National Directory of "Rightest" Groups, Publications
    and Some Individuals in the United States (and Some Foreign
    Countries), 1048
The First Ten Years, 857
The First Twenty Years: A Segment of Film History, 960
Fischer, Heinz-Dietrich, 63
Fischer, Thomas, 662
Fisher, Desmond, 373
Fisher, Harold A., 728
Fishman, Barry, 518
Five Hundred Years of Printing, 310
A Flick of the Switch, 1930-1950, 494
The Flicks, or Whatever Became of Andy Hardy?, 831
Flynn, Charles, 927
Fodor, Gabor, 39
Fonseca, Jaime M., 39
Forbes, Dorothy, 414
The Foreign Press: A Survey of the World's Journalism, 727
Foremost Women in Communications, 64
Forty Years of Screen Credits, 1929-1969, 1035
Forum for Protest: The Black Press during World War II, 674
Four Theories of the Press, 188
The Fourth Estate: An Informal Appraisal of the News and
    Opinion Media, 99
The Fowler Report, 364
Fraenkel, Heinrich, 935
France: An Illustrated Guide to 400 Key Figures in the French
    Cinema, 938

Franck, Irene M., 855
Francois, William E., 65
Franklin, Marc A., 66-67
Franklin, Ruth Korzenik, 67
Fraser, Robert S., 1041
Frederick, John T., 1059
A Free and Responsible Press, 37, 68
A Free and Responsive Press, 638
Freedom of the Movies: A Report on Self-Regulation, 37, 888
Freedom of the Press: A Framework of Principle, 37
Freedom Press: Development of the Progressive Press in West-
    ern Europe and the U.S.A., 772
Freidrich, Lynette Kohn, 583
French, Philip, 858
French Cinema since 1946, 796
Friedman, Leslie J., 69
From Caligari to Hitler: A Psychological History of the Ger-
    man Film, 907
From Mary Noble to Mary Hartman: The Complete Soap Opera
    Book, 405
From Radical Left to Extreme Right: A Bibliography of Current
    Periodicals of Protests, Controversy, Advocacy, or Dis-
    sent, 1060
From Sambo to Superspade: The Black Experience in Motion Pic-
    tures, 911
Fryburger, Vernon, 1125, 1138-39
Fulton, Albert R., 859
Fulton, Len, 272, 1046, 1052
Fundamentals of Public Relations, 1126
Fund Raising for Cable Television Projects, 363
Furhoff, Lars, 39
Future Directions of the Newspaper Industry, 652
The Future of Broadcasting: A Report Presented to the Social
    Morality Council, October, 1973, 415
The Future of Newsprint, 1970-2000, 639
The Future of Public Broadcasting, 376

Gadney, Allan, 70
Gadney's Guide to 1800 Contests, Festivals & Grants in Film &
    Video, Photography, TV-Radio Broadcasting, Writing, Poetry
    & Playwriting, Journalism, 70
Gallup, George H., 71
The Gallup Poll: Public Opinion, 1935-1977, 71
Gandy, Oscar H., Jr., 72
The Gangster Film, 813
Gans, Herbert J., 73, 675
Garbicz, Adam, 860
Gardner, Herbert S., Jr., 1106
Gardner, Mary A., 676

Garnham, Nicholas, 416
Gaynes, Martin J., 223
Gebbie House Magazine Directory, 1075
Geduld, Harry, 865
Gelfman, Judith S., 677
Gender Advertisements, 1107
George, John, 96
Georgi, Charlotte, 74
Gerani, Gary, 417
Gerbner, George, 75, 418
Gerlach, John C. and Lana, 861
The German Cinema, 935
German Exile Literature in America, 1935-1950, 258
The German-Language Press in America, 786
The German Language Press of the Americas, 635
Germany, 826
Getting into Film, 924
Gibson, George H., 419
Gifford, Denis, 862-64
Gillespie, Gilbert, 420
Gillmor, Donald, 51, 76
Ginsburg, Douglas H., 421
Gitelman, Zvi Y., 41
Glaister, Geoffrey Ashall, 273
Glattbach, Jack, 77-78
Glessing, Robert J., 678
Gloria, Ameria J., 3
A Glossary of Cable Terms, 363
Glut, Donald F., 422, 877
Goffman, Erving, 1107
Golden Multitudes: The Story of Best Sellers in the United
    States, 292
Golden Throats and Golden Tongues: The Radio Announcers, 532
Golding, Peter, 79
Goldwater, Walter, 1049
Goodgold, Ed, 1036
Goodhardt, G. J., 423
Goonetileke, H. A. I., 3
Gordon, George N., 80-81, 424
Gordon, Thomas F., 82
Gormley, William T., Jr., 679
Gorokhoff, Boris I., 274
Gottesman, Ronald, 865
Goulart, Ron, 1050
Government and Mass Communications, 37
Gowans, Alan, 83
"Go Watch TV!": What and How Much Should Children Really
    Watch?, 556
Graham, Irvin, 1108

Graham, Peter, 866
Grannis, Chandler, 275
The Great Audience, 185
Great Britain, Central Office of Information, Reference Division, The British Press, 680
Great Britain, Committee on Broadcasting, Report, 425
Great Britain, Home Department, Committee on the Future of Broadcasting, Report of the Committee on the Future of Broadcasting, 426
Great Britain, House of Commons, Monopolies Commission, Films: A Report on the Supply of Films for Exhibition in Cinemas, 867
Great Britain, Royal Commission on the Press, Analysis of Newspaper Content, 688; Memoranda on Evidence Submitted to the Royal Commission on the Press, 1947-48, 681; Minutes of Evidence Taken before the Royal Commission on the Press, 682; Report, 1962, 683; Documentary Evidence, 1962, 684; Minutes of Oral Evidence, 1962, 685; Interim Report: The National Newspaper Industry, 686; Final Report, 1977, 687; Periodicals and the Alternative Press, 1051
The Great British Picture Show from the Nineties to the Seventies, 972
The Great Funnies: A History of Film Comedy, 985
The Great Gangster Films, 965
The Great Movie Serials: Their Sound and Fury, 877
The Great Radio Heroes, 436
The Great Science Fiction Pictures, 966
The Great Spy Pictures, 967
The Great Television Heroes, 422
The Great Television Series, 555
The Great Western Pictures, 968
Green, Timothy, 427
Greenfeld, Howard, 276
Greenfield, Jeff, 428
Gregory, Winifred, 632
Grey, David L., 757
Griffith, Mrs. D. W. (Linda), 868
Griffith, Richard, 869-70, 990
Gross, Gerald, 277
Gross, Larry, 418
Grundfest, Joseph A., 429
Guback, Thomas H., 871
Guidebook to Film: An Eleven-in-One Reference, 865
A Guide to Book Publishing, 307
Guide to Book Publishing Courses, 305
Guide to Citizen Action in Radio and Television, 538
Guide to College Courses in Film and Television, 792
A Guide to Film and Television Courses in Canada, 1978-79, 872
A Guide to Satellite Communication, 531

Guide to Women's Publishing, 106
Guimary, Donald L., 430
Gurevitch, Michael, 43
Gustafsson, Karl Erik, 689
The Gutenberg Galaxy: The Making of Typographic Man, 129

Hachten, William A., 84
Hackett, Alice Payne, 278
Hadenius, Stig, 689
Haefner, James E., 1137
Hahn, Taeyoul, 3
Haight, Timothy R., 195
Hale, Julian, 431
Hale, Oran J., 690
Hale, William Storm, 887
Hall, Sandra J., 137
Hall, Stuart, 85
Halliwell, Leslie, 873-74
Halliwell's Film Guide: A Survey of 8000 English-Language
    Movies, 873
Hallman, E. S., 373
Halloran, James D., 86-87, 432-35
Hallowell, Mary Louise, 359
Halmos, Paul, 88
Hammel, William, 89
Hampton, Benjamin B., 875
A Handbook of Canadian Films, 814
Handbook of Communication, 159
Handbook of News Agencies, 691
Handbook on International Public Relations, 1111
Hanson, Philip, 1109
Harasymiw, Bohdan, 90
Hardware Software: A Background Guide to the Study of the
    Mass Media, 220
Hardy, Forsythe, 876
Harmon, Jim, 422, 436, 877
Harmon, R. Joyce, 493
Harmonay, Maureen, 437
Haroldsen, Edwin O., 18
Harris, Paul, 438
Harrison, Stanley, 692
Hart, James D., 279
Hartog, Simon, 995
Hasan, Abul, 280
Hausman, Linda Wiener, 693
Haven't I Seen You Somewhere Before? Remakes, Sequels and
    Series in Motion Pictures and Television, 1896-1978, 920
Head, Sydney W., 439-40
The Heavies, 829

Hecquet, Marie-Claude, 872
Hellack, Georg, 91
Heller, Melvin S., 441
Hendricks, Gordon, 878-80
Henstell, Bruce, 899
Hepburn, James, 281
Hepple, Alex, 694
Hibben, Nina, 881
Higgins, Patricia Beaulieu, 442
Higham, Charles, 882-83
Hill, Harold E., 443
Hill and Knowlton Executives, Critical Issues in Public Relations, 1110
Hill and Knowlton International, Handbook on International Public Relations, 1111
Hillier, Jim, 884
Himmelweit, Hilde T., 444
Hindley, H., 373
Hindley, M. Patricia, 92
Hirsch, Leon V., 595
The Historian and Film, 1009
History and Bibliography of American Newspapers, 1690-1820, 645
The History and Development of Advertising, 1132
The History Makers: The Press of Europe from Its Beginnings through 1965, 739
A History of American Magazines, 1059
A History of Book Publishing in the United States, 315
History of Broadcasting in the United Kingdom, 345
A History of Broadcasting in the United States, 333
History of Cooperative Newsgathering in the United States, 756
A History of English Advertising, 1102
History of Indian Journalism, 750
A History of Journalism in Canada, 708
The History of Motion Pictures, 807
A History of Scientific and Technical Periodicals, 1054
History of the American Film Industry from Its Beginnings to 1931, 875
History of the Book, 262
The History of the British Film, 925
A History of the Catholic Press Association, 1911-1968, 751
A History of the Cinema: From Its Origins to 1970, 982
A History of the Movies, 875
A History of the Press in India, 733
The History of World Cinema, 986
Hocking, William Ernest, 37
Hoffman, Frederick J., 1055
Hoggart, Richard, 93
Hohenberg, John, 94

397

Holden, W. Sprague, 695
Hollander, Gayle Durham, 95
Holloway, Harry, 96
Hollywood: The Movie Colony, the Movie Makers, 989
Hollywood, UK: The British Film Industry in the Sixties, 1032
Hollywood at Sunset, 882
Hollywood Now, 850
Hollywood's Canada: The Americanization of Our National
    Image, 816
Holmgren, Rod, 97
Homberg, Erentraud, 535
Hopkins, Mark W., 696
Horecky, Paul L., 1069
Howard, John A., 1112
Howe, Michael J. A., 445
How to Build a Profitable Newspaper: Printing Impressions, 754
How to Protect Your Rights in Television and Radio, 453
How to Talk Back to Your Television Set, 454
Hudson, Howard Penn and Mary Elizabeth, 697
Hudson's Washington News Media Contacts Directory, 697
Huettig, Mae D., 885
Hulbert, James, 1112
Hull, David Stewart, 886
Hulteng, John L., 98-99
Humanities Index, 1160
Hummel, Lani S., 446
Hurst, Walter E., 887
Huszezo, Adaline, 41
Hynds, Ernest C., 698

Ichinohe, H., 406
IENS Press Handbook, 1113
The Illustrated Dictionary of Broadcast-CATV-Telecommunica-
    tions, 407
ILPA Directory of Member Publications, 699
Image and Influence: Studies in the Sociology of Film, 1025
The Image of the Media, 219
Impact of Television on Children and Youth, 583
The Independent Film Community: A Report on the Status of
    Independent Film in the United States, 851
Independent Radio: The Story of Commercial Radio in the United
    Kingdom, 334
Independent Television Networks in Italy at the Turning Point
    from Cable, 412
Index to Characters in the Performing Arts: Radio and Tele-
    vision, 564
Index to Legal Periodicals, 1161
Indian Film, 810

The Indian Institute of Mass Communication, Mass Communica-
tion in India, 3
Indian Journalism, 731
The Indian Press: Profession to Industry, 642
Indonesian Government and Press during Guided Democracy, 738
Industry Statistics, 1972: Newspapers, Periodicals, Books
and Miscellaneous Publishing, 204
INFA Press and Advertisers Year Book, 1114
The Influence of International Communication on Develop-
ment, 158
The Information Bank, 1162
The Information Film, 1031
The Information Machines: Their Impact on Men and the
Media, 10
The Information Process: World News Reporting to the Twentieth
Century, 658
Information Sources in Advertising History, 1131
Inglis, Ruth A., 37, 888
Inkeles, Alex, 100
Innis, Harold A., 101-103
In Quest of Freedom: Finland's Press, 1771-1971, 767
Instant World: A Report on Telecommunications in Canada, 447
Institute of Practitioners in Advertising, 1115
The INTELSAT Definitive Arrangements, 382
International and Intercultural Communication, 63
International Commercial Satellite Communications, 579
International Commission for the Study of Communication
Problems, Documents for the Study of Communication Prob-
lems, 104
International Communications, 1975-1977, 483
International Communications and Political Opinion, 119
International Communications Services, 607
International Directory of Little Magazines and Small
Presses, 1052
The International Encyclopedia of Film, 889
International Film Guide, 890
The International Film Industry, 871
International Index, 1160
International Index to Film Periodicals, 1163
International Inventory of Television Programme Structure and
the Flow of TV Programmes between Nations, 612
The International Law of Communications, 134
International Literary Marketplace, 282
International Motion Picture Almanac, 891
International News and the Press, 732
International Studies of Broadcasting, with Special Reference
to the Japanese Studies, 406

International Telecommunication Control: International Law
   and the Ordering of Satellite and Other Forms of Inter-
   national Broadcasting, 576
International Telecommunications Bibliography, 411
International Telecommunications Policies, 610
International Telecommunications Union, Catalogue of Films
   on Telecommunications, 1978-79, 448
International Television Almanac, 449
In the Public Interest: A Report by the National News Council,
   1973-1975, 700
An Introduction to the American Underground Film, 981
Invention and Innovation in the Radio Industry, 493
The Invisable Resource: Use and Regulation of the Radio Spec-
   trum, 481
An Irish Publisher and His World, 271
Irving, John A., 190
Irwin, Manley R., 450
Isber, Caroline, 551
Ismach, Arnold H., 51
Issues in Broadcasting: Radio, Television, and Cable, 578
Issues in International Broadcasting, 451
Is This Your Life? Images of Women in the Media, 112
The Italian Anti-Fascist Press (1919-1945), 755
The Italian Cinema, 915
Ito, Masami, 373

Jacobs, Lewis, 892-94
Jacobs, Norman, 105
Jacobson, Robert E., 452
Janowitz, Morris, 14
Japan, 1019
Japan: Film Image, 1024
Japanese Cinema: Film Style and National Character, 984
The Japanese Press, 701
Japanese Research on Mass Communication, 108
Jarvie, Ian C., 895
Jennings, Ralph M., 453
Jensen, Jay, 25
Jesus, Emilinda V. de, 3
Joan, Polly, 106
Jobes, Gertrude, 896
Johnson, Leland L., 518
Johnson, Michael L., 702
Johnson, Nicholas, 454
Johnson, Richard B., 455
Johnstone, Ian Anthony, 456
Johnstone, John W. C., 703
Jones, Greta, 107
Jones, William H., 704

Jones, William K., 457
Jonsson, Lennart, 39
Journalism: A Bibliography, 648
Journalism, Communication and the Law, 628
Journalism Abstracts, 1164
Journalism in America before Emancipation, 647
Journalism Quarterly Cumulative Index, 1165
Journalism Scholarship Guide and Directory of College Journal-
    ism Programs, 705
Jowett, Garth S., 897

Kaftanov, S. V., 458
Kahn, Frank J., 459
Kalba, Kas, 460
Kamen, Ira, 461
Kaplan, Frank L., 706
Kaplan, Harold J., 56
Kardish, Laurence, 898
Kato, Hidetoshi, 39, 108
Katz, Elihu, 109, 462
Katzen, May, 110-11
Katzman, Natan, 387-463
Kauffmann, Stanley, 899
Kaye, Evelyn, 464
Kelly, Terence, 900
Kendall, Patricia, 475
Kent, Ruth K., 707
Kerr, Chester, 283
Kesterton, Wilfred H., 708
Kimbrough, Marvin, 1053
The Kinetoscope: America's First Commercially Successful
    Motion Picture Exhibitor, 880
King, Clyde L., 951
King, Frank H. H., 709
King, Josephine, 112
Kingsford, R. J. L., 284
Kings of the Bs: Working within the Hollywood System, 927
Kino: A History of the Russian and Soviet Film, 917
Kinsley, Michael E., 465
Kirsch, Donald, 710-11
Kittross, John M., 399, 466, 586
Klapper, Joseph T., 113
Klein, Walter J., 901
Kletter, Richard C., 550
Klever, Anita, 467
Kline, F. Gerald, 114
Klingender, F. D., 902
Klinowski, Jacek, 860
Knight, Arthur, 903
Knight, Derrick, 904

Kobal, John, 905
Kobre, Sidney, 712
Koenig, Allen E., 468
Kowalski, Rosemary Ribich, 906
Kracauer, Siegfried, 907-908
Krasnow, Erwin G., 469
Kraus, Sidney, 115
Krekel, Kimberly A., 411
Krishnaswamy, Subrahmanyam, 810
Kronick, David A., 1054
Kurien, George Thomas, 285
Kwan, Shirley, 346

LaBrie, Henry G., 713
Lackmann, Ron, 470
Lahue, Kalton C., 909
Land, Herman W., Associates, Inc., 471
Language and Language Behavior Abstracts, 1166
The Language of Journalism: A Glossary of Print-Communications
    Terms, 707
Lannon, Judy, 529
Laskin, Paul, 472
Lasswell, Harold D., 116-118
Lathem, Edward C., 645
Laudon, Kenneth C., 120
The Law of Advertising, 1136
Law of Mass Communications, 150
Layng, Sanderson, 414
Lazarsfeld, Paul F., 109, 342, 473-78
Leab, Daniel J., 911
The Least Worst Television in the World, 568
Lee, Alfred McClung, 714
Legal Bibliography: Synopsis of Cases on Cable Television, 363
Legal Control of the Press, 150
Legg, Stuart, 902
LeGrice, Malcolm, 912
Lehde-White, Neva S., 730
Lehmann-Haupt, Hellmut, 286
Leigh, Robert D., 37, 212
Leiser, Erwin, 913
Lejeune, Caroline A., 914
Lekovic, Zdravko, 39
Leng, Woon Ai, 373
Lent, John A., 121-23, 479, 715
Leprohon, Pierre, 915
Lerner, Daniel, 116
LeRoy, David J., 716
Levin, Harvey J., 480-81
Lewels, Francisco J., Jr., 482

Lewis, Roger, 717
Leyda, Jay, 916-17
Libraries and the Book Trade, 233
Lichty, Lawrence W., 483-84
Liebert, Robert M., 485
Liehm, Antonin and Mira, 918
Light and Shadows: A History of Motion Pictures, 821
Light Entertainment, 404
Lim, Khor Yoke, 373
Limbacher, James L., 919-21
Lindsay, Vachel, 922
Lippmann, Walter, 124
Lipstein, Benjamin, 1116
Lisann, Maury, 486
Lists Showing the Ownership of Radio and Television Stations
    Licensed by the Canadian Radio-Television Commission, 369
Literary Marketplace, with Names and Numbers: The Directory
    of American Book Publishing, 287
Literary Taste, Culture and Mass Communication, 125
Literature and Society, 125
The Literature of Journalism: An Annotated Bibliography, 747
The Little Magazine: A History and a Bibliography, 1055
The Little Magazine in America, a Modern Documentary His-
    tory, 1055
Liu, Alan P. L., 126, 718, 923
Liu, Peter Yi-Chih, 1117
The Liveliest Art: A Panoramic History of the Movies, 903
Local Government Uses of Cable Television, 363
Local Origination Directory, 508
Lofgren, M. Violet, 27
London, Mel, 924
The (London) Times Index, 1167
A Long, Long Look at Short Films, 904
Longley, Lawrence D., 469
Longman, Kenneth A., 1118
The Long Revolution, 217
The Long View, 1039
Love, Barbara J., 64
Low, Rachael, 925
Lowenstein, Ralph L., 148
Lutz, William D., 774
Lyle, Jack, 38, 558-60

MacCann, Richard Dyer, 926
McCarthy, Todd, 927
McCavitt, William E., 487
McClure, Arthur F., 928
McClure, Robert D., 521
McCombs, Maxwell E., 127, 387

McGarry, K. J., 128
MacGowen, Kenneth, 929
McGowen, John J., 513
McGraw, Walter, 488
McGregor, O. R., 686, 688
McGuire, William J., 1116
MacKay, Ian K., 489-92
Maclauren, W. Rupert, 493
McLean, Eva, 301
McLuhan, Marshall, 55, 129-30
McMahon, Morgan E., 494
McMurtrie, Douglas, 288
McNicoll, David, 872
McNulty, Jean, 92
McQuail, Denis, 131-33, 688, 720
McVey, Sheila, 298
McWhinney, Edward, 134
Macy, John W., Jr., 495
Madden, Lionel, 1056
Maddison, John, 496
Maddox, Brenda, 497
Madison, Charles A., 289
Magazine Circulation and Rate Trends, 1940-1976, 1057
Magazine Index, 1172
Magazine Profiles: Studies of a Dozen Contemporary Magazine
    Groupings, 1058
Magazines in the Twentieth Century, 1061
Magazines in the United States, 1072
Magic Shadows: The Story of the Origin of Motion Pictures, 976
Magnant, Robert S., 498
Mahle, Walter A., 39
Make It Again, Sam: A Survey of Movie Remakes, 845
Maltin, Leonard, 803, 930
The Manipulators: America in the Media Age, 192
Mankiewicz, Frank, 499
Manning, Willard G., Jr., 500, 515
A Manual on Bookselling: How to Open and Run Your Own Book-
    store, 290
Manvell, Roger, 889, 925, 931-36
Mapp, Edward, 937
Marbut, F. B., 721
Market Structure and the Business of Book Publishing, 316
Markham, James W., 135
Marlowe, J. Orrin, 600
Marsh, Earl, 354
Martin, Gail M., 92
Martin, Henri-Jean, 270
Martin, John L., 168
Martin, Marcel, 938

Marty, Martin E., 722
Marxism and the Mass Media: Toward a Basic Bibliography, 136
Marzio, Peter C., 723
Marzolf, Marion, 724
Mass Communication, 33
Mass Communication: A Sociological Perspective, 222
Mass Communication: Teaching and Studies at Universities, 110
Mass Communication: A World View, 209
Mass Communication and Economics: A Bibliography, 153
Mass Communication and Society, 43
Mass Communication Effects and Processes, 82
Mass Communication in Africa: An Annotated Bibliography, 84
Mass Communication in Hong Kong and Macao, . . . in India,
    . . . in Indonesia, . . . in Korea, . . . in Malaysia,
    . . . in Nepal, . . . in Pakistan, . . . in Singapore,
    . . . in Sri Lanka, . . . in Taiwan, . . . in Thailand,
    . . . in the Philippines, 3
Mass Communication Law: Cases and Comments, 76
Mass Communication Law in a Nutshell, 223
Mass Communication Research: Major Issues and Future Direc-
    tions, 46
Mass Communications: A Book of Readings, 181
Mass Communications: Selected Readings for Librarians, 128
Mass Communications and the American Empire, 178
Mass Culture: The Popular Arts in America, 169
Mass Culture Revisited, 170
Mass Entertainment, 146
Mass Entertainment: The Origins of a Modern Industry, 24
The Mass Media, 79
The Mass Media: Aspen Institute Guide to Communication Indus-
    try Trends, 195
Mass Media: Systems and Effects, 47
Mass Media and Cultural Relationships, 157
Mass Media and Mass Communication, 125
Mass Media and Mass Man, 31
Mass Media and Modern Society, 25
Mass Media and Socialization, 87
Mass Media and Society, 210
Mass Media and Violence, 137
The Mass Media Book, 97
Mass Media Booknotes, 138
Mass Media in America, 155
The Mass Media in a Violent World, 26
Mass Media in Black Africa: Philosophy and Control, 213
Mass Media in Canada, 190
Mass Media in C.M.E.A. Countries, 139
Mass Media in Society: The Need of Research, 86
Mass Media in the Federal Republic of Germany, 91
Mass Media in the Soviet Union, 100, 696

405

Mass Media Issues, 186
The Mass Media of the German-Speaking Countries, 176
Mass Media Law, 156
Mass Media Law and Regulation, 65
Mass Media Periodicals: An Annotated Bibliography, 214
Mass Media Policies in Changing Cultures, 75
Mass News: Practices, Controversies, and Alternatives, 716
Mass News Media and the Third World Challenge, 768
Masson, Peter, 1119
Mast, Gerald, 939
Mastroianni, George A., 578
Mayer, Arthur, 870
Mayer, Henry, 725
Mayer, Michael F., 940
Meadows, Jack, 107
Measuring Payout: An Annotated Bibliography on the Dollar
    Effectiveness of Advertising, 1120
Media: An Introductory Analysis of American Mass Communica-
    tions, 177
Media, Messages and Men: New Perspectives in Communication, 148
Media, Politics, Democracy, 172
Media Access: Your Rights to Express Your Views on Radio and
    Television, 563
The Media and Business, 140
Media and Government: An Annotated Bibliography, 72
The Media and Terrorism, 141
The Media and the People, 25
The Media are American, 202
The Media Book, 1121
Media Casebook: An Introductory Reader in Mass Communica-
    tions, 177
Media Daten, 1143
The Media Environment: Mass Communications in American
    Society, 193
The Media in America, 198
The Media in France, 12
The Media Law Dictionary, 149
Media Law Reporter, 142
Mediamerica: Form, Content, and Consequences of Mass Communi-
    cation, 211
Media Japan, 613
The Media Society: Evidence about Mass Communication in
    America, 49
Media Sociology, 203
The Media Sourcebook: Comparative Reviews and Listings of
    Textbooks in Mass Communications, 194
Media Studies in Education, 143
Medium Rare: A Look at the Book and Its People, 317
Meeting of Experts on Book Development Planning in Asia, 291

Meeting of Experts on Development of Information Media in
    Latin America, 144
Meeting of Experts on the Use of Space Communication by the
    Mass Media, 501
Meetings of Experts on the Development of News Agencies in
    Africa, 726
Mehr, Linda Harris, 941
Mehrotra, R. K., 3
Mellen, Joan, 942-43
Melody, William, 145, 1122
Men, Messages, and Media: A Look at Human Communication, 182
The Men and Machines of American Journalism, 723
Mendelsohn, Harold, 146
Merrill, John C., 63, 147-48, 727-28
The Messenger's Motives: Ethical Theory in the Mass Media, 98
Method to the Madness: (Hollywood Explained), 799
Mexican Media Rates and Data, 1143
Meyers, Robin, 294
Meyersohn, Rolf, 125
Miller, Arthur C., 805
Miller, Peter, 114
Miller, Susan, 72
A Million and One Nights: A History of the Motion Picture, 979
The Mind Managers, 179
Minowa, Shigeo, 304
Mirror, Mirror: Images of Women Reflected in Popular Cul-
    ture, 207
A Mirror for England: British Movies from Austerity to Afflu-
    ence, 846
Mitchell, D. Craig, 214
Modern Communication Technology in a Changing Society, 36
The Modern News Library, 779
Monaco, James, 944-46
Monaco, Paul, 947
Money behind the Screen: A Report Prepared on Behalf of the
    Film Council, 902
Montgomery, John, 948
Morella, Joe, 1123
Morin, Edgar, 949
Morris, Norman S., 503
Morris, Peter, 993-94
Mosco, Vincent, 504
The Most Important Art: East European Film after 1945, 918
Motion Picture Distribution (Business and/or Racket?!?), 887
Motion Picture Empire, 896
The Motion Picture Industry, 950
The Motion Picture in Its Economic and Social Aspects, 951
Motion Picture Marketplace, 952

407

Motion Pictures, 1894-1969, Identified from the Records of the
    United States Copyright Office, 953
Motion Pictures: The Development of an Art from Silent Films
    to the Age of Television, 859
Motion Pictures, Television and Radio: A Union Catalogue of
    Manuscripts and Special Collections in the Western United
    States, 941
Motion Pictures and the Arts in Canada, 844
Motion Pictures and Youth, 970
Mott, Frank Luther, 292, 729, 1059
Moulds, Michael, 823
The Movie Business: American Film Industry Practice, 819
Movie Comedy Teams, 930
Movie-Made America: A Social History of American Movies, 1003
Movie Monsters, 864
The Movies, 870
The Movies, an American Idiom, 928
Movies and Society, 895
The Movies Begin: Making Movies in New Jersey, 1887-1920, 1011
Movies on TV, 1978-79, 954
The Movie Stars, 869
The Muckrakers, 672
Muffled Drums: The News Media in Africa, 84
Muller, Robert H., 1060
Muller-Strauss, Maurice, 801
Mullick, K. S., 505
Mumby, Frank A., 293
Municipal Control of Cable Communications, 452
Murphy, James E. and Sharon, 730
Murray, James P., 955
Murray, John, 149, 591
Murthy, Nadig Krishna, 731
Musolf, Lloyd D., 506

Nachbar, John G., 956
Nafziger, Ralph O., 732
Names and Numbers: A Journalist's Guide to the Most Needed
    Information Sources and Contacts, 737
Namurois, Albert, 507
Natarajan, Swaminath, 733
National and International Systems of Broadcasting, 409
The National Association of Educational Broadcasters, 443
National Directory of Weekly Newspapers, 734
National Film Archive Catalogue, 957
National Rate Book and College Newspaper Directory, 1124
National Sovereignty and International Communication, 151
Nazi Cinema, 913
NCTA Cable Services Directory, 508
Neale, John M., 485

The Negro in Films, 961
Nelson, Harold L., 150
Nelson, Jack, 651
Nelson, Lyle, 557
Nelson, Roy Paul, 99
Nemeyer, Carol A., 295
Network Rates and Data, 1143
New Cinema in Europe, 932
New Cinema in the USA: The Feature Film since 1946, 933
Newcomb, Horace, 509-10
The New Communications: A Guide to Community Programming, 414
New Directions in Mass Communications Policy: Implications
    for Citizen Education and Participation, 171
A New Guide to Federal Cable Television Regulations, 550
The New Journalism: The Underground Press, the Artists of
    Nonfiction, and Changes in the Established Media, 702
New Perspectives in International Communication, 164
News Agencies: Their Structure and Operation, 735
News Broadcasting on Soviet Radio and Television, 661
News Bureaus in the United States, 777
New Serials Titles, 1068
News from Nowhere: Television and the News, 667
News from the Capital: The Story of Washington Reporting, 721
The Newsmongers, 758
The Newspaper Business, 704
Newspaper Index, 1168
The Newspaper Press in New South Wales, 1803-1920, 776
Newspaper Rates and Data, 1143
Newspapers of East Central and Southeastern Europe in the
    Library of Congress, 775
The News People: A Sociological Portrait of American Journal-
    ists and Their Work, 703
Newsprint Data: Statistics of World Demand and Supply, 736
Newsreels across the World, 801
The New World of Advertising, 1125
The New York Times Encyclopedia of Television, 355
New York Times Film Reviews, 958
The New York Times Guide to Movies on TV, 959
The New York Times Index, 1169
New Zealand, Committee on Broadcasting, The Future of Broad-
    casting for New Zealand, 511
Nilsson, Lennart, 39
The Nineteenth-Century Periodical Press in Britain, 1056
Niver, Kemp R., 960
Noble, Grant, 512
Noble, Peter, 961
Noll, Roger G., 513
Nolte, Lawrence W., 1126
Nonfiction Film: A Critical History, 811

409

Nordberg, E. Wayne, 264
Nordenstreng, Kaarle, 151, 514, 596
Norland, Rod, 737
Norrie, Ian, 293
Norton, Alice, 1127
Norton, William, 97
Nunn, Godfrey Raymond, 296
Nye, Russel, 152
Nyhau, Michael J., 6, 376

Oakley, Charles Allen, 962
O'Dwyer's Directory of Corporate Communications, 1128
O'Dwyer's Directory of Public Relations Firms, 1129
Oettinger, Mal, 381
Oey, Hong Lee, 738
Olson, Kenneth E., 739
Olson, May E., 635
Oluwasanmi, Edwina, 301
One Hundred Years of the Yiddish Press in America, 1870-
     1970, 740
One Reel a Week, 805
One Week of Educational Television, 463
On the Cable: The Television of Abundance, 572
Oppenheim, A. N., 444
Orientations to Mass Communication, 62
Ortega, Carlos, 39
Orton, Barry, 7
Other Voices: Black, Chicano, and American Indian Press, 730
Other Voices: The New Journalism in America, 50
Outer Space and Inner Sanctums: Government, Business, and
     Satellite Communication, 465
Outlaws of America: The Underground Press and Its Context:
     Notes on a Cultural Revolution, 717
Overseas Press Club of America and American Correspondents
     Overseas, 1975 Membership Directory, 741
Owen, Bill, 358
Owen, Bruce M., 153, 515, 757
The Oxford Companion to Film, 812

Page, Roger, 297
Palek, David L., 1130
Panday, Narendra R., 3
Paperback Parnassus, 309
The Parade's Gone By, 825
Parch, Grace D., 659
Parish, James Robert, 516-17, 963-68
Park, Rolla Edward, 518
Parker, Derek, 519
Parker, Edwin B., 560

Parties in Interest: A Citizen's Guide to Improving Televi-
    sion and Radio, 566
Patterns of Discrimination against Women in the Film and Tele-
    vision Industries, 520
Patterson, Lindsay, 969
Patterson, Thomas E., 521
Paule, Milton, 1075
Paulu, Burton, 522-24
The Payne Fund Studies, Motion Pictures and Youth, 970
Pearson, Robert E., 1130
Pec, Merton J., 513
Pecans, Aida B., 3
Peers, Frank W., 525-26
Pelletier, Gerad, 154
Pelton, Joseph N., 527
Pember, Don R., 155-56
Penn, I. Garland, 742
Pennybacker, John H., 588
The People Look at Educational Television, 558
The People Look at Public Television, 1974, 559
The People Look at Radio, 474
The People Look at Television: A Study of Audience Atti-
    tudes, 584
The People's Films, 926
Peoples Speaking to Peoples, 212
Periodicals and the Alternative Press, 1051
Periodicals on the Socialist Countries and on Marxism, 1063
Perlmutter, Tom, 971
Perry, George, 972
Perry, Martin Kent, 528
Personal Influence: The Part Played by People in the Flow of
    Communications, 109
Perspectives of the Black Press, 1974, 713
Perspectives on Publishing, 298
Peters, Jean, 248
Peterson, Theodore, 188, 1059, 1061
Petrick, Michael J., 32
Philippine Mass Communications before 1811, after 1966, 122
Pichard, R. A. E., 973
Pickett, Calder, 748
Picture-Tube Imperialism? The Impact of U.S. Television on
    Latin America, 618
Piepe, Anthony, 157, 529
The Pilkington Report, 425
Pinto, Virgilio B. Noya, 39
Pitts, Michael R., 530, 963-68
Plant, Marjorie, 299
Ploman, Edward W., 373, 531
The Plug-in Drug: Television, Children and the Family, 624

411

Poindexter, Ray, 532
Politella, Dario, 660
The Political Impact of Mass Media, 187
Politics in Public Service Advertising on Television, 1130
The Politics of Broadcast Regulation, 469
The Politics of Canadian Broadcasting, 1920-1951, 525
The Politics of Information: Problems of Policy in the
    Modern Media, 191
The Politics of International Standards: France and the
    Color TV War, 392
Polley, Richard W., 1131
Polsky, Samuel, 441
Pool, Ithiel de Sola, 158-59, 558
Poor Men's Guardians: A Record of the Struggles for a
    Democratic Newspaper Press, 1763-1973, 692
The Popular Arts, 85
The Popular Arts in America: A Reader, 89
The Popular Book: A History of America's Literary Taste, 279
Popular Culture and High Culture, 73
Popular Media in China: Shaping New Cultural Patterns, 35
Porter, Vincent, 904
Poteet, G. Howard, 533
Potter, Elaine, 743
Powers, Anne, 974
Powledge, Fred, 534
The Practice of Mass Communication, 162
Prakoso, Mastini Hardjo, 3
Pratt, George C., 975
Presbrey, Frank, 1132
Pre-School Children and Television, 535
The Presentation of Science by the Media, 107
Press, Film, Radio, 160
Press and Advertisers Year Book, 744
The Press and America, 666
The Press and Journals in Communist China, 718
The Press and Society: From Caxton to Northcliffe, 653
The Press as Opposition: The Political Role of South African
    Newspapers, 743
Press Councils and Press Codes, 745
The Press in Africa: A Handbook for Economics and Advertis-
    ing, 670
The Press in Asia and Oceania: A Handbook for Economics and
    Advertising, 670
The Press in Australia, 725
The Press in Developing Countries, 764
The Press in Europe: A Handbook for Economics and Advertis-
    ing, 670
Press in India, Report of the Registrar of Newspapers for
    India under the Press and Registration of Books Act, 746

The Press in Latin America: A Handbook for Economics and
    Advertising, 670
The Press of Guatemala, 676
Press under Apartheid, 694
Price, Jonathan, 1133
Price, Warren C., 747-48
The Print and Broadcasting Media in Malaysia, 77
The Print and Broadcasting Media in Singapore, 78
The Printing Industry, 312
The Printing Press as an Agent of Change, 665
Print Media Production Data, 1143
The Private Press, 257
The Process and Effects of Mass Communication, 183
Program Material Available from Government and Civic Agencies
    for Use by Radio Stations, 536
Program Material Available from Government and Civic Agencies
    for Use by Television Stations, 537
Projecting the Growth of Television Broadcasting, 518
Promise and Performance: Children with Special Needs. ACT's
    Guide to TV Programming for Children, 437
Propaganda, Communication, and Public Opinion, 118
Propaganda and Communication in World History, 116
Propaganda and Promotional Activities, 117
Proposals for a Communications Policy for Canada, 154
Prowitt, Marsha O'Bannon, 538
Psychological Abstracts, 1170
The Psychologique of Small Press Publishing, 272
Public Access Cable Television in the United States and
    Canada, 420
Public Affairs Information Service, 1171
Public Broadcasting: The Role of the Federal Government,
    1912-76, 419
The Public Eye: Television and the Politics of Canadian
    Broadcasting, 1952-1968, 526
Public Opinion, 124
Public Opinion: Coalitions, Elites, and Masses, 96
Public Opinion: Its Formation, Measurement, and Impact, 208
Public Opinion, 1935-46, 71
Public Opinion in European Socialist Systems, 41
Public Opinion in Soviet Russia: A Study in Mass Persua-
    sion, 100
Public Perceptions of Television and Other Mass Media, 539
The Public Persuader: Government Advertising, 1105
Public Relations, a Comprehensive Bibliography, 1090
Public Relations: Information Sources, 1127
A Public Relations Bibliography, 1100
Public Relations Law, 1140
Public Television: A Program for Action, 540
Public Television: A Question of Survival, 534

Public Television: Toward Higher Ground, 542
Public Television Program Content, 1974, 463
Public Television Programming by Category, 1976, 463
A Public Trust: The Report of the Carnegie Commission on the
    Future of Public Broadcasting, 541
Published Radio, Television, and Film Scripts, 533
The Publishers' Association, 1896-1946, with an Epilogue, 284
Publishers' International Directory, 300
Publishers on Publishing, 277
Publishing and Bookselling, 293
Publishing in Africa in the Seventies, 301
Publishing in India: An Analysis, 227
Publishing in Mainland China, 296
Publishing in Nigeria, 302
Publishing in the U.S.S.R., 274
The Pulitzer Prizes, 94

A Qualitative Study: The Effect of Television on People's
    Lives, 543
Queeney, K. M., 544
Questions and Answers about Pay TV, 461
Quicke, Andrew, 545
Quigley, Martin, Jr., 976
Quinn, James, 977

Radical Periodicals in America, 1890-1950, 1049
Radio: The Great Years, 519
Radio, Television and Society, 570
Radio and Television: A Selected, Annotated Bibliography, 487
Radio and Television Bibliography, 546
Radio and Television Broadcasting in Eastern Europe, 524
Radio and Television in Literacy, 496
Radio and Television in the Soviet Union, 403
Radio and Television in the U.S.S.R., 458
Radio and the Printed Page, 473
The Radio Code, 547
Radio Comedy, 619
Radio Listening in America, 475
The Radio Phenomenon in Italy, 412
Radio Power: Propaganda and International Broadcasting, 431
Radio Programming Profile, 549
Radio Research, 1941, 476; Radio Research, 1942-43, 477
Radio Soundtracks: A Reference Guide, 530
Rafferty, Keen, 749
Ragan, David, 978
Rahim, Syed A., 161
Rajan, S. P. Thiaga, 750
Ramond, Charles, 1134
Ramsaye, Terry, 979

RAND Cable Television Series, 550
Rao, Y. V. Lakshmana, 162
The Ravenous Eye, 569
Ray, Marla Wilson, 442
Read, William H , 163
Reader in Public Opinion and Communication, 14
The Readers' Guide to Periodical Literature, 1172
Readings in Mass Communication, 53
Recent Trends in the Structure of the Cable Television Indus-
    try, 528
Reel Plastic Magic: A History of Films and Filmmaking in
    America, 898
Reeves, Earl, 637
Regulating Cable Television Subscriber Rates, 363
Regulation of Broadcasting, 421
Rehrauer, George, 980
Reilly, Mary Lonan, 751
The Religious Press in America, 722
The Reluctant Reformation: On Criticizing the Press in Amer-
    ica, 646
Reluctant Regulators: The FCC and the Broadcast Audience, 381
Remember Radio, 470
Remote Control: Television and the Manipulation of American
    Life, 499
Renan, Sheldon, 981
Reporters' Ethics, 769
Reporting Africa, 196
Report of the Task Force on Women in Public Broadcasting, 551
A Report on American University Presses, 283
A Report on Cable Television and Cable Telecommunications in
    New York City, 552
Report on the Mass Media, 29
A Research Guide to China-Coast Newspapers, 1822-1911, 709
Research in Education, 1966-1974, 1173
Research on the Effects of Television Advertising on Child-
    ren, 1135
Resources in Education, 1173
Responsibility in Mass Communication, 165
Review of Sociological Writing on the Press, 720
Rhode, Eric, 982
Richard, Pamela, 453
Richards, Jeffrey, 983
Richie, Donald, 984
Richstead, Jim, 164
Richter, Rolf, 39
The Right Channel, 456
Righter, Rosemary, 752
The Right to Know: The Rise of the World Press, 783
Rimberg, John, 800

The Rise and Fall of British Documentary, 1017
The Rise of the American Film: A Critical History, 893
The Rise of the Novel, 319
Rivers, Gail Ann, 72
Rivers, William L., 6, 25, 50, 72, 165, 186, 637
Rivkin, Steven R., 550
Road, Sinclair, 990
Roberts, Donald F., 183, 387
Robinson, David, 985-86
Robinson, Gertrude Joch, 11, 753
Robinson, Glen O., 166
Rodney, James C., 987
Rogers, Everett M., 167
The Role of Advertising: A Book of Readings, 1139
Role of Private Foundations in Public Broadcasting, 611
Role of the Mass Media in American Politics, 168
Romano, Frank J., 754
Romero, Carlo, 39
Rosden, George Eric and Peter Eric, 1136
Rose, Ernest D., 553
Rosenberg, Bernard, 169-70
Rosengarten, Frank, 755
Rosewater, Victor, 756
Rosnow, Eugene, 988
Rosse, James N., 757
Rosten, Leo C., 989
Rotha, Paul, 990-91
Rothafel, Samuel L., 554
Rothstein, Larry, 171
Rotzoll, Kim B., 1137-38
Rounds, David, 405
Rovin, Jeff, 555
Ruben, Brent D., 40
Rubenstein, Eli A., 591
Rubin, Bernard, 172-73
Rubin, David M., 177
Rucker, Bryce W., 54, 174
Rutland, Robert A., 758
Rutstein, Nat, 556

Sachsmand, David B., 177
Sadoul, Georges, 992-94
Salcedo, Rudolfo N., 1047
Salinas, Raquel, 175
Salmane, Hala, 995
Sampson, Henry T., 996
Sandage, Charles H., 1137-39
Sanders, Ron, 373
Sandford, John, 176

Sandman, Peter M., 177
Sankaranarayanan, N., 303
Sarashandran, V. V., 3
Sarkar, Chanchal, 759
Sarris, Andrew, 997
Scandinavian Film, 876
Schacht, John A., 1062
Schenker, Susan, 945-46
Scheuer, Steven H., 954
Schiller, Herbert I., 151, 178-80
Schmacke, Ernst, 670
Schmidt, Georg, 998
Scholarly Publishing in Asia, 304
Scholarly Reprint Publishing in the United States, 295
Schramm, Wilbur, 159, 165, 181-83, 188, 557-58, 560
Schreibman, Fay, 629
Schudson, Michael, 760
Schulman, Paul H., 417
Schulte, Henry F., 761
Scott, Mary, 112
Screen World, 999
Seiden, Martin H., 561
Seldes, Gilbert, 184-85
A Selected Bibliography in the Economics of the Mass Media, 153
Selecting Advertising Media: A Guide for Small Business, 1097
Sellers, Leonard L., 186
Seng, Wong Hock, 373
The Serial: Suspense and Drama by Installment, 1014
The Seven Lively Arts, 184
Sex and Violence on TV, 608
Sex Role Stereotyping in the Mass Media, 69
Seymour-Ure, Colin, 187
The Shadow in the Cave: The Broadcaster, the Audience and the
   State, 574
Shaffer, Harry G., 1063
Shaffer, Susan E., 305
Shale, Richard, 1000
Shales, Tom, 1001
Shanks, Bob, 562
Shapiro, Andrew O., 563
Sharp, Harold S. and Marjorie Z., 564
The Shawncross Report, 683
Shayon, Robert Lewis, 565-66
Sheehan, Donald, 306
Sherman, Charles, 451
Shiers, George, 396, 567, 589
Shiers, May, 567
Shils, Edward, 125
A Short History of the Movies, 939

Shulman, Milton, 568–69
Siebert, Fred S., 188
Siepman, Charles A., 570
Signitzer, Benno, 189, 483
Silver, Rollo G., 286
Silver, Sheila, 13
Simmons, Howard, 140
Simon, Morton J., 1140
Singer, Benjamin, 190
Siriwardene, Reggie, 39
Sitney, P. Adams, 1002
Sklar, Robert, 1003
Skornia, Harry J., 571, 762
Skvorecky, Josef, 1004
Slawski, Edward J., 703
Slide, Anthony, 1005–1007
Sloan Commission on Cable Communications, On the Cable: The
    Television of Abundance, 572
Slow Fade to Black: The Negro in American Film, 1900–1942, 839
Smith, Anthony, 191, 573–75, 763
Smith, Bruce Lannes, 117–19
Smith, Chita M., 119
Smith, Datus C., 251, 307–308
Smith, Delbert D., 576
Smith, G. Royce, 290
Smith, John M., 1008
Smith, Paul, 1009
Smith, Robert Rutherford, 577
Smith, Roger H., 309
Smith, Sharon, 1010
Smythe, Ted Curtis, 53, 578
Snow, Marcellus S., 527, 579
The Soap Opera Book, 580
Soares, Manuela, 580
Sobel, Robert, 192
Social Communication Media in Belgium, 19
Social Sciences and Humanities Index, 1160
Social Sciences Citation Index, 1174
Social Sciences Index, 1175
Sociological Abstracts, 1176
The Sociology of Literature, 125
Sociology of Mass Communications, 132
The Sociology of Mass-Media Communicators, 88
Solberg, Janet, 581
Sommerlad, Ernest Lloyd, 764
SOS: The Story of Radio Communication, 615
A Sourcebook on Radio's Role in Development, 582
Soviet Book Publishing Policy, 318
Soviet Cinema, 842

418

Soviet Cinema: Directors and Films, 818
The Soviet Film Industry, 800
Soviet Political Indoctrination, 95
Spahn, Janet M. and Theodore Jurgen, 1060
The Spanish Press, 1470-1966: Print, Power, and Politics, 761
Spaulding, William E., 251
Speaking of a Free Press, 765
Special Commission on the Student Press, The Student News-
    paper, 766
Spehr, Paul C., 1011
Speier, Hans, 116
Spellbound in Darkness: A History of the Silent Film, 975
Spicer, Joanna, 373
The Sponsor: Notes on a Modern Potentate, 1089
The Sponsored Film, 901
Spot Radio Rates and Data, 1143
Spot Radio Small Markets Edition, 1143
Spot Television Rates and Data, 1143
Spraos, John, 1012
Squire, Jason E., 819
Standard Directory of Advertisers, 1141
Standard Directory of Advertising Agencies, 1142
Standard Periodical Directory, 1979-80, 1064
Standard Rate and Data Services, Inc., 1143
Stanley, Robert H., 193, 1013
Stanton, Frank N., 476-78
Stapleton, John, 39
Starch, Kenneth, 637
Stardom: The Hollywood Phenomenon, 1033
The Stars, 949
Statistical Trends in Broadcasting, 1144
Stay Tuned: A Concise History of American Broadcasting, 586
Stedman, Raymond William, 1014
Stein, Aletha Huston, 583
Steinberg, Charles S., 193, 349
Steinberg, S. H., 310
Steinby, Torsten, 767
Steiner, Gary A., 584
Sterling, Christopher H., 138, 194-95, 585-86, 716
Stewart, John, 1015
Stiehl, Ulrich, 311
Stoil, Michael Jon, 1016
Stokke, Olav, 196
Stomgren, Richard L., 821
The Story of Advertising, 1150
Strauss, Victor, 312
Strentz, Herbert J., 197
Stridsberg, Albert B., 1145
Structure and Organization of Broadcasting in the Framework
    of Radiocommunications, 507

Structure of Television, 416
The Struggle for National Broadcasting in Canada, 617
The Student Newspaper, 766
Studies in Violence and Television, 441
Summers, Harrison B., 587-88
Summers, Robert E., 588
The Sunday TIMES Guide to Movies on Television, 790
The Supply of Primetime Entertainment Television Programs, 500
The Surgeon-General's Report on Violence, 592
Sussex, Elizabeth, 1017
Sussman, Leonard R., 768
Sutherland, J. A., 313
Svensson, Arne, 838, 1019
Swain, Bruce M., 769
Sweden, 838
The Swedish Film Institute, 1018
Swedish Press Policy, 689
Swerdlow, Joel, 499
Swordsmen of the Screen: From Douglas Fairbanks to Michael
    York, 983
Symposium on Television Violence, 372
Syndicated Columnists, 778
Szecsko, Tamas, 39

Tangled Tapes: The Inside Story of Indian Broadcasting, 505
The Tangled Web: Basic Issues in Canadian Communications, 92
Tarif Media, 1143
Tate, Charles, 362
Taubert, Sigfried, 247, 314
A Taxonomy of Communication Media, 23
A Taxonomy of Concepts in Communication, 18
Taylor, Henry A., 770
Tebbel, John, 198, 315, 771, 1065
Technical Development of Television, 589
The Technique of Film Music, 936
Technology of Cable Television, 363
Tee, Lim Huck, 3
Teeter, Dwight L., Jr., 150
Telecommunications: The Booming Technology, 356
Telecommunications for Canada, 410
The Telecommunications Industry, 450
Television: The Critical View, 510
Television: The First Fifty Years, 428
Television: The First Forty Years, 393
Television: Here Is the News, 394
Television: Technology and Cultural Form, 622
Television Advertising Conditions in Europe, 1119
Television and Children, 445
Television and Delinquency, 435

Television and Growing Up: The Impact of Television Vio-
    lence, 592
Television and Human Behavior, 387
Television and Media Effect, 1098
Television and Political Life, 575
Television and Radio, 590
Television and Social Behavior, 591
Television and Society, 571
Television and the Child, 444
Television and the News, 762
Television and the Public, 342
Television and the "Wired City," 471
Television and the Working Class, 529
Television as a Cultural Force, 375
Television as a Social Force: New Approaches to TV Criti-
    cism, 374
The Television Audience: Patterns of Viewing, 423
The Television Code, 548
Television Economics, 515
Television Factbook, 593
Television for Children and Young People, 434
Television Index, 594
Television in the Corporate Interest, 357
Television in the Lives of Our Children, 560
Television Journalism, 644
Television Network News, 629
Television News, 650
Television News Index and Abstracts, 1177
Television Programming for News and Public Affairs, 625
Television's Action Arsenal: Weapon Use in Prime Time, 442
Television's Child, 503
Television Station Ownership, 595
Television Traffic--A One-Way Street?, 514
Television Violence and the Adolescent Boy, 336
Television Yearbook of the Republic of China, 1961-1975, 597
Terrace, Vincent, 598
Test Pattern for Living, 454
That's What They Said about the Press, 749
Thayer, Frank, 150
Theater and Song, 125
Theories of Mass Communication, 48
Theory of Film: The Redemption of Physical Reality, 908
Thesaurus: Mass Communication, 205
Third World Mass Media and Their Search for Modernity: The
    Case of Commonwealth Caribbean, 1717-1976, 123
A Thirty-Year History of Programs Carried on National Radio
    Networks in the United States, 1926-1956, 587
This Was Publishing, 306
Thomas, David Bowen, 1020

Thomas, Ruth, 599
Thomassen, Cora, 323
Thompson, Howard, 959
Thompson (J. Walter) Co., Advertising, 1146
Thompson, Wallace, 6
Thomson, David, 1021
Thorp, Margaret Farrand, 1022
Those Great Movie Ads, 1123
The Three Faces of Advertising, 1088
Tichenor, Frank A., 951
Tichensor, Phillip J., 114
A Title Guide to the Talkies, 1927-1974, 798
Tito's Maverick Media, 753
Titus, Edna Brown, 1068
To Be Continued. . . , 1036
Todorov, Dafin, 772
To Find an Image: Black Films from Uncle Tom to Super-
    fly, 955
To Irrigate a Wasteland: The Struggle to Shape a Public
    Television System in the United States, 495
Tomorrow's Television: An Examination of British Broadcast-
    ing, 545
Toms, Coons, Mulattoes, Mammies and Bucks: An Interpretative
    History of Blacks in American Films, 820
Topicator, 1178
Topping, Malachi C., 484
Toward a Sociology of Mass Communications, 131
Toward a Sociology of the Cinema, 895
Toward the Public Dividend: A Report on Satellite Telecom-
    munications and the Public Interest Satellite Associa-
    tion, 488
Townsend, George R., 600
Training for Mass Communication, 200
The Training of Journalists, 201
Trager, Robert, 199
Transmitting World News, 784
Trends in Network Television Drama and Viewer Concept of
    Social Reality, 1967-1976, 418
Trends in Scholarly Communication in the United States and
    Western Europe, 111
Trost, Mark, 517
Truitt, Evelyn Mack, 1023
The Tube of Plenty, 333
Tucker, Richard, 1024
Tudor, Andrew, 1025
Tune in Yesterday, 402
Tunstall, Jeremy, 202-203
Tuska, Jon, 1026-27
TV: The Most Popular Art, 509

TV Broadcast Financial Data, 601
The TV-Guided American, 337
TV Movies, 803
TV Season, 602
Twenty Years of Silents, 1908-1928, 1034
Twomey, John E., 603
Tyler, Parker, 1028

Udell, Jon G., 773
U.K. Advertising Statistics, 1099
Ulrich, Carolyn F., 1055
Ulrich's International Periodical Directory, 1066
The Unchanging Arts: New Forms for the Traditional Functions
   of Art in Society, 83
The Underground and Alternative Press in Great Britain, 1067
Underground Film: A Critical History, 1028
Underground Press Directory, 774
The Underground Press in America, 678
Understanding Media: The Extensions of Man, 130
The Unembarrassed Muse: The Popular Arts in America, 152
UNESCO, Basic Facts and Figures, 236
Union List of Serials in Libraries of the United States and
   Canada, 1068
The Universal Eye: The World of Television, 427
The Unseeing Eye: The Myth of Television Power in National
   Politics, 521
Up from the Footnote: A History of Women Journalists, 724
UPS Directory, 634
Urdang, Laurence, 1147
U.S. Bureau of the Census, Census of Manufactures, Industry
   Statistics, 1972: Newspapers, Periodicals, Books and Mis-
   cellaneous Publishing, 204
U.S. Congress, Joint Committee on Congressional Operations,
   Congress and Mass Communications, 604
U.S. Department of Commerce, Office of Telecommunications,
   Cable Television for Europe, 605
U.S. Foreign Broadcast Information Service, Broadcasting
   Stations around the World, 606
U.S. House, Committee on Interstate and Foreign Commerce, Sub-
   committee on Communications, International Communications
   Services, 607; Sex and Violence on TV, 608
U.S. Library of Congress, Slavic and Central European Division,
   Newspapers of East Central and Southeastern Europe in the
   Library of Congress, 775; The U.S.S.R. and Eastern Europe:
   Periodicals in Western Languages, 1069
U.S. President's Task Force on Communications Policy, Final
   Report, 609

U.S. Senate, Committee on Commerce, Science, and Transportation, Subcommittee on Communications, International Telecommunications Policies, 610
U.S. Senate, Committee on Finance, Subcommittee on Foundations, Role of Private Foundations in Public Broadcasting, 611
The Use of Mass Media in the Developing Countries, 20
The Uses of Cable Communications, 363
The Uses of Literacy: Aspects of Working-Class Life, 93
Uses of Literacy: Media, 125
The Uses of the Media by the Chicano Movement, 482
Using Mass Communication Theory, 127
Using the Mass Media: Communication Problems in American Society, 32
The U.S.S.R. and Eastern Europe: Periodicals in Western Languages, 1069

Vallance, Tom, 1029
van der Haak, Kees, 373
Vanier, Dinno J., 316
Varis, Tapio, 514, 596, 612
Vaughan, Samuel S., 317
Vedin, Bengt-Arne, 613
Vesterman, William, 7
The Video Implosion: Models for Reinventing Television, 460
Viet, Jean, 205
Vince, Pamela, 444
Vintage Radio, 494
Visionary Film: The American Avant-Garde, 1943-1978, 1002
Voices from the Japanese Cinema, 943
Voices of the Red Giants: Communications in Russia and China, 100, 135
Vronskaya, Jeanne, 1030

Waldron, Gloria, 1031
Walker, Alexander, 1032-33
Walker, Gregory, 318
Walker, R. B., 776
Walls, Howard Lamarr, 953
The Wall Street Journal, 1179
The War Film, 827
War Movies, 971
Waterman, David, 153
Watkins, Gordon S., 950
Watt, Ian, 319
The Waves at Genji's Door: Japan through Its Cinema, 942
Weaver, John T., 1034-35
Webster, B. R., 614
Wechsler, Andrew R., 153, 206
Wedel, Mildred Mott, 1059

Wedell, George, 462
Wedlake, G. E. C., 615
Weibel, Kathryn, 207
Weil, Gordon L., 616
Weiner, Richard, 777-78
Weir, Earnest Austin, 617
Weiss, Ken, 1036
Welch, Susan, 208
Wells, Alan, 209-10, 618
Wertheim, Arthur Frank, 619
The Western: From Silents to the Seventies, 852
Western Films: An Annotated Critical Bibliography, 956
Westerns: Aspects of a Movie Genre, 858
Whannel, Paddy, 85
What Happens in Book Publishing, 275
Whatmore, Geoffrey, 779
When Pirates Ruled the Waves, 438
When the Movies Were Young, 868
Where We Came In: Seventy Years of the British Film Indus-
    try, 962
Whetmore, Edward Jay, 211
White, Cynthia Leslie, 1070
White, David Manning, 169-70, 1037
White, Llewellyn, 37, 212, 620
White Paper on a Domestic Satellite Communications System of
    Canada, 400
Whose News? Politics, the Press and the Third World, 752
Who's Who in Hollywood, 1900-1976, 978
Who Was Who in Journalism, 780
Who Was Who on the Screen, 1023
Who Wrote the Movie and What Else Did He Write?, 1038
Wilcox, Dennis L., 213, 781
Wilhoit, Frances Goins, 214
Wilhoit, G. C., Jr., 45
Williams, Arthur, 621
Williams, Francis, 782-84
Williams, Raymond, 215-17, 622
Williamson, Judith, 1148
Willing's Press Guide, 785
Willis, Donald L., 1130
Wilson, Alexander, 1149
Wilson, David, 995
Window Dressing on the Set: Women and Minorities in Televi-
    sion, 623
Winick, Charles, 218
Winn, Marie, 624
Winston, Brian, 219-20
Winter into Spring: The Czechoslovak Press and the Reform
    Movement, 1963-1968, 706

Wirt, Kenneth, 463
Wittke, Carl, 786
Wolf, Frank, 625
Wolkin, Rachel, 332
Wolseley, Roland E., 787, 1071
Women and Film: A Bibliography, 906
Women and the News, 668
Women in Media: A Documentary Source Book, 13
Women in Television, 467
Women in Television News, 677
Women's Magazines, 1963-1968, 1070
Women Who Make Movies, 1010
Wood, James Playsted, 1072, 1150
Woodsworth, Anne, 1073
Woollacott, Janet, 43
The Working Press of the Nation, 1151; Feature Writer, Photo-
    grapher and Syndicate Directory, 1074; Internal Publica-
    tions Directory, 1075; Magazine and Editorial Directory,
    1076; Newspaper and Allied Services Directory, 788; Radio
    and Television Directory, 626; World Advertising Expendi-
    tures, 1152
World and International Broadcasting: A Bibliography, 483
World Communication: Threat or Promise?, 34
World Communications, 221
The World Encyclopedia of the Film, 1008
World Film and Television Study Resources, 553
World Filmography, 1967; World Filmography, 1968, 837
World Radio TV Handbook, 627
The World's Greatest Dailies, 728
Worlds of Laughter: The Motion Picture Comedy Short, 910
Wright, Basil, 1039
Wright, Charles R., 222
The Writer and Politics, 125
Writer's Market, 1077
Wroth, Lawrence C., 286
Wynar, Anna T. and Lubomyr, 789

Yang, Shou-Jung, 3
Yates, Raymond Francis, 554
Yin, Robert K., 550
York, Michael, 1055
Young Soviet Film Makers, 1030
Yu, Frederick T. C., 46-47
Yu, Timothy L. M., 3
Yurovsky, A., 644

Zell, Hans M., 226, 301
Zuckman, Harvey, 223

426

A native of Meridian, Mississippi, Eleanor Blum holds a master's degree in library science from Columbia University and a doctorate in communications from the University of Illinois. She taught at the George Peabody College for Teachers, the University of North Carolina, and, until her recent retirement, was professor of library administration and communications librarian at the University of Illinois. In addition to various professional articles and a regular feature in Journalism Quarterly, Miss Blum has published Communications Research in U.S. Universities. She is the first recipient of an award named in her honor--the Eleanor Blum Distinguished Service to Research Award--given by the Association for Education in Journalism.